The Politics of the
Asian Economic Crisis

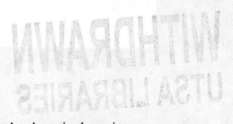

A volume in the series

Cornell Studies in Political Economy

Edited by Peter J. Katzenstein

A full list of titles in the series appears at the end of the book.

The Politics of the
Asian Economic Crisis

Edited by

T. J. PEMPEL

Cornell University Press

Ithaca and London

First published 1999 by Cornell University Press

First printing, Cornell Paperbacks, 1999

Printed in the United States of America

Library of Congress Cataloging-in-Publication Data

The politics of the Asian economic crisis / T. J. Pempel.
        p.   cm.
    Includes index.
    ISBN 0-8014-3722-9. — ISBN 0-8014-8634-3 (pbk.)
    1. Financial crises—Asia. 2. Asia—Politics and
government—1945-   I. Pempel, T. J., 1942-   .
HB3808.P65   1999
332'.095—dc21   99-38107
                                                        CIP

Cornell University Press strives to use environmentally responsible suppliers and materials to the fullest extent possible in the publishing of its books. Such materials include vegetable-based, low-VOC inks, and acid-free papers that are recycled, totally chlorine-free, or partly composed of nonwood fibers. Books that bear the logo of the FSC (Forest Stewardship Council) use paper taken from forests that have been inspected and certified as meeting the highest standards for environmental and social responsibility. For further information, visit our website at www.cornellpress.cornell.edu.

Cloth printing   10 9 8 7 6 5 4 3 2 1
Paperback printing   10 9 8 7 6 5 4 3 2 1

CONTENTS

v

CONTRIBUTORS

Yun-han Chu is professor of political science at National Taiwan University.

Bruce Cumings is Norman and Edna Freehling professor of international history and East Asian political economy at the University of Chicago.

Gary Hamilton is professor of sociology at the University of Washington.

Paul Hutchcroft is assistant professor of international business and director of the Southeast Asia Business Program in the School of Business Administration at the University of Michigan, Ann Arbor.

Linda Y. C. Lim is associate professor of international business and director of the Southeast Asia Business Program in the School of Business Administration at the University of Michigan, Ann Arbor.

Andrew MacIntyre is associate professor of Pacific International Affairs in the Graduate School of International Relations and Pacific Studies at the University of California, San Diego.

Barry Naughton is Sokwanlok professor of Chinese international affairs in the Graduate School of International Relations and Pacific Studies at the University of California, San Diego.

T. J. Pempel is Boeing professor of international studies at the University of Washington.

Jeffrey A. Winters is associate professor of political science at Northwestern University.

Meredith Woo-Cumings is associate professor of political science and director of the Roundtable on Political Economy at Northwestern University.

ACKNOWLEDGMENTS

The idea for this book was born in a conference held on October 30 and 31 and November 1, 1998, in Seattle, at the Jackson School of International Studies, University of Washington. The conference received financial support from the Jackson Foundation; for this, the editor and authors are most grateful. Jere Bachrach, director of the Jackson School of International Studies, was also very helpful in the planning and implementation of the conference. Mary Alice Pickert provided valuable research help to me as organizer and editor.

In addition to the authors whose work is presented here, David Asher, Alasdair Bowie, and Susan Whiting delivered papers to be published in other forums. Benjamin J. Cohen and Donald Emmerson attended as commentators and made invaluable suggestions during the meetings and in subsequent reworkings of various chapters. I thank all five scholars for their contributions. As editor, I also express my thanks to the individual contributors; they responded with a surprisingly generous mixture of cooperation, cheer, and speed that made the project far more pleasurable than is usually the case with such collective ventures.

Neither the conference nor the subsequent editing would have been as smooth without the fluid administrative and editorial support of Martha Walsh. Staff at Cornell University Press, and most particularly Roger Haydon, were exceptionally valuable supporters of this project from its inception. I thank them also for their expeditiousness.

T. J. P.

ABBREVIATIONS

AFTA	ASEAN Free Trade Association
ANSP	Agency for National Security Planning
APEC	Asia–Pacific Economic Cooperation
ASEAN	Association of South East Asian Nations
BAP	Bankers Association of the Philippines
BBC	Bangkok Bank of Commerce
BIS	Bank for International Settlements
BSP	*Bangko Sentral ng Pilipinas*
CBC	Central Bank of China
CIA	Central Intelligence Agency
CPF	Central Provident Fund
DBS	Development Bank of Singapore
DLP	Democratic Liberal Party
DPP	Democratic Progressive Party
DRAM	dynamic random access memory
EAEC	East Asia Economic Caucus
EMFMs	emerging market fund managers
EPB	Economic Planning Board
fdi	foreign direct investment
FKI	Federation of Korean Industries
FSC	Financial Supervisory Commission
GATT	General Agreement on Tariffs and Trade
GDP	gross domestic product
GLCs	government-linked companies
GNP	gross national product
HDB	Housing Development Board
ILO	International Labour Organization
IMF	International Monetary Fund
JEEP	Joseph E. Estrada for President

KCIA	Korean Central Intelligence Agency
KCTU	Korean Confederation of Trade Unions
KFTU	Korean Federation of Trade Unions
KMT	Kuomintang
LIBOR	London Interbank Offer Rate
NAFTA	North Atlantic Free Trade Agreement
NAP	New Aspiration Party
NEP	New Economic Policy
NICs	newly industrializing countries
NIEs	newly industrializing economies
NSC	National Security Council
NSC 48	National Security Council document 48/2
NT	New Taiwan
OECD	Organisation for Economic Co-Operation and Development
OEM	original equipment manufacturing
OPEC	Organization of the Petroleum Exporting Countries
PAP	People's Action Party
PRC	People's Republic of China
ROK	Republic of Korea
SES	Stock Exchange of Singapore
SIMEX	Singapore International Monetary Exchange
SMEs	small and medium-sized enterprises
SOEs	state-owned enterprises
WTO	World Trade Organization
UMNO	United Malay National Organization
USSR	United Soviet Socialist Republic

The Politics of the
Asian Economic Crisis

Introduction

T. J. Pempel

In July 1997, there was a massive run on the Thai baht. Despite a $26 billion effort by the Thai government, the currency lost 48.7 percent of its value over the next six months, triggering a sharp downturn in Thai assets and growth. Thailand's problems were quickly replicated, with variations, in several neighboring countries, most notably Malaysia, South Korea, Indonesia, Singapore, and the Philippines. Each experienced a tidal wave of troubles centering on the rapid outflow of foreign capital, 30 to 50 percent plunges in their stock markets, and significant declines in the exchange rates of their national currencies. Most also faced banking crises, problems of short-term debt repayment, recessions, sharp decelerations in their previously soaring economic growth rates, or some combination of these. Between July 1997 and April 1998, some 150 Asian financial institutions were shut down, suspended, nationalized, or placed under the care of a government restructuring agency. Another fifty announced plans to merge (*FEER* 4 April 1998, 81). Within several months, three of these countries—Thailand, Indonesia, and South Korea—had petitioned the IMF for complex financial assistance packages. Suddenly, many of Asia's most rapidly advancing countries found themselves sliding down the rungs of the hierarchical world income ladder instead of enjoying the steady climb up they had experienced for the previous decade or more.

Economic problems brought political repercussions. Massive street demonstrations forced the resignation of Indonesia's ruler of thirty-two years, President Suharto; power transfers overlaid by the economic turmoil took place in Thailand, the Philippines, and South Korea. Malaysia's finance minister and erstwhile prime-ministerial heir apparent, Anwar Ibraham, sought to set the country on a course of fiscal and monetary austerity, thereby threatening many Malay and Chinese business leaders who had been close supporters of Prime Minister Mahathir and the ruling party, UMNO. Mahathir eventually reversed Anwar's policy directions and

1

introduced strict capital controls that effectively ended the international convertibility of the Malaysian ringgit. Simultaneously, sweeping criminal charges were leveled against Anwar, whose arrest and trial triggered street protests from his supporters, demanding sweeping governmental and economic reforms.

The rich tableau that surrounded these activities commanded months of worldwide attention. Headlines that for a decade or more had proclaimed the arrival of the "Asian miracle" were replaced with boldface blazonings about "the Asian economic crisis" or "the Asian flu." The speed and magnitude of Asia's collective stumble, the erosion of wealth, and the increases in poverty and social insecurity were the regional equivalent of the Great Depression of the 1930s (Wade 1998, 1–2).

These cascading events triggered a host of far-ranging debates about the roots of the problem, appropriate and inappropriate roles for investment capital, the desirability of competing models of political economy, the future of Asia, and the dangers of moral hazard. Explanations for the sudden outbreak of this regional epidemic of economic ill health ranged widely, as did, naturally enough, the prescriptions for its cure. Indeed, like economic meltdowns in earlier times and other locations, the web of events in Asia became an ideological Rorschach test onto which various and competing interpretations of a host of complex and normative issues have been projected.

Market Economics and Asia

The economics of the Asian crisis have been widely reported. Among the most frequently proffered explanations for Asia's sudden straits are exchange rate and currency misalignments, exorbitant credit expansion, asset bubbles in real estate and stocks, liquidity excesses, productive overcapacity, and trade-linked ripple effects throughout the region. All of these were compounded by panic, the effects of demonstrations, and other psychoeconomic contagions (see *Economist* 15 November 1998, 19; *Financial Times* 31 December 1997).

Woven through the macroeconomic technicalities are varying strands of criticisms tracing the Asian crisis to endogenous institutional debilities and "crony capitalism." To many, the problems centered on industrial policies predicated on excessively close government targeting of investment capital (*Economist* 15 November 1997; *Financial Times* 4 December 1997). To others, the principal flaws lay in political patronage and close personal connections between powerful politicians, bankers, regulators, and business people. In particular, these were said to have led to poor quality regulation within many Asian financial institutions. The result was a morally hazardous public guarantee for nominally private business transactions.

How to weigh these elements has generated considerable debate among professional economists inside and outside international financial institutions, but the bulk of the blame has been laid on a mélange of alleged shortcomings in Asian capitalism. East Asia, in this view, set itself up for problems because its financial systems were rife with corruption, insider trading, and weak corporate governance, or because Asian political and economic leaders operated in ways that interfered with the unfettered interplay of the two key macroeconomic principles of free markets—fear and greed. Certainly, there is no shortage of analyses, most powerfully from within the IMF, charging that Asia's economic problems should be attributed largely to Asian mistakes.

Tempting as it may be to place the blame solely on the borrower, the dual nature of any loan, as Radelet and Sachs (1998b), for example, have pointed out, makes it hard to absolve the lender from all blame. If the borrower was so patently inept, ill advised, or evil, why did the lender provide the money in the first place? Important and regionally concentrated as the Asian crisis was in 1997, the world historically has had no shortage of financial crises. Indeed, Eichengreen and Fishlow (1998, 23) contend that periods of debt crises are perhaps more "normal" than are periods in which capital flows smoothly. Several regions suffered financial crises in the 1980s: Mexico had one in 1995, Brazil and Russia were beset by financial crises soon after that in Asia, albeit for different reasons. It is difficult to contend that Asia's problems were exclusively the result of debilities germinated in some "Asian" Petri dish and subsequently transmitted through "Asian contagion."

Without denying the importance of domestic flaws, Asia's problems were more complex than can be grasped by an exclusive focus on poor macroeconomic or structural arrangements in Thailand, Indonesia, and elsewhere. The other side of the problem involved excessive and poorly monitored foreign capital inflows coming primarily from the United States, Europe, and Japan. Only when the excesses of external funds collided with internal misallocations did Asia's meltdown occur. Ed Lincoln of the Brookings Institution has proffered one succinct and not untypical summary of such an analysis: "If a common thread weaves through most of Asia, it is a combination of weakly developed domestic banking systems exposed to deregulation of international capital flows" (1998, 4; see also Asian Development Bank 1998).

A More Politically Sensitive Perspective

The contributors to this volume provide interpretations that are often orthogonal to most prevailing economic analyses. We do this in at least three significant ways. First, all of us bring to our analyses a depth of country and regional expertise that makes us inherently skeptical of any "one size fits all" explanation for what happened "across Asia." Unlike most economic explanations, which grow predominantly out of deductive reasoning and consequently are predisposed toward parsimony, those offered here stress inductive nuance and detail. They are concerned not with presenting one explanation for the crisis as a whole, but rather with explicating the various aspects of a broader mosaic.

Second, all of the chapters in this volume stress the importance of politics. It is not that the authors believe economic factors were less important than the somehow more compelling political factors. This volume is not intended to be another fusillade in the ongoing disciplinary turf war—"my variables can swallow your variables"—between politics and markets. In their past work, as here, the contributors continually engage in the exploration of problems of an economic nature. Yet, they share the belief that many of the most intriguing and puzzling aspects of the Asian crisis involve the kinds of power relationships and institutional configurations that are not subject to resolution through an exclusively economic analysis, which typically marginalizes those relationships and configurations as "externalities."

What happened in Asia, we argue, took place at the intersection of economics and politics. We thus collectively investigate the ways in which the problems that arose in Asia in 1997–98 involved not only property values, financial flows, loan portfolio makeup, and debt ratios, but also the power relationships that undergirded them. Rather than accepting generic generalizations about "rent seekers" or "crony capitalism," we try to unravel precisely which capitalists were whose cronies and why they got the rents they did—in short, what groups and institutions were most responsible for the ways in which the crisis played out.

We believe that politics and economics in Asia, as more generally, are locked in an ongoing dance in which actions by one partner are matched by responses from the other. One moves forward and the other moves back, only to be followed by turns and spins that shift direction and sometimes reverse the lead. For us, the national differences in how the economic crises played out suggest that different Asian dancers moved to distinctly different beats: the liquidity crisis cha-cha in South Korea was quite distinct from the rupiah rumba in Indonesia; in Taiwan, politics and economics spun together in a waltz that could remain rather gracefully oblivious to the crises elsewhere.

Moreover, to continue the metaphor, like Ginger Rogers and Fred Astaire, economics and politics often dance up and down various staircases and move across different levels. Here, we differ in a third way from many existing analyses. The problems in Asia had unquestionably domestic political and economic roots, but our collective analysis argues that such domestic underpinnings were interlaced with political and economic linkages at two other levels: international and regional.

Collectively, these essays suggest that a complicated multilevel dynamic between economics and politics was at play in the Asian crisis of 1997–98. The currency and financial problems that rocked a number of East Asian economies during 1997–98 had unquestionably endogenous roots—the kind of ontological bias built into terminology such as *the Asian crisis*. At the same time, we stress that many of the most powerful seismic repercussions rippling across Asia had epicenters well outside the region.

The chapters following this introduction provide two different perspectives on the complex dynamics of the Asian crisis. Part I focuses primarily on international and regional forces, showing how interlinked economic and political factors contributed to the problems that affected so much of Asia. At the same time, these external shocks reverberated differently throughout the region. Their impacts were quite strong in a half dozen or more of Asia's rapidly growing economies; in others, they were far less severe. Part II examines different national economies, analyzing the domestic political causes of and responses to the broader regional crisis. Finally, in the conclusion, I highlight some of the broad lessons that can be drawn from the crisis.

International and Regional Politics of the Asian Crisis

In 1960, the richest fifth of the world's population held thirty times more of the world's income than did the poorest fifth. This ratio widened to 32 to 1 in 1970, 45 to 1 in 1980, and 59 to 1 in 1989 (Frieden and Lake 1995, 417). These and related data demonstrate the tremendous relative reallocation of wealth that has taken place between rich and poor countries over the last three decades. Despite absolute improvements in many parts of the world, relatively speaking, the world's rich have gotten richer and its poor have gotten poorer.

The stunningly rapid advance of most of the national economies in East Asia marked a substantial deviation from this broad trend. In 1960, Japan and Northeast Asia accounted for only 4 percent of world GNP, compared to 37 percent for the United States, Canada, and Mexico. By the early 1990s, the combined economies of Japan, South Korea, Taiwan, Hong Kong, the ASEAN countries, and Greater China contributed roughly 30 percent of world GNP, approximately the same share as that held by North America on the one hand and Western Europe on the other.

Except for the relatively short-term spurt in riches to the OPEC countries during the 1970s, East Asia's economic success marked the most meaningful reallocation of wealth between rich and poor countries since the end of World War II. And unlike the oil-producing countries, the nations of Asia enhanced their wealth through deep-seated structural changes in their national production profiles, rather than through the fortuities of natural resource endowment and the temporary production limits of an oil-producing cartel. Asia's successes thus garnered significantly larger shares in the production and export of the world's high-value-added manufactured goods.

As I have argued elsewhere (Pempel 1999), Asia's collective economic success was over-determined, politically constructed, and yet far from easy. Ultimately, it involved a complex mixture of politics and economics played out across three different levels—international, regional, and national. A similarly complex interaction was involved in the Asian economic crisis.

The economic havoc that crystallized in the summer of 1997 was catalyzed by a witches' brew that contained at least four major ingredients largely external to the countries themselves. First, there were changes in the international and regional balance of power. Second, the once diffuse and separate national economies of Asia had become increasingly interconnected. Third, important changes occurred in the nature of corporate production processes. Fourth and finally, the size and speed of cross-national capital movements expanded geometrically. Together, these four provided a substantially altered international and regional context for Asia's national political economies. All four are closely connected and are explored throughout this book, but they are tackled most explicitly in the four chapters that constitute Part I.

In his chapter for this volume, as in other work, Bruce Cumings (1987, for example) stresses how changes in U.S. strategic and military interests were a structuring backdrop, first, for the economic success of Japan and the Northeast Asian NICs during the first four decades after World War II and second, for various of their economic problems in the mid-1990s. He notes how American policy makers encouraged Japan, Taiwan, and South Korea to pursue mercantilist domestic economies that relied on export-led growth, largely to the U.S. market. In exchange, America got military installations and anticommunist regimes in Asia.

By the late 1980s and early 1990s, the collapse of communism and the end of the Cold War; the changing power balance in Asia; economic competitiveness from Japan, South Korea, and Taiwan; the economic integration of Europe and the formulation of NAFTA; and changing U.S. domestic politics combined to reduce America's indulgence of Asian trade policies. Although the military links between the United States and Japan, South Korea, and Taiwan changed very little, the predominant profiles of these latter three metamorphosed from unquestioned strategic allies into unscrupulous economic competitors.

In keeping with the prevalence of neoclassical economic thinking and a rising faith in monetarism, American policy makers turned increasingly to exchange rate policies in an effort to rectify bilateral trade imbalances with Asia. The Plaza and Louvre Accords, primarily between the United States and Japan, reduced the export prices of goods denominated in dollars while raising those denominated in yen, wón, or NT dollars. Subsequently, in an ad hoc agreement in April 1995, the United States and Japan cooperated to enhance the value of the dollar, thereby triggering much of the export slowdown and currency instability within Asian countries whose currencies were pegged to the dollar.

Currency realignments were important to a second major trend, namely the deepening of Asian regional ties. In chapter 3, I show, among other things, how exchange rate recalibrations in the mid-1980s strengthened the national currencies of Japan, South Korea, and Taiwan, and how these, along with changing domestic economic conditions and government policy shifts, stimulated the outflow of investment capital from all three countries to other parts of Asia. This new investment money, combined with a long-standing base of Japanese official assistance, fueled a surge in manufacturing production, national growth, and intra-Asian trade, particularly among the ASEAN countries. These in turn wove ever-denser webs of economic connections among the previously rather separated Asian economies. Initially, the results were increased production and growth through much of Asia; subsequently, however, excess capital led to the overproduction and asset bubbles that catalyzed the crisis of 1997.

Gary G. Hamilton also takes up the theme of Asian regionalism in chapter 2, with a focus on the ways in which corporations and sectors organize their production networks across national borders. World production, he points out, was once dominated by "vertically integrated" economic organizations within single nation-states (page 50). This pattern, he argues, has since shifted toward an increase in demand-responsive "reflexive manufacturing systems" involving truly international divisions of intracorporate labor and management (page 51). Many Southeast Asian and Chinese firms drawing on cheap labor became integrated in very different ways into these two patterns of corporate organization. Japanese and Korean corporations that had previously been almost exclusively domestic replicated their own vertically integrated systems in various parts of Southeast Asia. Meanwhile, ethnic Chinese capital (particularly from Taiwan, Hong Kong, and Singapore) created numerous networks of reflexive manufacturing operations within the PRC and ASEAN. For Hamilton, as for me, the result was to create an Asia driven not by any one homogenous "Asian model" or the simple regional aggregation of discrete national economies, but rather by complicated and hierarchical webs involving complex cross-national fusions.

Interestingly, and in contrast to the deeply institutionalized regionalism in Europe and even NAFTA and Mercosur, the regional ties linking Asia remained largely commercial in character. There was very little institutionalization of political authority (Katzenstein and Shiraishi 1997). As I examine more fully in chapter 3, Asia has no equivalent of a Brussels secretariat issuing regionwide regulations on trucking or social welfare for the whole region. Instead, ASEAN, and to a large extent APEC, rely on *musyawarah mufakat*, the Indonesian phrase for simple consultation and consensus. The institutional focus has been on regional trade liberalization, and, to the extent that intraregional trade has increased, so has regionwide vulnerability to trade-induced contagions.

The commercial and nonpolitical character of Asian regionalism also eliminated the possibility of any authoritative Asia-wide response to the external tremors as they began to ripple across the Asian region. Instead, Asia's heightened commercial integration left a host of seemingly national economies highly vulnerable to the various contagions that swept across the region. Cross-border downturns raced forward with none of the buffering protections that might have come from regionwide political or financial institutions.

The cross-national capital flows that linked various national economies and production networks throughout Asia were simultaneously part of the fourth and final major international change: the geometric increases and changing character, particularly during the 1990s, in cross-national capital mobility. I deal with this process in chapter 3, as does Jeffrey A. Winters in greater detail in chapter 4.

Capital flows now total more than seventy times the volume of world trade. Once the major flows of cross-border money involved government-to-government or bank-to-government transactions. Long-term capital and foreign aid projects such as factories, roads, harbors, hospitals, and schools were the result. The new monies, in contrast, are increasingly composed of private capital. Such capital has the enhanced ability to move quickly and autonomously, subject to political restraints from neither host government nor home government.

By the early 1990s, these private capital flows were rising throughout the developing world, going not only into Asia but into Latin America and central and east-

Table I.1. Sources of External Commercial Bank Debt to End of June 1997

	Loans (US$ billion)	% of Total* from Japan	% of Total* from United States	% of Total* from Britain	% of Total* from Rest of Europe	% of Total* from Others
Indonesia	58.7	39.4	7.8	7.4	30.9	14.5
Malaysia	28.8	36.4	8.3	7.0	37.0	11.3
Philippines	14.1	14.9	20.0	7.6	40.5	17.0
South Korea	103.4	22.9	9.6	5.9	29.3	32.3
Thailand	69.4	54.4	5.8	4.1	24.5	11.3
Total	274.5	33.6	10.3	6.4	32.4	17.3

*Total equals total debt loaned by country.
Source: Bank for International Settlements, as cited in *FEER* 23 July 1998, 38.

ern Europe as well (Kahler 1998, 1). In 1995, private capital accounted for three-fourths of all investment resources to the developing world. Much of this new investment money involved "hot money" such as short-term loans and portfolio investments. Eighty percent of net global foreign exchange transactions now have a maturity date of seven days or less (Wade 1998, 3).

From the 1990s onward, Japan presented one important source of such "hot money." Huge amounts of new money entered Asia as a consequence of Japanese domestic monetary policies seeking to bail out the Japanese banks and financial institutions from upward of $1 trillion in bad debt accumulated during the "bubble economy" (Asher 1996; Asher and Smithers 1998; Pempel 1998a). The Japanese government reduced its official discount rate to virtually zero, giving Japanese banks attractive incentives to borrow yen cheaply and lend it at higher rates to Asia's eagerly expanding firms and banks. By mid-1997, Japanese banks accounted for more than one-third of the total outstanding commercial bank debt in the five ASEAN member countries (with 54 percent of the loans in Thailand) (Table I.1). Moreover, while Japanese banks were lending at such low rates, U.S. and European banks were able to borrow yen in Japan and lend it throughout Asia and elsewhere in what was known as the *carry trade*.

Equally important as a source of "hot money" was new portfolio investment capital, particularly, but not exclusively, from the United States. In the United States, an explosion of middle-aged savers worried about their retirement prospects deposited huge pools of capital into an ever-expanding number of privately managed mutual funds. The search for ever-higher rates of return led many of these funds to invest in the growing economies of East Asia. As of 1994, nineteen U.S. closed-end funds with assets of $4.2 billion specialized in East Asia; twelve had been established since 1990. These included several country funds investing exclusively in South Korea, Malaysia, Indonesia, and Thailand. Another $1.8 billion was held in open-ended East Asian funds. For each fund launched in the United States during 1990 and 1991, seven others were formed in other countries, including, importantly, Hong Kong and Singapore (Petri 1995, 40). (By early 1999, the number of American funds focusing on Pacific Asia or its component economies was up to at least twenty-nine; this was over and above the developing-markets funds, world funds, and the like, which included but were not limited to investments in Asia. My calculations are from *Barron's* 11 January 1999.)

Portfolio capital, as Winters points out, rose from just 2 percent of total net financial capital flows to developing countries in 1987 to nearly 50 percent by 1996. The bulk of this staggering sum is in the hands of fewer than one hundred developing-markets fund managers operating out of financial centers within Asia but also across the world (see also Armijo 1999a).

The first "Asian contagion" was a contagion of unfettered optimism in the investment decisions of portfolio managers and short-term lenders. A herding instinct led most to sprinkle ever-expanding amounts of portfolio money and short-term loans liberally across rapidly growing Asian markets, convinced that past growth (and not a little bit of cronyism) would ensure that the new monies would be uniformly safe, take seed, and generate consistently high returns and expanding multiples. Ultimately, much of this money generated overproduction or found its way into bubble-prone property markets and thinly traded stocks.

For Winters, a key part of the "Asian contagion" involved the speed with which much of this money was pulled out as the asset bubbles burst, trade slowed, and currency values dropped. For him, a critical element was what he calls Asia's "plugging in" to world capital markets, often without the benefit of institutional surge protectors to prevent massive fluctuations and deadly jolts.

Just as an optimistic "Asian contagion" involved the failure by many lenders to differentiate among individual Asian borrowers, when the crisis began, the contagion of pessimism was often insensitive to national borders. The first whiff of economic problems in one country led outside investors to question the economic underpinnings of its neighbors. In chapter 7, Andrew MacIntyre shows how loss of investor confidence in Thailand led to similar questionings, but for different structural reasons, in Indonesia (see also Cerra and Saxena 1998). Even more problematic, once crisis struck, unrelated markets fell as investors sold securities or redeemed loans to maintain their overall risk profiles or to raise cash to cover losses elsewhere. Several contributors to this book explore how generic doubts about "Asia" swept through the Philippines, Taiwan, South Korea, Hong Kong, Singapore, and Malaysia despite the widely differing economic conditions and political structures in each.

International politics also played a role, as I explore in the conclusion, in the changing character of the IMF and its analysis of what had happened in Asia. American responses to the crisis in different countries were quite different, as both Cumings and Meredith Woo-Cumings examine (chapters 1 and 6, respectively). The United States was anxious to assist South Korea, where it had thirty-five thousand troops and where its American-based banks had substantial exposure, in contrast to its much less animated response to the problems in Indonesia, which had no U.S. bases and limited U.S. banking exposure.

With time, the importance of intra-Asian differences became apparent. As several of the authors demonstrate in Part II, discrete national political biases and institutional configurations created highly differentiated levels of vulnerability and resistance to investment withdrawals, currency attacks, and debt repayment demands. In short, just as international and regional politics were vital ingredients in the outbreak of the economic havoc, so individual countries demonstrated varying degrees of vulnerability or inoculation against their worst effects.

Politics of National Responses

A generic phrase such as *the Asian crisis* masks the widely varied experiences of different countries, both in the impact of the crisis and in responses to it. Although some countries were hard hit, others, notably Taiwan, China, and Singapore, escaped with only minor damage. Some countries, such as South Korea, responded with official efforts at greater capital integration, but others, such as Malaysia and Hong Kong, opted for restrictions on capital movement and monetary flexibility. Such differences reflected the specific market economics and policy choices of individual countries. Yet, as the essays in this volume demonstrate, neither economic fundamentals nor policy choices were created within a political vacuum. On the contrary, they were fundamentally the consequences of the intranational divisions of power and the nationally differentiated institutional arrangements that reflected these divisions.

For purposes of analysis, these political forces can be said to have played out during two rather separate periods. At first, there were differences in the degree of vulnerability to the various short-term capital and currency movements. Then, individual countries demonstrated widely disparate political biases in their efforts to make adjustments, once the first waves of the crisis had rolled over them.

Initial vulnerabilities were undeniably tied to a nation's financial openness. Which individual Asian economies were most shocked by, or immune to, the currency speculations, short-term capital withdrawals, and liquidity crises that swept through much of Asia was the direct result of how they were, or were not, "plugged in" to international capital markets. Countries such as Burma, Vietnam, China, and, to a lesser extent, Taiwan, stood at one pole, with only minimal connection to the international capital grid. Investment in Taiwan, as Yun-han Chu demonstrates in chapter 9, was sharply constricted by government regulations and CBC policy oversights, particularly over portfolio investment. In chapter 10, Barry Naughton points out that although the PRC attracted substantial sums of fdi, its communist government retained restrictions over capital flows, foreign trade, and currency convertibility that were among the most severe in the region. As a consequence of such insulation, these countries were largely immune to short-term property and stock bubbles, currency speculations, and "hot money" outflows.

In contrast, South Korea had recently qualified for membership in the OECD, thereby incurring that organization's requirement to open its capital markets.

Singapore, as Linda Y. G. Lim analyzes in chapter 5, also had a deeply institution-alized commitment to relative capital openness through a monetary regime predi-cated on the managed float of exchange rates. Hong Kong, although generally open, retained a currency board that restricted free-floating exchange rates. Between these two extremes, but having undergone varying degrees of financial liberalization over the previous decade or two, were countries such as Thailand, Indonesia, Malaysia, and the Philippines.

Choices about currency convertibility and openness to short-term foreign capi-tal movements, however, were clearly politically rooted. Taiwan, for example, had an ever-narrowing circle of strategic allies in its dealings with a hostile China. KMT leaders thus opted for policy mechanisms designed to ensure high levels of monetary and financial stability and fiscal balance. Economic stability became a foreign policy weapon critical to Taiwan's international acceptance and external security. To retain maximum political control over the process, financial liberaliza-tion in Taiwan gave priority to deregulation of the domestic capital market rather than to foreign participation.

In their efforts to restrict openness to international capital, the government was greatly aided by the fact that Taiwanese business was fragmented into numerous small and medium-sized industries, rather than being dominated by highly capi-talized mega-corporations such as Japan's *keiretsu* or Korea's *chaebŏl* or by huge, internationally sensitive financial institutions. Taiwan's few large industrial com-plexes were almost exclusively under the politically safe control of the KMT itself. The end result was an economy that was highly buffered politically from the worst excesses of international capital movement.

Rather a different picture emerges for South Korea. Close ties among the gov-ernment bureaucracy, the political parties, and the large and primarily family-owned *chaebŏl* gave the latter a virtual public guarantee for their highly leveraged borrowing practices (Wade 1990; Woo 1991). Serious credit analysis was frowned on. Instead, intra-*chaebŏl* loan guarantees became a way of life that allowed Korean and foreign banks to soften their exposure. As Woo-Cumings has suggested, the idea was that the loan guarantee turned the entire *chaebŏl* group into a gigantic chunk of collateral. This system came under political attack with Korea's democ-ratization and internationalization as early as 1993, but the institutionalized power of the *chaebŏl* left the excess borrowing highly resistant to change. As a result, the Korean private sector remained highly vulnerable to the short-term liquidity crisis it eventually confronted in 1997. Yet Korea's crisis of short-term debt was quite different from the currency and investment outflows that hit Thailand, Indonesia, and Malaysia. And in an additional twist of political fate, it was the crisis and the subsequent IMF assistance package that allowed the new government of Kim Dae Jung to force through policies designed to break up the long-standing and cozy ties among the *chaebŏl*, the government, the banks, and the previously governing par-ties that were Kim's political enemies.

Finally, and in contrast to the banking reforms being carried out in South Korea, stands the Philippines. As Paul Hutchcroft demonstrates for that country in chapter 8, simple openness or closedness of capital markets and investment opportunities were hardly unilateral determinants of the amounts of outside money flowing into countries.

Far more important, there as elsewhere, were the politics behind government monetary policies. Banking in the Philippines epitomized "crony capitalism": throughout the late 1980s and early 1990s, the government provided selected banks with high-interest, low-risk treasury bills that became "a major pot of gold" for the few chosen banks. As Hutchcroft puts it, "funds borrowed *from* the government were re-lent *to* the government at much higher rates!" (page 67). This lucrative intranational deal allowed Philippine banks to earn high levels of profits with low risk and hence to avoid the temptation to turn to international borrowings. When capital accounts were opened to foreign participation, the Philippines' long history of banking oligarchy, comparative macroeconomic disappointment, and high levels of political risk meant that the country initially attracted far smaller shares of outside fdi and portfolio money than did neighboring Thailand, Indonesia, Hong Kong, Singapore, and South Korea. Ironically, the country's lower economic elevation left it was far less vulnerable to the "hot money" outflows that affected so many of its neighbors.

In addition to such socioeconomic underpinnings of political power, institutional structures were also politically critical in the unfolding of the economic crisis within different countries. Thus, as MacIntyre demonstrates, Indonesia and Thailand were both highly vulnerable to "hot money" flight, but for very different institutional reasons. Thailand, with its highly fragmented electoral and parliamentary system, had governments that found it impossible to make and carry out consistent policies. Investors were thus highly skittish of even the mildest short-term Thai economic problems. In contrast, Indonesia, with far better economic fundamentals, also proved to be vulnerable, but for precisely the opposite reason. Suharto's one-man rule made it relatively certain that his decisions would be carried out; but to the dismay of change-averse investors, his policy preferences zigged and zagged erratically in response to the unfolding crisis.

Lim offers another example of how politics affected national responses during and after the crisis; she focuses more on socioeconomic support than on institutional differences in her examination of Hong Kong's retention of a currency board and its commitment to maintaining the local currency's "peg" to the U.S. dollar (even though this meant exceptionally high short-term interest rates and massive infusion of government monies into the previously mostly private stock market). This contrasted with Singapore's early ending of its currency board and its consequently far greater tolerance of currency devaluation during 1997–98. Economic policy choices in Hong Kong, Lim shows, rested heavily on the politically institutionalized power of Hong Kong property barons and property-dependent banks, a power that increased as Hong Kong reverted to PRC control. In Singapore, even though much of the property market was, like Hong Kong's, under government control, there, government ownership was used to provide politically popular low-cost housing, giving policy a very different official bias. Meanwhile, Singapore's manufacturing and export sectors remained stronger than Hong Kong's, democratic elections were far more constraining of public economic choices, and the Singaporean national bureaucracy was far more insulated from the local business community than was its Hong Kong counterpart. Such political differences exerted a profound influence over the contrasting economic choices made by the two city-states.

Building from that approach, one can note the different base of political power shaping responses within Malaysia. Cronyesque ties among many business and political leaders were woven together through the dominant party, UMNO. Meanwhile, the country's NEP provided a long-standing affirmative-action plan for the Malay population, which in turn ensured that group's strong electoral support for UMNO. Because this socioeconomic power base would have been sharply challenged as part of any IMF assistance package, Prime Minister Mahathir eventually rejected outside aid in favor of closing off Malaysian capital markets, arresting former Finance Minister Anwar, and providing government-induced stimulation to the economy.

Interestingly, despite greater levels of electoral democracy in Malaysia, Prime Minister Mahathir enjoyed much the same autocratic power as did Indonesia's Suharto, and Mahathir too spooked foreign investors. For Malaysia, however, as Winters point out, the problem was hardly uncertainty. Instead, it was outright hostility. Foreign investors had little incentive to keep capital in a country whose prime minister made unending pronouncements about the dangers of an international Jewish conspiracy and of foreign investors, and who issued nationalistic warnings that IMF assistance would carry strings binding Malaysian assets inflexibly to foreign controls.

Singapore's far more deeply institutionalized commitments to open markets, free capital flows, and integration with the world economy allowed it to do far better, after the first wave of problems, than many of its neighbors. Singapore was able both to hold on to much invested capital and to re-attract it quickly after the meltdown. Indeed, as Lim points out, after the crisis of 1997 foreign fund managers were given incentives by Singapore's government to establish operations there, to manage portions of the government's huge CPF, and, against the objections of Hong Kong, the Singapore exchange (SIMEX) began trading Hong Kong index futures.

Finally, it is worth highlighting how politics has shaped China's post-crisis activities. Most important, as Naughton underscores, China's leaders have been reinforced in their recognition of just how dependent political power can be on economic stability. For this reason, Chinese political leaders, but especially Zhu Rongji, remain convinced of the need to maintain tough political controls while simultaneously moving ahead with economic reforms "because those who fail to develop will not survive" (page 210). Particularly difficult, however, as Naughton makes clear, will be a "redefining [of] the urban social compact" through the privatization of SOEs (page 217). These SOEs remain extremely problematic, because their role in maintaining employment levels and social welfare benefits make them critical to domestic political stability despite their high levels of economic inefficiency.

The Asian crisis of 1997–98 raises a host of important and complicated questions, many of which are addressed in greater detail in the subsequent chapters and in the conclusion. But as I have tried to highlight in this introduction, and as the remaining chapters bring out in greater detail, what happened in Asia can be at best only partially understood by focusing exclusively on domestic macroeconomic forces. The crisis was the result of a complicated interweaving of economics and politics; a sensitivity to these political forces is vital to understanding why the crisis began and how it unfolded.

Acknowledgements

In addition to comments from the conference participants, this introduction benefitted from extensive suggestions from Benjamin J. Cohen, Linda Lim, and Andrew MacIntyre.

P A R T I

INTERNATIONAL AND REGIONAL CONTRIBUTIONS

CHAPTER ONE

The Asian Crisis, Democracy, and
the End of "Late" Development

Bruce Cumings

The global financial crisis that began in the summer of 1997 and spread from Thailand and Singapore to Indonesia and South Korea created a watershed in contemporary history: a systematic failure of capitalism struck precisely those economies long held up as models of industrial efficiency—the Asian "tigers"—and no one is quite sure what to do about it or where the crisis will end. A sober and influential American economist wrote recently that this turmoil "produced financial contagion on a scale unprecedented since the collapse of the Creditanstalt in 1931," and that he could not be sure the ministrations of the IMF had halted its progress (Hale 1998a).[1] In 1999, with the meltdown of Brazil's economy, it claimed another casualty. Standing behind the travail of the smaller afflicted countries is perhaps a more stunning phenomenon: the shaky financial condition and political Immobilism of the world's second largest economy, Japan, with perhaps $1 trillion in bad loans and (for a country long praised for its efficient "administrative guidance") a truly amazing crisis of governance.

Nothing has come close to this financial crisis as a defining moment that tells us what the post–Cold War world will really look like and the problems it will present. The international crises of the 1990s over Bosnia, Iraq, and North Korea might fall under the rubric "what's my atavism?"; all were holdovers or recuperations of old problems. But the financial crisis is no atavism, and it poses a host of different questions: What if markets don't work? What if investors panic? What if the IMF doesn't know what it is doing? (IMF remedies have been sharply criticized by the IMF's sister organization, the World Bank.) Who pays the costs of economic disaster? And what is the relationship between capitalism and democracy?

In the early stages of the crisis, two dominant views emerged among mainstream analysts: that Asian economies were at fault because of their "crony capitalism," with its many market irregularities and "moral hazards," and that the IMF was a secret organization, lacking accountability, that was itself interfering with normal market processes by bailing out investors who had made bad decisions. Henry Kissinger (*Los Angeles Times* 8 February 1998), for example, likened the IMF to "a doctor specializing in measles [who] tries to cure every illness with one remedy," and the *Wall Street Journal* editors (21 November 1997) called it "one of the most secretive institutions this side of an average missile base." Certainly these points are valid; the IMF is the global embodiment of the "new ecumenical gospel" of neoliberalism,[2] and its decision making is shrouded in mystery. But how can the "miracle" economies of Asia turn overnight into cesspools of "crony capitalism"? From the mid-1960s onward, South Korea and Taiwan were the fastest-growing economies in the world, with China outstripping them in the 1990s. In the 1990s, the East Asian countries accounted for nearly two-thirds of all capital investment (excluding Japan, with its long-term recession) and for one-half of the growth in world output, even though they constitute only 20 percent of the world's GDP.

In a recent article, Robert Wade and Frank Veneroso (1998, 3–22) therefore found IMF demands for "radical institutional change" in "the Asian High Debt Model" to be perplexing; to require a deep restructuring because of a temporary liquidity crisis struck them as inappropriate, given that the model had proved its manifold developmental advantages. But the model they describe, a national industrial strategy of state-mediated capital going to large firms trying to conquer foreign markets, with correspondingly high debt–equity ratios in the firms, is not an Asian but a Korean and Japanese model—as Meredith Woo-Cumings demonstrates in chapter 6 of this book. None of the Southeast Asian economies can be characterized in this way, except perhaps (and with many qualifications) Malaysia. China, however, finds this model deeply appealing and is far along the path of emulation.[3]

Japan, which pioneered the "developmental state," seemed just a few years ago to be the likely regional hegemon of the Pacific. It had a dominant economic position in Southeast Asia, and it appeared that Japan soon might organize China's entry into the world economy. But that did not happen, and the reason it did not lies in the history and practice of American hegemony in East Asia: South Korea and Japan have been sheltered economies, indulged in their neomercantilism and posted as engines of economic growth, because of the great value this had in the global struggle with communism. Now that this struggle is over, however, the issue of their "fit" with a new era of free markets and neoliberalism comes to the fore— to the surprise and shock of Koreans and to the consternation of the paralytic Japanese elite.

The deep meaning of the Asian crisis therefore lies in the American attempt to ring down the curtain on "late" development of the Japan/Korea type and in the likelihood that the attempt will be successful, because the strong, nationalistic neomercantilism of Japan and South Korea was propagated in the soft soil of semi-sovereignty, and because the Americans have had willing accomplices in Northeast Asian peoples who have sought to reform or nullify this model themselves, in the interest of economic equity and democratic politics. The unexpected liquidity crunch in 1997 had a certain serendipity for a resurgent United States with an ever-deepening global position and the strongest foreign economic policy in decades; it gave American leaders the chance to dismantle the remaining alternative model of capitalist political economy, before it organized not just Japan and South Korea, but China as well. Paradoxically, the economic debacle also gave the people of these countries a new and sudden chance at democratic opening. They are thus Washington's best allies in implementing lasting reform, because just as politics could not be separated from economics during the era of the "Asian miracle," today, demands for democratization go hand in hand with a crippling depression in the Asian region. The best place to witness this conjuncture is South Korea, but the Korean case also holds important lessons for China and Japan.

The Anomalous States of Northeast Asia

If the Cold War is over on a world scale, that does not mean structures built during that forty-year struggle have disappeared. Indeed, the watershed changes of 1989–91 had relatively little effect on Northeast Asia: no communist state collapsed, and the United States did not retreat; Soviet power in the region evaporated, leaving the structure of unilateral American power in place. The rationale for containment collapsed, of course, but that was merely one part of American strategy. The American bases that still dot Japan and South Korea (containing nearly one hundred thousand troops) were meant both to contain the communist enemy and to constrain the capitalist ally. After World War II, Japan and South Korea were the subjects of this dual containment policy, while their economies were posted as engines of growth for the broader world economy. Americans revived Japan's formidable industrial base, reconnected former colonial hinterland territories that were still accessible to it (South Korea and Taiwan above all), and enmeshed these territories in security structures that rendered them semi-sovereign states.

Since that distant but determining point of origin, American generals have had operational control of the huge South Korean army, and Japan, long the second-largest economy in the world, has depended on the United States for defenses and its vital resources. Meanwhile, both countries were showered with all manner of support in the early postwar period, as part of a Cold War project to remake both of them into paragons of noncommunist development. Japan became the paradigmatic example of non-Western growth for the "modernization school" that dominated American policy and scholarship in the 1950s and 1960s, just as South Korea subsequently became the first Asian "tiger."

The Korean War (1950–53) decisively interrupted U.S. plans to re-stitch American and Japanese economic relations with other parts of East Asia; indeed, the repositioning of Japan as a major industrial producer in response to a raging anti-imperial revolution on the Asian mainland is the key to explaining most of East and Southeast Asian history until the Indochina War finally ended in 1975. This regional Cold War structure thus resulted from unanticipated consequences that led American planners to forge a second-best world that divided Asia for a generation, when their first-best world was a single global economy under American leadership that would have yielded a unified Asian region. Ever since the publication of the "open door notes" in 1900 amid an imperial scramble for Chinese real estate, Washington's ultimate goal has always been unimpeded access to the East Asian region; it wanted native governments strong enough to maintain independence but not strong enough to throw off Western capital. The Cold War forced a number of temporary compromises in this vision that lasted far longer than anyone expected, and East Asia remained divided for decades. But these expedients began to erode dramatically after the Indochina War ended, as People's China was slowly brought into the world economy. Now, with the growing integration of the economies of the region, Cold War impediments have nearly disappeared. In that sense, the East Asian region is now poised to return to the "first principles" that American planners thought appropriate before the Chinese revolution and the Korean War demolished their plans.

The intricate and inseparable mingling of security and economic goals that marked American policy is visible in the operative documents for the postwar reconstruction of the region, ultimately embodied in a long analysis known as NSC 48, "Policy for Asia," approved by President Harry Truman at the end of 1949. In earlier papers that informed the final draft, American officials enumerated several principles that they thought should regulate economic exchange in a unified East Asian region (including China): "the establishment of conditions favorable to the export of technology and capital and to a liberal trade policy throughout the world," "reciprocal exchange and mutual advantage," "production and trade which truly reflect comparative advantage," and opposition to what they called "general industrialization"—something that could be achieved "only at a high cost as a result of sacrificing production in fields of comparative advantage." NSC 48 planners anticipated nationalist objections in the grand manner of the nineteenth-century Rothschilds:

> The complexity of international trade makes it well to bear in mind that such ephemeral matters as national pride and ambition can inhibit or prevent the necessary degree of international cooperation or the development of a favorable atmosphere and conditions to promote economic expansion. (Cumings 1991, 171–75)

Yet "general industrialization" is just what Japan and South Korea later pursued—nationalist strategies to build a comprehensive industrial base, a policy that contrasts sharply with the Southeast Asian countries (which tend to be "niche" economies, like the smaller states in Europe). As the favored countries in the East Asian region, Japan, South Korea, and Taiwan each developed states appropriate to the long era of division that began in 1950 and lasted through the 1980s. Japan was shorn of its military and political clout to become an American-sponsored "economic animal," with coercive functions transferred to bloated authoritarian states in Taiwan and South Korea that each had mammoth armies and spent almost all the income they extracted from their people on coercion, getting whatever else

they needed from direct American aid grants (Cumings 1999). These state appara-
tuses thus completed the regional configuration; without such front-line defenses,
Japan's military forces and its defense spending would have been much higher. At
the same time, all three states were deeply penetrated by American power and
interests, yielding profound lateral weakness. They were strong and weak at once,
and not by accident, because external shaping had its origins in the workings of an
American-led world economy. But East Asians were also actors in this milieu. If
the "developmental state" was their answer, this was not a new form of political
economy that emerged *sui generis*; they were devotees of European continental
theory—something that requires some elaboration, for it explains both what they
did and how the United States can undo it.

National Economy and State Science

In his 1994 book on Japan, James Fallows begins one chapter with a story about
finding an English translation of Friedrich List's *The Natural System of Political
Economy* in a bookshop in Tokyo. He writes that it had taken him five years to find
an English version of List's work, and that on doing so he exhaled his version of
Eureka: "*Friedrich List*!!!" (179). He goes on to argue that the German List, not
Adam Smith, was the economic theorist behind Japan's industrial growth. Now
compare E. H. Norman, writing in 1941, who begins a passage about German
influence on post-1868 Japan by saying, "It is a commonplace that Ito [Hirobumi]
modeled the Japanese constitution [and much else] very closely upon the Prussian"
(1975, 451). Or compare Karl Marx, who in 1857 analyzed the thought of a prominent American economist of the time, a follower of List named Henry Carey. The
natural and normal to Carey was tariff protection and hothouse development of
industry, and the unnatural and abnormal was the British doctrine of free trade,
which he saw as a form of highway robbery: "Carey sees the contradictions in the
economic relations as soon as they appear on the world market as *English* relations," Marx (1973, 88) wrote. Marx also writes that

> Originally [for Carey], the English relations were distorted by the false theories of her
> [England's] economists, internally. Now, externally, as the commanding power of the
> world market, England distorts the harmony of economic relations in all the countries
> of the world. . . . Having dissolved this fundamental harmony in its own interior, Eng-
> land, by its competition, proceeds to destroy it throughout the world market. . . . The
> only defence lies in protective tariffs—the forcible, national barricade against the
> destructive power of large-scale English industry. Hence, the state, which was at first
> branded the sole disturber of these "*harmonies économiques*," is now these harmonies'
> last refuge . . . with Carey the harmony of the bourgeois relations of production ends
> with the most complete disharmony of these relations on the grandest terrain where
> they appear, the world market, and in their grandest development, as the relations of
> producing nations. (886)

We can extract the implicit theory of the state here as follows: under conditions of national competition, the state becomes the "national barricade" (as part of what List called *nationalekönomie*). But elsewhere Carey had branded the state as the disturber of the domestic economy—therefore, he must think the state is good for some things (protection), but not good for others (intervention in the "free market"). Exactly so. Historically, this is nothing more than Republican Party praxis (Smoot-Hawley plus J. Edgar Hoover plus laissez-faire), but analytically it means the state is not simply a domestic expression, but is also formed from without by something else: national competition ("the grandest development") in the world market ("the grandest terrain"). *Nationalekönomie* is therefore not just for Germans but for everyone coming to the world of industry "late." The *arriviste* state should regulate competition by opening and closing within the grand terrain of the world market—in other words, something close to Karl Polanyi's theory of the state, which in the milieu of the world economy becomes a guarantor of Polanyi's "principle of social protection" against the backwash and the ravages of world market competition (Polanyi 1957).

The state is—in part—a historic and domestic product: Ito Hirobumi discovered German "state science" (*staatswissenschaften*) as opposed to our "political science." But it is also more than that; states differ according to time and place and are also residua of international competition. The state has a *lateral* dimension that may be strong or weak (penetrated or autonomous, to make it simple). If this is so, then state formation will again differ according to world time and position within the world system. Strong states are those whose citizens are habituated to the existing forms at home and those capable of imposing their wills abroad; the latter, in its hegemonic form, involves everything from consumption of the strong state's products to consumption of its exported culture. Immanuel Wallerstein is one of the few who understand this point, even if his discussions of it have been subject to endless misreading. Here is his definition of the modern world's array of "strong" and "weak" states:

> States have been located in a hierarchy of effective power which can be measured neither by the size and coherence of their bureaucracies and armies nor by their ideological formulations about themselves but by their effective capacities over time to further the concentration of accumulated capital within their frontiers as against those rival states.
>
> Nor were these states fully sovereign: "the very existence of this hierarchy provided the major limitation." (1983, 56–57)

For Marx, the state's "autonomy" consisted of the state's separating itself from society and becoming a power over and above it, much as Polanyi saw, in the rise of the world market, the extrusion of economic relations from social relations and the subordination of society by economic imperatives (the unregulated market separating itself and becoming a power over and above society, and, perhaps, the state). Thus, for Marx, the *modern state* means

The separation of the state from the body of society, or (as Marx writes), "The abstraction of the *state as such* . . . was not created until modern times. The abstraction of the *political state* is a modern product." (Coletti 1975, 33)

For Hegel (who found a home among Japanese and Korean thinkers that would no doubt surprise him), however, modern society establishes the distinction between public and private, and because individuals are atomized by the market (Marx says of Hegel's theory), therefore the state itself must provide a new form of unity—in Hegel's thought, an abstracted unity that substitutes for a lost organic community. It then follows that the state may become a conservator of past "protections" threatened by market relations or international competition:

> It is precisely *because* Hegel's vision of the contradictory and self-destructive character of modern society is so lively that he tried so hard to resuscitate and adapt to modern conditions certain aspects of the "organic" feudal order which still survived in the Prussia of his day. Hegel sees these more organic institutions as an elementary way of compensating for the newly unleashed individualism of bourgeois society. . . . The task of a modern state, in this sense, must be to restore the ethic and the organic wholeness of the antique *polis* . . . and to do this without sacrificing the principle of subjective freedom. (Coletti 1975, 30–31)

If John Locke presents the state (or "civil government") as the separated "impartial judge" of private conflicts, for Hegel this separation of state and civil society was a contradiction of his deepest understanding of human society, and so he hypothesized a state that would restore the lost organic wholeness for which he yearned, yielding a fusion of what we call state and society.

And here we come to the nub of the problem between the contemporary hegemony of neoliberalism and the realities of East Asian practice: *all* the modern states of the region, including the communist ones, have responded in some fashion to Hegel's passion for conserving a threatened organic heritage—leading to what Meiji thinkers called the "family state," what interwar Japanese ideologues referred to as *kokutai* (often translated as "national body"), or what became, in North Korea, a state/society modeled on the ruling family and the doctrine of Juche (*chuch'e*, a form of nationalist subjectivity pronounced *shutai* in Japanese and a central intellectual theme in modern Japanese and Korean history—see Koschmann 1996). The material foundations of this sheltered independence are also remarkable. The agency of *dependencia* in Latin America, fdi, remained amazingly low in Northeast Asia: in the mid-1990s, 0.4 percent of GDP in Japan and 2.5 percent in Korea, as compared to China's 20 percent, Taiwan's 7.4 percent, the United States' 8.5 percent, and the United Kingdom's 30 percent.

The central experience of Northeast Asia in the postwar period, in short, has not been a realm of independence in which autonomy and equality reign, but an alternative form of political economy enmeshed in a hegemonic web. Japan, South Korea, and Taiwan industrialized within this web, and thus their states were "strong" for the struggle to industrialize but "weak" because of the web of enmeshment; they are semi-sovereign states. North Korea and China defined themselves as outside the web, thereby endowing the web with overriding significance—and so they structured their states to resist enmeshment. Their states have been "strong" for industrialization and "total" for hegemonic resistance, but as the century ends, both are being drawn into the web. This suggests that the nearest thing to a new truth about the state since List, Hegel, and Marx is that state machineries are embedded in the world system, that their autonomy within it is quite limited, and that the specific institutional forms states may take around the world cannot be understood apart from the workings of the whole. That whole is the one Marx called "the grandest terrain," the world market.

In the 1990s, the second-best world, the world of blocs, of iron and bamboo curtains, unexpectedly disappeared—and, therefore, so has American indulgence for the neomercantilism of its East Asian allies, which was always a function of the Cold War struggle with their opposites (*Wall Street Journal* 8 December 1997). If there has been a "Clinton Doctrine" since 1993, it has been one of aggressive foreign economic policy designed to promote exports and to open targeted economies to American goods and investment (especially in service industries, which now dominate the U.S. economy, accounting for 85 percent of GDP, and in which the United States has a barely challenged global lead) while maintaining the Cold War positions that give Washington a diffuse leverage over allies like Japan and Germany and pose a subtle but distinct threat to potential adversaries like China.

Just as one would predict of a mature hegemonic power, the United States now prefers the virtues of a multilateral economism to the vices of direct coercion and intervention, and thus the IMF and the World Bank have vastly enhanced their usefulness in Washington's eyes, and even the abandoned Bretton Woods mechanism—an international trade organization—has materialized in the form of the WTO. As China waxed and Japan waned on American horizons in the 1990s,[4] perhaps the breadth of American hegemony can be appreciated in China's beleaguered efforts to polish its application to the WTO, while Washington continues to demand more reform before approving Beijing's entry. A central preoccupation of American policy is to shape and channel China's position in the world market so as to block the emergence of "another Japan," and the deep meaning and intent of the American and IMF response to the Asian liquidity crisis is to close the historical chapter in which the sheltered "developmental states" have prospered. All this goes on, of course, under the neoliberal legitimation of Smithean free markets and Lockean democracy and civil society.

South Korea is an exemplary case for all these points, because the liquidity crunch hit in the middle of a defining presidential election in a country long touted as a miracle of industrial development, a country just given the highest credit ratings by key Japanese agencies, one that had happily slurped at the trough of abundant Japanese and Western bank lending for thirty years.[5] But South Korea continued to be socked into the structure of American hegemony, and so key American officials rode herd on the IMF, with the goal of transforming Korea's "developmental state" into an American-defined normalcy that would essentially end, at least in its present form, the Korean ascendancy into the hallowed realm of advanced industrial states.

How Robert Rubin Rewrote the Rules of Korean Political Economy

A mark of Washington's unipolar preeminence and the potency of its foreign economic policy under Clinton is that even mainstream pundits found the IMF to be merely the creature of Treasury Secretary Robert Rubin and Deputy Secretary Lawrence H. Summers. Rubin and Summers, with Federal Reserve Chairman Alan Greenspan, have been the three horsemen of Clintonomics, and they were deeply enmeshed in fashioning appropriate remedies for the Asian crisis.[6] As the liquidity crunch hit Northeast Asia in the fall of 1997, American influence was critical in deflecting Japan's attempt to create an "Asian fund" to bail out threatened banks and in demanding far-reaching restructuring in return for IMF bailouts. Overnight came a stunning reversal of verdicts: Korea was less a miracle than a nightmare of "crony capitalism," collusive practice, and opaque governance.

To say that South Korea's finances "lacked transparency" at this time was an understatement, if not a joke; the highest officials were lying through their teeth. In November of 1997, the Governor of the Bank of Korea pretended that short-term nonperforming loans totaled only $20 billion, whereas private analysts placed the figure as high as $80 billion; foreign reserves were said to total $31 billion, when in fact Korea had but $6 billion left and all of it was committed in the near term—meaning that the country itself was bankrupt. Seoul was "burning through its reserves by as much as $2 billion a day to help banks that needed cash" (*New York Times* 10 December 1997).[7] By this time, the wón had plunged from 800 to 1,000 to the dollar. But the Kim Young Sam government was desperate to avoid an IMF bailout before the December 19 presidential election and sought help from Japan instead; in mid-November, South Korean Finance Minister Lim Chang Ryul openly pleaded with Tokyo to intervene: "If the Korean economy goes wrong, so does the Japanese economy" (*Korea Herald* 22 November 1997). The Bank of Korea head flew off to New York for a meeting with currency arbitrage master George Soros. Washington, however, wanted a quick bailout *during* the electoral campaign, so that candidates could commit to it—or be alienated from it, as the case might be.

The critical moment came when Rubin gave up his Thanksgiving vacation to huddle with Greenspan and then dispatched two senior officials to Seoul, including Summers (later called "a modern version of General Douglas MacArthur, reshaping Asia in America's interest"[8]), who told reporters that "financial support . . . should only be provided in the context of an IMF program" (*New York Times* 20 November 1997; *Wall Street Journal* 20 November 1997, 8 December 1997; *Washington Post* 21 November 1997; *Korea Herald* 26 November 1997). After an all-night negotiating session on 1 and 2 December between the finance minister and the IMF team, agreement was reached on a $57 billion bailout package made up of $21 billion in standby credits from the IMF, $10 billion from the World Bank, and $4 billion from the Asian Development Bank, with the United States, Japan, and other countries anteing up an additional $22 billion.

In return for the $57 billion package, the IMF demanded drastic restructuring. The classified text of the IMF agreement aimed directly at the Korea, Inc. model. It had a "highly leveraged corporate sector that lacks effective market discipline," with debt-to-equity ratios so high that most *chaebŏl* (conglomerates) were technically bankrupt at any give time; easy credit had led to "excessive investment in certain sectors such as steel and autos." Korea had to "restructure and recapitalize the financial sector and make it more transparent, market-oriented, and better supervised." It would have to cut its 1998 growth-rate projection by half (6 to 3 percent), lift ceilings on foreign investment in Korean firms from 26 to 50 percent, facilitate foreign mergers and acquisitions, open domestic markets (especially the capital and auto markets), and create flexibilities in the labor market that would allow enormous layoffs. The government would create revenue by raising taxes and interest rates and cutting budgets. Large financial institutions would now be audited by internationally recognized firms, and the vastly diversified *chaebŏl* would be forced to stop intersubsidiary loan guarantees and other kinds of internal deals. Rubin personally held up the agreement for ten hours while he pushed for new standards of accounting. For their part, Korean officials pleaded to include anti-labor provisions in the reform package, hoping the IMF could do for Kim Young Sam what he was unable to do for himself.

Kim Young Sam may still be ruminating about the stunning contrast between his last two Decembers in office. Riding a wave of popularity after cashiering the preceding two military dictators, in December 1996 he had proudly announced that South Korea had come of age as an advanced economy by joining the OECD, a group of top industrial nations. To polish Korea's application, President Kim had abolished the Economic Planning Board, which had been the central Korean locus of "administrative guidance." Under severe pressure from big business throughout his term to lower labor costs and restore comparative export advantage, in the same month President Kim and his ruling party rammed a new labor law through the National Assembly at dawn, with no notice to the still-sleeping opposition members. The new law retained the KFTU, a large, state-controlled trade union, as the only officially approved labor organization for five more years, leaving the independent, five hundred thousand–strong KCTU out in the cold, tarred as "illegal," even though the KCTU is one of the strongest unions in the world. The same law gave Korean businesses the legal right to lay off workers and the leeway to replace strikers with scabs.

Because Korea has no unemployment compensation or safety net, the December 1996 law severely undercut workers' interests. Korea never had "lifetime employment" like Japan, but for decades workers had traded reasonably good job security for the absence of independent representation and the right to work the longest hours in the industrial world at wages barely enough to sustain a family.

But, since the military dictatorship ended in 1987, Korean labor organization had expanded dramatically, especially in the flagship heavy industries: steel, automobiles, shipbuilding, and chemicals. Severe repression of labor under three decades of American-supported dictatorships finally gave way to modest improvement in wages and working conditions since 1987, but at the end of 1996 Korean labor was supposed to pay the cost of business excesses, thus to restore global competitiveness. The response to the new labor law was not long in coming. In January 1997, hundreds of thousands of Korean workers occupied the streets of Seoul for weeks on end, in what approached a general strike, until the government finally relented and agreed to shelve the law. Come the November liquidity crisis, the IMF adopted the task of doing what the Kim government could not: enforcing millions of layoffs. This could be accomplished without too much distress, the IMF said, if (virtually bankrupt) Korea enacted unemployment compensation laws.

The massive labor protests in early 1997 shocked the Korean elite and turned Kim Young Sam into a lame duck for the remainder of the year (Korean presidents can serve only one five-year term). He was further weakened when a gigantic steel firm, Hanbo, went belly-up under $6 billion in bad loans, some of which had been arranged with the political intervention of President Kim's son, who was soon arrested. Relaxed controls on the financial sector, also put in place with an eye toward joining the OECD, encouraged even more lending by Japanese and Western banks. Indeed, foreign bankers fell all over themselves to spread money around: "We were all standing in line trying to help these countries borrow money," said Klaus Friedrich, the chief economist at Dresdner Bank AG. "We would all see each other at the same places." Korea was especially favored because a foreign loan to a Korean firm was "tantamount to making a loan to the government," according to Vivien Levy-Garboua, of the Banque Nationale de Paris. "It was a Korea Inc. loan" (*New York Times* 28 January 1998). The heaviest lenders were Japan, France, and Germany, followed by American banks.

Japan's exposure, however, was triple Germany's ($119 billion compared to $34 billion, with the United States at $26 billion). When the run on the Thai baht began in July, all the banks began slashing their lending (by $100 billion in the second half of 1997) and made "a headlong rush for the exits," in the words of an American banker.[9] Kim's lame-duck status and the disappearance of the Economic Planning Board meant that Korea's usually astute economic planners did not have the political backing to take the measures necessary to head off the ballooning debt and liquidity problems, which were soon vastly accelerated by spooked foreign investors. Kim Young Sam was the first civilian president since 1960; he will have an indelible place in history for his courage in bringing former militarists Chun Doo Hwan and Roh Tae Woo to trial on sedition and corruption charges (Chun was sentenced to die and Roh to a long prison term; both were pardoned in early 1998, after spending a long time in jail). Otherwise, Kim was in every way a conservative and a child of the postwar South Korean system, and he showed it in 1996–97.

After the bailout, influential analysts inveighed against a model of development that had been the apple of Washington's eye during the decades of authoritarianism in Korea. Deputy IMF Director Stanley Fischer[10] said true restructuring would not be possible "within the Korean model or the Japan Inc. model." "Korean leaders are wedded to economic ideals born in a 1960s dictatorship," an editorial in the *Wall Street Journal* (24 November 1997) said, leading to "hands-on government regulation, ceaseless corporate expansion, distrust of foreign capital and competition." The thirty largest *chaebŏl*, accounting for one-third of the country's wealth, were "big monsters" that "gobbled up available credit" and relied on "outdated notions of vertical integration for strength." Perhaps the chief economist at Deutsche Morgan Grenfell, Ed Yardeni, trumped all the pundits in heaping scorn on Seoul: "the truth of the matter is that Korea, Inc. is already bankrupt. . . . All that's left is to file the papers. This is a zombie economy."[11] If it wasn't a zombie, the crisis certainly cut the economy down to size. In November 1997, South Korea ostensibly had a GNP of almost $500 billion and a per capita GNP of approximately $11,000; it accounted for about 6 percent of total world GDP (compared to 2.5 percent in 1980) and ranked eleventh among industrial countries. By January 1998, per capita GNP had fallen to $6,600 and GNP to $312 billion, or seventeenth place (behind Mexico, India, and Russia) (*World Bank* 1997b; Asian Development Bank 1996).[12] (By the end of 1998, the economy had lost a further 6 percent of GNP.)

Koreans accused the IMF of attacking "major pillars" of the economic system; reporters wrote that *chaebŏl* leaders were now "gripped with an unprecedented sense of crisis," with "dismemberment" perhaps in the offing. A spokesman for the Federation of Korean Industries asked how Samsung and Hyundai could have developed the nation's profitable semiconductor and auto industries "without the conglomerate system" and suggested delicately that U.S. and Japanese competitors might have had some "behind-the-scenes influence" on the IMF, "with an intention to weaken the competitiveness of Korean major industries" (*Korea Herald* 4 and 5 December 1997). An editorial in a leading daily charged that "a senior U.S. Treasury official backhandedly manipulated IMF negotiators to push for market opening . . . while Japan used financial aid as a weapon to prop open the [Korean] domestic market for their goods" (*Dong-A Ilbo* 3 December 1997).[13] But Koreans didn't know the half of it. Sources in Washington acknowledged that several reforms had been specifically demanded by U.S. Treasury officials, in keeping with former U.S. Trade Representative Mickey Kanter's view that the IMF could be a "battering ram" for American interests (see also *Korea Herald* 4 December 1997).[14]

Had Japan stepped in instead of the IMF, it would have signaled an unprecedented move toward a hegemonic role in the region, something that the Americans neatly blocked, supported by Chinese leaders equally adamant against a leadership role for Japan. But Japan was hardly in a position to do much, with its own banking system so shaky. Japan's financial authorities had injected up to $30 billion in the last week of November alone to prevent "an unmanageable run on the banking system"; experts estimated that up to one-half of the major Japanese banks might have to be closed or merged, and that an initial bailout of Japan's financial sector would take at least $80 billion, with nonperforming loans estimated at more than $600 billion at the end of 1997 (and $1 trillion by mid-1998). In panics, the good go down with the bad, of course, and as Japanese citizens—good savers all—began queuing up outside their savings banks, it momentarily appeared that the second-largest economy in the world might be crashing (all-purpose pundit C. Fred Bergston had Japan "teetering very close to the brink") (*Washington Post* 11 December 1997).[15] Thus, Rubin worked feverishly for days (albeit trying "to avoid conveying the slightest hint of panic"), not to block an enhanced role for Tokyo in Asia, but to keep the crisis from taking down Japan, Russia, and, probably, the world economy: "We have regarded Korea as a firewall that could not be breached," an anonymous high official in Washington said, "for fear of other 'teetering' dominoes like Russia—and even Japan" (*New York Times* 10 December 1997[16]). Rubin's frantic maneuvering perhaps made the executive theory of the state seem too subtle to capture the reality, except that he had now become executive for the world economy—or what the *Wall Street Journal* called a "socialist international" after German Finance Minister Theo Waigel flew to Washington to huddle with Rubin, Greenspan, and IMF director Michael Camdessus.[17]

Unfortunately, the Korean bailout lasted for only three weeks. The wón began tumbling again, and Rubin lost his holiday a second time when on Christmas Eve he and Greenspan huddled with top American bankers at the Federal Reserve Bank of New York, arranging $10 billion more in emergency loans to Seoul to back up a package that would enable it to roll over bad short-term loans, now said to total over $100 billion (with nonperforming loans of all types equaling 51 percent of Korea's GNP). Rubin then materialized as a national security manager, using tried-and-true Cold War tropes to declare that South Korea was a place in which there were still "enormous security concerns for the United States" and therefore could not be allowed to fail.[18] Major international banks agreed to swap $24 billion in Korean short-term loans for new government-guaranteed debt, and the Wall Street firm Goldman, Sachs arranged subsequent Korean bond offerings to soak up still more bad debt. (This firm, where Rubin was a partner for three decades, and Salomon Smith Barney, run by the former Treasury official who arranged the 1995 Mexican bailout, were working with failing Korean banks from late November onward.)

By the new year, Rubin had neatly accomplished three goals: to stop a run on Korean and Japanese banks, to rewrite the rules of Korea's political economy as a prelude to the (still ongoing) struggle to do the same in Japan, and to maintain American hegemony in the region. Alan Greenspan waxed ecstatic before a Senate panel: the result of the Asian crisis was "a worldwide move toward 'the Western form of free market capitalism.' " Another analyst exclaimed that "Wall Street won" (*Wall Street Journal* 8 December 1997).[19] Except, of course, that the panic of 1997 came close to detonating a collapse of the world economy worthy of 1929, a specter that still hangs over all of us and reached home in September 1998 with the collapse of Long-Term Credit, a huge hedge fund that also got its bailout courtesy of the Federal Reserve Bank of New York.

How Koreans Rewrote the Rules of Dictatorship and Democracy

It is an irony, one that perhaps only those who know South Korea's history can appreciate, that the worst economic crisis in the country's history should come just as the Korean people were about to elect dissident Kim Dae Jung, who suffered under the dictators as much as any political leader in the world. But it was not an accident, because Kim embodied the courageous and resilient resistance to decades of dictatorship that marked Korea as much as its high-growth economy did. Korean democracy has come from the bottom up, fertilized by the sacrifices of millions of people. If they have not yet built a perfect democratic system, they have constructed a remarkable civil society that gives the lie to common stereotypes about Asian culture and values. Paradoxically, this maturing civil society is a key enabling mechanism for Washington and the IMF's getting their way in Korea. Why? Because Kim's election has brought to power people who have long criticized the state-bank-conglomerate nexus and who, like the new president, have long been its victims. The irony grows; the global managers feared Kim's election (he might be a "populist"), and Washington backed the dictators who tormented him, with one U.S. ambassador after another refusing to meet Kim Dae Jung publicly while badmouthing him in "off-the-record" conversations with reporters. Meanwhile, back at home Americans increasingly question the quality of their own politics.

An economically booming America has a political spectrum from right to left that has lately been suffused with conflicted concerns about American civil society, as people grope for a politics of authenticity and meaningful participation.[20] A majority of Americans prefer not to vote (the 1998 Congressional elections had the lowest turnout in fifty years [*New York Times* 12 February 1999]) and reserve for Washington politicians a contempt unprecedented in American history. Simultaneously, contemporary writers of great influence argue that civil society is inherently a Western concept, and that it is absent in East Asia—whether in authoritarian Singapore, democratic Japan, or the NICs of South Korea and Taiwan. Samuel Huntington has made this view notorious in his book *The Clash of Civilizations* but it is a view by no means limited to conservatives. Korea's experience illustrates a different point: the truth that "Orient and Occident are chalk lines drawn before us to fool our timidity" (Nietzsche 1983, 128). Civil society and democracy are products of industrial modernity, not civilizational difference.

It is instructive, in judging where South Korea is today, to see how far it has come since 1987. From its inception, the ROK has been a country with a rebellious civil society amid weak or nonexistent democracy. Every Korean republic until the one elected in 1992, under Kim Young Sam, began or ended in massive uprisings or military coups. The longest, the Third Republic, under Park Chung Hee (1961–79), began with a coup and ended with Park's murder at the hands of his own intelligence chief. The next longest, under Syngman Rhee (1948–60), ended in a massive rebellion and his expulsion from office. Chun Doo Hwan's Fourth Republic (1980–87) began and ended with popular uprisings that shook the foundations of the system. For three decades, the core coercive power of the regime was the KCIA; set up by Kim Chong-p'il with American CIA help in 1961 (as the late Gregory Henderson wrote), it

> replaced ancient vagueness with modern secrecy and added investigation, arrest, terror, censorship, massive files, and thousands of agents, stool pigeons, and spies both at home and abroad. . . . In [Korean] history's most sensational expansion of . . . function, it broadly advised and inspected the government, did much of its planning, produced many of its legislative ideas and most of the research on which they were based, recruited for government agencies, encouraged relations with Japan, sponsored business companies, shook down millionaires, watched over and organized students . . . and supported theaters, dance groups, an orchestra, and a great tourist center [Walker Hill]. (1968, 264)

To make a long and bloody story very short, we can say that Park and Chun misjudged the hidden strengths and growing maturity of Korean civil society, which was overdeveloped in relation to the economy and was therefore the object of the ubiquitous agencies of the expanding authoritarian state: a vast administrative bureaucracy; huge, distended armed forces; extensive national police; an omnipresent CIA with operatives at every conceivable site of potential resistance; and thorough ideological blanketing of every alternative idea in the name of forced-pace industrialization. Park's authoritarian practice, learned at the knee of Japanese militarists in 1930s Manchuria, established an unending crisis of civil society that culminated in the urban civil disorders in Masan and Pusan in August and September 1979, leading to Park's assassination by his own intelligence chief in October, the military coup mounted by Chun Doo Hwan and Roh Tae Woo in December 1979, and the bloody denouement at Kwangju in May 1980.

The period between 1980 and 1987 will appear in history as a classic Brumairean event, with the luckless "nephew" (Chun) acting on behalf of the dispatched "uncle" (Park), using the jail and the gnout all the way, but compounding into farce the tragedy of Park Chung Hee (who truly was Korea's industrial sovereign, if not its Napoleon). The real tragedy, of course, had taken place at Kwangju in May 1980, where an aroused and self-organized citizenry (i.e., not a bunch of rioters and miscreants) sought desperately to save itself from the new martial law regime that Chun had just announced, only to be slaughtered (a minimum of six hundred killed, a maximum of two thousand—like Tiananmen in 1989).[21] Kwangju became the touchstone for resistance to dictatorship thereafter. As the capital of South Chôlla province, the disorders in this city expressed the problems of underdevelopment and disenfranchisement that have marked the southwestern region in the modern period; Kwangju is also the home base of Kim Dae Jung.

Amid this squalid history, it would be difficult to overestimate the lack of concern for democracy and human rights in Korea evinced by one American president after another. Kwangju occurred on the watch of President Jimmy Carter, who prided himself on his "human rights" policy; his main response was to send an aircraft carrier task force to Korean waters as a warning to North Korea and (within a week of the rebellion) to send the U.S. Ex-Im Bank chairman to Seoul to assure the junta of American economic support, including a $600 million loan that Carter had just approved. Carter told the *New York Times* that "the Koreans are not ready for democracy . . . according to their own judgement" (Lee 1988, 22–23). Meanwhile, for decades a chorus of praise met every new gain in South Korea's GNP. Multitudes of American economists, business pundits, and political scientists thought it their solemn duty to extol the virtues of Korean capitalism to the heights—not once but a thousand times. "Miracle" was the trope on everyone's lips, with "dynamic" not far behind. In September 1977, *Fortune* magazine had this to say about business in Korea:

> What positively delights American business men in Korea is the Confucian work ethic. . . . Work, as Koreans see it, is not a hardship. It is a heaven-sent opportunity to help family and nation. The fact that filial piety extends to the boss-worker relationship comes as a further surprise to Americans accustomed to labor wrangling at home. (Ogle 1990, 76)

Chun Doo Hwan had himself designated president shortly after Kwangju. In the next year, he purged or proscribed the political activities of eight hundred politicians and eight thousand officials in government and business and threw some thirty-seven thousand journalists, students, teachers, labor organizers, and civil servants into "purification camps" in remote mountain areas, where they underwent a harsh "re-education." Some two hundred labor leaders were among them. Chun's "Act for the Protection of Society" authorized preventive detention for seven to ten years, and yet more than six thousand people were given additional terms under this act in 1980–86. The National Security Law defined as "anti-state" (and therefore treasonable) any association or group "organized for the purpose of assuming a title of the government or disturbing the state" and any group that "operates along with the line of the communists" or praises North Korea; the leader of such an organization could be punished by death or life in prison (W. Park 1993).

An indication of just how arbitrary Korea, Inc. was under Chun can be gathered from the story of Chón Pong-gu, once the owner and chairman of the Samho conglomerate, which made glass and textiles and was involved in construction in the Middle East. Chón's son had been handing out $700,000 three times a year to General Chun's cronies as protection money. But it wasn't enough, so in 1984 his son urged that Chun be given a hotel or a golf course to keep him happy. Mr. Chón (the father) refused, and within months Chun transferred the Samho *chaebŏl* in toto to the rival Daelim group—and for good measure, he took Mr. Chón's personal assets as well. Chón retired to exile in California, where, since the new Korean government came in. he has been pursuing a lawsuit to regain his firm and his fortune, estimated at $2 billion in current prices (*New York Times* 25 March 1998).

Another man, Yi T'ae-bok, was sentenced to life in prison for publishing books "calling for class struggle" (such as those authored by G. D. H. Cole, Maurice Dobb, and Christopher Hill). He was jailed from 1981 to 1986. Meanwhile, Secretary of State George Shultz visited Seoul (in May 1986), praising the government for "a progressive movement going in the terms of the institutions of democracy" while criticizing "an opposition which seeks to incite violence" and refusing to meet with either Kim Young Sam or Kim Dae Jung.[22] But support for Chun's dictatorship was completely bipartisan, as we have seen.

At the end of 1986, American policy shifted, however, as Washington began to worry about a popular revolution in South Korea and U.S. policy shifted on a world scale toward support for limited forms of democracy, demonstrated by the primary evidence that William Robinson has now brought to light. Robinson argues that the Philippines was a key test case for the Reagan administration, after the murder of Benigno Aquino in 1983; a secret National Security Council directive approved in November 1984 called for American intervention in Philippine politics: "we are urging revitalization of democratic institutions, dismantling 'crony' monopoly capitalism and allowing the economy to respond to free market forces." This was followed by personal meetings in Manila between Ferdinand Marcos and the CIA director, William Casey (May 1985), and Senator Paul Laxalt, President Reagan's personal emissary (October 1985); Washington also vastly augmented the Manila Embassy's political staff (Robinson 1996, 91–92, 121–25; Cumings 1989). The same thing happened in late 1986 in Korea, when long-time CIA officer James R. Lilley became ambassador to Seoul and began meeting with opposition forces for the first time since 1980.

Korean politics had begun to reawaken with the February 1985 National Assembly elections, and by spring 1987 an aroused, self-organized citizenry again took over the streets of the major cities, with late-coming but substantial middle-class participation. Catholic leaders played a critical role in this episode. Korean civil society has a core strength in a myriad of Christian organizations; there are nearly 12 million Christians in Korea now, about one-fourth of the Korean population, and the 3 million Catholics there represent the country's fastest-growing group. Cardinal Kim Sô-hwan is the most influential religious leader in the country, and the Myóngdong Cathedral in downtown Seoul was one of the few sanctuaries where the dictators feared to tread. It was a center of protest in the 1970s and 1980s and played a critical role in shielding dissident students in May and June 1987, just before the downfall of the Chun regime. In the 1990s, it has worked closely with independent labor unions (Kim 1996).

In June 1987, amid a popular urban rebellion threatening to spread beyond control, various Americans—and especially Lilley—pressured Chun and Roh to change their policies. On 29 June, Roh Tae Woo grabbed the bull by the horns and announced direct presidential elections (to be held in December 1987); an open campaign without threats of repression; amnesties for political prisoners, including Kim Dae Jung; guarantees of basic rights; and revision or abolishment of the current Press Law. In an episode that still needs to be explored, American electioneering specialists went to Seoul to help elect General Roh, with some Koreans later charging that computerized election results were altered in favor of Roh. But the main factor enabling the emergence of an interim regime under the other, somewhat shrewder "nephew" (Roh) was the opposition's split between Kim Young Sam and Kim Dae Jung (both of whom ran and lost).

Roh's regime first accommodated and then sought to suppress a newly energized civil society, now including the liberated and very strong forces of labor (more strikes and labor actions occurred in 1987–88 than at any point in Korean history, or most national histories). The political system under Roh, wrote one expert, was by no means "a civilian regime . . . the military coexisted with the ruling bloc while it exercised veto power over opposition groups." When one courageous journalist, O Hong-gun, suggested clearing the military culture completely out of politics, agents of the Army Intelligence Command stabbed him with a bayonet (K. Park 1993, 161, 170–71). The partial democratization that occurred in 1987–88 in South Korea also proceeded without dismantling the repressive state structures, like the successor to the KCIA known as the *Agency for National Security Planning*, or ANSP.

In 1990, this regime sought to fashion the Japanese solution to democratic pressures, a "Democratic Liberal Party" (reversing the characters of Japan's Liberal Democratic Party) that would encompass the moderate opposition in the form of Kim Young Sam and his Pusan-based political machine, bringing them under the tent of the southeastern Taegu-Kyôngsang elites (or "T-K Group") that had dominated the ROK since 1961, thus to form a single-party democracy that would rule for the ages—or at least for the next generation. A host of analysts (not the least being the U.S. Embassy in Seoul) came forward to laud this "pact" between softliners and hard-liners among the elite, which seemed to mimic the democratic transitions of the 1980s in Latin America.

The Democratic Liberal Party solution could not last because, unlike Japan's system, it excluded labor (even today, no political party has roots in Korea's massive working class, and labor unions were prevented by law from involving themselves in politics until early 1998), failed to reckon with unresolved crises in postwar Korean history (especially Kwangju), and merely masked over sharp splits within the political elite—the continuing repression of anything smacking of a serious left (through the National Security Law), the restiveness of the *chaebŏl* groups under continuing strong state regulation, and, above all, the continuing exclusion of representation for the southwestern Chôlla people in the politics of Seoul. But Roh Tae Woo made a major contribution to democratization in 1992 by retiring and taking himself and his many fellow militarists back to the barracks, thereby enabling the election of the first civilian president since 1960, Kim Young Sam.

In 1995, a series of dramatic events and actions unfolded, with consequences no doubt unforeseen at the time, but having the result of an audacious assault on the dictators who ruled Korea from 1961 onward. Unlike any other former military dictatorship in the world, the new democratic regime in Korea did not allow bygones to be bygones: two former presidents ended up in jail, convicted of monumental bribery and treason against the state. Kim Young Sam probably allowed the prosecution of Chun and Roh on the initial charges of bribery because that would help him overcome the influence of the Taegu-Kyôngsang group within the ruling party, but he then was forced in November 1995 to allow both of them to be indicted for treason for their December 1979 coup and the suppression of the Kwangju citizenry, because the slush fund scandal was lapping too close to his own door. Also important was the emergence of a new generation of prosecutors, formed by the struggles of civil society that accompanied their education and coming of age, who now ingeniously use "the rule of law" to go after their dictatorial antagonists. The falling out among the ruling groups and the trials of Chun and Roh, as well as the full glare of publicity on the slush fund scandals (big business groups had supplied more than $1.5 billion to Chun and Roh in the 1980s), bathed the state and the *chaebŏl* groups in a highly critical light and definitively put an end to the military's role in politics. This was the finest moment for Korean democracy in history up to that point, vindicating the masses of Koreans who had fought for democratic rule over the past fifty years and opening the way to the election in 1997 of Korea's most prominent dissident, Kim Dae Jung.

But it still wasn't a democracy, and, even with Kim's election, it still isn't. The National Security Law is still on the books and is still used to punish peaceful dissent and heterodox speech—in spite of an unusual State Department entreaty (in August 1994) that Seoul do away with this anachronistic and draconian framework. The law, which was adopted in its original form in 1948, still embraces every aspect of political, social, and artistic life. In the summer of 1994, even a professor's lecture notes were introduced in court as evidence of his subversive activity, yet his actions never went beyond peaceful advocacy (W. Park 1993, 122–23). With the continuing exclusion of labor from the governing coalition and the continuing suppression of the nonviolent left under the National Security Law, the ROK falls short of either the Japanese or the American model of pluralist democracy; still, it has achieved a politics that is more democratic than the halting and temporary, jerry-built transitions to weak democracy in Latin America, the former Soviet Union and East Europe, and the Philippines.

We can conclude this brief consideration of recent Korean history with the observation that the contribution of protest to Korean democracy cannot be overstated; it is a classic case of "the civilizing force of a new vision of society . . . created in struggle" (Williams 1975, 231). A significant student movement emerged in Western Europe and the United States in the mid-1960s and had a heyday of perhaps five years. Korean students were central activists in the politics of liberation in the late 1940s, in the overthrow of the Rhee regime in 1960, in the repudiation of Korea-Japan normalization in 1965, and in the resistance to the Park and Chun dictatorships in the period between 1971 and 1988. Particularly in the 1980s, through the mediation of *minjung* ideology and praxis (a kind of liberation theology stimulated by Latin American examples), Korean students, workers, and young people brought into the public space uniquely original and autonomous con-figurations of political and social protest—configurations that threatened many times to overturn the structure of American hegemony and military dictatorship. It fit Habermas' characterization of student protest in terms of a blurring of bor-ders "between demonstration and civil disobedience, between discussion, festival, and expressive self-presentation" (Habermas 1992, 234).

Korea also has had one of the strongest labor movements in the world, one that organized itself through much of this century and has suffered under truly terri-ble repression. From the inception of the movement in the early 1920s under Japanese colonial rule through the decisive American role in shutting down wide-spread independent labor unions during the U.S. occupation (1945–48), and under the often stunningly harsh repression of the dictatorships that followed for the next four decades, Korean labor kept organizing and kept growing—or suffering the consequences. Today, the unions hold the key to whether Kim Dae Jung's—and the IMF's—reform program will succeed.

The IMF's Man in Seoul: Kim Dae Jung

Robert Rubin's ministrations came in the middle of the most important presiden-tial campaign in South Korean history. For the first time, it appeared that a former dissident, a person of unquestioned democratic credentials with a base in the abused and underdeveloped Southwest, might finally come to power. And so Washington and Wall Street insiders openly suggested that Kim was the wrong leader at the wrong time in the wrong place: a U.S. diplomat told a reporter, "We could be in a position in which Kim Dae Jung takes office in the midst of a finan-cial emergency that is going to require a lot of pain and downsizing of South Korean businesses. . . . Almost no one thinks he will command the authority to pull it off."[23] In fact, no other conceivable political leader was better positioned than Kim to truly change the Korean system; indeed, he had called for reforms analo-gous to those of the IMF throughout his long career (see, for example, Kim 1985).

Kim Dae Jung hit the political scene like a tornado in the 1960s, rousing large crowds and accumulating 46 percent of the vote in a 1971 election, in spite of all manner of rigging by the ruling party, which lubricated the electorate with hogsheads of cash, both homegrown and foreign ($7 million in political funds came from Gulf Oil and Caltex alone). And so it came to pass that there were no more contested presidential elections until the military dictatorship ended in 1987. In between, Kim Dae Jung was the loathed-beyond-measure *bête noire* of the dictators.

Kim has limped badly ever since a suspicious accident in 1971, shortly after the election, in which a large truck rammed his car, killing several passengers and badly injuring him. Two years later, KCIA agents kidnapped him from the Grand Palace Hotel in Tokyo and plunked him in a boat to return him to Seoul or, more likely, to kill him—given that they had chained him and weighted his body with cement. American intervention, in the form of a helicopter sent buzzing over the boat, may well have saved his life. After his coup, General Chun sought to execute Kim on trumped-up sedition charges, blaming him for the 1980 Kwangju rebellion; Kim was lucky to escape into exile in the United States. He returned to Seoul in 1985 and was under house arrest for most of the next two years. Dozens of buses full of riot police were always parked near his home, and his neighbors' houses were occupied by agents who surveilled his every move. He could not give interviews, attend rallies, or write for any publications, nor could his picture appear in any media. Ultimately, Kim spent a total of six years in prison, seven more under house arrest, and five years in exile.

Kim Dae Jung has never been a radical and has not had a strong base in labor for two reasons: first, until 1998 it was illegal for labor to involve itself in politics; second, over the years Kim has been much more a champion of the southwestern region and of small and medium-sized business than he has of labor (and, of course, supporting labor was a ticket to political oblivion in Korea's McCarthyite milieu). It is true that he is more sympathetic to labor demands than previous leaders, and labor clearly prefers him to the past run of dictators. But that isn't saying much, given the harsh anti-labor environment of the past fifty years. The KFTU was for decades the only legal union—it was controlled by the state in the interests of owners, through what the late James West called "corporatism without labor," whereby the state, the conglomerates, and the banks worked hand-in-glove, but labor was systematically excluded. From 1970 to 1987, the state also controlled the recognition of unions at foreign-invested companies, banning strikes and all unapproved union organizers, "to placate uneasy foreign investors" (West 1987, 494–95). The other large union is the KCTU, which grew rapidly after 1987 but was illegal until early 1998. Both unions have about half a million members, but the KFTU was built on an enterprise union base controlled from the top down, which allowed but one union per enterprise and thus dispersed horizontal solidarity across sectors. The Trade Union Act in force for decades barred intervention in the workplace by "third parties" (anyone who is not an employed worker or manager) and banned political activities by unions, making support of a specific political party illegal. All unions had to be approved by the Ministry of Labor (KCTU 1997).

In spite of all this—or because of it?—South Korea today is a remarkable country in which even white-collar bank employees strap on identical headbands saying "Down with IMF trusteeship!" and march through the streets yelling slogans in unison. Students on the raucous campuses ten years ago, they are now united with blue-collar workers in the KCTU. But because of labor's strength even in white-collar ranks, foreign companies are reluctant to buy firms without being given the right to reduce the number of employees. An anonymous senior official of a foreign brokerage firm said in January 1998, "There's no point in taking over a [Korean] bank if you can't lay off anyone" (*New York Times* 15 January 1998). President Kim allayed labor's fears with a master stroke in the same month, however, one that augers a far-reaching political transformation: under his direction, for the first time in Korean history, labor leaders met with leaders of business and government to work out fair and equitable policies for dealing with the IMF crisis, a kind of "peak bargaining" arrangement that represents labor's biggest gain ever.

After tough negotiations, Kim got labor to agree to large layoffs (which would triple the pre-crisis unemployment rate, albeit from 2 to 6 percent, not a high rate by Western standards[24]) in return for the right to exist legally and to participate in politics and field candidates for elections. When labor leaders took this deal back to the rank and file, it was soundly rejected, and many called for a general strike. The ROK has virtually no social security or unemployment compensation system; a puny unemployment law passed in 1995 allows 50 percent of wages for 30 to 210 days, depending on how long a worker has been employed—measures that are well below International Labor Organization standards. But months of labor peace followed the January agreement, punctuated by a sudden day-long shutdown by 130,000 unionists on 28 February and sporadic actions that continued as unemployment approached nearly 7 percent of the work force by mid-summer. In July, both major unions approved large strikes (involving fifty thousand to seventy thousand metal and auto workers). But they only lasted a day or two, did not lead to a general strike, and were designed not to shut down the economy but to pressure the Kim administration to halt layoffs. In late July, both big unions returned to the "tripartite" talks with business and government (*Hanguk Ilbo* 28 July 1998), and the arrangement continues today.

The key to the reform process has been a fair and across-the-board sharing of the IMF pain and not just more layoffs of workers, which required serious reform of Korea's octopus-like conglomerates. President Kim has been a lifelong critic of these firms, and they have reciprocated. Samsung, for example, one of the top three firms in Korea, whose founder was an inveterate pro-Japanese reactionary, hates Kim and has funded his rivals for decades. Their mammoth and extraordinarily diversified structure, combined with an open spigot of state-mediated loans, was essential to Korea's success in grabbing market share around the world (rather than simply pursuing price advantages), because losses in one subsidiary could be made up by gains in another. In 1993 (according to none other than Kim Dae Jung), the top five *chaebŏl* accounted for 66 percent of total sales and 53 percent of Korean GNP, and the top 30 accounted for 80 percent of GNP (Kim, Aquino, and Arias 1995, 79).

In an interview given shortly after he was elected (*Washington Post* 9 January 1998), Kim blamed the financial crisis on military dictatorships that lied to the people and concentrated only on economic development to the detriment of democracy, leading to a "collusive intimacy between business and government." He said the way out of the crisis was to reform the government-bank-business nexus, induce foreign investment, and then increase exports.[25] By and large, that is exactly what has happened: this "nexus" is now far more transparent than at any time in Korean history, with the widespread adoption of contemporary accounting practices and the supervision by the government of lending to the private sector (rather than the government's handing out policy loans—see chapter 6, by Meredith Woo-Cumings). Kim's *chaebŏl* reform package went along with IMF demands to eliminate intersubsidiary loan guarantees, lower debt-to-equity ratios, and improve transparency. Early threats to dismantle the conglomerates, however, have given way to breaking the nexus between the state and the firms. Kim Dae Jung has indicated more than once that he has no plans to change the size or purpose of the *chaebŏl*.[26] Instead, he has promoted a "big deal" in which the conglomerates would swap subsidiaries to concentrate on core businesses. For example, Samsung's automobile factory would go to Hyundai, in return for Hyundai's giving its semiconductor business to Samsung (*Korea Herald* 11 July 1998). As Meredith Woo-Cumings argues, this state-managed "big deal" is unfortunately reminiscent of Chun's early-1980s demands that each *chaebŏl* concentrate on the industry it does best, something that also occurs in the wake of an economic downturn. But, as Woo-Cumings points out, Kim's desire to preserve the conglomerates is not surprising, given their history, their importance to Korean development, and the recent merger mania (in the name of enhancing global competitiveness) among many Western transnationals. Korea's reformers have no alternative but to work within this *chaebŏl* system.

The clearest break with the past is in Kim's economic team, which includes several well-known critics of Korea, Inc. and the *chaebŏl*, most of them from the disadvantaged southwest, several of whom lost their jobs for political activities during the Chun period. Chon Ch'ŏl-hwan, a progressive economist and human rights activist, heads the Bank of Korea; North Chôlla Province Governor You Jong-keun, a free-market advocate and former economist at Rutgers University, is a special advisor to President Kim; Lee Jin-soon, Kim Tae-dong, and several others were key members of the Citizen's Coalition for Economic Justice, which promoted labor and criticized *chaebŏl* concentration in the past.[27] They (with IMF and World Bank support) have advocated new safety nets for laid-off workers and New Deal–style public works projects (roads, bridges) to employ the jobless. Kim's team has also published lists of firms and banks that are threatened with closure (including fully twenty-four of twenty-six commercial banks) if they cannot remedy their insolvency; only the "fittest" firms would survive. For the first time, the government is planning to sell shares in state-run monopolies to foreigners; for example, Philip Morris and British-American Tobacco hope to buy as much of Korea Tobacco and Ginseng as they can (*Korea Herald* 8 June 1998).

Democratic reforms have proceeded rapidly under Kim Dae Jung. Kim Young Sam did nothing to change Korea's ubiquitous ANSP, merely putting his own allies in control of it. This intelligence agency prosecuted hundreds of cases under the National Security Law in the mid-1990s, including that of labor organizer Pak Chông-yul, who was arrested in the middle of the night in November 1995. Ten men rushed into his home and dragged him off to an unheated cell, where for the next twenty-two days his tormentors beat him, poured cold water over him, and limited him to thirty minutes of sleep each day, all to get him to confess to being a North Korean spy—which he wasn't. An anonymous government official told a reporter such measures were necessary because "We found the whole society had been influenced by North Korean ideology." He estimated that upward of forty thousand North Korean agents existed in the South (*New York Times* 22 February 1997).

An investigation in early 1998 proved that the ANSP had run an operation just before the election to tar Kim Dae Jung as procommunist, and incoming officials also unearthed for reporters the list of KCIA agents who had kidnapped Kim in 1973. In February 1998, the *Sisa Journal* published the full administrative structure of the ANSP for the first time, showing that it had more than seventy thousand employees (and any number of informal agents and spies), an annual budget of approximately 800 billion wón (about $1 billion), and almost no senior officials from the southwest (three from among the seventy highest-ranking officials, one among thirty-five section chiefs). It controlled eight academic institutes, including several that provide grants to foreign academics and publish well-known English-language "scholarly" journals. Kim Young Sam's son, Kim Hyón-ch'ól, ran his own private group inside the ANSP and gave critical information to his father; many therefore blamed Kim's inattention to the developing Asian crisis on the arrest of his son (for arranging huge preferential loans and massive bribery) in mid-1996, thus depriving the President of reliable information. The new government cut the "domestic" arm of the ANSP by 50 percent, reduced the rest of the agency's staff by 10 percent, fired twenty-four top officials and many lesser employees, and reoriented the agency away from domestic affairs, toward North Korea. A top official said the ANSP "will be reborn to fit the era of international economic war" (*Korea Herald* 19 March 1998) (not a bad characterization of the contemporary world economy).

Kim Dae Jung's most far-reaching changes have involved North Korea, and here Kim has the support of top *chaebŏl* leaders, all of whom see the North's well-trained, well-educated, but low-paid workers as a key to restoring Korean comparative advantage. At his inauguration, he pledged to "actively pursue reconciliation and cooperation" with North Korea and declared his support for P'yóngyang's attempts to better relations with Washington and Tokyo—in complete contrast with his predecessors, who chafed mightily at any hint of such rapprochement. He underlined his pledges in early March of 1998 by approving large shipments of food aid to the North, lifting limits on business deals between the North and southern firms in April, and calling for an end to the American economic embargo against the North in June. He has explicitly rejected "unification by absorption" (which was the de facto policy of his predecessors) and has in effect committed Seoul to a prolonged period of peaceful coexistence.

Kim Dae Jung's presidency, in short, has achieved major changes in the economy, the political system, and relations with the North. He is more popular today than when he was elected, with his party winning about 60 percent of the vote in local elections in June 1998 and his own approval ratings rising above 80 percent late in that year. South Korea's foreign reserves reached $50 billion by the end of 1998, with industrial leaders urging that they be built up to $100 billion—that is, about the level of reserves that so far has enabled Taiwan, Hong Kong, and China to avoid runs on their currency. It therefore may turn out that a curious confluence of liquidity crisis, IMF reform, Washington's desire to rein in Northeast Asian late development, and Korean democratization will put the ROK on much better footing than other countries now trying to ride out the Asian crisis. (Many early 1999 estimates were that the economy would actually begin growing again, albeit at a predicted 2 percent for the year.)

Strong counter-tendencies exist, however. Some foreign analysts say Korea has not yet attracted significant foreign investment, that progress on "transparency" is slow, and that incentives to foreign investors (e.g., tax favors and bureaucratic services) are not as good as in Southeast Asia. State bureaucrats are perceived to be dragging their feet on real reform, and labor militancy also discourages foreign businessmen (*Korea Herald* 17 June 1998). More important, perhaps, is David Hale's observation that "the magnitude of the debt overhang in East Asia is massive compared to the pool of speculative capital available for corporate restructuring from foreign investors" and worse than the Latin American debt problem in the 1980s (1998a).[28] Furthermore, the competitiveness of the smaller countries is being squeezed from the top by Japan, with its superior production technology, and from below by China, with its labor cost advantages. China's share of the region's exports has gone from 6 to 26 percent in the past decade, and today it is difficult to think of export products that Korea or Thailand can make that China cannot. (In 1997, China replaced Korea in electronics sales: with nearly $50 billion in annual sales, China ranked fourth after the United States, Japan, and Germany; Korea is now fifth).[29] Meanwhile, Japan is still the largest creditor nation, with $285 billion in foreign exchange reserves making it invulnerable to the kind of liquidity crisis that affected Seoul—in spite of a "bad debt overhang" now estimated at $1 trillion.

Conclusion

During the Cold War, as a key ally and front-line state, South Korea would have gotten its bailout with an immediate and overriding emphasis on issues of security, as it did in 1983 when Reagan and Prime Minister Nakasone arranged a $4 billion package for Seoul that amounted to 10 percent of its entire outstanding debt at a time when Latin America got no such help. But the Northeast Asian pattern of late development only worked when Japan and Korea were sheltered economies. Today, apparently autonomous Asian "tigers," having prospered within an indulgent hegemonic net for thirty years, find themselves rendered dependent and bewildered by a dimly understood hegemonic mechanism that now places their entire society and economy under global jurisdiction. Strong conservative forces in South Korea and Japan are fighting to preserve what they perceive to be their postwar social compact, and thus their modern civilization, against the IMF gospel. Others, like former Prime Minister Lee Hong Koo (now Korea's ambassador to Washington), argue that "the model is now clear. . . . It's not Japan, it's the West. The current crisis has convinced almost all people that the old style doesn't work" (*New York Times* 17 January 1998). I would put my money on the latter view (one also held by Kim Dae Jung), because South Korea and Japan are ultimately incapable of resisting Washington's ministrations, short of breaking out of the postwar settlement.

The Cold War order in East Asia took shape through a positive policy of industrial growth, designed to restart the world economy after the devastation of global depression and war, and in reaction to the revolutions on the Asian mainland that transformed and divided the region after World War II. The United States established distinct outer limits on its allies, the transgression of which was rare or even inconceivable and provoked immediate crisis—the orientation of Seoul or Tokyo toward the Soviet bloc, for example. The typical experience of this hegemony, however, has been a mundane and mostly unremarked daily life of subtle constraint, in which the United States kept allied states on defense, resource, and, for many years, technological and financial dependencies. This is a potent form of hegemony, and it has a message: In the 1940s, it crushed one form of statist empire, and in the 1980s, another. Today it is eroding, if not erasing, the last formidable alternative system, the Japan-Korea model of state-directed neomercantilism (one undermined and made vulnerable by its inclusion in the postwar regional order). What is the message? The open door, pluralist democracy, and self-determination.

If the last point seems odd (was not Korea, Inc. an aspect of self-determination?), it is not. The willing accomplice of these successive victories has been a self-energized populace that demands reform and opening in the name of liberal values. Look at the collective behavior of the vanquished: postwar Japan as a constitutional democracy and exemplar of pacifism; Germany as the most self-conscious adherent of liberal values in Europe; the rush toward markets and representative government in Russia and Eastern Europe in the 1990s; and the burgeoning recognition in Japan and Korea that "economies are all going the American way," in the words of a former top trade official in Japan.[30] Taiwan has not been my subject, but it, too, now has a pluralist democracy and, with its historical pattern of dispersed industry and relatively small business in comparison to Korea, a mostly unproblematic economy that prospers within a diffuse American hegemonic net.[31] Now, even North Korea has invited the World Bank to tutor its experts in capitalist economics. Here is a system, in other words, with clearly established boundaries of its own but incessant frontier violations of the Other.

Still, it is by no means clear that the major regional economic power, Japan, is "going the American way." Japan was mired in recession throughout the 1990s, and, since the LDP coalition fell in 1993, it has been politically sandbagged by the inability of bureaucratic and political elites to agree on the necessary measures to restore growth to the economy; politically, as a parliamentary democracy, it lacks the top-down powers of Korea's executive-dominant system. To say this so dryly detracts from Tokyo's truly amazing record of inanity in the past decade, from its catatonia at the time of the Gulf War (while the United States succeeded in getting it to foot much of the bill) to Prime Minister Hosokawa's evanescent "new politics" (instantly welcomed by Clinton, however fleeting that moment proved to be), to Prime Minister Hata's empty rhetoric about Japan becoming a "normal power," to, finally, Prime Minister Murayama's "socialist" recapitulation of all three (followed by more dithering and the bringing of one of the most tried and true political hacks of the LDP, Prime Minister Obuchi, into power).

Meanwhile, Clinton administration officials (exemplified by the successive U.S. trade representatives, Mickey Kanter and Charlene Barshefsky) have been breathing hotly on the Japanese neck all through the same period, from the failed "Structural Impediments Initiative" to a host of trade disputes and attempts to adjust Japanese interest rates by remote control from afar to the steel-dumping charges that Washington brought against Japan in February 1999. But they can't perform the kind of open-heart surgery on the Japanese system that they did in Korea, because Japan is a creditor nation that hardly requires an IMF bailout and does not have to listen to a lot of hectoring advice from Western economists—even if a great deal has been proffered in the past few years, especially by Treasury Secretary Robert Rubin and Mrs. Barshefsky. But then South Korea listened up and, thus far, is much the better for it. Perhaps the remaining obstacle to Japanese recovery is precisely the unwillingness of its leaders to renovate thoroughly Japan's industrial strategy: long the wonder of the world for its fluid flexibility, now it may be the most formidable rigidity in the system. Externally, Japan is still situated so that it cannot help but cooperate in any regime that Washington develops, whether it be the United Nations (where it still lacks a seat on the Security Council), the trilateralism of the 1970s, NAFTA and APEC in the recent period, the new WTO, or something else. Twenty years ago, Seisaburo Sato called Japan's pusillanimous foreign policy a kind of "irresponsible immobilism," but that was in the context of Tokyo's very dynamic and mobile foreign economic policy. Now, it appears immobilized both at home and abroad.

Washington's enduring regional configuration is also shaky, however. The Asian crisis rippled through the region as the world market began to approximate the globe itself, with the recent addition of hundreds of millions of people in China and former Soviet bloc territories. Capital is entangling "all peoples in the net of the world market," in Marx's words, accounting for both the current economic boom in the core and the widespread sense that the dynamics of the whole are unstable. Americans now envision "communist" China as an anchor of stability in East Asia, something that led Rubin and Clinton dramatically to cozy up to Beijing during Clinton's visit in June 1998 and to praise it for keeping its currency stable. Because the renminbi is nonconvertible, hedge fund speculators couldn't traffic in it, and because China (like Taiwan and Hong Kong) has maintained large foreign currency reserves, it has continued to grow (8 percent in 1997, approximately 7 percent in 1998, and a projected 7 percent again in 1999). Meanwhile, the capitalization of the American equity market is now approaching 140 percent of GDP (compared to 82 percent in 1929), and the mutual fund industry has assets higher than all the banks ($5 trillion). Right now, the Asian crisis is keeping American monetary policy expansionary, but a stock market crash has been a constant threat for two years and is easily imaginable in the near future (Hale 1998a).

The point man for the new ecumenical gospel, the IMF, attempts to impose hegemonic rules on everyone, creating a level playing field in conditions of structural inequality and hierarchy that tilt the game toward the United States and the advanced industrial countries. Meanwhile, free-market advocates castigate the IMF's secrecy, and even the global managers wonder if a world in which trillions of dollars slosh around uncontrolled might be the source of financial chaos. This calls forth a demand for global regulation, for international macroeconomic policies to stabilize the whole. Here is the essence of the conundrum that not just ordinary people, but the global managers themselves, cannot predict: can this brave new world, in which capital spins out its telos in a historically unprecedented vacuum of alternatives, be controlled?

CHAPTER TWO

Asian Business Networks in Transition:

or, What Alan Greenspan Does Not Know

about the Asian Business Crisis

Gary Hamilton

In January and February of 1998, Alan Greenspan (1998a, 1998b, 1998c), the chairman of America's Federal Board of Reserve, made a number of presentations before committees of the U.S. Congress. In his testimony, as well as in the question-and-answer session afterward, he explained the reasons for the economic crisis that had gripped Asia since the previous summer. He also outlined a rationale for congressional support of the IMF's so-called aid packages to Korea, Thailand, and Indonesia. The reasoning in his speeches echoed that expressed in many articles—really editorials and thought pieces—by other economists that appeared in major newspapers and magazines beginning in October 1997.[1] The economic reasoning that Greenspan and other writers used to interpret the first year of Asia's financial crisis draws on a set of images of how the capitalist world economy works and of how the Asian countries got themselves into such an awful fix.

Many students of Asian societies, myself included, interpret Asian economies, and also the Asian crisis, in a very different way. In this chapter, I use Alan Greenspan's interpretation as a proxy for the general views of the most prominent economic analysts and contrast this rather conventional economic interpretation to what I believe is a more realistic interpretation of the economic and social background—the so-called secondary causes—that shaped the crisis without actually causing its occurrence. I argue that the crisis results from fundamental shifts both in the organization of global capitalism and in the integration of Asian economies into this global system.

What Alan Greenspan Predicts

In asking the U.S. Congress for money to support the IMF, Greenspan predicted that the Asian business crisis would have two positive long-term consequences.

The successful resolution of the crisis would first bring an end to crony capitalism and, second, hasten the convergence of capitalism into one global pattern, or what Greenspan (1988b) referred to as "the Western form of free market capitalism." Both predictions hinge on what he means by two crucial terms: "crony capitalism" and "free market capitalism."

The term *crony capitalism* is an interesting one. When the seriousness of the crisis became clear, Greenspan, in chorus with many other observers, began to use it retrospectively to interpret crucial organizational dimensions of Asian economies before the crisis began and to single out these dimensions as the fundamental causes of the current emergency. To economists, the term *cronyism* generally implies that collusion of any kind undermines market processes. In the Asian context, the meaning is more nuanced. These observers charge that there are two forms of cronyism at work.

The first form of cronyism is a systemic linkage between government and business. These linkages are so strong and so unidirectional that they amount to straightforward government interventions in the marketplace. Until the crisis, political economists often praised such interventions as the source of the Asian miracle. Remember Alice Amsden's proclamation (1989) that Korea's success came from the government's "getting the prices wrong" and Robert Wade's (1990) persuasive argument that Asian states were able to "govern the market" and thereby to create their own success. Now these same scenarios, we are told, create what economists call *moral hazard*, "situations in which someone can reap the rewards from their actions when events go well but do not suffer the full consequences when they go badly" (Greenspan 1998b, 2). Most commentaries, including Greenspan's, use South Korea as the key example of moral hazard. The Korean state officials targeted industrial sectors for rapid growth. Korean banks, largely controlled by the state, gave huge loans to the businesses selected to develop the targeted sectors. Such government support also signaled other investors, both local and foreign, to lend large sums of money, on the assumption that everyone could share in the profits when times were good, but the government would cover the loans if times turned sour. Such no-lose situations of government-induced moral hazard, reiterated the economists, resulted in very high levels of firm indebtedness (leverage as a ratio of debt to equity) in South Korea, Thailand, and Indonesia. The high levels of leverage made the firms vulnerable to currency fluctuations, thus precipitating the crisis.

Most commentators, however, see crony capitalism as something more than collusion between government and business. It is also a term they apply to the interfirm networks that made up the business groups for which many Asian economies are so well known. The *keiretsu* in Japan, the *chaebŏl* in South Korea, the overseas family-owned Chinese conglomerates in Southeast Asia—these all are cited as the prime and undifferentiated examples of "crony capitalism." The logic that establishes them equally as examples of cronyism is subtler than for blatant government intervention in the economy. In the case of business groups, accusations of cronyism arise from the common practice of firms in a group owning each other's shares and loaning each other money, creating a web of interlocking ownership and indebtedness. In such cases, says Alan Greenspan (1998b, 10), stocks are purchased and loans are made "on the basis of association, not economic value." It is at this point that the analysts begin to equate cronyism with *guanxi*, that ubiquitous term meaning, in Chinese, relationship or connection. Equating cronyism and *guanxi* implies that networks based on interpersonal associations look a lot like market-distorting cartels.

In his statements before the congressional committee, Greenspan predicted that the Asian business crisis would have the effect of lessening, if not ending, crony capitalism in Asia. The IMF-imposed economic reforms would spell an end to artificial government supports, an end to cross-holding, and, most important, an end to Asian forms of capitalism, all of which rest on some form of cronyism. An end to these kinds of market distortions, he further predicted, would encourage the major Asian economies to converge toward one pattern of global capitalism, which Greenspan identified as the Western form of free market capitalism.

The free market capitalism that Greenspan described in his presentation has four clearly defined features. These features would, supposedly, become more obvious in Asia as crony capitalism recedes. First, transparency in accounting and in public disclosure of information is an "essential" element of free market capitalism. The broad "dissemination of detailed disclosures of governments, financial institutions, and firms, is required if the risks inherent in our global financial structures are to be contained." Without clear signals about "product and asset prices, interests rates, debt by maturity, detailed accounts of central banks, and private enterprises . . . a competitive free-market system cannot reach a firm balance except by chance" (Greenspan 1998b, 9). Second, when there is transparency in the economic system, both "private transactors and government policymakers" can "discipline" themselves, meaning that they can accurately assess the risks before them and act prudently. Third, this discipline leads to price structures in credit, equity, and product markets that reflect "true" value, rather than "distorted" value based on some form of moral hazard. Fourth and finally, "an effective competitive economy," said Greenspan (1998c, 8), "requires a rule of law" that would limit arbitrary government intrusion in commercial disputes and establish a regulatory system to structure the incentives of economic players.

Greenspan's Picture of Global Capitalism

In Greenspan's portrayal of the Asian crisis, there is a clear indictment of Asian business practices and a valorization of Western economic institutions. There is an equally clear presumption that, were Asian economic institutions more like the Western ones, the crisis would have been much less severe, if not averted altogether. This portrayal is, of course, not Greenspan's alone, but rather a view that many commentators share. If we examine this view closely, we see that it is based on a set of assumptions that form a more or less coherent image of the nature of global capitalism.

Let me quickly sketch out the main features of this portrait of the capitalism. The first thing to note is that this picture of global capitalism has a very clear foreground and a very fuzzy background. In the clear foreground are the institutions of capitalism, and in the blurred background are the economic activities of manufacturing, distributing, and consuming. If we set this image in motion, Greenspan's narrative of the Asian crisis directs our attention only to what happens in the foreground. The picture of global capitalism that we get is the following:

First, capitalism is perceived to be a country-based phenomenon. Free market capitalism is equated with clearly defined and relatively stable economic institutions, which one might call "institutionalized markets," rather than with the less-well-defined and ever-changing economic activities of manufacturing and distributing products. In the foreground, we see that capitalism corresponds to a system of ownership (equity systems are a market for ownership), a system of banking and credit, an established and distant relationship between governments and markets, and a country-based means of monitoring these institutions. If these conditions are met, then the presumption is that the economy will be free market capitalism. In this system of capitalism, price setting occurs in markets for ownership, in markets for money, in markets for labor, and in markets for undifferentiated products (e.g., commodity markets, ranging from gold to orange juice).

Second, this country-based capitalism is presumed to rest on market institutions that are objective and neutral with respect to society and culture. In this view, institutions are systems of incentives that can be engineered to produce transparency and market discipline. Such systems of incentives are, in essence, sets of rules that constrain all economic actors in the same way, regardless of their social and cultural affiliations. Keeping the institutional rules in the foreground and the society and culture in the background provides the level playing field that American trade negotiators so often find missing in Asian economies.

Third, it is assumed that free market capitalism automatically arises if the incentive structures are correctly constructed and strictly and fairly enforced. The intent of the IMF bailout is to impose such incentive structures on each of the troubled economies. The desired outcome of these measures is to install economic institutions that are similar, if not identical, everywhere in the world. When economists talk about the global convergence toward free market capitalism, the capitalism they have in mind is the capitalism that presumably flows from creating consistent foreground institutions—call it *institutionalized free market capitalism*. Markets are only "free" if incentive structures are constructed and institutionalized that way and if the participants, as well as the system as a whole, are strictly and fairly monitored—hence, a capitalism of "institutionalized free markets."

A fourth feature of this image of capitalism occurs in the fuzzy background. The actual activities of manufacturing, distributing, and selling products are not in clear view, but are assumed to occur somewhere out of sight, more or less automatically, and to follow the laws of supply and demand.[2] Even though economic activities and price-setting processes occur out of view, most analysts would argue that the conceptual fuzziness is not a problem because economic activities are inherently dynamic and ever-changing. The principles of efficiency and profit and the laws of supply and demand parsimoniously drive the system of global capitalism, making predictable what would otherwise be uninterpretable and chaotic.

Using this interpretation of global capitalism, Greenspan locates the sources of the current crisis in the foreground features of Asian economies: in the lack of transparency (which is only a feature of institutionalized markets), in unformed or weak markets for credit, in an excess of government intervention, and in inadequate equity markets that might buffer currency fluctuations. In most analyses, including Greenspan's, the background factors—the actual processes of making and selling products—are hardly mentioned.

What Is Missing in This Vision of Capitalism?

Greenspan conceives of capitalism in terms of the paraphernalia of economic activities, rather than in terms of the economic activities themselves. He focuses on the institutional structures that frame business activities. In his view, free market capitalism is a particular kind of institutional framing that, when correctly built and strictly monitored, clarifies all economic activities, making them transparent without artificially constraining them. This framing supposedly produces reliable economic outcomes that faithfully reflect the laws of supply and demand and the principles of efficiency and profit, so much so that those activities may be left in the background.

Writing as an economic sociologist and not as an economist, I find that the features missing from this image of capitalism are the very features without which capitalism would not exist at all: industrial production and mass consumption. For me, these are the core features of capitalism, the up-front characteristics, but for many (though by no means all) economists, they are the background factors, blurred and indistinct.

Even more important, the country metaphor used to conceptualize global capitalism is perniciously inadequate. Capitalism cannot be characterized, even metaphorically, as a state-based economic system in equilibrium. As a sociologist, I see capitalism as a moving story, a historical narrative. The main protagonists are not countries but people, firms, products, capital, institutions, and the interrelationships among all of these. The setting of the story is not confined to national boundaries but rather follows the protagonists wherever they move in time and space. Finally, I see the narrative as being shaped by active attempts to control the working of all these things. In other words, capitalism is complexly organized through the efforts of people, firms, and governments, each attempting to control the actions of the others. Alan Greenspan's free market institutions are forms of control that one set of actors (e.g., the state or the IMF) tries to impose on other sets of actors, sometimes against their wishes. The point is that capitalism is always contested terrain. The notions of movement, change, organization, and contestation are all missing in the Greenspan version of capitalism.

This is not the place to discuss the theoretical differences between these two versions of capitalism. The reader, however, should keep in mind what I mean by *capitalism*, for the simple reason that Greenspan's characterization misses the very things that have been driving globalization in the first place, the very things that have integrated Asian economies into the world economy: the spread of capitalistic activities in the form of industrial production and mass consumerism. These are noncyclic changes and cannot be viewed as aspects of a larger equilibrium that has now gotten out of kilter. Rather, these transformations in production and consumption have occurred worldwide and have resulted in profound structural changes in most of world's economies, particularly those in Asia. Do we, as analysts of Asian economies, really believe that the Asian crisis was simply the result of inadequate institutional framing? Or do we believe that the current crisis has something to do with these worldwide capitalist transformations?

Transformations in the Global Economy

What are some of these transformations? There have, of course, been many changes, but two *organizational* changes that have occurred at the level of the global economy in the past twenty years seem particularly important: the rise of demand-driven economies and the creation of reflexive manufacturing systems.[3]

Not so many years ago, most capitalist economies in the world could be characterized as producer-driven, in the sense that consumers largely bought what large manufacturing firms produced (Chandler 1977, 1990; Chandler and Daems 1980; Piore and Sabel 1984). In the immediate post–World War II era, very large vertically integrated corporations and business groups supplied the major consuming regions of the world with whatever manufactured goods were consumed. The first great manufacturing enterprises were American, but by the 1960s, the German and Japanese corporations became effective competitors. These manufacturing giants are the General Motors, IBMs, General Electrics, Boeings, Volkswagens, Sonys, and Toyotas of the world economy. The major economic contests occurred between these giant producers; by and large, what they produced, we consumed. They defined the product and manufactured it mainly from within their own firm or group of firms, and we, the consumers, purchased whatever they made. As Piore and Sabel (1984) observed so insightfully, adopting an economy-of-scale, Fordist production system was the only viable route to major economic success for most firms.

In the 1960s and early 1970s, an alternative approach to manufacturing began small and then accelerated (Piore and Sabel 1984; Harvey 1990; Gereffi 1994; Gereffi and Korzeniewicz 1994; Saxenian 1994; Harrison 1994).[4] Largely because of technological advances in mass communications (e.g., television), firms that emphasized retailing and merchandising—for example, department stores such as JCPenney, Wal-Mart, and Kmart, and brand-name merchandisers such as Calvin Klein and Nike—started to appear. These firms specialized in selling fashion goods and goods with rapidly changing product cycles, such as televisions and computers. Department stores have been around for a long time, as have brand-name producers, but this time brand-name producers began to merchandise products that they did not make. They did not own factories; they designed the goods, subcontracted their manufacture, and then merchandised them through their own retail outlets (e.g., Gap) or outlets run by someone else (e.g., The Bon Marché and Nordstrom). This type of manufacturing started with the demand side, with what would sell, with products whose qualities were purposefully constructed for carefully selected segments of the mass market. Emphasizing the products themselves, as opposed to how, where, or by whom the products were made, created an awareness of niche markets—an awareness of demand. By the late 1970s and early 1980s, merchandisers computerized their inventory systems, based on such innovations as bar codes, so that they could reduce inventory and cut costs. They would only design and order from their subcontractors products that appeared to be selling. This manufacturing process started in textiles, but entrepreneurs, understanding the logic behind this type of manufacturing, soon began to apply these techniques to almost every category of consumer goods.

Consider this alternative approach to manufacturing. The shift involves a fundamental transfer of economic power from the manufacturing end to the merchandising and distribution end of the commodity chain.[5] The principal barrier to entry into the making and selling of goods shifted into the hands of merchandisers and retailers. The marketability of products was all that mattered. Quality, of course, counted, but quality was guaranteed through the branding and retailing process. If Nike's name was on the shoe, then of course the shoe was good. If Wal-Mart or The Bon Marché sold the goods, then of course they would stand behind the quality. The importance of manufacturing in and of itself began to recede, relative to the product that was being made and merchandised.

In the 1980s and 1990s, the effects of this trend so intensified that no part of the global capitalist economy remained unaffected (Dicken 1992; Castells 1996). One should remember the crisis that shook, and to some extent still shakes, the industrial structure of the United States (Harrison 1994). It was in the late 1970s and early 1980s that the industrial heartland of American became known as the rust belt, when such world-renowned companies as IBM and Chrysler almost went bankrupt, and when a number of core American cities did, in fact, go bankrupt and had to be bailed out, such as Detroit, Cleveland, and New York (see Bluestone and Harrison 1982). It was during this period of profound industrial restructuring in the United States that the U.S. economy began to shift from a producer-driven to a demand-responsive economy, an economy in which super-discount retailers and brand-name merchandisers emerged victorious (Gereffi 1994; Gereffi and Hamilton 1996).

This shift toward demand responsiveness led to the creation of what I call *reflexive manufacturing systems*.[6] Once the product is designed and the niche market targeted, demand is calculated. Based on calculated demand, a manufacturing process is put together that will result in the targeted price and quality. This requires that merchandisers standardize the product (e.g., the hamburger, the cup of coffee, the running shoe, the computer) and then design a manufacturing process that achieves the desired goals. Because the merchandisers do not own the factories, this requires backward engineering, or reflexive manufacturing, which segments the production process into explicit steps whose efficiency and profitability can be calculated in advance of production so that each step can be allocated to a least-cost producer.

The creation of reflexive manufacturing capabilities occurred gradually. Initially, coordination between the merchandisers and the subcontractors was difficult, and few service providers could handle the intermediate and subsidiary steps in getting a product made and delivered to the merchandisers. But it was not too long before the intermediate roles—the shippers, the fast-freight forwarders, the custom handlers, the banking services—were identified and filled, and the whole process of reflexive manufacturing was made routine.

Changing Integration of Asian Business Networks into the Global Economy

What do these trends have to do with Asian business networks and the Asian business crisis? The answer is a great deal.

The story of Asian economic development is not a country-by-country story, is not a story told through such bestiary metaphors as tigers, dragons, or the flying geese. Most analysts emphasize Asia's export-led development, but when they explain how the development occurred, they give country-by-country accounts of industrial policies designed to capture fdi, or of infrastructural and institutional factors that attract or put off would-be investors.[7] As evidence for their accounts, the same analysts typically present macroeconomic data that have been collected by individual countries, such as bilateral trade flows and fdi. This mode of analysis tends to push the understanding of economic development patterns toward the state-centered, "institutionalized free market" model of capitalism that I outlined earlier.[8]

What analysts do not often examine, however, is the actual organization of a country's or region's economy and the integration of that economy into the organization of global capitalism. The trade figures are there, so the integration is assumed. But if Asia's integration into the global economy is looked at carefully, it becomes apparent that the linkages in the manufacturing and distribution of goods within and between Asian and Western economies are complexly organized. The linkages are organized globally through processes of manufacturing, merchandising, distributing, and consuming, and not merely through constraints imposed by political economies. A close examination would also show that these interlinked commodity chains simultaneously are embedded in the social and political institutions of locales and are extremely sensitive to such global conditions as price and currency fluctuations.[9] Because they are so sensitive, the economic power in many of these global commodity chains has shifted from producer driven to demand responsive. As I show in the following discussion, this shift is not a simple case of changing competitive advantage, but of what Nicole Biggart and I (Orrù, Biggart, and Hamilton 1997, 97–110) have called *societal competitive advantage*, a situation in which distinctive and nontransferable social patterns lend themselves to particular organizing strategies that subsequently become integral elements in highly competitive manufacturing and distribution chains in the global economy.

Large Japanese business networks were the first of Asia's business networks to achieve global significance. As is well known, post–World War II Japanese enterprises organized themselves by creatively reconstructing the patterns of the prewar business groups, the *zaibatsu*. In the 1950s and 1960s, when the new Japanese business groups, the new *zaibatsu*—the intermarket groups, such as Mitsubishi and Sumitomo—first began to organize themselves, their major competitors were the vertically integrated corporations in the United States and Europe. The Japanese countered those industrial giants by creating some of their own.

These new business groups, composed of tiers of independent firms, were more flexibly organized and more all-encompassing than were their American counterparts in the 1960s and 1970s (Gerlach 1992; Fruin 1992; Aoki and Dore 1994; Westney 1996; Orrù, Biggart, and Hamilton 1997). The Japanese groups created horizontal synergies by linking upstream firms that produced intermediate goods, such as steel, to downstream assembly firms that manufactured such things as ships and automobiles. They also created vertical synergies in each area of final production by developing *keiretsu*, vertically tiered hierarchies of firms that constituted "one-setism," the principle of self-sufficient production systems (Gerlach 1992, 85–86; Westney 1996). To make this economic organization work as a self-sustaining system, they situated financial services—banking and insurance—and trading companies at the center of each group. Ownership of the business groups was accomplished collectively through members' jointly holding each other's shares, a practice that protected the group from hostile incursions from the outside. The main banks coordinated the loans for member firms, and, because equity holding conserved ownership in the group, bank indebtedness became the way to finance growth and daily operations (Sheard 1986; Gerlach 1992). The trading companies handled most transactions among member firms and served as the main trading arm, selling products produced by the group to the rest of the world. Although group structure draws its models from Japanese social organization (Aoki 1992), these groups are examples not of cronyism, but of vertical integration carried to its logical conclusion. That there are six or more groups so organized and that these six groups hotly compete among each other for domestic and global market share means that these are not monopolies, but rather vertically integrated groups geared first, last, and always to the production and distribution of goods (Westney 1996).

By the 1970s and 1980s, Japanese business groups had become so institutionalized in their practices and so adept at manufacturing that they succeeded in capturing a sizable share of the global market in many product areas, from automobiles to high-technology electronics. To a large extent, the success of these giant business groups precipitated the industrial crisis in the United States, which, in turn, promoted the shift of American corporations from vertical integration to product creation, reflexive manufacturing, and merchandising (see Bluestone and Harrison 1982; Prestowitz 1988; Womack, Jones, and Roos 1990; Reich 1991; Harrison 1994).

At the same time that Japanese industrial might was rising, the economies in South Korea, Taiwan, and Hong Kong were developing. But if we look closely at these three economies, we see considerable differences in how they were linked to global capitalism. Beginning in the early 1960s, South Korean state officials decided to industrialize the Korean economy by supporting the development of large enterprises that could compete with Japanese firms in the same global markets in which the Japanese were selling their products. The story of the *chaebŏl* is well known (Amsden 1989; Woo 1991; Kim 1997; Orrù, Biggart, and Hamilton 1997). The government selected key entrepreneurs, favored them with preferential loans, allowed their enterprises to grow into very large diversified and vertically integrated business groups, and then attempted to control them through the state's control of the banking system and a system of perpetual indebtedness.[10] By the late 1970s, the top five *chaebŏl* were so large that their output alone represented approximately 20 percent of the valued added in the Korean economy, or nearly 70 percent of the economy if their sales are represented as a ratio to the Korean GDP. By the 1980s, the state-of-the-art production facilities of the *chaebŏl* had successfully challenged the dominance of Japanese firms in the same product lines at a price point that was slightly cheaper and at a level of quality that was slightly lower than the Japanese products themselves—so much so that some writers began to ask, "Is Korea the next Japan?" (Kang 1989; Amsden 1989).

Japanese and Korean manufacturers are examples of producer-driven mass production systems. Capital-intensive, heavily subsidized, and highly leveraged, both enterprise systems rely very heavily on government infrastructure to allow them to encompass the industrial structure of each country. The network structure of these enterprise groups allowed considerable flexibility in the organization of export production, but the interdependent networks of firms themselves were a fixed, not a flexible, feature of both Japan's and South Korea's enterprise systems. Speaking of Japan, Ronald Dore (1986) described this system as "flexible rigidities": flexible production and organizational and structural rigidities. Amsden (1989) implies much the same conclusion for South Korea.

The organizational rigidity in these enterprise systems arises from their being doubly embedded in their respective societies, first in social institutions and, second, in an institutionalized political economy. The organizational structures of enterprises are socially constructed, metaphorically, on norms of kinship and community, the main tenets of which are reconstructed and reified in the course of making these enterprises work economically (Aoki 1988, 1992; Orrù, Biggart, and Hamilton 1997). Embedded in the social organization of these societies, the enterprise systems also become institutionalized into the larger political economy of the societies, so that the different segments of the society become mutually supportive (Whitley 1992; Brinton and Kariya 1998). The internal organization of these economies, in turn, structures the integration of each country's export-led trade regime. The goal of this regime was for the major Japanese and South Korean business groups to compete head-on with other business groups in their own societies so that they could be particularly competitive with major manufacturers elsewhere in Asia and in the West. This strategy worked extremely well for a while.[11]

Whereas Japan and Korea developed their own forms of industrial giantism, entrepreneurs in Taiwan and Hong Kong adopted a very different approach to building their respective economies. From the outset, Chinese social organization, based on differentially structured relationships among family and friends, made it difficult for entrepreneurs to create large vertically integrated firms that were similar in scope and scale to those in Japan and South Korea (Wong 1985; Redding 1990; Chen 1994, 1995). Elsewhere, I have described at length some of the reasons that it is so difficult for the Chinese to create such enterprises, so I will not repeat myself here (Hamilton and Biggart 1988; Orrù, Biggart, and Hamilton 1997). It is enough to say that the push toward individual ownership and toward certain forms of interpersonal cooperation within and between families led to economies in Hong Kong and Taiwan that were composed primarily of modest-sized firms in the manufacturing sectors. Large firms do exist in both Hong Kong and Taiwan, but they are primarily producers of intermediate goods, such as polyurethane or textiles, where advantages associated with economies of scale allow firms to grow large and where some vertical integration in the upstream production process is possible. Large firms are also found in property and services sectors, for different reasons. But by and large, small and medium-sized firms predominate in sectors specializing in manufacturing final products.

Given these propensities, Chinese entrepreneurs never thought they could or should compete with large vertically integrated corporations elsewhere. Instead, outside of the state-dominated sectors, Chinese entrepreneurs began to produce products and parts of products that would be merchandised by others (Shieh 1992; Hamilton 1997). By the 1960s, Hong Kong manufacturers were producing garments, a range of plastic products, and fairly simple electrical appliances for American and European retailers (Wong 1988). Taiwan manufacturers also specialized in textiles and garments, but in addition served as small-time subcontract manufacturers for Japanese enterprises (Gold 1986). By the 1970s, when the first merchandising boom started in the United States, Hong Kong and Taiwanese entrepreneurs began to play important manufacturing roles in the reflexive manufacturing systems that Western retailers and brand-name merchandisers were just figuring out how to create (see Turner 1996; Gereffi 1994; Hamilton 1999). The availability of flexible manufacturing options in Taiwan and Hong Kong, as well as the OEM production in Korea and Japan, promoted the ability of Western firms to figure out how backward-engineered manufacturing might work. Textiles, garments, footwear, and high-technology products are all examples of Western-merchandised, brand-name goods that Korea and Japan, on the one hand, and Hong Kong and Taiwan, on the other, began to produce not only in competition with each other, but also within commodity chains that were organized in very different ways (Levy 1988, 1991). Whereas Korea's and Japan's vertically integrated commodity chains produced finished export goods, Taiwan's and Hong Kong's small and medium-sized firms produced parts of export products that could be flexibly assembled in many different locations.

As the demand-responsive trend accelerated in the 1980s, the competitive advantage of Taiwan and Hong Kong nearly equaled that of Japan and Korea, as is shown dramatically by rapid increases in exports from Taiwan and Hong Kong and by the fact that Taiwan took Japan's place as the holder of the world's largest foreign reserves. In 1985, on the eve of the Plaza Accord (the agreement that forced most currencies in East Asia to float against the U.S. dollar), Japan and Korea, on one side, and Taiwan and Hong Kong, on the other, represented alternative systems of production that were in demand in the global economy.[12] With the signing of the Plaza Accord, however, the relative advantages of each alternative shifted suddenly.[13]

In a matter of a year, East Asian currencies increased their value, in some cases by nearly 40 percent. In Taiwan, the currency shift soon created an economic crisis. In a relatively short time, the stock market lost nearly 75 percent of its value, the property bubble burst, and bankruptcies were ubiquitous. Faced with much higher labor costs, networks of Taiwanese manufacturers making garments, footwear, and household appliances could not produce at the price points demanded by Western buyers. Many of the networks abruptly dissolved. In some cases, they were reconstituted in very different ways in the PRC and Southeast Asia, where labor costs were much lower (Hsing 1998). Those entrepreneurs who remained in Taiwan searched for new partners, new products to make, or new and lower-cost ways to make what they had previously made (Chen 1995). In Hong Kong, exempt from the Plaza Accord then as well as now, so that the HK dollar remains pegged to the U.S. dollar, wages had still moved high enough that most labor-intensive manufacturing moved out of Hong Kong into the Guangdong hinterland. The movement of industry out Hong Kong rapidly accelerated after 1985 (Naughton 1997a; Soulard 1997).

These changes in Hong Kong's and Taiwan's business networks were quite profound and amounted to a comprehensive industrial restructuring (Hsing 1998; Naughton 1997a). At first, this restructuring seemed to disadvantage the Hong Kong and Taiwanese manufacturers, many of whom had to relocate and reorganize their businesses. In just a few years, triangle manufacturing systems were created (Gereffi 1994) in which Western buyers continued to place orders with the Hong Kong and Taiwanese manufacturers they had used before. Now, however, these manufacturers had shifted the site of production to affiliated factories in China and Southeast Asia, and the production networks grew even larger and more cost sensitive. The restructuring, therefore, had the consequence of increasing Chinese involvement in the global development of Western-led subcontract manufacturing. Entrepreneurs from Taiwan and Hong Kong became specialists in and carriers of reflexive manufacturing techniques. They became better at producing in batches and more integrated into global manufacturing than ever before. In the 1990s, for example, the high-technology industry has swung decisively toward Taiwan's globalized manufacturing system, because they have become indispensable component and OEM suppliers for high-technology merchandisers such as Dell and Gateway. For another example, the PRC is now the largest exporter to the United States. Nearly 44 percent of China's exports come from Guangdong province, are produced in networks of firms coordinated by Hong Kong and Taiwanese entrepreneurs, and are trans-shipped out of Hong Kong with the help of services provided in Hong Kong (Naughton 1997a).

A careful analysis of the underlying causes of Asia's current financial crisis reveals that the difficulties of Korean and Japanese manufacturers today should be traced to their unwillingness, and perhaps inability, to respond organizationally to currency fluctuations that began in 1985 and continued with China's currency devaluation in 1991. The immediate effects of currency adjustments in 1985 in Japan and South Korea were much smaller than in Taiwan and Hong Kong, but the long-term effects have been much more severe. In the five years after 1985, Japanese manufacturing groups, suddenly richer than ever with upwardly valued money and seemingly invincible, began investing heavily and often unwisely around the world. Oblivious to valuations, global investors, including Japanese investors, pushed the Japanese stock market to unparalleled heights. By 1990, however, the Japanese bubble had reached its limit.

Although a few global firms (e.g., Sony and Toyota) continued to excel for a time, the profitability of the underlying system of production could not sustain the overhead network structure of Japanese business groups. The currency reevaluations increased the costs of domestic labor and reduced the competitiveness of locally produced goods as export products. Pricing their goods high in the relatively closed domestic economies, Japanese businesses kept the prices in global markets near or even below those of their international competitors. Some businesses also began to figure out how to produce the same goods in low-cost ways, usually by investing heavily in overseas capital-intensive production facilities (Hatch and Yamamura 1996). At the same time that Japanese business groups embarked on strategies of massive outward investment, Japan's domestic economy began to contract. The stock market collapsed, the property bubble began to deflate, and Japan slipped into a recession from which it has yet to emerge (Asher and Smithers 1998).

Finding some lucrative global niches, the four or five top Korean manufacturing groups remained highly competitive and even profitable in some sectors. These *chaebŏl* embarked on a tripartite strategy to upgrade existing products, find new, higher-value products to mass-produce, and relocate labor-intensive factories to foreign sites where labor was cheaper. They had sufficient low-cost borrowed capital to pursue this global expansion. Funded by ample loans from government and private sources, the top Korean *chaebŏl* built factories both locally and globally to mass-produce such products as semiconductor chips and automobiles. But for many of the *chaebŏl* outside of the huge top five groups, profit margins declined, and series of bankruptcies of lesser groups began to occur even before the 1997 financial crisis (*Financial Times* 8 August 1997, 17; *Wall Street Journal* 10 September 1997, A18).

The massive outward investment to reconstruct vertically integrated networks of Japanese and Korean business groups on a global, instead of national, basis had two consequences. Domestically, raising money for foreign investments lifted the debt leverage of firms and extended the search for additional capital to foreign banks and foreign credit markets.[14] Internationally, the direct foreign investments were targeted for only a few locations, with Southeast Asia among the principal sites for investment. Beginning in the early 1970s, but accelerating in the 1980s, Matsushita developed its production facilities in Malaysia, where it alone accounts for approximately 5 percent of Malaysia's GNP. Finding the Thai government very amenable, Japanese automobile firms moved many labor-intensive manufacturing plants to Thailand (Doner 1990). Korean garment and footwear firms primarily went to Indonesia. Many other Japanese and Korean firms began to follow suit. They were joined by other manufacturing firms and service providers from other locations around the world that wanted to get in on the action in Southeast Asia. Institutional investors (e.g., pension funds and banks) began to pour money into local stock markets, buying shares in those few Southeast Asian firms in which there was sufficient liquidity, and into local property markets. The result of this massive investment inflow was too much money chasing too few opportunities. A speculative bubble emerged in stocks, property, and financial services. The influx of capital led to a huge demand for imports, some for intermediate goods for manufacturing final products, but also a lot for luxury goods, such as cars and cognac.

Another, and equally important, consequence of the extended and greatly increased flow of funds to and from Asian countries, especially the funds from institutional investors, was the development of globalized financial institutions. This is an irony of the crisis. East Asian industrialization had been largely accomplished with local money administered through locally embedded financial institutions. For instance, the state-owned banking system controlled Korea's industrial development for most of the period between the 1960s and the early 1990s (Amsden 1989; Kim 1997). Foreign investors had only limited ability to invest in Korean firms and only limited ability to take money out of Korea. In Taiwan, investment capital for small and medium-sized firms came from the informal economy, in large part because the state-owned banking system would not readily loan money to small firms (Lee 1990; Lin 1991). Before the 1990s, in Southeast Asia, a lot of the investment capital for businesses owned by the ethnic Chinese came from local banks that were also owned by ethnic Chinese. These banks were only loosely connected to international financial networks. By the 1990s, however, the desire of international investors to invest their money in Asia pushed forward a series of liberalization measures that gradually opened Asian economies to the flow of Western money. Most Asian countries implemented globally standardized rules for stock exchanges, banking, and other financial institutions, and connected local financial organizations to globalized ones. The globalization of local finance set the stage for the Asian leg of the global crisis.

Current Crisis

The proximate cause of the so-called Asian financial crisis was another currency fluctuation, followed this time by an all-out panic. Running out of reserves to back its currency, the Thai government allowed the baht to float against the U.S. dollar. Recognizing that their investments were at stake, nearly everyone abandoned their assets in baht. As investors of all types moved their money into safe havens, in essence stopping the flow of money, the stock market crashed, currency plummeted, and credit vanished. Companies needing capital could no longer get it, and those owing money had nowhere to turn. Many went bankrupt in the process.

The same initial scenario was quickly repeated in one country after another. Among countries with convertible currencies, only Hong Kong successfully defended its currency from devaluation. Because Chinese yuan is not yet convertible, China did not have to support its currency. But the crisis was a general one, and global stock markets all developed what many referred to as the "Asian flu."

However, the crisis did not play itself out in the same way in every location. In Taiwan, the panic was momentary; Taiwan firms soon took the opportunity to expand at the expense of others. As the general period of economic decline extended through Asia, turning from slowdown to recession, Taiwan's economy suffered a crisis of falling demand. Otherwise, the economy remained sound, and only a few major bankruptcies occurred. In Hong Kong, the very high price of property receded and the stock market collapsed. The Hong Kong government intervened to slow the slide in property values and actively propped up stock prices by buying shares of major companies. Although shaken, manufacturing in both locations goes on unimpeded. Falling demand in Asia and elsewhere is the greatest danger, and, if the recession is a prolonged one, a new and potentially more serious crisis may emerge. In these places, the crisis in its earliest phases was relatively slight and was confined to the most speculative parts of the economy.

But in Korea and in Japan, the initial crisis was very large indeed, and it has continued to reverberate through both economies. The reason for this severity is that the financial nature of the crisis went straight to the heart of the industrial structure in both countries. The business groups, the *chaebŏl* in Korea and the *keiretsu* and intermarket groups in Japan, have found that they cannot sustain the debt-financed system of vertical integration that they have had in the past. The inability to sustain these systems intact started before the recent crisis, but now it appears that these two economies will have to find solutions to correct a manufacturing system that cannot now be adhered to in a world economy that has changed directions.

In Southeast Asia, the crisis at present is complicated by the fact that Indonesia also faced a domestic political crisis leading up to the resignation of Suharto and widespread civil unrest. The domestic violence and continued political uncertainty caused a massive flight of foreign and, more seriously, ethnic Chinese capital. Only time will tell when some of this investment capital will begin to return to Indonesia. Elsewhere in Southeast Asia, the economies are starting to rebuild. As some predictability returns to global industries, firms throughout Southeast Asia will return to the things that they do best and for which they can find buyers. The lessons learned in the financial crisis will put Asian entrepreneurs on a new footing. Manufacturing processes will be streamlined, debt diminished, and economic relationships tested for reliability and trustworthiness.

Conclusion

I'll conclude by returning to Alan Greenspan's analysis, in order to briefly contrast his argument with mine. Did cronyism and the lack of transparency cause the Asian business crisis? And as a result of the crisis, will the Asian economies converge toward the Western form of free market capitalism?

I hope my analysis shows that these are the wrong questions to ask. When we examine Asian economies, we should not look for what is not there, but for what is there and how it works. When economic analysts look at Asian economies, they often see what is not there. Treating Asian economies as negative cases, they try to explain the crisis in terms of how Asian economies differ from how Western economies are supposed to function (but actually do not). This is not a logical approach.

But if we look at how these economies actually work, we see something else. My own analysis suggests that the chief factors underlying the crisis involve a historical shift in the organization of the global economy from producer-driven manufacturing systems to demand-responsive reflexive manufacturing. The earlier successes of Japanese and Korean business groups rested on their ability to create giant producer-driven manufacturing systems. To accomplish this, they created negotiated alliances between the state and business groups and among firms in business groups. It is a mistake to think of these alliances as cronyism and of Japanese and Korean economies as examples of "crony capitalism." They are, in fact, a type of modern capitalism that does not rest on culture alone, but rather on the creation of distinctive and very advanced manufacturing systems. Different from the American system of capitalism, these manufacturing systems were globally extremely competitive with the same generation of American and European corporations; so efficient were they, in fact, that they forced Western firms into a global restructuring.

Good relationships are important in business and will remain so, but transparency is not all that it is cracked up to be. If anything, the strong linkages within the Japanese and Korean business groups have helped them survive thus far, largely through being able to resist restructuring. More transparency and less mutual commitment might have caused some of the business groups and perhaps the Japanese economy to collapse entirely and would have made the collapse in Korea much worse. In Southeast Asia, institutionalized currency and equity markets were sufficiently open that institutional investors could get their money out quickly enough to collapse the economy effectively. Just think what a little more openness would have done in China.

More important, Greenspan's prediction of a global convergence is based on an inadequate understanding not only of how these Asian economies work, but also of how the U.S. economy works. An analysis of global capitalism must look beyond the ways in which formal institutionalized markets operate and must put capitalist activities in the foreground of our understanding. This will not give us a model or an image, but rather an account of how capitalism has changed and continues to change.

Finally, if my analysis is correct, then we should also understand that there is, strictly speaking, no Western model of capitalism to converge to. The organization of American firms differs from the organization of German firms, which is different again from the organization of British or Italian firms, and, of course, there are plenty of differences within each country. To lump them all together for the purpose of arguing that Asian firms should become more like Western firms is to misunderstand the way capitalist economies build on social and political institutions to create organized firms and groups of firms that are effective in the global arena.

I believe that both Japanese and Korean business groups will have to reorganize, but I do not believe that either will end up resembling an American corporation or a Chinese family-owned enterprise. Instead, these groups will have to reinvent themselves, will have to find within their organizational repertoires new ways to become economically viable again. But rest assured, whatever the future brings, the relational foundation of Asian economies will continue.

Regional Ups, Regional Downs

T. J. Pempel

One of the most basic techniques in climbing a difficult mountain involves having all the climbers rope themselves together. In this way, individual weaknesses can be compensated for by the collective strengths of the others. Even if one or two climbers slip, collectively solid footing by the remainder prevents them from falling too far. Conversely, however, when every climber is lashed together, if too many individuals get into trouble, they will pull the whole group over with them. Asia's hyper-growth from the mid-1980s until the downturns of summer 1997 reflected the positive strengths of lashing together the region's component economies. Regionwide commercial and financial integration allowed most of Asia's national economies to climb together, collective strengths compensating for individual weaknesses. Yet, slippage by a few in 1997 quickly dragged a large number of their climbing partners down behind them, endangering the region as a whole.

This chapter analyzes the ways in which Asia's economic success was linked to its subsequent slippage. Both phenomena pivot around Asia's intersection with two far broader world trends: first, the growing transnational mobility of capital; and second, the rise in regionalism. Within Asia, the two trends became increasingly connected, and for nearly two decades the results were explosively positive economically. Only in 1997 did the shadow sides of each become apparent.

National sovereignty has always been, in Stephen Krasner's poignant phrase (1993, 18–19), "up for grabs," but transnational capital flows and regional linkages have recently challenged the long-standing assumption that the most significant actors in international politics will be national governments. Instead, both capital flows and regionalism increasingly influence, and not infrequently bypass, the decisions of national governments.

The transnational movement of capital has expanded geometrically since the mid-1980s. On a typical day in early 1999, nearly $2 trillion in international capital exchange crosses national borders. By far the largest proportion of this money is private, rather than governmental. This is quite different from the situation that prevailed as recently as the early 1980s.

Thus, in 1983, five major central banks (in the United States, Germany, Japan, Britain, and Switzerland) held $139 billion in foreign-exchange reserves, versus an average daily turnover of $39 billion in the major foreign-exchange markets. The combined firepower of these banks consequently dwarfed that of the marketplace by more than three to one. By 1986, the two were about even in size. By 1998, the balance of power was reversed. These major central banks had $426 billion in reserves against $1.8 trillion in daily trading activity. Market makers had gained a four-to-one advantage over central banks (Greider 1997, 245; *Economist* 23 May 1998, 97).

In the words of Walter Wriston, former chairman of (then) Citibank, today

> bad monetary and fiscal policies anywhere in the world are reflected within minutes on the Reuters screens in the trading rooms of the world. Money only goes where it's wanted, and only stays where it's well treated, and once you tie the world together with telecommunications and information, the ball game is over. . . . For the first time in history, the politicians of the world can't stop it. It's beyond the political control of the world, and that's the good news.[1]

Equally important has been the explosion of regional integration through various trade blocs and economic associations. The two most substantial have been the European Union and NAFTA. But elsewhere, whether in Latin America's Southern Cone, French East Africa, the Islamic nations of the former Soviet Union, or the Caribbean, various regional trade and manufacturing networks have also formed. Asia has been no exception. As with capital movements, the cumulative effect of regional ties has been to provide a competing arrangement for the organization of political space (Hughes 1997, 4–17).

This paper examines both trends—capital movements and regionalism—as they have played out in Asia. The central argument is straightforward: the countries of Asia have become increasingly interconnected. Political considerations have been important in fostering such ties, but most connections have been commercial and economic, rather than political. And it has been capital movements—most notably foreign aid, fdi, joint manufacturing networks, trade, and bank loans—that have been the thickest strands in weaving this regional Asian web. For a decade and a half at least, such ties were conducive to the "Asian economic miracle" that captured so much attention. But this web of connectedness was subsequently at the heart of the region's downturn.

Prelude to Regionalism

Regional integration in Asia since the 1970s presents a striking contrast to that area's earlier experiences. During the late nineteenth and early twentieth centuries,

Asia was largely a fragmented collection of disparate Western colonies. Only Japan and Thailand remained independent of Western colonial rule. The single serious bid for Asian integration was Japan's unsuccessful military attempt to form the Greater East Asia Co-Prosperity Sphere.

Fragmentation increased after World War II, largely as an outgrowth of the Cold War. The politically divided Asia-Pacific became the principal battleground for Cold War contestation. The communist victory in China set that country at odds with the United States and its allies in Asia. The Korean Peninsula was cleaved at its midpoint and plunged into a civil war. Indochina underwent a series of wars, first with the French, then with the Americans, and, throughout and subsequently, among its component countries. Indonesia was bathed in an anticommunist bloodbath in the mid-1960s that left the victorious regime at odds with many of its immediate neighbors. Guerrilla insurrections swept Thailand, Malaysia, Burma, and the Philippines. These were but the most prominent manifestations of intra-Asian divisions.

The two competing Cold War alliances offered some measure of integration to their respective members, but in contrast to NATO, for example, the U.S. links were predominantly bilateral and country-specific rather than regionwide. Security was linked to low-credit loans, technology assistance, and infrastructural development for America's major allies in Asia—Japan, Taiwan, South Korea, and ultimately Thailand and (South) Vietnam—in an effort to create stalwart allies in Asia whose economic systems could be held up as viable alternative models to those put forward by the Soviet Union and China. To retain maximum influence over each of these allies, however, America resisted the creation of intra-Asian ties. Instead, almost all connections bound individual Asian countries back to the United States; unmediated links among America's Asian allies were rare. Meanwhile, open rivalry between China and the USSR kept the communist countries divided. Asian regionalism and integration were at best a dream in the face of such overwhelming military and strategic forces pressing toward fragmentation.

Emerging Asian Regionalism

Just as the fragmentation of Asia was driven by political considerations, so were the earliest moves toward greater regional integration. Three important threads were central to greater cohesion. First, Japan entered into a series of official agreements with many of its Asian neighbors concerning war reparations and official aid. Second, China shifted its strategic orientation away from the USSR, opting for greater openness to Western capitalist economics. And third, beginning with the 1967 formation of ASEAN, the nations of Southeast Asia settled many of their security problems and became more closely linked economically.

All three of these intersected to create closer links among the previously divided nations of Asia. While the motivations behind these moves were often highly political, the mechanisms whereby they were implemented were predominantly economic and commercial.

As Japan recovered from the economic devastation and political isolation of World War II, it began to repair its diplomatic relations with the rest of Asia. In keeping with the country's overall approach to foreign policy, economics, trade, and aid became the principal mechanisms for such improvements. Between 1955 and 1967, Japan negotiated wartime reparations agreements with a total of ten East and Southeast Asian countries, transferring nearly $2 billion in economic and technical assistance. Most of this money was tied to the purchase of Japanese goods and services, thereby opening these markets to Japanese companies and creating important bilateral trade, technology, and infrastructural links between these countries and Japan.

Bilateral foreign aid also played a big role in improving Japan's ties to the rest of Asia (Arase 1995; Orr 1990). Approximately 70 percent of Japan's aid has consistently been targeted for that region. Unlike assistance accompanied by requirements for "structural reform," Japanese aid was usually delivered with no such macroeconomic demands. At the same time, public-private coordination within Japan meant that the commercial interests of Japanese corporations were systematically, albeit informally, incorporated into official government "aid" and "economic cooperation."

As the United States reduced its presence in the region after its military defeat in Vietnam and the articulation of the Guam Doctrine by Richard Nixon, Japanese government monies became ever more important to regionwide economic development, as well as to enhancing Japan's economic presence throughout the region. Thus, in 1989 Japan accounted for 69 percent of Thailand's total aid, 62 percent of Indonesia's, 57 percent of Malaysia's, 48 percent of the Philippines', and 39 percent of China's (Kato 1999, 4).

At least as critical to reshaping relations within Asia were changes in China. From the consolidation of communist control in 1949 through the Great Leap Forward (1953–60) and the Great Proletarian Cultural Revolution (1965), the PRC was mired in ideologically driven disasters that left it falling economically further and further behind many of its neighbors. Internal developments in China combined with the normalization of relations between the United States and Japan on the one hand and the PRC on the other to shift this focus. China began the tentative embrace of more pro-Western and capitalist-friendly policies. But whereas Japan's moves involved primarily reaching out to the rest of Asia, China's involved opening itself up (partially) to regional and worldwide investment and trade.

Finally, the formation of ASEAN was particularly important in connecting the countries of Southeast Asia. In 1967, the governments of Indonesia, Malaysia, the Philippines, Singapore, and Thailand formed the association, nominally as a non-communist arrangement to promote economic, social, and cultural cooperation and development among its members, but simultaneously as a way to resolve regional disputes and reduce the opportunities for big power interventions in Southeast Asia (Leifer 1989; Alagappa 1993). As internal security problems receded, the wars in Indochina ended, and the Cold War itself cooled, attention within ASEAN turned more explicitly to issues of trade, stabilization of commodity prices, market openings, and the effort to attract development assistance from the industrialized countries. ASEAN's economic efforts were aided by the 1967 creation of the Asian Development Bank. The countries of Southeast Asia tied their fortunes increasingly to one another and began a collective concentration on economic development.

Cumulatively, these changes greatly reduced the military and security tensions throughout the region. Equally important, they increased the range of economic ties among the countries of Asia. Still, in contrast to regional integration in Europe, Asian regional ties, including those within ASEAN, rested less on political institutionalization and the surrender of sovereignty and more on informal cooperation and coordination among member states.

Deep regional economic connections took time to develop. Aid improved Japan's bilateral ties to many countries, and ASEAN began to reduce intraregional barriers to trade. But into the mid-1970s, most Asian states continued to trade heavily with Japan and the United States and far less with one another. Complex economic transactions across the region were limited. Nor were intra-Asian relations particularly advanced by intraregional tourism, technology transfer, research and development, or cultural exchange.

Such linkages deepened by the mid-1970s and expanded dramatically from the middle of the 1980s onward, driven primarily by an explosion in investment from Japan, Taiwan, Korea, and Hong Kong. The result was an increasing complexification of trade and investment patterns across the region.

Regional Economic Integration

A significant expansion in fdi for plants and infrastructure as well as increased capital flows through bank loans and portfolio investments catalyzed a wave of regionwide growth and an expansion in Asian regional ties. This increase in capital movements, in turn, grew out of the strengthened economies, rising production costs, and enhanced currency values of first Japan and later South Korea, Taiwan, Hong Kong, and Singapore. As the national economies of each began to improve, so did their exports, their current-account balances, their currency values, and their domestic production costs. In keeping with the logic of product-cycle theory, enhanced investments overseas by firms in all of these countries followed.

Japan was the first to go through this process, with a sequence of products, such as textiles, electronics, and automobiles. Japanese products in these and other areas increased their world market shares. As they did so, U.S. policy makers in particular sought to reduce the American market penetration of such goods through monetary realignments. The United States abandoned the Bretton Woods monetary system (1971), subsequently, entered into the Plaza (1985) and Louvre (1987) Accords, and then negotiated a series of informally coordinated recalibrations during the late 1980s and early 1990s (Henning 1994). All led to de facto devaluations of the U.S. dollar and rises in the Japanese yen. Fixed at ¥360 to the U.S. dollar from 1947 until 1971, the yen more than quadrupled in value to about ¥80 (vis-à-vis the U.S. dollar) at one point in 1995.

The costs of land and labor in other parts of the world fell dramatically for holders of the rapidly appreciating yen. As costs of production rose in both nominal and real terms within Japan, Japanese firms found it financially compelling to invest in overseas production. Overseas investments were facilitated by the substantial liberalization of Japanese financial markets, the revision of the Foreign Exchange and Control Law (1980), and the deregulation of the corporate bond market. Meanwhile, the Japanese government provided encouragement and various forms of assistance for more and more Japanese firms, including many subcontractors, to move parts of their operations abroad in the search for enhanced market access and cheaper production (Shiraishi 1997, 188–89).

Roughly one-fourth of Japan's investment capital went to Asia (between 1992 and 1995, this meant $35 billion). Between 50 percent and 60 percent of this investment was in manufacturing. For many Japanese companies, Southeast Asia provided a "way out" of the pressures created by rising costs and monetary realignments; moving production overseas obviated the need to accept slower growth or corporate overhauls (Shiraishi 1997, 171). Numerous Japanese firms, particularly in the consumer electronics and automobile industries, began expanded, intraindustry division of labor throughout the Asian region. As Hatch and Yamamura (1996) have argued, this allowed firms to regionalize their previously national production networks. Correspondingly, the ASEAN countries into which Japanese production facilities were moved often lacked the "triangle of cooperation" found in more self-sustaining economies, a triangle based on strong ties between government and business, big and small business, and business and labor. Lacking such domestic connections, the economies of Malaysia, Indonesia, and Thailand in particular remained closely dependent on private investment and official aid from outside their national borders.

Japan's expanded investment represented a massive increase in the incoming monies for many countries. Thus, in 1989 Japanese firms were investing four times as much money in Taiwan as they had in 1985; five times as much in Malaysia; five times as much in South Korea; six times as much in Singapore; fifteen times as much in Hong Kong; and twenty-five times as much in Thailand (Courtis 1992). The investment wave continued through most of the 1990s, despite Japan's own economic slowdown. For the single year 1993, Asian fdi by Japan accounted for 33 percent of that country's total fdi (*Japan Times* 20 June 1994). This regionalization and internationalization of Japanese manufacturing production was most clearly demonstrated in the fact that by 1995, Japanese-owned companies were manufacturing more overseas (¥41.2 trillion) than they were exporting from the home islands (¥39.6 trillion) (*FEER* 4 July 1996, 45).

Japan also expanded its role in international financing during this period. In the late 1970s, Japanese investors accounted for 6 percent of direct investment outflows from the major industrial nations, 2 percent of equities outflows, 15 percent of bond outflows, and 12 percent of short-term bank outflows. By the late 1980s, these figures had swollen to 20 percent of international fdi, 25 percent of equities, 55 percent of bonds, and 50 percent of short-term bank loans (Frieden 1993, 434).

This broadened role was particularly noteworthy throughout the Asian region. Japanese banks had 99 banking offices in Asia in 1980, 313 in 1990, and 363 in 1994 (PEO 1995, 233). In 1991, 19 percent of all Japanese banks' overseas lending went to Asia; three years later, that had risen to 26 percent. By the middle of the 1990s, Japanese banks held 37 percent of Asia's private external liabilities. Japan also provided approximately $10 billion in bilateral loans to China, a figure that constituted approximately three-fourths of China's total bilateral borrowing. Only the World Bank offered financing on a comparable scale (Lardy 1994, 49–63). At the same time, however, the bulk of Japan's structural *investments* go to the NIEs and Southeast Asia, not to China. These waves of Japanese fdi spurred economic development in numerous economies across Asia and wove increasing ties between such countries and Japan and among the countries themselves.

Domestic economic development, current account surpluses, and subsequent currency revaluations energized similar investment outflows from other Asian countries. Most notably, the Taiwanese NT dollar rose by 28 percent from 1985 to 1987, and the Korean wón jumped 17 percent from 1986 to 1988. Like their Japanese counterparts, companies in both countries suddenly had strong motivations to move elements of their production facilities abroad.

Production in Taiwan, Hong Kong, Singapore, and the PRC was particularly affected. Hong Kong and Taiwan had achieved high levels of success with labor-intensive manufactured exports during the 1960s and 1970s. In response to rapidly rising wage rates and labor shortages and to increasing costs of land and growing environmental protection measures, businesses in Hong Kong and Taiwan, like their counterparts in Japan, began to restructure their production networks. The opening of the PRC to fdi provided companies from these locations with undeniable opportunities that were bolstered by common language, business customs, and low transaction costs. It was these other ethnically Chinese areas that provided the lion's share of China's incoming fdi during the 1980s and 1990s.

The PRC had established special economic zones as part of the country's overall move toward economic openness. Hong Kong firms were particularly heavy investors in Guangdong and, between 1979 and 1995, accounted for over 80 percent of that region's fdi. This in turn accounted for roughly 30 percent of the cumulative fdi in China (Sung 1997, 42, 47). The area of South China near Hong Kong became interlaced with complex production units that transcended political boundaries; this integration was enhanced in the run up to, and following, the July 1997 reversion of Hong Kong to Chinese control.

By moving its labor-intensive activities to Guangdong, Hong Kong became free to concentrate on more skill-intensive processes, such as product design, sourcing, production management, quality control, and marketing. China, meanwhile, became home to three-fourths of the manufacturing workers employed by Hong Kong firms, and before the 1997 reversion China was by far Hong Kong's biggest trading partner (*Economist* 31 October 1993, 11).

Taiwan also became highly integrated into the region through fdi. In 1980, China made the politically astonishing decision to allow Taiwanese products to enter the country duty free; Taiwanese businesses took advantage, and exports from Taiwan to China surged from $21 million in 1979 to $390 million in 1980. Ties between these "two Chinas" broadened further with the upward revision of the Taiwanese currency following the Plaza Accord. The 40 percent increase in its value against the U.S. dollar meant that Taiwan risked the loss of export competitiveness in a range of light manufactured goods. Like Hong Kong businesses, many firms in Taiwan were anxious to develop low-wage production facilities within the PRC. Government officials accepted the inevitability of revaluation and dramatically changed direction, especially toward the PRC.

China, meanwhile, had devalued its currency by approximately 50 percent in the same period, making it a particularly attractive target for potential Taiwanese investors. Straightforward economic appeals were bolstered by Premier Zhao Ziyang's policy of pushing what came to be known as the *coastal development strategy*. Taiwan, in turn, by relaxing a number of its more anti-PRC policies, enabled its businesses to operate on the mainland (Naughton 1997a, 81–110).

In 1989, approximately one-half of total Taiwanese fdi of $7 billion went to the PRC, and by 1991, Taiwanese investment constituted just over 11 percent of the total entering that country. The absolute amounts continued to rise steadily into 1993, falling off somewhat after that (Sung 1997, 48). Thus, in 1996, $3.4 billion was going out of Taiwan, with approximately one-third of that invested on the Chinese mainland.

Investment monies also flowed out of Singapore, particularly into Malaysia, but also to other areas in Southeast Asia. This allowed Singapore to deepen its provision of services in finance, law, accounting, advertising, information technology, medical services, and the like for the rest of the region, much as Hong Kong was doing farther to the north.

Such diverse sources of fdi meant that Japan's contribution to the total stake in Asian fdi dropped steadily from the mid-1980s to the mid-1990s. By then, Japanese money constituted only about 14 percent of the total investment capital pouring into the region; other Asian investment monies, in contrast, had risen to more than 58 percent (Bernard and Ravenhill 1995, 182).

Interlaced with such investment was the emergence of a host of "natural economic territories," or "growth triangles," geographically proximate sub-regions with very different levels of development and well-defined divisions of labor. The best known of these brought together Malaysia's Johor State, Singapore, and Indonesia's Riau Province. Others connected Taiwan to Fujian, Hong Kong to Guangdong, and China's Dailian export zone to Japan and South Korea (Gereffi 1995, 127). These growth triangles were but the most obvious manifestations of intra-regional complementarity.

Increased cross-border investment and production complementarity enhanced intra-Asian trade. Japanese exports to the rest of Asia rose from 25.7 percent in 1980 to 42.1 percent in 1995; for the first time in decades, Japanese exports to Asia were greater than those to the United States. ASEAN trade with the United States also gave way to intra-Asian trade. When the U.S. Congress eliminated General Special Preference status for several ASEAN countries in 1991, East Asian NIEs and the ASEAN countries were well positioned to absorb one another's products. Between 1986 and 1992, the intraregional share of exports from Asian countries increased from 31 to 43 percent, while dependence on the U.S. market fell from 34 to 24 percent (Kato 1999, 6; IMF 1995; Pempel 1995, 54, 66).

As Asian regionalism has progressed through commercial interests and market forces, it has retained a largely "open" character. Despite the growth of economic ties *within* the region, economic connections *outside* the region, most especially to the United States, remain critical. Japan, for example, in 1994, sent 30 percent of its exports to the United States and only 6.5 percent to its number two market, Hong Kong. America was also the largest export market for South Korea, Taiwan, Malaysia, and Thailand and the second-largest market for Hong Kong, Singapore, and Indonesia. Asian regionalism in the mid-1990s had certainly not developed as a closed loop. Economic success for the region depended heavily on access to non-Asian markets, most particularly those of the United States (Kokuseisha 1997/98, 387).

Not only trade, but also finance, linked the region's members to the outside. Following the slowdown in global commodity prices and electronics in 1985–86, for example, many Southeast Asian countries undertook various measures of financial reform and liberalization, increasingly opening their capital markets to those of the rest of the world. Domestic motivations were enhanced by incredibly strong pressures from U.S. administrations from Reagan through Clinton to liberalize conditions for investment by U.S.-owned banks, securities houses, and insurance firms. Similar pressures encouraged South Korea to undertake similar measures in preparation for its entry into the OECD. Most of these liberalizations were made with only limited structural reforms to buffer the impact of increased financial flows. This new openness allowed European (and Japanese) banks to become heavy lenders to Asia, with 25 to 45 percent of the loans for many Asian countries coming from European banks. In addition, considerable portfolio money flowed into the region, particularly, but not exclusively, from the United States. Investments from Hong Kong and Singapore were also important.

Overall, therefore, by the middle of the 1990s East Asia had become not only a far richer region through intraregional trade and investment, but also one far more integrated than had been the case in the 1950s or 1960s. Whereas early growth had centered on Japan and then expanded to include the NIEs (Taiwan, South Korea, Hong Kong, and Singapore), by the 1990s the miracle had embraced China and much of Southeast Asia. Moreover, intra-Asian trade and investment patterns had become quite complicated, involving multiple sources, increasing complementarity, high degrees of independent corporate- and market-driven decision making, and webs of overlap and interconnection. As a result, virtually all of the economies of Asia became far wealthier, less dependent on primary production, and more industrialized, and they were able to offer their citizens substantially longer lives and improved lifestyles. But the regional connections that had been so vital to collective improvement also magnified and projected across the region the problems that arose in the summer of 1997.

Politics of Regional Contagion

The economics of the 1997 downturn have been well examined, and the deep web of economic linkages and interconnections analyzed earlier make it intuitively clear why the contagion spread so quickly. Yet, too frequently ignored are the connections between economic fundamentals and underlying political forces. Political and institutional elements were particularly critical to the way in which the economics of the crisis played out.

Two factors were especially critical. First, as should be clear from the previous discussion, Asian regionalism was steeply hierarchical. This contrasted with regionalism in Western Europe in particular but with regional groups, such as NAFTA and Mercosur, as well. Western European integration brought together, for example, at least four relatively large countries: Germany, France, Italy, and Britain. Germany's primary role in the European Union has frequently been counterbalanced by one or more of the other three. In addition, although the European Union has several low-income members, most of its members have relatively comparable per capita incomes. Thirteen of the twenty countries in the world that rank highest in GNP per capita, for example, are from Europe; only two (Japan and Singapore) are from Asia.

Most other regional arrangements (including even NAFTA, with the United States somewhat balanced by Canada) involve less steep hierarchies, at least in the per capita incomes and production profiles of their members. Asian regionalism was characterized less by equality and similarity of national economies and more by a complementary economic hierarchy of unequals. Such an arrangement left national vulnerabilities highly skewed. This is particularly true if, as was true in Asia, institutional arrangements are not set up to buffer the group's weakest members.

Furthermore, most countries in Asia, despite the rise in their internal economic connections to one another, still draw heavily on capital from outside the region, especially from European banks, and depend heavily on the United States as their major export market. Capital coming into the region is at least double that going out. Moreover, in the mid-1990s the United States represented the largest or second-largest export market for Japan (30 percent of total exports), Hong Kong (23 percent), South Korea (22 percent), Singapore (19 percent), Taiwan (26 percent), Malaysia (21 percent), Thailand (21 percent), and Indonesia (15 percent) and was the third-largest export market for China (behind Hong Kong and Japan at 18 percent) (Kokuseisha 1997–98, 387). In contrast, Britain was the only country in Europe to send more than 10 percent of its exports to the United States. Both capital and export market dependency thus left the East Asian countries highly vulnerable, individually and as a group, to non-Asian policy preferences and commercial activities.

Japan is clearly the Gulliver in the region of Asian economic Lilliputs. Despite its own economic foundering since the bursting of its economic bubble in 1990, Japan continues to be the region's preeminent economic giant. With only 10 percent of Asia's population and an even smaller proportion of its total land mass, Japan accounted for nearly two-thirds of the region's total GNP. Its economy was more than ten times greater than that of the second-largest in Asia, China; twenty times as large as Taiwan's; and fifteen times as large as Korea's, not to mention approximately thirty times larger than Indonesia's and nearly one hundred times larger than Singapore's. In other words, the Japanese GNP was about six times greater than the combined GNPs of Taiwan, South Korea, Singapore, and Hong Kong. Japan's per capita income showed a similar gap—it was more than double that of Hong Kong, the second-richest economy in Asia, and more than ninety times that of China.

If the hierarchical character of Asian regionalism was important, so too was the nature of institutional development in the region. Institutions remained decidedly uneven at the national and the regional levels. This is not the place to review the extensive arguments about state strength in various parts of Asia (see Woo-Cumings 1999). Suffice to say that many have argued for the importance of bureaucratic and technocratic governmental powers either across Asia as a whole or within specific Asian countries. However, even those who stress the strength of states in Asia typically concede that any such strength is far more evident in Northeast than in Southeast Asia. Singapore, and perhaps Malaysia, demonstrate some measure of bureaucratic autonomy from special interests, but Hong Kong, Thailand, Indonesia, and the Philippines show far less.

Moreover, political democratization during the 1980s in South Korea and Taiwan—as well as in the Philippines and Thailand—further reduced whatever autonomy over the macroeconomy their governmental bureaucracies and economic technocrats might once have had. As Lim (1998, 30) has phrased it, "Whereas previous authoritarian regimes could impose high interest and taxation costs on local business communities almost at will, and had done so to maintain currency stability for decades prior, this became difficult with the increased political influence of businesses over elected legislatures whose members were either business persons themselves, or required business support to get elected."

Equally problematic was the fact, noted earlier, that capital liberalizations advanced more quickly in many parts of Asia than did the creation of institutions able to exercise financial regulation, monitoring, or management. As Paul Hutchcroft in his contribution to this book makes clear for the Philippines, but as was true elsewhere in the region, Asian entrepreneurialism generated an explosion of highly competitive, but rarely closely controlled, banking institutions.

Without a doubt, critics of Asia's alleged "crony capitalism" are too quick to attribute to it any or all of Asia's failings while remaining blind to the pervasiveness of cronyism elsewhere. The endemic links between politics and corruption were suggested 2,000 years ago by Juvenal, in his declaration in *Satires*, "I refuse to become an accomplice in theft—which means that no governor will accept me on his staff."

In most places, a general rule of politics is that money buys access and access buys influence. Strict regulatory institutions and bureaucratic professionalism are critical to tempering the free flow of such influence buying. Yet, in those countries most seriously affected during the collapse of 1997, such institutionalization and professionalism in finance and administration remained quite low. Financial liberalization typically ran well ahead of oversight regulatory institutions. Indeed, whether in Thailand, Indonesia, Malaysia, the Philippines, or South Korea, the lack of such institutional controls enhanced the incentives for many multinational firms and outside investors to enter "guaranteed" ventures with Asian powerholders and their cronies. These ties enlarged personal empires, corporate debts, and cumulative capital exposure.

Asia had few regionwide institutions with sufficient resources, sovereignty, and commitment to soften the economic blows when they began. The region has a host of informal, nonofficial institutions, such as the Pacific Economic Cooperation Council, the Pacific Basin Economic Council, and the Pacific Trade and Development Conference. Next to ASEAN, perhaps the most important governmental organization was APEC, created in 1989. But, like ASEAN, APEC and all the others remain highly informal and nonauthoritative. They operate mostly through ad hoc committees, have minimal secretariats, give large roles to business initiatives, and have little power to bypass national governmental authority. They exercise virtually no control over commercial transactions involving capital movements, fdi, and loans, and have only minimal influence over trade.

During the crisis, ASEAN struggled to play a role, but it was not equipped institutionally to do so without the voluntary cooperation of its members. Most governments resisted any surrender of their independence or any modification of the ASEAN principle of noninterference in domestic affairs. APEC was even more institutionally ineffective than ASEAN. The capacity of either to shape regional events was easily overshadowed by the entry of the IMF with its billions of dollars in credit and its corrolary demands for tight monetary policies and fiscal reform.

Institutional weaknesses were particularly noteworthy in the case of capital investment. The decades-long record of spectacular growth in much of Asia attracted outside capital at an ever-increasing rate. Although the developed countries of the world accounted for nearly 80 percent of the total inward fdi stock in 1990, this figure dropped to just over 70 percent in 1995 and to 68 percent in 1997. Meanwhile, monies coming into Asia represented just over 11 percent of the world total in 1990, a figure that was up to 15.6 percent in 1995 and 17.2 percent in 1997 (United Nations 1998, 7) By 1997, the Asia-Pacific accounted for nearly three-fifths of the fdi inflows received by all developing countries and more than one-half of the developing country fdi stock (United Nations: 1998, 14–15). Money was flowing into Asia at a rate well above the growth in GNP (Griffith-Jones and Stallings 1995, 147).

As Linda Lim (1995, 245) has pointed out in a different context, the ASEAN countries in particular struck investors as exceptionally desirable locations:

> With the partial exception of the Philippines, and in contrast to the much richer and more industrialized Latin American nations, the ASEAN countries were "model debtors." Their market-oriented economic reforms included phased-in trade and investment liberalization, privatization, and deregulation, all of which contributed to making their economies more efficient and more attractive and accessible to foreign investment—thereby facilitating the shift to export-oriented industrialization.

The bulk of the money that flowed into Asia, however, was unmediated by any government. Rather, most monies came through private sector arrangements subject to limited, if any, governmental oversight, often woven deeply into the fabric of existing cronyism. With very few exceptions, in countries such as Taiwan, China, and to some extent South Korea, national governments exercised no more than marginal control over incoming capital flows.

Some of these monies obviously fueled an expansion in infrastructure and productive capacity. But an increasing proportion of the inflow involved short-term loans and portfolio investment. Bank loans represented about 70 percent of the total capital inflows to Asia in the middle of the 1990s. (This compares to less than one-half in the West.) Moreover, local banks played an extremely large role in the domestic economies of many Asian states. For example, in the United States the largest bank (Chase Manhattan) controls assets equal to about 4 percent of the annual GDP; in contrast, Malaysia's biggest lender (Malayan Banking) controls assets equal to 37 percent of domestic GDP, and the assets of Thailand's top lender (Bangkok Bank) are equal to 25 percent (*FEER* 12 February 1998, 58).

The short-term loan situation became particularly problematic. Foreign capital was readily available at low interest rates. Meanwhile, rates on local debt were about double the rate for foreign debt. Consequently, local banks found it highly profitable to borrow overseas and lend locally; domestic loans were predominantly short term, with multiple roll overs required to complete long-term projects.

Much of the rapidly inflowing money, both loan and portfolio, found its way into highly speculative investments in stocks and property. Bello (1998), for example, shows that foreign investors became the largest buyers of equities on the Thai stock exchange, while in Jakarta, the influx of foreign money increased the capitalization of the stock market almost fourfold, from 69 trillion rupiah ($23.4 billion) in 1993 to 260 trillion rupiah in 1996. Foreign trading accounted for an astronomical 85 percent of the volume (See also *FEER* 25 September 1997, 43). Just as had happened in Japan in 1985–90, much of the rest of Asia began to experience asset bubbles in stocks and property markets.

Before 1990, flows of portfolio capital were trivial, but by 1996 they exceeded $30 billion per year; approximately one-half of this went to South Korea alone. Outstanding bank loans to Asia increased from $110 billion at the end of 1990 to

$367 billion at end of 1996; total loans peaked at $390 billion in mid-1997. Two-thirds of these loans had maturities of one year or less (Bosworth 1998, 8).

Such short-term money was extremely vulnerable to exchange rate shock. This shock came with the agreement on 24 April 1995 among the G-7 to strengthen the dollar vis-à-vis the yen. In addition to reducing the export competitiveness of countries with currencies pegged to the dollar, the declining value of the yen and the rise in the U.S. dollar increased the local currency burden on Asian borrowers for loans denominated in dollars and for holders of Asian stocks. Undoubtedly, a considerable portion of the capital inflow had been based on unrealistic assumptions about the rapidity and sustainability of growth combined with the belief that the exchange rates were stable, guaranteed by governments, or both. Certainly, governmental monetary policies that had long pegged local currencies to the U.S. dollar seemed to offer such guarantees. This in turn made the collapse of the Thai baht even more regionally explosive. But, in reality, most governments were equipped to do very little to protect exchange rates.

Countries with high foreign currency reserves were, of course, less subject to successful attack by financial speculators and stock market collapses. China, Hong Kong, Singapore, and Taiwan were particularly noteworthy in this regard. But fortuitous as such holdings proved during the crisis, large foreign reserves are not without costs. The same reserves could have been used to import new plants and equipment and to bolster long-term growth prospects, for example, or to reduce taxes or provide enhanced citizen benefits.

Furthermore, high debt leverage within most Asian economies made it politically unpalatable for governments to raise interest rates rapidly for fear of eroding the entire debt-based economic model that had been put in place. Devaluation, in turn, would increase a nation's total debt burden, because most debts were denominated in foreign currencies, especially the U.S. dollar. Such alternatives were equally unpalatable for many governments, and most lacked the institutional capability to enforce these unpopular policies had they tried. As currencies fell throughout the region, what began as a liquidity crisis turned into a solvency crisis (Bosworth 1998, 9).

A separate dimension of the regional problem also emerged from the unmediated inflow of capital. Whereas considerable amounts of short-term "hot money" flowed into stocks, property, and short-term loans, far more capital was directed toward a vast expansion in productive capacity for manufactured goods. As export-led economies, most of Asia's success stories had continually pursued expanding market shares. Corporate "success" was measured less through short-term profitability and more through continued expansion of capacity and high-volume sales abroad.

Yet overseas competitiveness in the face of expanding production hinged on stable or declining exchange rates for the exporter. Because the currencies of most of the Southeast Asian countries were pegged directly or indirectly to the U.S. dollar, exports from those countries did very well as the dollar depreciated relative to the currencies of Japan, Taiwan, and South Korea. In 1995, this pattern began to reverse, however. In particular, with the economy of Japan in the midst of what became almost decade-long doldrums, the yen depreciated substantially, thereby undercutting the export competitiveness of goods priced in currencies pegged to the rising U.S. dollar.

Exporting Asia also had to compete with increasingly price-competitive Chinese firms invigorated and expanding due to investments from Taiwanese and Hong Kong partners and parent firms. China's export competitiveness was further enhanced by that country's 1994 devaluation of the yuan. Chinese products increasingly undercut the cost competitiveness of those from Thailand, South Korea, and Malaysia. Companies in these latter countries had expected to move upscale to higher technology sectors and thereby to stay ahead of the China "threat." But conditions worldwide changed far more rapidly than many of them had anticipated, particularly as oversupply rose, making their adjustments more problematic.

Export-led growth works only so long as the exporter(s) makes up a relatively small part of the total world market. The world has a finite capacity for the consumption of particular products at a given time, and once that capacity is reached, subsequent productivity increases become counterproductive, involving an ever-more-vicious zero sum game among producers. This problem began to haunt many Japanese exporters by the mid-1990s. It was devastating to the numerous exporting firms in Thailand, Malaysia, Indonesia, and South Korea; manufacturers of semiconductor chips in particular began to face this problem in late 1996, but it was also true for consumer electronics, automobiles, frozen chicken, petrochemicals, steel, lumber, and basic metals, all of which were important to the developing Asian economies.

Problems of regional overproduction were exacerbated by Japan's long economic slowdown and its declining market for imports. Japan's stall, and the political unwillingness to undertake substantial structural reforms, had also enhanced internal pressures for more domestic protection against products from the rest of Asia (Pempel 1998a, chap. 6; Uriu 1996). These Japanese problems reduced any political impetus the country might otherwise have had to expand its imports from the rest of Asia and to adopt the role of "market of last resort" for the rest of the region.

The share of Asian exports absorbed by Japan fell steadily through the 1990s. Just under 20 percent of Asia's exports went to Japan in 1980; in 1995, this was down to 13.2 percent (IMF various). Thus, most Asian countries, with the exception of China, Thailand, and Malaysia, were running substantial trade deficits with Japan at the time of the crisis. And when the East Asia Economic Caucus had its first de facto meeting in December 1997, after the outbreak of the crisis, Japan was quick to veto a proposal by Malaysia and Singapore to develop an Asian free-trade zone. Japan's only substantial leadership effort was its proposal for a $30 billion Asian fund to support recovery, a proposal that was quickly squashed by the United States as too independent of the IMF. Only with the Kuala Lumpur meetings of APEC in 1998 did a scaled-down version of Japan's proposal gain acceptance, and then it was integrated with U.S., World Bank, and Asian Development Bank measures.

As a consequence of all these factors, exports, which had long been the source of Asian expansion for all the problem economies, fell sharply just before the crisis exploded in full force. In Thailand, they dropped from an annual growth rate of 24 percent in 1996 to 0.9 percent during the first eleven months of 1997. Export growth in Malaysia, at 30 percent in 1995, fell to 0.9 percent in 1996. For South Korea, the story was similar—export growth rates fell from 30 percent in 1995 to 3 percent in 1996. Only Indonesia (which, with more of its exports in agricultural business, faced less competition from Chinese manufactured exports) continued to do well, its rates remaining at approximately 10 to 11 percent annually over the same period (Sen 1998, 111). As exports fell, so did trade balances. In short, expanded capacity and export growth ceased to be a source of stimulus for these economies, becoming instead a source of currency concern. As current account balances weakened, currencies came under threat.

Decreasing export growth and rising current account deficits during 1995 and 1996 had raised some warning flags among international banks and money managers, but continued fast growth and a somewhat blind faith in its unstoppability overshadowed such worries. Investment capital continued to flow in. Thailand was the first of the countries to implode; in mid-1996, the BBC collapsed, exposing the failure of the Thai central bank to crack down on corrupt banking practices and flagging the probability that many other Asian banks had been no more diligent than had Thailand's. In February 1997, Samprasong Land, a real estate company, defaulted on a Euro Bond, signaling that foreign funds had been creating an unsustainable property bubble. Foreign bankers began to call in loans; in anticipation of the government's inability to hold the peg linking the baht to the U.S. dollar, hedge funds began selling the baht short. Within Thailand, locally owned companies were also dumping baht for dollars. Despite the Thai central bank's $26 billion effort to hold the peg, by the end of 1997 the baht was in free fall. As Bernard (1999, 18) has phrased it, "The sight of an under-funded central bank defending an over-valued currency that the entire world is selling off presented an irresistible opportunity for hedge funds." Various currency attacks and collapses subsequently drove down the Indonesian rupiah (44.6 percent), the Malaysian ringgit (44.8 percent), the Philippine peso (33.5 percent), and the HK dollar (29.4 percent) (Goldstein 1998, 3).

By December, the problems had spread to South Korea, which was especially vulnerable on account of its nearly $95 billion in short-term debt, mostly held by the private sector. As one indication of the herd behavior operating across the region, consider the stock markets of South Korea and Hong Kong. The two markets had moved independently of one another before July 1997. Afterward, movements in South Korea mimicked those in Hong Kong. When the Hong Kong stock market crashed in the third week of October, it helped to trigger the exodus of foreign banks and institutional investors from South Korea (Park 1998, 17). The capital exodus and the fall in stock prices led ultimately to the collapse of the wón, which fell nearly 50 percent.

In all of these cases, local financial systems proved to have been operating under lending standards far less stringent than those prevailing among Western banks.

Weak political and financial oversight and the inability to preserve currency values or to provide political guarantees for private loans led foreign bankers to demand full repayment of both the principal and interest while portfolio managers extracted their funds wholesale. In 1996, some $96 billion in capital flowed into just five countries: South Korea, Malaysia, Thailand, Indonesia, and Singapore. By the end of 1997, these five saw a net outflow of $100 billion (*FEER* 1999, 6).

The result was a serious capital shortage for highly leveraged local firms and a spiral of escalating bankruptcies, stock and property market collapses, and hedge fund shorting of the newly floating currencies. Ultimately the problems reverberated through numerous "real economies" in the form of decreased productivity, some 10 million jobs lost, corporate failures by thousands of companies, economic contraction, surging inflation, and collapsing imports.

The political fallout has been at least as consequential. Citizen protests in Indonesia led to the toppling of long-time strongman Suharto. Malaysia forcibly returned thousands of migrant workers to Indonesia and a domestic struggle between Prime Minister Mahathir and former Finance Minister Anwar broke out. Thailand, South Korea, and the Philippines all went through electoral transformations closely linked to the economic crisis. One could even argue that the toppling of Japanese Prime Minister Hashimoto was due in part to the spillover of regionwide economic problems to Japan's already slumping economy.

The preceding analysis demonstrates the intensely commercial stimulation behind Asia's collective growth. Waves of investment created deep networks of highly productive manufacturing and trade. These in turn allowed an ever-larger number of Asian economies to grow rapidly and to deliver substantial benefits to the citizens of those countries.

At the same time, the steep hierarchy of Asian regional development, combined with a dependence on outside capital and export markets, left many Asian countries vulnerable to decisions made in Japan, the United States, and Europe. This should not be surprising in itself. But the low levels of Asian institutional development meant that potential political barriers to unwanted commercial activities were almost nonexistent. National governments, bureaucracies, and financial regulators—whether national or regional—all found it difficult to buffer unwanted commercial transactions. Such issues became combustible fodder in the heated post-crisis debates, a point examined in the conclusion to this volume.

Acknowledgment

Andrew MacIntyre provided helpful suggestions for revision of this chapter.

CHAPTER FOUR

The Determinant of Financial Crisis in Asia

Jeffrey A. Winters

Recent events have underscored the inadequacy of models in coping with abrupt shifts in market liquidity and provided another illustration of the increasing convergence in the behavior of banks and other categories of market participants. It is now broadly acknowledged that national and sectoral regulatory oversight has significant short-comings in view of the globalisation of markets.

—Bank for International Settlements, November 1998

Although the effects of the Asian crisis that began in 1997 were felt by all countries in Asia, they were not felt with the same severity. Why were such varied countries as Indonesia, South Korea, Thailand, and Malaysia badly damaged, whereas the equally varied Singapore, Vietnam, the Philippines, Taiwan, Burma, and China were punched and bruised but not knocked to the ground? The answer to this question holds important clues for disentangling the political-economic forces behind the crisis itself. This chapter argues that a particular blend of external and internal factors accounts for the onset of the crisis and the peculiar path it has cut through the region. More concretely, I posit that the source of the crisis lay in systemic changes in international capitalism—specifically, in who controlled capital flows to developing countries and in the growing prominence of highly mobile and volatile forms of capital and transactions. But, equally important, the vulnerability of particular countries varied with the nature of their linkages and with their exposure to external capital flows that could change course more rapidly than ever before and on a scale that could easily overwhelm all but a few countries economically. To use the metaphor of a huge electrical grid, as the current in the system grows more unstable and potentially dangerous, what matters most are, first, the degree to which one is plugged in and second, whether surge protectors are in place to dampen the effects of massive fluctuations and deadly jolts.

The reglobalization of capitalism, especially for financial capital, was already well under way before the end of the Cold War. But the momentum of liberalization accelerated once security concerns for countries like the United States could no longer override long-standing domestic and international interests that demanded government help in forcing the world open for trade and investment. Although still concerned with security in the Asia-Pacific region, policy makers in the United States began to insist that market access be a two-way street and employed increasingly tough tactics to convince recalcitrant countries that they meant business. This meant separating the state from the private sector, lowering protective barriers, breaking up monopolies in the name of promoting fair competition, and liberalizing access, particularly for financial capital. Of course, this policy shift was not just limited to Asia. It became the centerpiece of the entire U.S. foreign policy and has been pursued aggressively through the WTO and various regional trade and investment groupings, such as APEC meetings and NAFTA.

Volatility Increases as Private Capital Supplants Official Capital

While these pressures were having the intended effect in postcolonial countries, the truly important change maturing in the external political economy was that private capital flows had decisively replaced bilateral and multilateral official flows as the dominant source of foreign capital for developing countries, and especially for the emerging markets of Asia and Latin America. The change in who supplied capital brought a change in why it was supplied. The motives, interests, and patterns of behavior associated with private capital flows introduced heightened instability. Whereas in the first decades after World War II, official capital was provided institutionally, for political goals, such as rolling back communism or maintaining regional security, private capital moves in a more atomized way in search of a combination of market shares and profits in an environment marked by competition. The significance of this trend has been magnified by changes not only in who controls capital, but in the mixture of forms of capital flowing to developing countries. The share of highly mobile—and thus potentially volatile—commercial loan and portfolio capital flows has grown rapidly in the 1990s, while the volume of foreign exchange transactions has increased even faster.

Private capital has thoroughly dwarfed flows of official capital to developing countries. One indication of the new significance of private-sector flows can be seen from comparisons with flows from the World Bank, the leading supplier of multilateral capital to poor countries. In its first fifty years of operation, the World Bank Group supplied approximately $300 billion in loans for 6,000 projects in 140 countries. By comparison, more than $300 billion was invested in developing countries by private capital controllers in just two years, 1996 and 1997.[1] In the 1950s and 1960s, bilateral and multilateral government loans provided the majority of all capital flows to developing countries. In 1984, official and private sources were roughly balanced, with total official flows to these states of $33.4 billion and total private

Table 4.1   Inflows and Outflows of Private Bank Credits, 1996–98 (US$ billion)

	1996 Total	1997 Total	1996 Q4	1997 Q1	1997 Q2	1997 Q3	1997 Q4	1998 Q1	1998 Q2
Total worldwide assets	141.4	99.1	44.1	41.9	34.0	25.8	–2.6	–2.1	–7.2
Developed countries	22.8	25.2	7.2	4.2	8.8	7.8	4.4	9.5	2.1
Eastern Europe	10.8	18.5	6.5	4.3	3.3	8.3	2.6	6.5	4.2
Developing countries	107.9	55.4	30.4	33.2	21.9	9.7	–9.4	–18.1	–13.5
Latin America	28.5	34.6	13.1	7.9	5.8	10.7	10.2	15.6	–0.2
Middle East	–0.1	10.5	–2.2	3.6	–0.6	0.3	7.2	–0.9	5.8
Africa	–0.4	2.7	1.3	0.8	0.9	0.7	0.3	1.0	–1.6
Asia	79.8	7.6	18.2	21.2	15.8	–2.0	–27.4	–33.8	–17.6

Q = quarter.
Source: BIS 1998b (9).

flows of $35.6 billion. But since 1984, private flows have increased five times faster than official flows. In 1995, private capital accounted for three-fourths of all investment resources delivered to the developing world. Portfolio capital, a particularly volatile form of investment, rose from just 2 percent of total net financial capital flows to developing countries in 1987 to nearly 50 percent by 1996. The majority of this staggering sum of money is in the hands of fewer than one hundred EMFMs.[2]

This augmented role for portfolio capital is based more on flows to Latin America than flows to Asia, where bank credits remain dominant. For every quarter from 1993 through the middle of 1998, private bank loans to Asia by outsiders have outpaced capital inflows in the form of securities (international money-market instruments, bonds, and other paper) by at least two to one, and in most years by a much larger factor. Except for the fourth quarter of 1997, when portfolio flows were negative and bank loans surged, the exact opposite was the case for Latin America, where portfolio flows predominated.[3]

Table 4.1 offers a glimpse into the staggering reversal in private banking funds to Asia. The steep drop in total inflows from $79.8 billion in 1996 to just $7.6 billion in 1997 tells a tale that is dramatic enough. But even more revealing of the jolt that hit Asia are the quarterly figures. Private bank credits to Asia continued their rapid growth through the first quarter of 1997, reaching $21.2 billion, but then began a precipitous decline caused by widespread nonrenewal of interbank credit lines. In less technical language, foreign bankers were suddenly unwilling to roll over the region's many billions in short-term loans as they came due, and the negative numbers in the table reflect the net repayments that had to be made. Starting with negative flows in the third quarter of 1997, and continuing through the second quarter of 1998, the losses representing outflows of bank credit from Asia reached a crippling $80.8 billion over the four quarters involved. Table 4.2 shows how rapidly

Table 4.2 External Debt of Selected Countries, 1992–97 (US$ billion)

	1992	1993	1994	1995	1996	1997
Indonesia						
Total external debt	88.0	89.2	107.8	124.4	129.0	120.7
Short-term debt	18.1	18.0	19.5	26.0	32.3	80.0
Private nonguaranteed debt	16.3	14.0	24.4	33.1	36.7	50.8
South Korea						
Total external debt	*	43.9	56.8	78.4	104.7	157.0
Short-term debt	*	19.2	30.4	45.3	61.0	92.2
Private nonguaranteed debt	*	*	*	*	*	*
Malaysia						
Total external debt	20.0	26.1	29.3	34.3	39.8	42.9
Short-term debt	3.6	7.0	6.2	7.3	11.1	14.6
Private nonguaranteed debt	4.0	5.7	9.5	11.0	13.0	25.9
Philippines						
Total external debt	33.0	35.4	40.0	39.4	41.2	42.6
Short-term debt	5.3	5.0	5.7	5.3	7.2	9.3
Private nonguaranteed debt	1.0	2.2	2.9	5.5	4.9	6.8
Thailand						
Total external debt	41.8	52.7	65.6	83.2	90.8	95.9
Short-term debt	14.7	22.6	29.2	41.1	37.6	36.5
Private nonguaranteed debt	13.8	15.3	20.2	25.1	36.2	66.8

* = Not available.
Sources: World Bank 1997; Global Development Finance; BIS 1998a.

total debt for selected countries increased and the share that was short term. The amount of short-term debt tells us how vulnerable different countries were to a sudden and even indiscriminate change of mood on roll overs. Short-term foreign debt is also the most sensitive to a rapid deterioration in currency exchange rates.

The rapid expansion in yen- and dollar-denominated private bank borrowing by selected Asian countries set the stage for a chain-reaction collapse in their economies. The spark, however, came not from defaults in private or public debt, but from the destabilizing impact of currency traders who, aware of mounting pressures from short-term debt roll overs and other latent economic problems, began placing forward contracts that bet heavily against the ability of many regional currencies (starting with the Thai baht) to hold their value.[4]

Forward contracts on exchange rates play an indispensable role in facilitating trade between nations by reducing uncertainty and risk. Forward contracts in currency allow private parties involved in a transaction that spans many months to know in advance exactly what exchange rate will be used when payment is finally made. Currency arbitragers taking on this time risk must, of course, anticipate positive and negative trends in economies to avoid incurring massive losses. As long as currency arbitrage remains linked to the volume and value of internationally traded goods, currency trade itself is unlikely to be an independent catalyst for sudden changes in currency value, but rather will adjust in tandem with broader and deeper

Table 4.3   Average Daily Turnover in Foreign
Exchange Markets, Selected Years (US$ billion)

Year	Volume	% Increase
1989	590	—
1992	820	39
1995	1,190	45
1998	1,490	25

Source: BIS 1998a (14).

trends within and between economies. But by the late 1990s, the average daily turnover in worldwide foreign exchange markets ballooned to roughly 50 times the daily turnover in goods and services. This occurred because currency traders seek profits not just from their risk-reducing and trade-supporting services, but from betting for and against currencies for the profits that can be made from speculation. The average daily turnover in foreign exchange markets continued to accelerate through 1995, when it started to moderate (Table 4.3). As recently as 1973, the average daily turnover in worldwide foreign exchange markets was $15 billion. In 1983, it was still only $60 billion. The 1998 average daily turnover of $1.5 trillion is equal to approximately 85 percent of the total foreign exchange reserves in the vaults of all the world's central banks (*Toronto Star* 29 August 1998, 1).

The vast majority of this currency trading is not subject to effective controls. For 1998, the Bank for International Settlements notes that "'trading' of various OTCs [over-the-counters], among banks themselves, rather than through the 'exchange' and 'clearing house' markets, is a whopping $1,360 billion, and this daily turnover is not subject to the general oversight and rules of exchange markets (and their boards) and built-in circuit breakers (to halt trade), but only subject to general bank oversights like capital adequacy ratios and reserves against value-at-risk of the trading" (BIS 1998a, 31).

The Domestic Side of the Equation

No country in Asia has been untouched by the destabilizing economic impact of the crisis that began in 1997. All have seen exports hurt, stock market capitalizations in decline, rates of foreign investment slowed, and values of currencies eroded. But where the crisis began, which countries were pulled in quickly and deeply, and where the devastation was greatest depended on the degree and nature of a country's exposure to the external financial system and its growing potential for massive disruptive fluctuations. There are myriad ways to slow financial capital flows by complicating transactions, stalling for time, imposing certain conditions, and, especially, frustrating the attempts by hedge funds and currency trading departments in banks to speculate against a currency for the sole purpose of making a large and fast profit. These are the flip side of the story just told about the rising volatility in external capital flows as globalization advances.

If the jolts from rapidly shifting capital flows pose a potential danger, of first importance is the degree to which a country is plugged in to these flows. Limited exposure to external flows helps explain why some Asian countries—such as Burma, Vietnam, and the Philippines—were drawn less severely into the crisis and felt the impact more gradually. But there were also countries—most notably Taiwan and Singapore—that were deeply plugged in and yet were not knocked to the ground when capital controllers unleashed their punishment on the region. For these countries, it was predominantly domestic factors that were crucial in mediating the impact of an increasingly volatile regime of global financial flows. It is in the nature of a country's external linkages, in its local policies and practices, that the surge protectors that dampen the jolts are found.

The key considerations in the Asian crisis were convertibility of currency; the existence, size, and international exposure of capital markets; the degree of private foreign borrowing by local corporations; the share of this borrowing that was short-term; and the ease with which currency traders could raise local credit to launch an attack on a national currency. These factors were more important than the economic fundamentals of the countries in question, their degree of crony capitalism, or even whether governments were resolute and skilled in adopting policies to dampen the crisis once it began to spread throughout the region. Although declining economic fundamentals and crony capitalism played a contributory role in some of the cases, they did not play a causal role in any.[5]

For a country to be among those hardest hit by the crisis, it was a necessary but not sufficient requirement that it be deeply integrated into external capital flows. Indonesia, Malaysia, Thailand, and South Korea all met this standard. All four countries enjoyed high convertibility of currency, borrowed aggressively from private foreign creditors[6] (although Malaysia showed some restraint), and had few obstacles in place to prevent currency traders from mounting an attack on the U.S. dollar–pegged exchange rates that predominated in the region. All four countries had active capital markets that were growing rapidly, as measured by daily volume of transactions, total market capitalization, and the frequency of initial public offerings. All four countries were relaxing the barriers to foreign equity participation and ownership on the local exchanges. But, as the Bank for International Settlements reports make clear, foreign bank credit remained more important than equities.

Liberal banking rules (or, when rules were tighter, the absence of strong enforcement) allowed currency traders and hedge funds to borrow massive amounts of local money; this money would first be used to buy foreign exchange from dwindling reserves and, once the currency collapsed, could be traded back into local funds to pay off outstanding loans at a steep discount, leaving a tidy profit for the trader. Indonesia's banking system—which had undergone reckless deregulation in the 1980s at the incessant urging of the IMF, World Bank, and U.S. government—was one of the easiest to abuse. Hundreds of banks were opened by large conglomerates that were connected politically and financially to the Suharto

regime. The central bank had neither the expertise nor the political will (or inclination) to set lending limits and basic prudential controls. Currency speculators
faced virtually no limits in raising the local resources needed to attack the rupiah.

The contrasts with the countries that were hit less severely are striking. Some of
the less-affected countries were only minimally plugged in to external financial
flows (by design or by circumstance) and had plenty of surge protectors in place;
others were maximally plugged in to the global grid but had important domestic
limits that weakened the effects of shocks. Vietnam and Burma were among the relatively closed countries. The Vietnamese dong is nonconvertible, and exchange
rates are fixed by the State Bank of Vietnam. The State Bank imposes strict limitations on the conversion of dong to hard currency, and only specially designated
industries are permitted to convert dong reserves to dollars. The launching of
Vietnam's capital market was still in the early planning stages in 1997, when it was
postponed by conservatives as the crisis hit the region. Although Vietnam has considerable foreign debt, most of it is medium- and long-term loans from bilateral and
multilateral bodies and is used either by the government or by state-owned firms.
Private firms, which played such a crucial role in building up short-term private
borrowing in the hardest-hit countries, remain small in number and scale in
Vietnam and have not yet enjoyed much success in attracting private foreign credit.
The banking sector is dominated by state banks, and their borrowing from foreign
private banks has been limited and highly controlled. Vietnam suffered gradually
from the crisis, but the dong has not gyrated wildly, and what economic decline the
country did see in late 1997 and through 1998 was caused more by downward trends
in investment already evident in the two years leading up to the Asian crisis.

Burma had been attempting to liberalize in the 1990s, but the refusal by the junta
in power in Rangoon to allow a democratic opening has rendered the country an
international pariah that attracts only minimal attention from foreign capital—with
most of that in infrastructure and extraction. Liberalization had stalled by 1993,
and Burma declined further with the onset of the Asian crisis in 1997. But the country was already too ravaged and destabilized by that point to separate the corrosive
impact of the Asian crisis from the downward economic momentum acquired in
previous years. Like Vietnam, Burma was virtually off the map for global financial
capital. When financial capital controllers began punishing countries in the region
(mainly by withdrawing their capital, selling shares, or reducing their exposure),
very little sudden damage could be done to countries in which the controllers had
hardly gained a toehold in the first place. For these countries the impact came later,
and, especially for Vietnam, the pressures entered through the back door of trade
and declining long-term capital investments.

The Philippines is an interesting bridge case. The country has maintained a relatively open and integrated posture toward the international economy. There are
also a number of large local firms that, under the right circumstances, could have
fueled the sort of speculative property and stock market bubbles seen in Thailand,
Indonesia, and Malaysia. It is also the case that the Philippines has a large foreign
debt. But two things about the debt are notable. First, the proportion of short-

term debt is relatively low,[7] and second, the share of total external debt owed to official bilateral and multilateral creditors is 48 percent, with loans due to private foreign banks and other financial institutions amounting to only 20 percent. To their advantage, the Philippines had only recently reappeared on the radar screens of international financial interests when the crisis hit. Unlike their counterparts in neighboring countries, even the largest domestic companies had neither the credit rating nor the lure of a vibrant economy to attract billions in foreign bank credits that could be deployed at home in various speculative assets. Had the Philippines accelerated the process of making itself more attractive to foreign capital after President Ferdinand Marcos was deposed in 1986, it is very likely that the country would have been as ravaged by the Asian crisis as Thailand and Malaysia were. The peso is highly convertible, and the banking sector would have been an easy target for speculators. Instead, the Philippines posted one of the best economic growth records in the region and was one of the few that could attract new private loan capital from abroad after 1997.

Taiwan is highly embedded in flows of goods, services, and considerable financial capital. The NT dollar has a medium degree of convertibility, and the country's stock market is vibrant but has only limited involvement of foreign capital. Taiwan had several lines of defense against the Asian crisis. First, firms in Taiwan are much smaller than in South Korea or Japan.[8] This makes them unlikely players in the global credit game. They also have the lowest debt-to-equity ratios in Asia. Indonesian companies are leveraged at a rate of more than 400 percent; for listed Taiwanese firms, the average ratio is only 30 percent. Most companies borrow locally or finance their growth out of retained earnings.

State banks play a major role in Taiwan's economy, and they lend most heavily to other state-linked enterprises. This also tends to reduce the debt exposure of private firms. The central bank in Taiwan imposes many restrictions on commercial currency trading, and banks face limits on how much local currency they can lend for foreign exchange dealings. This is a major brake on speculators. Not surprisingly, the average daily turnover in Taiwan's foreign exchange markets is only US$150 million to US$200 million. Foreign investors are allowed to play in the Taiwanese stock market, but foreign capital that is invested in stocks can be withdrawn only under a variety of restrictions that depend on how it was originally invested (*Economist* 7 November 1998).

It is hard to be more exposed to the external economic environment than Singapore. The country's total trade is roughly three times the size of its GDP. Although foreign funds made up 70 percent of Singapore's total investment in manufacturing in 1997, the manufacturing sector is dwarfed by the financial and business services sectors, which comprise 29 and 23 percent of GDP, respectively. Foreign capital is much less represented in these two main sectors than in manufacturing. And although Singapore is seen as a paragon of capitalism, GLCs account for 60 percent of GDP (State Department 1998). Singapore has virtually no controls on the convertibility of the national currency, although the government does impose limitations on lending of the Singapore dollar to nonresidents

($5 million) or to local residents for use abroad. This is an important check against speculative uses of the currency.

Thanks to the CPF—a compulsory savings plan requiring that 20 percent of individuals' incomes be placed in tax-exempt accounts with matching funds from employers—Singapore has a savings rate of roughly 50 percent of GDP. Not surprisingly, gross national savings routinely exceeds investment, allowing corporate investment capital to be drawn overwhelmingly from local, rather than external, sources. Singapore imposes dollar-lending limits on off-shore banks lending to Singapore-based firms. At the onset of the crisis, that limit was only $100 million, although it was raised in 1998 to $300 million. Large foreign reserves permitted Singapore to hold back most attacks on its currency, leaving the country to enjoy one of the lowest currency depreciations in the region. Singapore completely retired its external debt in 1995.

The Onset of the Crisis

"In nearly every economic crisis, the root cause is political, not economic," concluded Singapore's senior minister, Lee Kuan Yew, in an October 1997 address to leading American businessmen at the Fortune 500 Forum in Boston.[9] Mr. Lee did not mean political in the same sense as the Malaysian prime minister, Dr. Mahathir Mohamad, who blamed the crisis on an international conspiracy of Jews (who, he implied, were upset to see Muslims prosper economically, a view that is not only odious but odd, since the crisis began in Thailand). He meant that the behaviors of economic actors are a response to previous decisions and policies of governments. Governments oversee and enforce the context in which economic activity unfolds. Their policies make the opportunities and set the rules. They also create the sort of time bomb that exploded in Southeast Asia at the beginning of July 1997. This is because the interaction does not stop with the context created by governments—economic actors react in an increasingly connected transnational environment according to their own interests. Speaking from the perspective of policy makers, one analyst expressed the resulting impact on state sovereignty succinctly: "We are free to do what we want, but we do not control the consequences" (Harberger et al. 1993, 2).

When the stakes are high, information is crucial. Investors operate well with *risk*, for which probabilities of different outcomes can be calculated. They do not operate well with *uncertainty*, which means the absence of quality information on which to base investment decisions. Transparency transforms uncertainty into risk. In the world of Asian business, transparency means bringing into public view much more information—who is doing what; who owns what; who is borrowing and from where, how much, and for what; how well all parties are profiting (including the government itself); and who is being bailed out, protected, and subsidized at whose expense. These questions strike at the heart of power relations across Asia. Failing to answer them satisfactorily over extended periods, which was the norm during the Cold War decades, is no longer a viable option. Indeed, as hidden information about the economies of Southeast Asia seeped out in July 1997, it triggered an escape psychology among private capital controllers that by November had erased some $400 billion of value in the region's capital markets measured from the beginning of 1997. All the economies in the region saw their growth rates hurt in 1998, and several fell into recessions and contractions that continued well into 1999. Scores of billions of dollars in production and hundreds of millions of jobs are being lost (Chowhury and Paul 1997). According to estimates in October of 1998, $1 trillion in loans had gone bad, $2 trillion in equity capitalization for Asian stock markets had been vaporized, and $3 trillion in GDP growth had been lost (*AWSJ* 14 October 1998).

Three aspects of the crisis are particularly surprising: first, that a region believed to be so strong could stumble and crumble so rapidly; second, that so many countries could be swept simultaneously into the crisis; and third, that despite domestic and international efforts to restore stability and confidence, including some $120 billion in rescue packages sponsored by the IMF, the crisis remained so deep and enduring through 1998 and well into 1999. Indeed, what began as crises in Thailand, Malaysia, and Indonesia soon spread to South Korea, shook Hong Kong, and threatened China and Japan. The Asian crises caused ripple effects that disrupted the capital markets of Europe and North America, with daily gyrations on the New York Stock Exchange resembling the brain waves of a patient having a nightmare.

Before analyzing the crisis and crises in greater detail, it would be well to bear certain considerations in mind. One is that the crises are the result not only of government policies, but specifically of their interactions in an international environment dominated by private controllers of capital who are willing and able to relocate massive resources away from perceived danger in a very short time frame—though not necessarily willing to bring them back as quickly as they withdrew them. Significantly, once this process starts, it does not matter if the danger is real or perceived. This leads to important lessons regarding transparency and information.

Another is that even if analysts or policy makers can successfully diagnose the superficial and deep causes of crises, it is not obvious what sorts of policies will stabilize the situation. Indeed, even the Mexican crisis in 1994 and 1995 provides few clear parallels and lessons for dealing with the disaster that spread like wildfire across Asia. It appears that many policy makers in the region, together with powerful international institutions like the IMF, took actions that were tailored more to standard balance-of-payments difficulties than to the specific kind of crisis that hit Asia. As they groped for a policy combination that worked, their actions sometimes helped to deepen and prolong the crisis.[10]

Phase One: Triggering a Reaction from Mobile Capital and Arbitragers

To the casual observer, the floating of the Thai baht in July 1997 was a curious development, but hardly worth more attention than the thousands of other facts filling the newspapers that day. To individuals controlling huge pools of investment resources in Southeast Asia, the float was a flashing red light signaling danger for the whole region. Within weeks, the Indonesian government also floated the rupiah—another stunning announcement for investors, both local and global, whose entire game plan for Southeast Asia was founded on stable exchange rates pegged to the U.S. dollar.[11] It was in this moment that the changes in the nature of control over investment flows into and out of developing countries made their impact felt with a vengeance. It was also the moment at which the latent vulnerabilities linked to high external exposure, especially to private and short-term bank debt, became explosive for countries without any built-in surge protectors.

The already thin level of economic analysis prevailing among capital controllers before these announcements was soon replaced by a pure psychology of escape. All controllers of liquid capital, including domestic actors, began behaving like spooked wildebeest on the Serengeti. Frustrated policy makers, economists, and even managers and analysts at major institutional investing firms tried desperately to break the grip of the escape syndrome by pointing out that despite some obvious and even deep problems with the political economies of Southeast Asia, the economic fundamentals in the region simply did not warrant such a mass exodus. But when the managers and analysts finished talking to reporters, most of them went back to their terminals and phones and continued selling shares and local currency, because they knew that words of assurance would not be enough to stop the stampede.

In the weeks and months that followed, several countries in Southeast Asia endured devaluations in their currencies averaging more than 50 percent and declines in local stock markets that were even higher. Scores of millions of workers and managers were fired from companies that either went bankrupt or had to scale back their operations because economic growth rates were suddenly much lower, imported components were much more expensive, or major government projects were postponed or canceled. At the epicenter of the crisis were the region's ailing banking and property sectors, which grew more unstable as the crisis deepened.

If it is true that there were serious underlying problems in the political economies of Southeast Asia, then why did the crisis not occur six, twelve, or even eighteen months earlier? All of the difficulties experienced by the economies of the region—weak banks, wasteful and nonproductive investment, overbuilding in the property sector, excessive borrowing by private-sector firms, and speculation in local stock markets with borrowed funds—had been chronic for years. An important part of the answer concerns information, or the lack of it, and a psychology among investors that inflates an economic bubble and then triggers its collapse. A moment came when currency traders, suspecting that Thailand's economic situation was much worse than investors thought, were proved correct. The day was 2 July 1997, when policy makers in the Thai government, who spent a staggering $23 billion buying baht in a vain attempt to maintain the U.S. dollar peg, gave up their defensive effort because they realized that their foreign exchange reserves would run out long before there would be any good economic news to report about the country's property and banking sector. Only an immediate, genuine, and reliable upturn in the health of the economy could have stopped the pressure from the currency traders (by causing them to lose large amounts of money for betting the news would be bad). And given the realities in the Thai economy, there would be no such upturn.

It would be incorrect to conclude simply that the peg to the U.S. dollar was the chief problem. The peg was a smart policy and worked rather well as long as the dollar was weak. It gave Thai and other regional exporters a competitive edge, especially against producers based in Japan. This, in turn, generated high growth, which attracted capital and helped strengthen the belief (some would say hype) that the economies of Southeast Asia would be able to sustain high growth rates indefinitely. Those who pointed to serious and growing problems in the region's economies were shouted down by others who responded that the countries would grow out of the bottlenecks they faced, whether they be national debt, balance-of-payments problems, insolvent banks, or oversupplies in office space and expensive residential property.[12] No matter how accurately one demonstrated that there were serious problems in the structure and operation of the economy—and the excellent reports from the ECONIT Advisory Group, a private think tank in Jakarta, are probably the best examples—it was futile to argue with success. Between 1990 and 1995, when the dollar was weak and exports were still booming, Thailand ran current account deficits of 7.7 percent of GDP, a level that normally signals serious problems to investors, rating agencies like Moody's Investors Service and Standard & Poor's, and such watchdog institutions as the World Bank and the IMF. But no one seemed to care, and no public alarm bells were rung.

When the dollar appreciated in value, the peg went from blessing to curse as Thailand's exports became relatively more expensive and began to weaken. At the same time, there was a global slowdown in key Southeast Asian exports, especially electronics. With a massive devaluation in 1994, China laid the foundation for the competitive export pressures that would undercut exporters in Southeast Asia. By the first quarter of 1997, it was clear that Thai private companies, encouraged by the stable exchange rate, were running up their short-term debts even more aggressively by borrowing tens of billions of dollars from foreign commercial banks. Currency traders were the first to notice the sharp rise in Thailand's current account deficit. And because most currency traders are based in commercial banks, they were also the first to notice the surge in Thai businesses' and financial institutions' borrowing of large amounts of dollars with relatively short maturities.

Phase Two: Chain Reaction

A chain reaction was set in motion by currency traders and managers of large pools of portfolio capital, who operate under intense competitive pressures that cause them to behave in a manner that is objectively irrational and destructive for the whole system, especially for the countries involved, but subjectively both rational and necessary for any hope of individual investor survival. As an increasing proportion of private capital flowing to developing countries was in the form of commercial loans and portfolio investments, meaning stocks, bonds, and other securities, countries across Southeast Asia moved rapidly to open up capital markets, because selling shares is an important alternative to raising capital from commercial banks. But where does this capital originate and how does it reach the market? Here I focus on a group that is admittedly more important for Latin America, but had been rising in importance for Asia after 1995.

Panic and Emerging Market Fund Managers

The majority of capital invested in Southeast Asia's capital markets is owned and managed by local actors. But a substantial portion of the capital invested in the region's capital markets comes from many millions of private citizens from around the world. These people usually do not buy shares in individual companies in emerging markets directly, in part because they have no idea where to put their money, and it would be very costly for them to collect the needed information to make such decisions. This money is gathered in a variety of institutional forms, such as pension funds and mutual funds. These institutions have management teams that decide where to invest the capital and how much to allocate, on the basis of individual companies but also through much broader categories, such as sectors, geographic regions, and types of market. Various formulae that balance risk, profitability, and other factors are used. The person responsible for a fund is called a *fund manager*.

Collectively, these large institutional investors put tens of billions of dollars in portfolio capital into the capital markets of developing countries. However, there is still another stage before the money reaches capital markets in areas like Southeast Asia. Often, even the largest institutional investors lack the staff and expertise to invest intelligently in emerging markets. To solve this problem, specialized mutual funds arose that were specifically designed to invest in emerging markets. At the head of these funds are EMFMs. Institutional investors allocate different percentages of their total portfolio at the macro level to different types of investments in different world regions; the portion allocated to emerging markets ends up in the hands of EMFMs. The EMFMs make the micro-level decisions about which specific countries and companies in emerging markets will receive the investments as purchases of shares in capital markets around the world. This structure for channeling investment capital produces a precarious funnel effect (Haley 1999). Hundreds of millions of independent investors and savers entrust their money to a much smaller number of institutional investors, who entrust a portion of their capital to an even smaller number of EMFMs. The disturbing result is that most of the portfolio capital supplied to developing countries ends up in the hands of just one hundred extremely important EMFMs.

Of course, EMFMs are paid very handsomely for serving this specialized role as the eyes, ears, and decision-makers for millions of people and their money. Justified or not, these individual investors (plus a range of institutional investors) expect that EMFMs will act prudently and responsibly with the capital under their control.[13] Even when they are at their analytical best, EMFMs have two major problems: intense pressure to outperform all the other EMFMs in a highly competitive environment, and the poor quality of available information about the world's emerging markets. The combination of all three elements—the funnel effect, intense competitive pressures, and bad information—produced the explosive volatility and the chain reaction that rocked Asia. Currency traders lost confidence, started betting that local currencies would go down in value, and unloaded those currencies en masse, setting off a self-fulfilling downward spiral that was exceedingly difficult for government officials with limited reserves and a convertible currency to counter. Meanwhile, EMFMs started selling shares across the region and then beyond it. Entire banking and corporate sectors that had borrowed heavily in yen- and dollar-denominated currencies sank into immediate insolvency. One of the least-understood aspects of investments channeled through capital markets or, indeed, deposits in banks, is that the decision to invest, to keep the capital where it is, or to pull the capital out is only partly based on direct information about the quality, safety, and stability of the investment—whether it is in a country's capital market, a bank, or an individual company. The decision to invest is also based on what the investor believes other investors will do.[14]

And so there is a paradox: even if there is no good reason to panic, the more individual controllers of money and capital act to protect themselves in times of uncertainty, the more genuine reason there is to panic. Subjectively, escape is the only course of action that makes sense, even if, objectively, rushing out of a market is unwarranted.[15] And the logic of the escape syndrome applies equally to foreign and domestic capital controllers. A chain reaction is triggered by an event like the float of the Thai baht, which caused EMFMs to realize that the positive (buy/bullish) psychology regarding similar emerging markets (which is a very delicate bubble, rarely based on solid data and information) can burst and cause tremendous financial losses. A trigger such as that seen in Thailand also causes EMFMs to ask tougher questions, look much more closely at the data on the economies in which they are invested, and demand better answers and immediate policy actions to prevent a loss of confidence. If the answers and policies are late or never come, the chain reaction deepens as it widens. Once a crisis starts, it also exposes weaknesses in an economy that previously were well hidden, such as high debt levels, poor sales or export performance, problem loans in the banking sector, or dangerous interlocking relationships between capital markets, banks, and the property sector. What begins narrowly as a financial crisis enters a vicious cycle and quickly becomes a full-scale economic crisis.

Phase Three: Vicious Cycle

Although the poor condition of the Southeast Asian economies did not cause the crisis, the fact remains that the political economies of the region were not especially healthy on the eve of it. For years, Asia's corporate and political leaders had borrowed more money than they could invest productively. Believing growth rates would remain strong indefinitely, they built hundreds of office towers, thousands of luxury condominiums (although the real shortage is in low-cost housing), and scores of resorts and used borrowed funds to speculate in the capital markets. According to one estimate, Asian (excluding Japanese) companies had borrowed at least $700 billion from the rest of the world between 1992 and the onset of the crisis. Japanese banks loaned Asian firms $263 billion; European banks, $155 billion; and American banks, $55 billion. Conservative estimates were that by the middle of 1997, Indonesia, Malaysia, Thailand, Singapore, and the Philippines had accumulated bad bank loans that totaled $73 billion, or 13 percent of these countries' combined GDPs. That makes Southeast Asia's banking mess larger in relative terms than the savings and loans crisis in the United States in the 1980s and the Japanese bubble in the 1990s (Bremner et al. 1997, 116). Economic ministers in the region had a hard time passing legislation that would regulate all of this reckless activity, and when they succeeded in getting laws on the books, they found enforcement an even greater challenge.

A highly damaging downward spiral was triggered by initial pressures on the region's currencies and capital markets. In Indonesia, as the economic ministers raised interest rates to try to pull rupiah liquidity out of the market and defend the currency, they unwittingly deepened the crisis by increasing investors' alarm about how serious circumstances were in Indonesia and by tempting them to shift their money out of the potentially volatile Jakarta Stock Exchange and into the banking system, especially the large state banks. In Malaysia, Prime Minister Mahathir played to domestic nationalist and religious sentiment by lashing out at currency speculators and others who he felt had turned against the Malaysian economy for no good reason. His accusations overlooked the fact that Malaysian investors, being no less self-interested than any other capital controllers determined to protect their assets in the face of tremendous threats, were themselves deeply involved in the selling of Malaysian ringgit and shares on the Kuala Lumpur exchange for the logical reasons explained earlier. And it is worth recalling that Datuk Ahmad, governor of Malaysia's central bank until September 1998, was appointed in the aftermath of a scandalous outbreak of currency speculation in 1992 and 1993 that was undertaken by directors of the central bank. This speculation resulted in losses of 16 billion ringgit. Mahathir's statements, combined with other signs that his government would not produce any serious policy responses to the spreading crisis, caused the pressure on Malaysia to increase. In Thailand, the crisis provoked infighting among coalition partners in the government, leading to the resignation of the prime minister and the formation of a new government. The initial Thai government response was fragmented and contradictory, and it caused investor confidence in the country and economy to drop to unprecedented levels.

The vicious cycle of the crisis was given added momentum in the early months by an attitude of denial that suggested that leaders in the region did not understand the dimensions of the problems they faced. In August 1997, Indonesia announced that it planned to build the world's longest bridge across the Strait of Malacca, connecting Sumatra to Malaysia. The project belonged to one of former president Suharto's daughters. Malaysia refused to cut back on its "megaprojects," which included plans to build the world's biggest dam and longest building (after having already built the tallest). Despite rapidly deteriorating conditions in Thailand, the Thai armed forces insisted on delivery of what they claimed was Southeast Asia's first aircraft carrier, built in Spain and priced at $250 million. By November, the Thais were still bickering among themselves and showing insufficient will to implement IMF conditions for a rescue plan. Meanwhile, Indonesia's President Suharto was sending a dizzying series of mixed signals. First, he canceled and postponed a number of large and expensive projects of dubious developmental and productive value, only to reinstate several that were connected to his children and to businessmen close to the president. After hammering out a $43 billion IMF-sponsored rescue package, Suharto quietly reneged on most of what he had agreed to in public. When the rupiah fell to seventeen thousand to the dollar in January 1998, from twenty-four hundred before the crisis started, Suharto revised the national budget and readopted the reforms pushed by the IMF, only to fail again to implement them seriously. In Malaysia, a major and decidedly nontransparent stock deal that effectively bailed out a company closely linked to Mahathir's party apparatus, UMNO, stunned investors on the already weak Kuala Lumpur exchange, causing a sell-off that plunged the market to its lowest level in nine years.

One of the most striking examples of self-inflicted harm is evident in the Indonesian case. This example also serves as an illustration of how political power and business power weave together to produce an economic fabric in many parts of Asia that is worn increasingly thin by the vicissitudes of contemporary investor motives and capital movements. Bambang Trihatmodjo, one of President Suharto's entrepreneurial children, opened up a bank, accepted deposits from thousands of Indonesian citizens, and then loaned a big chunk of those deposits to his own company—one that happened to be highly unprofitable despite generous government protections. Strictly speaking, such reckless banking practices are against Indonesian law. But no one was strict with the president's children or, for that matter, with any of the other cronies made rich by their links to state power in Indonesia.

When Mr. Bambang's institution appeared on the list of sixteen troubled banks to be closed as part of the first IMF rescue package, he protested loudly and then, with a newfound respect for the rule of law and Indonesia's courts, filed suit against the minister of finance and the governor of the central bank. The essence of his claim? That he was being treated unfairly, since "90 percent of banks in Indonesia violated that requirement [on legal lending]" (*AAP Newsfeed* 7 November 1997). Observers were not sure whether to gasp at what he said or at his audacity in saying it. Mr. Bambang's tragic story, multiplied countless times across Asia and mixed with foreign financiers who were eager to play along, captures in a nutshell how billions on billions of dollars in bad debt and unprofitable investments could have accumulated into a massive bubble that has now burst.[16] The Indonesian case is extreme, which helps explain why the crisis was predominantly economic and financial for every other country in the region but predominantly political for Indonesia.

Institutional Failures

Apart from the structural factors emphasized in the first sections of this chapter, blame for the crisis spreads in several directions. The IMF and the World Bank are supposed to be watchdogs that alert governments and capital controllers to serious trouble on the horizon, but these institutions did not perform their jobs. The IMF failed to anticipate the Mexican peso fiasco of 1994–95. After that record bailout, a new "early warning system," meant to provide more extensive and timely information to policy makers and market actors, was created. But the IMF provided no warnings in the weeks and months before 2 July 1997. In May, the IMF had issued its "World Economic Outlook," but it contained no clear signals that Thailand or the other countries in Southeast Asia were in serious trouble. In response to these criticisms, the IMF claimed that it knew there were problems and that it had the internal documents to prove it. But as one observer asked pointedly, "Is secrecy the hallmark of an early warning system?"[17]

Rating agencies, such as Standard & Poor's and Moody's Investors Service, are given "privileged access to the books and boardrooms of companies, as well as to finance ministries and central banks." Yet businesses and banks that these agencies rated highly were crumbling under the weight of the region's financial crisis. Executives from these firms defended themselves by saying that as far back as two years before the crisis, they had already sent clear signals of problems, but that these concerns did not appear in their credit ratings. Why? Because, according to a top manager at Moody's, such signals are not supposed to appear in the ratings. "An institution run by a bunch of bureaucrats who couldn't run a corner candy store is not necessarily a bad credit risk," the manager pointed out. What matters is the willingness of governments to intervene and bail out management teams that the man from Moody's admits may in fact be "dumbos." A high credit rating does not mean that a company or bank is well managed. It means that despite "bad management, lax regulations, corrupt lending practices and all other maladies," creditors will be paid, because governments can be expected to provide public funds as backing. It happens that these rating agencies provide another measure, called *financial ratings*, that reflect what the agency thinks of a company's or bank's actual management and operation. But investors do not appear to consult these ratings.[18]

Lessons from the Crisis

It is evident that the reemergence of global finance on a scale last seen at the end of the nineteenth century, in combination with late-twentieth-century technology and communications, is a volatile mix that wrenches governments and populations alike. Federal Reserve Chairman Alan Greenspan suggested that "these virulent episodes" seen in the Mexican and Asian crises may be "a defining characteristic of the new high-tech financial system." Greenspan admitted that no one fully understands the workings of that system. "At one point, the economic system appears stable," he said, and "the next it behaves as though a dam has reached a breaking point, and water—confidence—evacuates its reservoir." Hinting at a crack in the dam known as *neoclassical economic theory*, Greenspan concludes, "We have observed that global financial markets, as currently organized, do not always achieve an appropriate equilibrium" (1998a, 186). The political question is whether people want their fates to be determined so thoroughly, randomly, suddenly, and irrationally by the controllers of mobile capital. Although it would be a difficult struggle, with capital controllers putting up a mighty fight, steps can be taken to severely limit the power and influence of hot money and those who wield it. Many people around the globe feel immobilized by abstractions like "globalization." The fact remains that it is not technology, but rather the policies of states that confer so much power on those controlling and moving investment resources around the globe. In September of 1998, Mahathir decided to pull the plug and impose capital controls—an attempt at a strong dose of Keynesian management—in an effort to regain some semblance of control over the domestic economy. On balance, the policy has helped, more than it has hurt, him and the Malaysian economy.

On the question of political participation, arguments about the wonders of authoritarianism for rapid economic development have been floating around government, business, and academic circles for several decades. It is striking, however, that Thailand and South Korea handled their crises better than Indonesia and both managed to have peaceful changes in government leadership at the peak of economic disruption. And they did so without violence and bloodshed. In Indonesia, the country faced a political impasse for months while Suharto clung to power despite his age and poor health and despite being fully implicated in making the country vulnerable to crisis in the first place. This impasse played a central role in prolonging the country's economic pain, because capital controllers stayed on the sidelines waiting for a resolution to the succession crisis, largely ignoring the huge IMF rescue package. Suharto was finally deposed, at a cost of more than one thousand Indonesian lives. The relatively more participatory political systems in Thailand and South Korea allowed discredited leaders to be eased out and new leaders to take the reins and push through painful reforms with a legitimacy that was utterly lacking in the half-hearted efforts of Suharto's New Order regime and the Habibie government that followed.[19]

How this crisis will affect Asian countries or international capitalism is not yet clear. For the present, controllers of mobile capital are in charge, particularly for those countries drawn into their grid. Either through the direct signals of their capital investments and withdrawals or through the spins and policy reforms pushed by organizations like the IMF or individuals like Alan Greenspan, these capital controllers are able to punish or reward countries they dislike or favor. Of course, along the way jobs and goods are created. But over time, and with successive crises, especially in finance, it becomes apparent that the motives of these investors have little to do with jobs and production. These are by-products of the profit-making drive, not its central concern or goal. Neoclassical economists consider this to be the genius of market systems—one does not have to want to create employment or develop a society. It happens as if by magic.

In fact, it does not happen automatically or magically. Nor does it happen without a good dose of coercion, conflict, and now the constant threat of tremendous economic upheaval on short notice. Private investors are choosy. Some 80 percent of total private capital flowing to developing countries goes to a dozen countries. This means that until major changes are made in how capital is controlled, countries are going to face intense pressures to be responsive to the demands of capital controllers. These pressures will yield reforms in the short and medium term that could undermine much of what defines business-government relations across many parts of Asia. But just as these crises produce reforms, they could also build and strengthen the resolve of governments and their populations over the medium and long term to gain more leverage over how capital is controlled. Certainly, among conservatives in the countries that were hit hard and in countries that escaped with lighter punishment, there is growing agreement on this point.

PART II

NATIONAL RESPONSES

CHAPTER FIVE

Free Market Fancies: Hong Kong, Singapore, and the Asian Financial Crisis

Linda Y. C. Lim

The urban-industrial entrepôts of Hong Kong and Singapore have long been widely recognized as the first and second most liberal economies in the world. Although internally well-managed in public and private sectors, both economies were adversely affected by regional "contagion" from the financial crisis affecting their Southeast Asian neighbors and trade partners. Despite similarities in economic structure, particularly in dependence on trade intermediation and regional service exports, there was a dramatic difference in the policy response of each government to the domestic economic downturn that was a consequence of the regional crisis. Whereas Hong Kong retreated from its long tradition of open capital markets with unprecedented market interventions, Singapore moved in the other direction, announcing not only the continuation of its open market policies, but also the further liberalization of financial markets and openness to foreign capital market actors. This chapter argues that this policy difference is due to differences in the domestic political systems and circumstances of each location.

The Economics of Crisis

The regionwide Asian economic crisis began with the symptoms of a classic currency crisis in Thailand, which then spread, through "contagion effects," to its Southeast Asian neighbors and Korea and deepened into a financial, and finally an economic, crisis characterized by severe recession in most of the affected countries. A currency crisis arises when a country with a more or less fixed exchange rate runs cumulatively large current account deficits (when imports exceed exports of goods and services) that can no longer be funded by inflows of foreign capital (required to cover the gap in foreign exchange) in the forms of debt and direct and portfolio

101

investment. This is usually an indicator that the currency is overvalued (i.e., imports and foreign liabilities are artificially cheap, and exports and domestic assets are artificially expensive). Maintaining the overvalued exchange rate depletes the country's foreign exchange reserves, resulting eventually in capital flight as owners of capital anticipate a devaluation. In economies with capital account convertibility, such a devaluation is likely to be precipitated by speculative attacks.

The standard economic policy solutions for such a balance-of-payments crisis are to (1) float (i.e., depreciate) the overvalued currency and/or (2) deflate the domestic economy by raising interest rates, tightening credit, cutting government spending, and raising taxes. Each measure makes exports and assets cheaper for foreigners and imports and foreign assets dearer for residents, while reducing domestic demand for imports and exportables and curbing inflation (which is likely to result from currency depreciation that raises the prices of imports). The resulting reduction in foreign exchange outflows to pay for imports and increase in foreign exchange inflows from greater export earnings and new inward foreign investment helps rebuild foreign reserves, stabilize the domestic currency, and reflate the economy. A country that does not allow its exchange rate to depreciate must endure a more severe deflation to bring its external accounts into balance.

There are well-known limitations to the effectiveness of this standard policy (which will not be discussed here), but it remains by and large the conventional path to economic recovery from a currency crisis—both recommended by the IMF (and followed by governments not reliant on IMF funds and thus not constrained by the conditions that accompany such funding) and expected by financial market actors. Economists tend to differ only in the extent to which they favor either devaluation or deflation as the principal mechanism for recovery. For example, economists who favor a currency board (see the discussion of Hong Kong, later) prefer that all the adjustment be borne by domestic deflation, particularly higher interest rates and reduced domestic liquidity, whereas those opposed to domestic deflation prefer to rely on currency depreciation alone. A third policy option, imposing currency controls to restrict the outflow of depleted foreign exchange reserves, attempts to avoid both devaluation and deflation but is rarely recommended by economists because of resulting inefficiencies. During the Asian crisis, however, this extreme move was implemented by Malaysia.

The Politics of Crisis

The main problem with applying the standard economic policy of devaluation, deflation, or both lies in the realm not of economics, but of politics. The deflationary prescription of raising interest rates, restricting credit, cutting government expenditure, and increasing taxes is bound to be politically unpopular, because it raises business costs and reduces incomes and living standards. Devaluation also raises the cost of importing foreign inputs and of servicing foreign debt, and reduces consumption, living standards, and domestic wealth valued in terms of foreign currency. Business communities and populations at large, quite under-standably, do not appreciate being made poorer.

In theory, this means that any government that relies on popular support or on support from the local business community for its existence is likely to oppose or delay such policies, especially if an election is approaching, when the government may even resort to short-term stimulus measures that worsen the external imbalance (e.g., tax cuts, pork-barrel expenditures, and easy-credit policies) as in Mexico in 1994. This is why financial market actors watch elections and election outcomes so closely, as they did in Brazil and Venezuela in late 1998, for example. As I have argued elsewhere (Lim 1998), immature and unstable democracies, such as those established in Asia since the mid-1980s are particularly vulnerable to political influence on eco-nomic policy, and this influence is most likely to run in opposition to deflationary policies and devaluation that impose costs on the electorate. But authoritarian gov-ernments that are beholden or related to powerful business constituencies are simi-larly vulnerable. At the same time, governments of economies that rely on the inflow of foreign capital must balance this domestic electoral or interest-group pressure against the need to conform to domestic and external financial market actors' expec-tations of prudent fiscal and monetary policies that preserve currency values and, hence, the value in foreign exchange of their investments in the host country. Government macroeconomic policy responses are thus constrained by both external economic and domestic political demands. Hong Kong and Singapore face similar external economic pressures from global capital markets, whose players include their own citizens (the source of potential "capital flight"). The following discussion argues that the two governments' different macro policy responses to the crisis reflect the dominance of domestic political factors in each case.

Hong Kong

Nearly all former colonies abandoned the colonial currency board system that rigidly linked their currencies to those of their respective "mother countries." Hong Kong did not, not only because it remained a colony much longer than most—until July 1997—but also because a stable currency was widely believed to be necessary for political confidence in the territory, on the part of both outsiders and, more important, its own otherwise politically insecure residents. Domestic financial pan-ics in the late 1970s and early 1980s led to the decision in 1983 to peg the Hong Kong currency to the U.S. dollar—the dominant currency of international trade and investment in the world at large. It was believed that this would deliver long-term benefits to the economy in terms of financial stability, domestic and foreign confidence in the value of the currency, and the removal of currency risk.

Under a "pure" currency board system, there is no autonomous government monetary policy. The home currency is backed 100 percent (or more) by equiva-lent units of the key foreign currency to which it is pegged. If foreign currency reserves decline, so does the domestic money supply, resulting in a contraction in the domestic economy and a rise in real interest rates that will attract an inflow of the foreign currency, expanding the domestic money supply again and causing interest rates to fall. Domestic balance is thus achieved purely by the inflow and outflow of capital responding to interest rate differentials—in this case, between Hong Kong and the United States. The Hong Kong system has in the 1990s evolved to a less than "pure" currency board, allowing the territory's financial authorities to intervene at the margins to limit fluctuations in currency reserves (*Economist* 1 November 1997, 80).

A currency board is supposed to protect a currency from speculation, since investors know that any attempt to sell the currency short simply penalizes the speculator by raising his borrowing costs without permitting him to buy back the shorted currency at a lower rate in the future.[1] This automatic adjustment mechanism depends, however, on the interest rate's being allowed to soar to whatever level is required to achieve equilibrium (i.e., to reduce domestic demand for foreign currency while increasing foreign demand for the local currency). Speculators may still attack a currency if they suspect that the authorities are unwilling to tolerate sustained high interest rates and the high unemployment that accompanies them.[2]

After more than a decade of stability, Hong Kong's currency was attacked by speculators in October 1997, a few months after the collapse of the Thai baht in July and while "contagion" was rapidly decimating the currencies of its other Southeast Asian neighbors. The reasons for this were twofold. First, speculators do not attack unless economic fundamentals suggest that their attack might be successful, by moving other holders of the currency to sell it en masse. Hong Kong's export-oriented services sectors (e.g., finance and tourism) had become uncompetitive with the fall in the currencies of its major customers and competitors in the region. Domestic industry and services also suffered from severe import competition. The anticipated result was a fall in Hong Kong's ample foreign currency reserves, which would eventually reach the point at which the domestic money supply would contract and interest rates would rise.

The second factor motivating the speculative attack was speculators' bet that the Hong Kong authorities would be reluctant to let this corrective mechanism play out because of the political consequences of the heavy deflationary cost it would impose on the domestic economy. The Hong Kong authorities had not previously shown such reluctance, but Hong Kong's July 1 1997 reversion to Chinese rule introduced an element of uncertainty into market actors' guesses about the authorities' likely response to a now overvalued exchange rate. Leading Hong Kong businessmen, some known to be favorably inclined toward and thus supported by the territory's new sovereign power, China, publicly complained that the peg and overvalued exchange rate were hurting their businesses. Given both changed economic fundamentals and a changed political environment in which the (pro-China) business community—which now dominated the territory's semi-elected representative bodies—was now more powerful than it had been under British colonial rule, it was reasonable, if still risky, for speculators to assume that the Hong Kong authorities' commitment to maintaining the peg might waver.

The speculators' gamble failed, but they attacked the HK dollar again in August 1998, when high interest rates and the now even more overvalued exchange rate had already plunged the territory into recession, with concomitantly huge (40 percent) drops in property values and the stock market, which is disproportionately populated by publicly listed property development firms and by banks and financial institutions heavily exposed to the property sector, to which almost one-half of all bank loans go (*FEER* 5 March 1998, 49). Interest rates had already doubled, and further increases would threaten not only deeper recession, more bankruptcies, and unemployment, but also more loan defaults and insolvency of big companies and financial institutions—on whose health Hong Kong's key financial services sector depended. Speculators shorted both the HK dollar and stocks, increasing the probability that they would win on one count or the other: under the currency board system, massive HK dollar selling would send interest rates soaring, which in turn would send the stock market plunging further, whereas if the peg were abandoned, the currency would plunge.

In defense, the Hong Kong Monetary Authority and treasury department embarked on historically unprecedented moves to foil the speculators' attacks. These included the imposition of a raft of new restrictions on speculative activity, particularly short selling and futures trades, and massive government stock purchases to prop up the stock market (*Wall Street Journal* 17 August 1998; *South China Morning Post* 8 September 1998). The measures worked to stabilize the stock market and interest rates while preserving the currency peg and received both support (*South China Morning Post* 27 August 1998; *FEER* 3 September 1998, 29; *Wall Street Journal* 20 August 1998; *AWSJ* 20 August 1998) and criticism (*Wall Street Journal* 17 August 1998; Liu 1998; *Wall Street Journal* 3 September 1998, A19; Clifford and Prasso 1998; *South China Morning Post* 8 September 1998) from local and foreign economists and financial market actors. Support came from local and foreign investors grateful for the protection of their asset values and angry at the actions of speculators, while criticism was based on the belief that the intervention called into question the integrity of Hong Kong's currency board, all but ensuring future speculative attacks[3] and undermining the credibility and consistency of government policy, on which the territory heavily relies for its competitive edge in business and financial services and its reputation as a good location for investment. Elected representatives in the legislature also voiced concern at the large amount (an estimated US$10 billion to US$15 billion) of government funds spent to prop up the wealth of stockholders in particular companies and about conflicts of interest in the management and future disposal of now government-owned stocks (*Economist* 31 October 1998, 79).

The purpose of this chapter is not to examine the economic pros and cons of Hong Kong's intervention policies, but rather to consider the likely political motivations behind these policies, which I argue center on the extreme interest-sensitivity of the territory's economy, particularly its inordinate dependence on the property sector.[4] This arises because the territory has never had a free market in land, although the markets in labor and (until recently) capital have been relatively free.

In part because of the territory's much-vaunted low tax regime (a flat 15 percent income tax), the government has long relied on sales of land, which it totally controls, and on land taxes for as much as 40 percent of its revenues.

This artificially induced land scarcity (even after taking into account the territory's hilly topography) has steadily pushed up property values and prices. Land costs typically amount to 70 percent of the total cost of building in Hong Kong, the inverse of the relationship in most markets (*Wall Street Journal* 14 September 1998). Thus, before the crisis, Hong Kong residents paid three times as much as Singaporeans for the same residential space (Bacani 1998), even though Singapore has a similar population density (but flatter land) and income level. A high proportion of Hong Kong residents' household wealth is invested in property and in the stocks of property companies and financial institutions with heavy property loan exposure. At the same time, the government must supply public housing developments for the roughly 50 percent of the population who cannot afford prevailing private market housing prices. High property prices are also the main reason that Hong Kong routinely ranks as the most expensive city in the world in terms of cost of living, which adversely affects its competitiveness.

Recognizing the welfare and efficiency costs of Hong Kong's land policy—the result of a deviation from market forces that arguably amounted to a tax on Hong Kong's population and businesses for the benefit of the British colonial regime—chief executive Tung Chee Hwa made reforming the property sector and making housing affordable a "defining policy" of his new administration when he took office on 1 July 1997, pledging "to increase supply, gradually bringing down prices, thereby reducing the role property plays in the economy, and the volatility that engenders" (Wang 1997).

Instead, barely a year later, in June 1998, the Tung administration announced a freeze on government land sales until 31 March 1999; a series of tax cuts, including a rebate on certain property taxes; an easing of credit; and a doubling of the amount of special low-interest loans available to first-time home buyers. The goals were to stabilize property prices, which had fallen by 40 percent from 1997's peaks, and to protect the banking system, which had a large exposure to the property market (*Wall Street Journal* 23 June 1998)—this despite the fact that most private-sector analysts believed that prices had to fall still further to restore Hong Kong's competitiveness, given its exchange rate rigidity and that "Hong Kong's stock and property markets are simply too big for the government to try to support" (*Wall Street Journal* 11 June 1998). As part of the package of market interventions unveiled in August and September 1998, the government added more measures to stimulate the property market, including halving the 10 percent deposit a property buyer must pay on signing a preliminary agreement and removing the minimum 20 percent of total purchase price that a buyer must pay after signing the formal transaction agreement (*Wall Street Journal* 14 September 1998, A25).

These and other intervention measures—particularly the government's massive stock purchases—have led to inevitable accusations that they are designed to salvage the fortunes of Hong Kong's property barons, "the handful of powerful tycoons who control much of this city's wealth" and are close to Tung, whose "cabinet is a virtual plutocracy of senior business leaders" (*Wall Street Journal* 17 August 1998). The property sector—dominated by only seven companies in 1996—accounts for the bulk of the Hong Kong Stock Exchange, the world's fifth largest exchange. Before the crash, property and, hence, stock market values had been bolstered by the Sino-British agreement to limit land sales to 124 acres a year in the run-up to 1 July 1997 and by property purchases by Chinese state-owned companies "anxious to show their support for Hong Kong" (*Wall Street Journal* 14 September 1998). The high cost of entry (residential tracts auctioned off by the government between 1993 and 1995 started at more than a quarter billion U.S. dollars each) kept the number of developers small, so much so that "The parcels got very big and the dollars got very big. It got to the point that I phoned [Financial Secretary] Donald Tsang to say we need more competition."[5] Hong Kong–based fund manager Marc Faber has further noted that "the heaviest share buybacks of this year took place on Aug. 11, 12 and 13—the three days leading up to the initial (government stock-purchase) intervention. What an unusual coincidence, especially considering that these heavy purchases were carried out by some of Hong Kong's largest property tycoons" (Faber 1998). He concludes that "A number of well-placed government officials and businessmen must have had prior knowledge of the intervention" (Faber 1998).

Even defenders of the government's intervention have pointed to the "property cartel" as a major source of Hong Kong's current problems (*FEER* 3 September 1998, 29). Faber (1998) and others (*Wall Street Journal* 14 September 1998, 18) have also noted that besides the "property barons," other members of the local elite—in stockbroking, banking, law, and other cartelized professions—have also benefited from state interventions. This despite the fact that the majority of top executives in Hong Kong recently surveyed disagreed with the government's intervention to prop up markets (64.4 percent) and did not think that this effort would help the economy as a whole in the long run (61.1 percent) (*FEER* 30 April 1998, 34).

This discussion suggests something that the Hong Kong government denies: that the territory's difficulty in recovering from its current economic problems, and its government's choice of unorthodox state interventions as the means of limiting the damage, result from dual domestic political pressures—the overdependence of half of the population on property wealth (populist pressure), and the influence that a few large property developers are suspected of wielding over the nonelected chief executive (elite pressure). In the short run, the interests of both coincide with respect to the lowering of interest rates and the rise of the stock market, and this has been achieved with the help of government interventions and fortuitous developments in the world economy.[6]

In the long run, however, there is a conflict of interest between sizable government ownership of large property conglomerates like New World and Cheung Kong and the government's role as sole supplier of land for development; also, the size of the government's holdings (now estimated at between 15 and 25 percent of total stock market capitalization) reduces stock market liquidity and increases volatility and the risk that stock prices will be set primarily by government sales and purchase decisions (through a new asset-management corporation supervised by the monetary authority, which also regulates the banks the government now owns), rather than by "the market." This in turn politicizes both capital and property markets, making them vulnerable to real or perceived shifts in political sentiments in both Hong Kong and China and compromising the allocative efficiency that markets are assumed to deliver.

The relationship between Hong Kong and China complicates the prospects for the Hong Kong economy and thus affects domestic and foreign capital market actors' perceptions and decisions in a number of ways. China's support of the Hong Kong peg—including its presumed willingness to commit some of its own sizable foreign exchange reserves to a defense against speculators and its apparent unwillingness to devalue its own currency[7]—makes the peg more credible and increases the likelihood that both territories' currencies will remain overvalued and their economic growth slow for the time being. But China is also eager for the territory's property-dependent economy to be stable and prosperous after its reversion to Chinese rule, and many Chinese SOEs are heavily invested in the Hong Kong property markets. This would incline the Chinese government to support the Hong Kong authorities' move toward more state intervention in the property and capital markets to push up property and stock prices, which parallels its own heightened interventions to stimulate the sluggish Chinese domestic economy through loose monetary policy and delayed state enterprise reforms. To the extent that these measures do succeed in "pump priming the Chinese economy," they also limit the severity of Hong Kong's current recession. In short, the presence and support of China add further "external" political weight to the domestically generated political pressures that have set the Hong Kong authorities on the path of extensive domestic market intervention in the wake of the Asian financial crisis.

Singapore

Singapore has so far weathered the regional economic storm much better than Hong Kong, despite the fact that its hinterland—primarily Malaysia and Indonesia—has been devastated, whereas Hong Kong's hinterland—China and Taiwan—has continued to grow. The city-state maintained growth of 1.5 percent of GDP in 1998, when Hong Kong suffered a 5.1 percent decline in GDP, and is expected to grow at 1 percent in 1999, whereas Hong Kong continues to contract by 1.5 percent.

The chief economic reason for this superior performance is Singapore's managed-float exchange rate regime. Singapore abandoned the colonial currency board regime long ago, and its dollar now floats against a weighted basket of currencies including the U.S. dollar, the Japanese yen, and the Malaysian ringgit (Malaysia being Singapore's largest trade partner) in undefined ("secret") ratios. With the weakening of the yen and the ringgit over the past two years, Singapore's currency has "naturally" also weakened against the U.S. dollar, the HK dollar, and the Chinese renminbi, although it has strengthened against all other regional currencies and has remained roughly at par with the NT dollar. This flexibility has limited the loss of competitiveness suffered by Singapore's export sectors—including global high-technology manufacturing and the regional tourism, financial, and commercial services found in Hong Kong—during its neighbors' currency meltdown.

As a sovereign nation-state with a credible independent (and elected) government, Singapore, although equally open and vulnerable to world market forces and international capital flows, has not shared Hong Kong's psychological need for an external currency peg to maintain the political confidence of its citizens in the stability of their economy and currency. Some degree of currency flexibility has also been important to Singapore because, unlike Hong Kong, it has maintained a manufacturing sector despite the shift of comparative advantage away from labor-intensive activities that affected both economies beginning in the late 1970s. Hong Kong's response was to relocate its mostly locally owned labor-intensive manufacturing activities across the border in China, reallocating resources into the services sector (particularly financial and business services) and skill-based segments of the manufacturing value chain (design, marketing, distribution). Although Singapore also relocated some labor-intensive manufacturing activities to its lower-wage neighbors Malaysia and Indonesia, it has not abandoned the manufacturing sector. Rather, the government has invested heavily in upgrading its manufacturing industry through direct and indirect state subsidies to create a more capital- and technology-intensive sector that still uses some relatively unskilled labor.[8] Manufacturing remains dominated by multinationals, as it has been since export-oriented industrialization began in the late 1960s, with multinationals' suppliers accounting for most of the locally owned sector. In the regional economic crisis, this globally oriented multinational manufacturing sector has continued to be buoyed by exports to the still healthy U.S. and European economies, partially offsetting the decline in the trade and services sectors resulting from the severe recessions in Malaysia and Indonesia and stagnation in Japan.[9]

Over time, Singapore's managed-float currency and industrial policy have delivered higher income, faster GDP growth, and lower inflation and interest rates than Hong Kong's currency peg and reliance on market forces (static comparative advantage) for resource allocation. Their domestic political systems are also very different. Unlike Hong Kong's government, Singapore's has had to be accountable to an electorate that votes in general elections held every four to five years. Despite tight control of the media, constant fine-tuning of the electoral system in ways that disadvantage opposition parties, and periodic legal intimidation of opposition candidates, the ruling People's Action Party has never won more than 70 percent of the popular vote (voting is compulsory), and, until the most recent general election in 1996, its popular vote share had actually been declining to as little as 60 percent of votes cast (although this has always translated into more than 90 percent of parliamentary seats held). This periodic electoral test has made it necessary for the government to work to maintain its popularity.

Maintaining economic prosperity and full employment has played an important role in passing this electoral test. The unskilled segment of the labor force, although declining in relative share, is still the most numerous in the electorate, and in Singapore, as in other advanced industrial countries, it has progressively rejected participation in more arduous manual jobs, such as construction and domestic service, as overall incomes have risen and affluence has increased. Thus, it has been necessary to create and maintain relatively high-wage, high-productivity, if low-skilled, jobs in mostly high-technology manufacturing for these workers—in combination with imported labor if necessary.[10] Exchange rate flexibility has been crucial for the maintenance of international competitiveness and, thus, jobs in manufacturing. Hedge fund operators and other currency speculators correctly reasoned that the government would not defend the Singapore dollar when it came under speculative attack in October 1997, despite the huge current account surplus and foreign exchange reserves (more than twice those of Hong Kong on a per capita basis) that it commanded. In short, the political costs of deflation ensured that Singapore's government, unlike Hong Kong's, would prefer depreciation to maintain the competitiveness of the manufacturing (and other export-oriented) sectors.[11]

But like Hong Kong, Singapore's government also controls the land market and houses an even higher proportion—more than 80 percent—of the population. That the result of this intervention has been somewhat different than in Hong Kong reflects the different politics of housing in each location. This is not the place to explain in comprehensive detail how and why public housing in Singapore has been and will likely remain highly politicized (see Lim 1989, 182–86; Pugh 1989). I highlight only those features of this politicization that affect the social impact of and public policy responses to the economic crisis.

Briefly, "Housing policy is the very cornerstone of the PAP's political legitimacy. The policy dimension is a very big one in the housing equation."[12]

The primary goal of the public housing program has always been to win the electoral support of the population by providing decent, affordable housing, with a secondary goal of building a sense of community and national commitment through financing occupants' ownership of their public housing units through the forced-savings CPF scheme (which Hong Kong, under Tung Chee-Hwa, has also started emulating). To achieve this has required massive government investment (funded to a large extent by citizens' own compulsory savings) and an inevitable "crowding out" of the private sector, alleviated by the fact that CPF savings may be used by the higher-income segment of the population to purchase private housing units. A "two-tier" housing market thus developed, with relatively reasonable prices for government-built units in HDB estates, allowing 80 percent of HDB occupants to become home owners, and much higher prices for privately developed units purchased by individuals and families in the top 15 percent of the income distribution.

Over time, policy shifts allowing the resale of HDB units and the use of CPF funds to purchase multiple properties and private sector units, together with homeowners' strong inclination to "upgrade" their properties as affluence spread, resulted in a sharp rise in the prices of both public and private housing units. Property began to be viewed as an "investment" and a means of maximizing the long-term return on one's CPF forced savings through anticipated capital gains, because

> What else does one do with CPF money earning miserly interest barely ahead of inflation, than to dump as much of it as possible into property?
>
> Even Senior Minister Lee Kuan Yew has said that if he were a young man again, he would buy a HDB flat and trade it in for the capital gain.
>
> The belief that the Government will not allow the bottom to fall out of the property market is a deeply ingrained one. . . . The Government has a vested interest in keeping prices of HDB resale flats high to protect the value of public housing. Resale prices in turn support the private residential property market, and so on it goes.[13]

The sharp rise in prices from this strong demand elicited an equally strong supply response, which came not only from private developers, but also increasingly from GLCs diversifying out of their traditional businesses. Previously state-owned companies that were being privatized and listed on the local stock exchange started building luxury condominium units, hotels, and office blocks—not only in Singapore, but also in less-developed neighboring countries like Cambodia, Myanmar, Vietnam, and Indonesia—as part of a state-promoted "regionalization" drive. In addition to Pidemco Land (formerly the Urban Redevelopment Authority), GLCs in shipping (the Sembawang and Keppel groups), technology (Singapore Technologies) and banking (DBS Land, part of the Development Bank of Singapore group), and even Singapore Bus Services (now known as DelGro), among others, ventured into property development. They may have been emboldened to take this risk because of moral hazard—the "deep pockets" with which their monopolistic positions in other markets provided them; the implicit backing and guarantee of the government's huge accumulated surpluses and foreign reserves; and, many in the private sector argue, the "crony capitalism" that ensures that GLC managers have the security of tenure of civil servants in a politicized bureaucracy, regardless of the mistakes they may make in the market.[14] To a lesser extent than in Hong Kong, property companies, conglomerates (including GLCs) with property divisions, and banks with substantial exposure to property loans began to make up a sizable proportion of the capitalization of the Stock Exchange of Singapore.

In a nation in which close to 90 percent of the population were already home-owners, this ballooning property bubble—directly and indirectly encouraged by government policy and GLC strategy—set the stage for the subsequent market meltdown. The private condominium market relied heavily on dubious assumptions that the continued rapid rise of domestic incomes would result in accelerated "upgrading" out of HDB into private housing units, and anticipated strong demand from foreigners—Hong Kong residents worried about the 1997 reversion to Chinese rule, affluent Chinese-Indonesians and Malaysians, and expatriates working for multinational corporations engaged in regional business. To its credit, the government acted in 1996 to deflate the bubble by releasing more public land for housing, but this was too little, too late: "we were overbuilt in properties. We started to choke that off in 1996, by taking the froth off—if we had done that in 1995, we would be better off."[15]

When the regional crisis broke, the combination of collapsed demand and increased sales by foreigners, rising interest rates, and a plunging stock market (with its attendant negative wealth effect) resulted in property values falling, in some cases below their purchase prices of a few years earlier, and banks accordingly asked buyers to "top up" their loans with additional cash payments (*FEER* 5 March 1998, 45). But many buyers, particularly self-employed professionals and small business owners, were already overleveraged and suffering from falling incomes and asset values. Overseas property investments were also hurt by the economic crisis and by unfavorable political developments in neighboring countries, resulting, for example, in low occupancy rates in expensive new hotels and causing massive revenue and asset value losses to listed companies (including GLCs) on the Stock Exchange of Singapore, further depressing their share values.

The political importance of housing values to a population whose retirement savings were, in response to government policy, invested in now rapidly depreciating assets, has also limited the state's ability to respond to the larger macroeconomic downturn. Reducing CPF contribution rates (which have ranged as high as 50 percent of salaries) has in the past been a standard tool of the government's counter-cyclical policy, used to reduce labor costs and thus increase employment in recessions. But to reduce rates now would jeopardize the ability of even more households to service their housing loans out of their CPF contributions,[16] threatening more defaults and foreclosures and further risking the government's popularity among the electorate and the health of the financial sector (which, encouraged by the state-sponsored "regionalization" drive, had increased its loan exposure to companies in crisis-hit neighboring countries). Still, after months of deliberation, and as the economy sank further into zero-growth territory, the difficult step was taken of cutting CPF contributions by 10 percent to stimulate employment, with "bridging loans" provided to homeowners who would have difficulty paying their mortgages as a result (Osman 1998).

In contrast to the situation in Hong Kong, the government in Singapore is not closely linked to private-property developers, who also wield less influence in the more sectorally diversified, more multinational- and GLC-dominated economy. There have been isolated incidents involving, for example, a member of Parliament who was also a paid adviser to a large local property development company and who asked the government not to release more land into the private market, because it was already saturated and developers would suffer; another large local property developer suggested that GLCs prop up the market by buying and holding properties. But these suggestions were shot down by other political figures and by the public, and the aforesaid member of Parliament was subsequently forced to resign from his paid advisory position. The government may also face pressure to prop up the property market from GLCs that are heavily invested in this sector, but it is restrained from doing so by its accountability to the electorate at large, which includes buyers as well as owners/sellers of property.

As I have argued elsewhere (Lim 1987), a distinctive feature of Singapore's domestic political economy is the division between the private business elite and the ruling public-sector elite—a situation in sharp contrast to that prevailing in post-British Hong Kong. Although this division has weakened over time—for example, through the increasing popularity of practices such as the previously mentioned employment by private companies of ruling-party members of Parliament as paid advisers and the employment of former government officials in highly paid senior management positions in private companies—it remains sufficient to ensure some autonomy in government economic decision making. Government policy remains guided primarily by considerations of economic efficiency and, ultimately, electoral accountability.

Thus, unlike Hong Kong, Singapore's political leaders have decisively reaffirmed their commitment to open markets, free capital flows, and integration into the global economy,[17] and indeed the city-state stands to enhance its competitive advantage in relation to these and other regional neighbors in attracting fdi and regionally or globally oriented financial services. Protection of local financial and professional services is slated to be reduced, not increased, as a result of the crisis, and foreign fund managers are being given incentives to establish operations in Singapore to manage a portion of the government's huge CPF portfolio. Against the objections of Hong Kong, Singapore has also started trading the Hong Kong futures index on its SIMEX futures exchange (Chan 1998).

Singapore's financial liberalization at a time of crisis should not, however, be taken as an unqualified proof of the superiority of free market mechanisms over controls and state interventions. Rather, it is arguable that its openness to external capital flows and world market forces has been possible and beneficial only because the government exerts considerable control over the domestic economy and polity, control that it can exercise if necessary to counterbalance external shocks. The state's heavy intervention in the land, labor, and capital markets provides many potential policy levers—such as large accumulated budget and current account surpluses—with which it can adjust the economy to cyclic downturns and external shocks like the recent crisis. One example of this has been the government's ability to fiscally stimulate the economy through tax cuts and spending increases in the current recession (Ibrahim 1998). In short, strong domestic controls are the flip side of the world's most open economy.

Conclusion

The preceding discussion shows that domestic political interests and institutions, as well as international and domestic economic forces, have played a major role in Asian countries' vulnerability and responses to regional economic crises. In the realm of economics, the Hong Kong experience illustrates the textbook trade-off between exchange rate stability and economic growth, with devaluation and deflation the only alternative orthodox solutions to a currency crisis. Either policy could work if properly applied, but in Hong Kong, political forces intervened. The power of the property cartel arguably limited the deflationary pain the territory could tolerate, and the psychological importance of the currency peg removed devaluation as a policy option. This made restrictions on speculation and stock market intervention the only other course of action open to the authorities. But without currency controls to support its overvalued currency, the Hong Kong economy suffered two years of negative GDP growth and a steep decline in asset prices. Longer-term recovery depends on more fundamental restructuring of the economy away from overdependence on the property sector and on confidence in the political management of the territory, including management of the government's recently acquired corporate stock.

In Singapore, in contrast, the relative autonomy of the state from local private sector (including property market) interests and its institutionalized accountability to an electorate for whom economic prosperity is the paramount concern have given the government a much freer hand to implement adjustment policies (initial currency depreciation, property market deflation, and budgetary stimulus) within a continued open market system—with more, rather than less, liberalization planned for the financial sector. Politically motivated housing and housing-finance (CPF) policies and bad investment decisions by GLCs in the property sector, perhaps on account of a form of moral hazard, did worsen the local impact of the crisis and constrain government policy responses to it, but these are now being dealt with, with the assistance of the government's legendary "deep pockets."

This chapter suggests that Hong Kong's retreat from and Singapore's embrace of free market forces in response to financial crisis have as much, if not more, to do with domestic political interests (the property cartel in Hong Kong) and institutions (electoral accountability in Singapore) that dictate economic policy choices as with the economic policy possibilities that confront them. I have not evaluated these policy possibilities from an economic perspective, about which there is much controversy (*Wall Street Journal* 25 September 1998, A1, A6). And despite their recent actions, both economies remain relatively free compared with others in the world.

At the same time, although Singapore has followed a different path from Hong Kong's in reaffirming its commitment to open capital markets and its economy has held up better, this should not necessarily be taken as an indicator of the wisdom of relying on free market forces. On the contrary, much of Singapore's greater ability to withstand the crisis may be considered the fortuitous result of both the state's desire to hold on to its political monopoly in an electoral system and its long-term heavy control of and participation in the economy (Lim 1983b)—including the massive siphoning off and channeling of household savings, the maintenance of cumulatively huge budget and current account surpluses and foreign reserves (which have an opportunity cost), a managed-float exchange rate, the control of the housing and labor markets, a sophisticated industrial policy based on state subsidies that has helped maintain a diversified economy, and the operation of large, monopolistic, GLCs that have diversified into many sectors otherwise occupied by private firms. Overall, these state activities, although sometimes costly and allocatively inefficient, have probably helped stabilize the economy.

In the realm of politics, international relations have also played a role in the impact on the economies involved in the regional crisis and their respective policy responses to it. Relations with China have played a role protective and supportive of Hong Kong's policy—and limited its economic downturn, given integration into the still-growing Chinese national economy. But relations between Malaysia and Singapore, having reached a historic low in conflicts over transportation, water, stock market, and financial aid links, and the publication of the controversial memoirs of former Singapore prime minister Lee Kuan Yew, have hampered the recovery of both nations by dampening trade and investment and increasing political risk. This risk has been heightened by the economic near-collapse and political and social unrest in neighboring Indonesia, and by the less-than-warm relations between the new Indonesian administration and Singapore—based in part on the financial "safe haven" that Singapore provides to (especially ethnic Chinese) Indonesian flight capital and its refusal to release a promised $5 billion in financial aid to its giant neighbor until certain conditions are met. Because of its close economic and fraught political ties with its neighbors, Singapore's own recovery from the crisis will be delayed, just as Hong Kong's much deeper recession may be prolonged if its giant hinterland, China, takes an economic turn for the worse, as is entirely possible (Lardy 1998b).

Finally, although domestic politics may play the dominant role in government policy responses to the economic crisis, these responses also need to be tempered by the need to consider the views of foreign and local capital market actors, because their capital is needed for recovery to occur more swiftly. Uncertainty about the investment strategies of the Hong Kong government's new asset management corporation (whose actions, because of its size, must affect stock values) and its other financial sector policies may be expected to dampen foreign investor interest in Hong Kong—at least until continued deflation restores the purchasing power parity value of its assets, given the still overvalued exchange rate. Singapore, on the other hand, has seized the initiative in ingratiating itself with foreign capital market actors through regulatory liberalization and active promotion of the financial sector that will enable it to attract some of Hong Kong's business in this sector. Singapore is also cutting costs much more aggressively than Hong Kong, where government workers have recently refused to take wage cuts that have already been implemented in Singapore. But Singapore's long-term attractiveness as a financial and business center for the region still depends on its neighbors' economic recovery and its own political relations with them.

CHAPTER SIX

The State, Democracy, and the Reform of the Corporate Sector in Korea

Meredith Woo-Cumings

Nineteenth century civilization was not destroyed by the external or internal attack of barbarians; its vitality was not sapped by the devastation of World War I nor by the revolt of a socialist proletariat or a fascist lower middle class. Its failure was not the outcome of some alleged laws of economics such as that of the falling rate of profit or of underconsumption or overproduction. It disintegrated as the result of an entirely different set of causes: the measures which society adopted in order not to be, in its turn, annihilated by the action of the self-regulating market. Apart from exceptional circumstances such as existed in North America in the age of open frontier, the conflict between the market and the elementary requirement of an organized social life provided the century with its dynamics and produced the typical strains and stresses which ultimately destroyed that society. External wars merely hastened its destruction.

—Karl Polanyi, *The Great Transformation*

In the Asian crisis of 1997–98, the financial system that had held together the political economy of the ROK collapsed of its own weight. This collapse was triggered by contagion and currency speculation, much like the wars that had hastened the demise of Polanyi's "nineteenth century civilization," but the deeper roots of this collapse were internal, stemming from the contradictions in Korea's developmental system—or, in the parlance of political science, its "regime."[1] In the Korean context, this regime consisted of a highly effective state that, in its quest for national security and rapid industrialization, created a set of institutions and public policies to promote the rise of world-class entrepreneurs, known as the *chaebŏl*. The *chaebŏl* in turn provided support for the state and performed a kind of employment and indispensable welfare function in a society largely bereft of a social safety net.

The most critical mechanism that allowed for this give-and-take between the state and the corporate sector in Korea was state control of the banking sector, from the 1960s and 1970s era of heavy-handed "financial repression" to the highly controlled and protracted financial liberalization of the 1980s. This intervention resulted in a heavily indebted corporate sector; the debt-to-equity ratio for the *chaebŏl* has remained near 300 to 400 percent, and sometimes risen higher, for the last thirty years. By the 1990s, the state had withdrawn from day-to-day allocation decisions in the banking sector, but it was still a hovering presence, fretting about the hugely leveraged corporate sector that kept devouring the majority of domestic credit and remained profoundly vulnerable to external shocks and business downturns that would have an impact on their ability to service debt. In this sense, the current corporate crisis in Korea is a thirty-year crisis.[2]

This chapter has three purposes: first, to explain the cause of the corporate and financial crisis in Korea; second, to examine the current reform in Korea and its relevance for other countries; and third, to consider future trajectories for Korea's corporate-sector development. Scholars have interpreted the Korean crisis as the result of either an excess *or* a deficit of industrial policy. There was no excess—by 1997, Korea was a country bereft of industrial policy, save in research and development for high technology. Nor was the problem caused by the lack of "coordination"; corporate crisis, not coordination, has been the perennial and integral feature of Korean developmentalism for thirty years. Others have blamed "cronyism," but that term is analytically meaningless. It refers to anything from state-sanctioned theft—the frenzied feeding of Ferdinand Marcos and his associates at the trough of the state (the original meaning of the term "cronyism")—to the Federal Reserve–led bailout of Long Term Capital Management in 1998 (Chang 1999). "Cronyism" in Korea was as prevalent in 1967 as in 1997 and has different causes and, therefore, cures than "cronyism" in multiethnic states in Southeast Asia.

I argue instead that the financial crisis in Korea was born of an inability to resolve the long-standing and widely recognized dilemma of its developmentalism. Twenty years of "financial liberalization" notwithstanding, the Korean state was unable to sever the Gordian knot between the state and the banking sector on the one hand and the hugely leveraged corporate sector on the other. This was because the state was hamstrung between a highly effective bureaucracy that sought to regulate the corporate sector and a political ruling group that, relying on the financial support of big business, ended up circumventing the best efforts of the bureaucrats. Unable to extricate itself from the corporate/banking quagmire, and equally unable to implicate itself effectively in managing the crisis, the Korean state dawdled along, creating a nightmarish web of credit controls and loan ceilings in the hope of keeping the *chaebŏl* away from the loan window. In the end, it took a massive banking and corporate crisis and the institution of a democratic regime to break this logjam.

I also discuss the lessons for other countries of Korea's experience in restructuring the corporate sector. This experience is especially relevant for China, which has occasionally expressed an interest in developing Korean-type conglomerates and where the state-SOEs relationship seems to contain elements of the Korean developmental dilemma. The Korean experience may also shed light on the banking restructuring effort under way in Japan—a country that has provided Korea with a political and economic template for rapid growth, but which is now mired in a similar developmental quandary.

Finally, I reverse gears and examine state-business relations in other countries, in search of useful lessons for Korea. A developmental regime thirty years in the making—or sixty years, if its origins are traced to the wartime mobilization during the colonial period—does not change its path overnight. It is possible, however, that some learning can take place, perhaps from corporate systems in similar environments that have some developmental, cultural, or other systemic propinquity to Korea's. I focus in particular on the Chinese model of state-corporate relations and governance, both in Taiwan and Southeast Asia; the Japanese *keiretsu* system, even as it undergoes profound transformations; and (given the force of global institutional convergence) the relevance of some aspects of the Anglo–American style of corporate governance.

The Problem of Developmentalism and the Crisis of the Corporate Sector in Korea

Rethinking Max Weber's East Asian Capitalism

There is remarkable consistency in the way that Westerners have problematized capitalist enterprise in East Asia over the past century. As early as 1904, Max Weber (1958, 22) postulated that the modern rational enterprise was predicated on "the separation of business from the household" and the "rational bookkeeping" that would issue forth from independent firms, thus presaging today's debate about family-controlled firms in East Asia and the lack of transparency in their business accounting. For Weber, the predominance of family-run enterprises and a relative absence of rational accounting were *prima facie* evidence not merely of bad corporate governance, but that capitalism in East Asia was not modern, rational, or normal—that is to say, not Occidental. Weber found it puzzling that the Chinese, who on the whole seemed to exhibit the appropriate "acquisitive virtuosity" and "deification of wealth" (in the Confucian sense that wealth was the means toward a virtuous and dignified life), should have failed to achieve the kind of depersonalization of business reflected in the commercial laws of the Italian city-states. The reason for the absence of legal forms and social foundations of capitalist enterprise, Weber concluded, was the social simultaneity of a premodern political order on the one hand, and a particular type of kinship structure ("acquisitive familial community") on the other (1951, 242–45). The *state* and the *family* did not simply hinder the rise of capitalism; they also sheltered and thus preserved the society against it. This aspect of Weber's argument is little understood.

It is true that Weber had an extensive lexicon for describing the political order that connived with the Confucian and Taoist predilection to deny modernity and rationality to East Asia, a lexicon that formed the well of ideas and definitions from which many scholars continue to draw. China had what Weber called "political capitalism," or sometimes "bureaucratic capitalism," in the form of "usury connected with office, emergency loans, wholesale trade and industrial *ergasteria*" or capital connected with extortionist practices in office. His lexicon has been continually replayed in discussions of capitalism in East Asia—used to explain why no capitalism existed in the past or what kind of capitalism can be observed now. Weber also used the term "booty capitalism," which experts still use to describe the worst excesses of the government and the oligarchy in the Philippines, and "pariah capitalism," which remains a common description of Chinese entrepreneurship in Southeast Asia.[3] In other words, East Asia possessed a system of capitalism that is anything but what Werner Sombart might call "high capitalism," whether in the pre-capitalist dynasties of a century ago or in the "miracle" economies that seemed to define the meaning of Third World development for a generation.

Weber, who spoke disparagingly of the kinship organization in China as the "sib-fetter" of the economy, understood that the communal, or the sib, economic organization "protected the individual against the dangers of proletarization and capitalist subjection." The patriarchal sib was, for him, an expression of "the abolition of feudal estates," as well as "the extensiveness of patrimonial bureaucratic organization" (1951, 96–97). Just as Marx thought religion was both the "sigh" and the opium of the oppressed, for Weber the Chinese sib-based economic organization seemed to work both as a protection against the incipient capitalism of late imperial China *and* as a barrier against the rise of a culture of universalistic trust. That is, in the absence of or amid the rise of a contract-based system of business trust, one's own family was still the best bet. Given the tenuous political exigencies of the Chinese diaspora and the prevalence of particularistic trust in East Asia, it is not surprising that this tried-and-true system of Chinese enterprise should persist to this day.

Why this century-old reminder of the conflict between the market economy and the self-preservation of society? First, it is not unrelated to the Korean developmental dilemma, a theme that I return to later. Second, it is useful to be reminded that East Asian business has developed in a cocoon of particular historic practice, in which what appears irrational from an ideal-typical Western standpoint may be an effective local adaptation in the interests of wealth accumulation. Third, when development is incredibly rapid, practices that might have been expected to die out have persisted, because everything seemed to work. For nearly fifty years, East Asian capitalism was most notable for the speed with which it developed, in many countries in a single generation; therefore, rapid growth was not so much the solvent of outdated practice as its preservative.

Korea's Capitalist Enterprises: Growth, Concentration, Diversification, Indebtedness

The ROK has been a security state in the global system since its division in 1945, with these security concerns used to justify the logic of industrialization since the end of the Korean War in 1953. Its critical position during the Cold War enabled it to attract huge amounts of external savings—foreign aid in the 1950s and 1960s and foreign loans in late 1970s and the 1980s. But Korea was also a postcolonial state born without a capitalist class of its own, so the first order of the day was the creation of a whole constellation of entrepreneurial elements by vetting foreign and domestic capital through the banking system, which was owned and controlled by the state. In the 1970s, big business relied heavily on cheap capital, so-called policy loans given at negative real rates (a 6 percent loan rate, in the context of a 12 percent inflation, for instance) to firms willing to conform to the dictates of government industrial strategy. Thus, the state created a structural incentive for the firms to rely on bank financing and retain entrepreneurial autonomy by staying closed to the public.

Because the firms were highly leveraged from the beginning, much more than in Latin America or Southeast Asia, business had to maintain good relations with the state to avert the possibility of default (through severance of friendly credits). The high rate of leverage meant that even small changes in the discount rate or in concessional credit rates between sectors could have dramatic effects on resource allocation, because the effect of such instruments on the firms' cash flow position was so much greater, given the high debt to equity ratios. The state manipulated this vulnerability to change the economy's investment pattern and to guide sectorial mobility. The Korean firms, therefore, exhibited an unusually high propensity to conform to the industrial policy goals of the state (Woo 1991).

The Korean *chaebŏl* grew as fast as they did because of the steady and massive provision of investment capital from the banks. Almost all of the *chaebŏl* groups began when Korea was in the phase of export-led, light industrial production. Lucky made toothpaste, Goldstar made radios, Samsung made clothes, and Hyundai began with U.S. military contracts during the Korean War to transport goods and people around in war surplus or cobbled-together trucks and buses. Daewoo was founded only in 1967. They acquired their typical large and diversified structure even more recently, during the Third Five-Year Plan in the early 1970s, which developed heavy industries: steel, chemicals, machine tools, automobiles, shipbuilding, and power generation. By the 1980s, electronics had also become a huge part of the *chaebŏl* repertoire. The expansion of these firms was stupendous: between 1970 and 1975, the three fastest-growing *chaebŏl* (Hyundai, Daewoo, Ssangyong) grew at annual rates of 33 percent, 35 percent, and 34 percent, respectively. This breakneck rate of growth, combined with reliance on politically mediated debt, encouraged high-risk taking and competitive overinvestment in various industries—such as integrated petrochemicals, which more than doubled the output of ethylene at a time when world prices were declining and surplus capacity was widely anticipated (Whitley 1992, 43). The same was often true of sectors like semiconductors, ships, steel, and cars, so that excess capacity bulked large as an explanation of Korea's serious economic downturn in 1979, leading to a loss of 6 percent of GNP in 1980.[4]

Still, there were great advantages to the state-directed heavy industrialization of the 1970s. Experience in managing complex technologies in heavy and capital-intensive industries, requiring effective coordination and integration of separate independent components, became the basis for generalizable managerial skills—skills transferable to other kinds of manufacturing. The largest firm, Hyundai, has carried on globe-ranging operations in automobiles, shipbuilding, construction, electronics, aircraft, machine-building, and many others. This organizational aspect of the *chaebŏl* has not received much scrutiny, but the fact that they kept increasing market share at home and abroad attests to their organizational ability. The effective presence of Korean firms today in the fledgling markets of Eastern Europe, the Central Asian Republics, and other emerging areas is testimony to the advantage that accrues to having a vast, flexible, and well-coordinated internal organization. This success should be considered alongside the well-known inefficiencies of the so-called convoy system, whereby even the most inefficient unit of the *chaebŏl* group is kept afloat through intricate cross-subsidiary financing agreements.

The Korean *chaebŏl* occupies an oligopolistic position running the gamut of the modern sector of the economy. There are many indicators of the size and the extensive market position of the big conglomerates. One indicator is the value-added of the *chaebŏl* as a percentage of total industry, which in 1989 stood at 9.2 percent for the top five *chaebŏl* and 16.3 percent for the top thirty. Alternatively, one could look at sales figures as a percentage of manufacturing industries; in 1990, the top thirty *chaebŏl* accounted for 35 percent of total sales. The same top thirty groups also employed some 16 percent of labor working in manufacturing. But because these numbers are liable to change with corporate restructuring and as some firms become independent of the group, one might also want to look at data for individual firms. Sales figures for the top one hundred firms in 1981 accounted for 46.2 percent of manufacturing, dropping to 38.5 percent in 1987 and 37.7 percent in 1990; this trend is also visible for value-added: 40.6 percent of manufacturing in 1981, down to 36.5 percent in 1987, and a small drop in 1990 to 35.1 percent. Just as the indicators for *chaebŏl* economic concentration can be variable depending on corporate definitional boundaries, the indicators using individual firms can change drastically with mergers and acquisitions (Yu 1996, 24).

Although these figures indicate a formidable level of concentration, it is also true that such is increasingly the trend in global economy, as firms scramble to survive in global competition by getting bigger and more competitive. The jury is out on just how economically concentrated Korea's *chaebŏl* are, or should be, given the uncertainty today about changes in corporate governance of the *chaebŏl* and how to interpret economic concentration in light of the accelerating global trends toward industry mergers. In any event, oligopoly in the context of "controlled competition" has been part and parcel of Korean (and Japanese) developmentalism, and the ongoing corporate reform seems to be creating monopolies through mergers and swaps.

The thornier issue is diversification. Unlike the level of market concentration, Korea's level of diversification remains high in comparison to advanced Western countries. In 1994, the number of affiliated firms for the top five *chaebŏl* averaged approximately 40, to a total of 210 firms, and the top thirty *chaebŏl* had some 616 affiliated firms (Yu 1996, 24). This extraordinary diversification was achieved pri-

marily by establishing new subsidiaries: the mammoth and extraordinarily diversified structure of the *chaebŏl*, combined with an open call on state-mediated loans,
was essential to Korea's success in gaining market share around the world, because
losses in one subsidiary could be made up by gains in another. This extensive diversification has been the main staple of public criticism of the *chaebŏl*, but perhaps
the criticism needs to be weighed against at least three considerations.

The first is the obvious point that while the *chaebŏl* have been criticized for failing to nurture "core competence," thereby to exploit more fully the gains from
economies of scale, diversification into many different sectors can be justified
through the gains from the economy of scope (as opposed to scale), from dynamic
back-and-forth synergy among firms, and, of course, from portfolio diversification
to reduce risk. The second and often forgotten point is that diversification went
hand in hand with specialization. Out of Samsung's fifty affiliated firms,
Hyundai's forty-nine, the LG Group's fifty-three, Daewoo's twenty-five, and
Sunkyung's thirty-three, only a select few firms in a few sectors were responsible
for the bulk of total sales figures. Three of Samsung's firms were responsible for
67 percent of its sales, and even in the case of Hyundai, which is evenly spread
across many different manufacturing sectors, five affiliated firms accounted for 70
percent of total sales. As for Daewoo, four firms accounted for 85 percent of total
sales (Yu 1996, 39). If the common complaint about *chaebŏl* diversification can be
summarized in the remark that "even in the Olympics there aren't gold medallists
who can win in both swimming and basketball,"[5] one might counter that the
chaebŏl were not truly intending to win in all categories—the incentive system
pushed them in that direction. The third and last point about the merits and
demerits of diversification also has to do with corporate governance: when the
structure of a given *chaebŏl* changes as firms become detached from the group, the
chaebŏl is instantly "specialized." Over the years, the government has tried to use
its elaborate system of credit control to curtail the *chaebŏl* tendency toward diversification and to coax the groups to "specialize" in a few sectors, but to little avail.

The question of diversification and specialization might have remained academic, except for this: are the family-run *chaebŏl* firms profitable? By the eve of the
financial crisis, it was clear that they were not. This is not surprising. The conventional wisdom is that the *chaebŏl* are not profitable and indeed are not even interested in profit. Their activity, it is said, has rarely been driven by ordinary market
concerns of price or supply and demand, and instead has long pursued market
share, and they have not only operated at a loss in so doing but have courted a kind
of habitual bankruptcy—should anyone call them to account on a given day. The
data for the decade before the crisis seem to validate such impressions.

In a comparative study of corporate profits in East Asia, Stijn Claessens, Simeon
Djankov, and Larry Lang (1998a) show that in 1988–96, profitability, as measured
by real return on assets in local currency,[6] was lowest in Korea in comparison with
nine East Asian countries, Germany, and the United States. The rate for Korea was
3.7 percent, whereas it was 4.6 percent for Hong Kong, 4.1 percent for Japan, 4.4
percent for Singapore, 7.1 percent for Indonesia, 7.9 percent for the Philippines,

6.7 percent for Taiwan, 6.3 percent for Malaysia, and 9.8 percent for Thailand. All Southeast Asian countries and Taiwan had rates higher than those recorded for Germany (4.7 percent) and the United States (5.3 percent). Likewise, the return on assets in U.S. dollars, adjusted for the effects of currency movements, show that for the same period, Korea again recorded relatively low rates (9.2 percent) compared to the Philippines (17.2 percent) and Thailand (14.7 percent), although it was higher than Japan (6.6 percent).

If the profits were falling, real sales were rising. In the same study, Claessens, Djankov, and Lang show that real sales growth, year on year, for the 1988–96 period was 8.2 percent for Korea, compared to 3.7 percent for the United States and 2.6 percent for Germany. Capital investments were also growing briskly. Korea, along with Thailand, had the highest rate of capital investment among the nine East Asian countries under study, at 13.6 percent and 13.8 percent, respectively. The rates were 3.4 percent for the United States and 2.5 percent for Germany. Japan showed a relatively low rate—8 percent—in comparison to other East Asian countries, reflecting continuing recession.

By 1996, Korea was sustaining one of the lowest profit rates and one of the highest capital investment rates in East Asia, meaning that external financing had to be large to make up for the very limited retained earnings. For the period between 1988 and 1996, the corporate indebtedness of the Korean firms was greater than that of practically any other firm in the world. A comparison of corporate leverage—total debt over equity—in some fifty countries shows that from 1988 to 1996, Korean firms had the highest ratio of leverage *by far* at 348 percent, followed by Japan at 230 percent. The leverage ratio in Taiwan was only 82 percent, less than one-fourth that in Korean firms. The ratios for the United States and Germany for the same time period were 103 and 151 percent, respectively (Claessens, Djankov, and Lang 1998a). This is not so different from the situation that prevailed in the 1970s, when the leverage ratio of Korean firms was between 300 and 400 percent; of Mexican and Brazilian firms, approximately 100 to 120 percent; and of Taiwanese firms, 160 to 200 percent (Woo 1991, 12)

If the corporate leverage ratio remained the same, so did the manner in which it came about. Banks in Korea allocated credit to the large corporations, relying for repayment on real collateral, a very complex system of cross-guarantees from the various subsidiaries and affiliates of the group, and personal guarantees from the group chairman and directors. Little attention was paid to the earnings performance and cash flow generation of their borrowers. Finally, the pattern of financial crisis in Korea also remained more or less the same: low return on assets, declining sales growth, excess capacity, stiff price competition, and high leverage. In many ways, 1997 was a rerun of the crisis of 1979.

By late 1997, the sharp rise in interest rates (used to defend the wón) pushed the *chaebŏl* over the brink. According to some analysts, the combination of interest rate and currency shocks left up to 49 percent of Korean firms illiquid and 40 percent technically insolvent. Five major groups—with a combined workforce of more than one hundred thousand employees and Wón 26.7 trillion in assets—quickly failed, unable to pay their debts. And more than half of the thirty largest *chaebŏl* (with combined employment of more than a quarter million people and liabilities of Won 103.4 trillion) were at risk of falling into bankruptcy (Lieberman and Mako 1998).

Why had economic reform proved so difficult in Korea?

The Regulatory Albatross

In the earlier discussion, I invoked Max Weber, not because he was correct in his opinions on China, but because he had a coherent argument about capitalism and capitalist institutions in East Asia, bits and pieces of which have ricocheted through the century to color our views on the region. Weber believed that the Western institutions of capitalism did not, or could not, take root in East Asia, that they were bound to be stymied between the bureaucratic state on the one hand and the family orientation of its enterprises, or the "sib-fetter," on the other. In this section, I reflect on the nature of the bureaucratic state in Korea and the difficulties it has encountered in its efforts at reform. In the section that follows, I examine the phenomenon of family-owned corporations in Korea—or the latter-day "sib-fetter"— as a rational entrepreneurial response to the incompleteness of capitalist institutions in Korea, especially with regard to property rights. To the extent that economic reform lagged in Korea, it was because of the complex and highly involuted dynamics between the state and the entrepreneurs, which in turn deeply prejudiced the emergence of the rule of law and transparency in corporate accounting.

In one sense, the dilemma of the developmental state in Korea is straightforward. The developmental state in Korea has provided a far greater trickle-down effect than any Reaganite ever imagined, yielding an egalitarian payoff at the end of the developmental tunnel. The critical part of this equation has been the corporations, most of which are in industry. Industry composes 42.9 percent of Korean GDP, compared with approximately 30 percent for the OECD as a whole. Layoffs as a result of bankruptcy, therefore, affect a large proportion of the work force, as Korea lacks the cushion against unemployment provided by the large agricultural sector of Southeast Asia and the service sector of the OECD countries (Lieberman and Mako 1998). The five largest *chaebŏl* alone employ more than six hundred thousand workers, and thus these large firms perform an indispensable welfare function in a society largely bereft of a social safety net. So even as the *chaebŏl* in Korea courted a habitual bankruptcy, it was not easy to sever the credit that sustained them and allow them to go bankrupt. This might be called the "state of permanent receivership"(Lowi 1975).

In Korea, politics was hostage to economics—and more. A developmental state like Korea's creates a permanent bind for itself with regard to big business. On the one hand, Korea is a paradise for big business; state industrial policy favors domestic producers over consumers and foreign producers in every manner imaginable. As domestic producers become more powerful economically and politically, however, the state attempts to rein in and tame them through regulatory means, creating an endless number of discretionary rules. These rules have been fickle, irrational, short lived, and, therefore, predictably ineffective in achieving their goals. Instead, they create the sense that the rules of the game in Korea are endlessly negotiable. Rather than institute the effective rule of law, or transparency throughout the nexus of the state, the banks, and the *chaebŏl*, the interventionist state in Korea has been profoundly "results-oriented," privileging outcomes over established rules. Administrative decrees were the norm, not transparent legal procedures.

By all accounts, the Korean state has been a relentless nag, trying to force firms to reform and failing every time because of the state-created incentive structure. For instance, in the aftermath of the financial crisis in 1972 and the bailout of big business through a sudden moratorium on corporate repayments of loans to the curb market, the government selected what it considered "blue chip" firms (based on profitability, equity, and asset position) and forced them to go public, by threatening to slap recalcitrants with a 40 percent corporate tax (versus the usual 27 percent). Overnight, new public stock offerings, valued at $48 million, inundated the Seoul Stock Exchange, and the number of companies listed jumped 50 percent. The stock market received a further boost in 1974, when a special presidential decree tightened the audit and supervision of bank credit for all nonlisted (but listable, according to government standards) firms. Many more measures like these followed in the 1970s. The government also sought to control the securities market by setting low prices on new issues and determining dividends and corporate reinvestment decisions.

Finding themselves between the state's punitive measures on the one hand, and costs of going public on the other (losing autonomy and cheap credit, the high costs of raising undervalued equity capital), the *chaebŏl* responded predictably. Some firms decided that it was better to resist the government order, pay the tax, and bypass the palliatives that the government offered to listed firms. Others obeyed the government, but without really complying: the owners themselves absorbed much of the newly issued stock (Woo 1991, 174–75). The equity market in Korea thus remained relatively small.

The state also tried to limit *chaebŏl* access to bank credit, through what surely must be one of the most arcane and intractable set of credit controls (*yoshin kwalli*) that the world has known. The system of credit controls had its origins in the era of industrial policy. In a country where bank credit was extended not on the basis of economic viability but on the exigencies of state economic policy, the only way to prevent default was to impose a system of incessant supervision and control, ranging from ubiquitous surveillance of the use of credit (to prevent speculation, for instance) to supervising the reform of corporate financing structures, to creating a web of credit ceilings. Attempting to prevent the concentration of credit, the government came up with complex rules limiting credits to the same borrower, limiting credit per individual bank for large borrowers, and establishing credit ceilings for *chaebŏl*-affiliated firms. To prevent default, the government developed a series of guidelines for "early warning," procedures for "modernizing" credit evaluation, and intricate rules for default management. A special set of decrees applying only to the *chaebŏl* sought to regulate the ratio between equity and debt in various industrial sectors and gave fiscal incentives for going public. Beginning in 1980, the government closely monitored *chaebŏl* use of bank credit and expanded external audits; by the middle of the 1980s, the state also instituted a consistent policy package based on fair trade laws. In 1992, the fair trade law was again fortified, the use of intersubsidiary loan guarantees was restricted, and relaxation of the loan ceiling was offered as an incentive for some *chaebŏl* to develop their "core" industries. The result was a regulatory albatross that, in the end, did not achieve its purpose. The state had to proliferate regulations to stem the worst effects of its own developmental strategy. Meanwhile, no regulation or special decree ever changed the essential structure of Korean corporate governance, right up to the crisis of late 1997.

Why did the state choose bureaucratic—and not market—means to rein in the *chaebŏl*, allowing regulations to hypertrophy, especially in light of three decades of the best advice by liberal economists in and out of Korea that the only effective solution to the *chaebŏl* problem is the reform and liberalization of the banking sector? Part of the answer may be political ("cronyism"!), but the larger reason lies in the habits of "late" development, of being results-oriented rather than rule-oriented. Korea may have grown very fast over the past four decades, but it did not overcome the fear of real competition and the free market. Even current democratic reformers are drawn to the use of discretionary measures by the government because Korea, after all, has one of the oldest and finest traditions of civil service in the world. In times of crisis, the temptation grows strong to use this ubiquitous state structure to force industrial reorganization; the bureaucrats—who come from the best universities and constitute a respected and experienced elite—always think that around the next corner is the regulation that will finally achieve real reform. Thus, almost all major reforms of the last two decades—import liberalization, financial liberalization, privatization—not only moved at a snail's pace, but went hand in hand with proliferation of more regulations to obtain an economically desirable outcome. And few of the new measures really worked.

The Family Albatross

To fully appreciate the failure of the developmental state to enforce corporate reform, attention must be paid to politics as it relates to the issue of property rights—or, going back to Weber, the absence of legal forms and social foundations for modern, legal-rational capitalist enterprise. Korea had a world-class meritocratic bureaucracy that modeled itself after Japan's (Woo-Cumings 1995), but this went hand in hand with a highly brittle form of authoritarian regime, lasting up to 1987, or 1992, when the first civilian regime was inaugurated. In this regard, I find similarities between Korea and Southeast Asia. In Korea, as in Southeast Asia, a charismatic political order is based on vast discretionary political power, rather than on the rule of law or norms that are legitimated over time. Both the small Chinese firm in Indonesia escaping from the burdensome legal realm to the extralegal "gray economy" and the Korean manufacturing behemoth that believes it still needs to get even bigger (or to provide bigger political contributions) are forestalling the threat of outright confiscation. In short, the problem of corporate governance cannot be resolved without addressing the problem of the continuing discretionary power of the politicians and the bureaucrats, residual industrial policy, and a host of other problems that come under the rubric of the rule of law.

The politics of confiscation has had a long pedigree in Korea, starting with an anti-corruption campaign in 1961 that rounded up the richest men in Korea and stamped them as profiteers with "illicit fortunes." In the end, the businessmen were allowed to use the huge fines levied on them to establish industrial firms, donating shares in the firms back to the government. Banks, however, were confiscated, swiftly nationalized, and lined up under the direction of the Ministry of Finance. From this point on, big corporations could anticipate that political regime changes would be accompanied by various kinds of shakedowns, ranging from the payment of huge bribes to so-called industrial rationalization (involving forced mergers and the like) or even outright confiscation of property.

Because the *chaebŏl* is a politically charged issue in Korea, all successive regimes—including the current one—have sought to mobilize support by forcing "industrial reorganization" or "industrial rationalization," which often meant swaps and mergers to force corporate specialization. In the 1980 industrial reorganization that followed Chun Doo Hwan's coup, for instance, the three biggest *chaebŏl* groups were ordered to give up firms specializing in the production of power-generating and heavy construction equipment, which were merged into Korean Heavy Industries and Construction; Saehan Autos was forced to merge with Hyundai so that there would be only two makers of passenger cars; Kia and Tong-a were merged into a monopoly on trucks and buses; the heavy electric subsidiaries of Ssangyong and Kolon were merged with another firm; and so on. Property rights were completely insecure unless the state (often meaning the ruling dictator) approved of the firm and what it was doing—something that was mightily helped along by large political contributions. Business leaders could lose not only their firms but also their own fortunes at the whim of the state.

A typical example would be the dismantling of Kukje, Korea's sixth largest conglomerate, in 1985. By that time, Kukje was involved in everything from jogging shoes to construction, securities, steel making, paper making, shipping, resorts, tires, farm tools, an aluminum smelting plant, and so on. But it was also massively indebted and split by a long-standing family feud. In February 1985, the government decided to pull the plug on the firm and its preferential funding, proceeding to dismantle it and turn its assets over to others "[without] due process, no bidding for assets, only a multimillion-dollar takeover operation shrouded in secrecy" (Clifford 1996, 218). The reason for this confiscation, the owner of Kukje claimed in 1988, was the paltriness of his contribution to the ruling group. There were other *chaebŏl* whose properties were expropriated, allegedly after the they ran afoul of President Chun Doo Hwan.[7]

The relationship between well-established rules and norms in society and corporate governance has been discussed elsewhere (Fukuyama 1995) and need not detain us, except for one glaring flaw in the Western argument. Democratic capitalism, the argument goes, cannot be achieved except in the presence of a thick web of civic institutions (Putnam 1993), but—here is the rub—a healthy "civil society," defined as a complex web of voluntary associations and intermediate institutions— is absent in the low-trust, Confucian societies. This leads to the predominance of family-based firms. Instead of civil society, Confucian (and Catholic) cultures exhibit amoral familism, meaning that people maximize the material, short-run advantages of the nuclear family, rather than individual or societal goals. The economic effects of amoral familism, Edward Banfield famously argued, create a "very important limiting factor in the way of economic development in most of the world. Except as people can create and maintain corporate organization, they cannot have a modern economy" (Banfield 1958; Fukuyama 1995, 99). Amoral familism (or the absent Anglo-Saxon civil society) gives you a premodern economy and the predominance of family firms.

To the extent that one accepts this characterization of places as diverse as Korea, China, and southern Italy (Banfield's locus of specialization), one can give up any hope of corporate reform, because family governance is the product of an indelible and ineradicable historical and cultural stamp. Fortunately, the argument is wrong; it does not explain family governance of Korean corporations.

The prevalence of family firms does reflect an absence of universalistic trust and the rule of law in Korea (not to mention a country like Indonesia), but such practices have their roots in decades of authoritarianism and the myriad discretionary rules that it has fostered to support and regulate big business, and not in some indelible (and therefore inescapable) cultural trait. The emergence and persistence of family-controlled firms is related to the prevalence of discretionary rule (rather than the rule of law) in Korea, growing out of institutional structures of "late" industrialization. That is different, however, from arguing that democracy and market capitalism are not possible in the absence of Anglo-Saxon civil society, the rule of law, and the resulting high levels of trust that such societies reflect and in turn foster.

Indeed, there is no such thing as an East Asian pattern of corporate governance that is true in all Confucian societies—a fact that Francis Fukuyama overlooks by refusing to call Japan a Confucian society. Corporations are publicly held in Japan, whereas they are not in Korea; in Muslim Indonesia and Buddhist Thailand, they are mainly family-controlled. In fact, in a study of corporate ownership in East Asia, Claessens, Djankov, and Lang (1998b) conclude that although ownership concentration in East Asian corporations is high, it is not significantly different from that in other countries at similar levels of economic and institutional development.

How serious is the problem of family ownership? For the top thirty Korean *chaebŏl*, family ownership (defined as the share held by the family members and affiliated firms) came to 43.3 percent in 1995. The figure for the top five *chaebŏl* in 1994 was 47.5 percent, combining the family share of 12.5 percent and the 35 percent share for the affiliated firms. These figures, although high in comparison to developed countries, are lower than they used to be. In 1987, family ownership in the top thirty firms averaged 56.2 percent, and that in the top five averaged 60.3 percent. So there has been a steady decline in relative shares owned by the family and affiliated firms, as might be expected from my earlier argument. But it is clear that individual families still exercise too much control over corporate governance of the *chaebŏl*, and public stockholding remains weak. For the top thirty *chaebŏl*, which together claimed possession of some 623 firms in 1995, the number of publicly listed firms was 172, or only 27.6 percent. This figure shows a marginal decline from 1991, when the number of listed firms was 161 out of 561 firms, or 28.7 percent (Yu 1996, 25–26).

In comparison to other East Asian countries, Korea stands somewhere in the middle in terms of the concentration of family control. If we look at the percentage of total market capitalization controlled by the top five families, the figure is 29 percent for Korea, whereas it is much higher in Indonesia (40.7 percent), the Philippines (42.8 percent), and Thailand (32.2 percent). The percentage is considerably lower in Singapore (19.5 percent), Taiwan (14.5 percent), and Malaysia (17.3 percent), and it is stunningly low in Japan (1.8 percent). The comparative ranking is about the same when we look at the top fifteen families. It is only when we look at the share of the top family that Korea begins to look more like Indonesia or the Philippines, because of the presence of Hyundai's Chung Ju-Yung family, which is the biggest family holder not only in Korea but in all of East Asia, with holdings worth $48 billion (Claessens, Djankov, and Lang 1998b). The manner in which family control is ensured is fairly common throughout East Asia, as it is in some developed countries—the use of pyramid schemes (owning a majority of the stock of one corporation that in turn holds a majority of the stock of another—a process that can be repeated a number of times), deviations from one–share–one-vote rules, cross-holdings, and the appointment of managers and directors who are related to the controlling family (Claessens, Djankov, and Lang 1998b).

Is family control of big business necessarily inefficient? The answer is not as simple as one might think and depends on many things—above all, the entrepreneurial talent of the family members running the business. Reflecting on the rise and fall of corporate families, Joseph Schumpeter (1951, 119) remarked that capital accumulation does not happen automatically: "the captured value *does not invest itself* but must be *invested.*" By this he meant that the study of capital accumulation should include behavior and motive—in other words, shifting focus from the social "force" to the responsible individual or family. The crucial factor, he argued, is that "the social logic or objective situation does not unequivocally determine *how much* profit shall be invested, and *how* it shall be invested, *unless individual disposition is taken into account.*" Thus, a private corporation run by able owner-managers can be more effective than one run by professional managers; it is just that there is no way to ensure that this will always be the case. For every advantage to owner-management of the big firm, such as speed and flexibility in corporate response, there is a disadvantage, such as a dearth of professional management skill. Likewise, the owner-manager, by assuming corporate responsibility, can either create stability for the firm or, by being dictatorial and arbitrary in his decision making, a sense of instability. Owner-managers can be more dedicated to the long-term development of the firm, using their own resources, but it is also easy to imagine a nefarious collusion between corporate and private accounting.

The Korean *chaebŏl* shows both the advantages and disadvantages of family control. In the early days of industrialization, the can-do spirit and dedication on the part of founding entrepreneurs who made strategic choices and resource-allocation decisions by themselves helped expand business by leaps and bounds. Strong central—even personal—control gave the *chaebŏl* much more integrated command and direction than conglomerates managed by professionals. But it is also true that there was too much personal charisma and too little routinization and institutionalization, so that, at the end of the day, Max Weber's insight that the essence of modernity is the rationalization as well as the professionalization of economic and political management, that modernity is unthinkable apart from rational bureaucracy and the separation of the household from the corporation, is still valid. In Korea, too, the predominance of the family-controlled firms must change, as routine replaces charisma and as what began in the 1960s as a frenetic attempt to emulate Japanese success becomes more settled and institutionalized. The change will come slowly but surely, paralleling increasing globalization of the Korean economy and, if our analysis is correct, increasing democratization as well.

Democracy and Corporate Reform

Corporate restructuring is still under way in Korea, but it may be said that a confluence of three factors has made the current reform effective thus far: first, the magnitude of the current crisis, drawing international financial institutions into the reform process; second, the inauguration of a reform leadership long committed to the project of severing the state-business tie and abiding by the rule of law to which the corporations and the government are both subject; and third, continuing use of the tools of industrial policy to bring about a liberal economic order. Liberal economic reform in Korea has not meant the retreat of the state from the market; on the contrary, it has meant a deep intervention by the state, using the tried and true method of industrial swaps and mergers, dictated or brokered from above. This heterodox mix of policies, backed by the vast power and prestige of a centralized polity, is what gives momentum to the reforms today.

The crisis of 1997–98 was a disaster waiting to happen, we have argued, but without it the resolution of the bad-debt problem in the Korean banking system would again have been postponed, as it had been for decades. The crisis and the subsequent bailout of Korea also inserted international financial institutions, mainly the IMF and the World Bank, deeply into the reform process in Korea, greatly raising the stakes of reform. The virtue of this is that the international financial institutions could run political interference for the new regime: every unpopular policy and outcome could be blamed on the IMF, from legalizing layoffs and skyrocketing unemployment to massive corporate bankruptcy. The inter-

national financial institutions thus reduced the political perils of reform and provided a shield for the regime.

The relationship between democratization and financial reform and liberalization
is difficult to establish. General Pinochet's Chile and President Suharto's Indonesia
brooked financial liberalization but not democracy, and Japan in the 1950s brooked
democracy but not financial liberalization. In the minds of Korean democrats, however, the two are inextricably connected. The most prominent Korean democrat to
have articulated this position was Kim Dae Jung, in the late 1960s. The policy of
financial repression, he argued, went hand in hand with political repression. The
power of military authoritarianism was based not only on the coercive capacity of
the state, but also on its capacity, through financial repression, to control the business class. For thirty years Kim advocated financial liberalization, not because he
valued allocative efficiency above all else, but because it was the most effective way
to sever the link between the repressive state and the *chaebŏl*.

In the trials of two former presidents, held in the mid-1990s, one *chaebŏl* leader
after another was brought into the docket and shown to have lined the pockets of
leading politicians from the 1960s on. If the images of the flagship firms that made
the Korean miracle were deeply tarnished, the revelation nonetheless was a hugely
important phenomenon: it signaled the arrival, finally, of democratic politics in
Korea, and it was only through democratic means that the deep nexus between the
chaebŏl and the authoritarian state could be broken. The best news for those interested in *chaebŏl* reform is simply that real reform is now possible, given the election
of two successive civilian presidents (Kim Young Sam in 1992 and Kim Dae Jung
in 1997) and the impetus of a crisis in the economy unparalleled since the Korean
War.

In the middle of an analogous crisis, President Franklin Roosevelt, in his message to Congress in 1938, called for an investigation of concentrated economic
power. "The liberty of a democracy," he said, "is not safe if the people tolerate the
growth of private power to a point where it becomes stronger than their democratic state itself."[8] In Korea, the problem of private power is as President
Roosevelt described it, but much more so: before the crisis, politicians and political parties extracted funds from the *chaebŏl*, offering in return loan guarantees to
sustain these highly leveraged firms. No firm could avoid paying out one day, lest
it be declared bankrupt the following day. The mid-1990s investigations, ultimately leading to the incarceration of two previous presidents and several big business leaders, revealed the operational method of patronage to the Korean people.
Korea, Inc. proved to be far more arbitrary than Japan, Inc.: especially in the 1980s,
a racketeering state was the flip side of the much-touted developmental state; the
earlier, more systemic pattern of *chaebŏl* support for the ruling groups changed
into a kind of mad extortionism.

President Kim Dae Jung, long a dissident who was the object of *chaebŏl*-provisioned
political funding (he nearly won his first presidential campaign in 1971 in spite of
widespread irregularities and munificent support for Park Chung Hee, whereupon
there were no more elections until 1987), needs no tutoring in the politics or the

economic liabilities of the state-*chaebŏl* relationship. He wrote, "The Korean economy . . . has been plagued by inefficient allocation of valuable resources . . . [which is] the result of government interference in almost every aspect of market functions, including pricing, credit allocation, industrial location decisions, and labor-management relations. This interference has left the Korean economy in a state of serious imbalance" (1985, 3). The economic crisis gave him the leverage he needed to pursue real reform of the Korean system for the first time since it got going in the 1960s.

The new Korean government has issued a number of measures to force corporate reform, including ending the system of intersubsidiary loan guarantees and posting deadlines to bring the corporate debt-to-equity ratio down. Kim Dae Jung has also demanded a "Big Deal," meaning a swap of key subsidiaries so that each of the top *chaebŏl* will emerge stronger in the areas of their "core competence." This would reduce overlapping investments and allow surplus production capacity to be closed down. Some of these measures are critically important departures from the past, such as the decisive ending of the intersubsidiary loans (which was mightily helped by the demands made by the IMF); others are not departures but continuations of the past government policy, although with more teeth.

The main difference from the past is the simultaneity of the banking and corporate restructuring. Because individual Korean banks made a substantial percentage of their loans to specific *chaebŏl*, banks have an incentive to prop up groups with fresh loans rather than let them collapse and bring the banks down with them. This situation, in which banks are de facto quasi–equity holders in corporations, highlights the necessity of simultaneous corporate- and financial-sector restructuring in Korea. Hence, corporate restructuring has been closely linked to bank restructuring and recapitalization and to resolution of the bad loans in the banking sector, and this is happening in tandem with the push to increase the equity and cash flows of the *chaebŏl* and extend the maturity profile of their debt.

To do this, the government created the FSC, an independent agency reporting directly to the prime minister with the mandate to restructure both the corporate sector and the financial institutions. The FSC has taken a step–by–step approach, focusing first on voluntary workouts for the medium-sized *chaebŏl* (i.e., those ranked after the big five). The medium-sized *chaebŏl* have been given priority because they are in deepest distress, and a large number of insolvencies in this group could bring severe social distress and political pressure on the government to abandon its reform program. A series of defaults, it is also feared, could provoke another crisis. Moreover, if the restructuring of the medium-sized *chaebŏl* worked, the recipe could then be applied to the big five *chaebŏl* (Lieberman and Mako 1998).

The government produced, in rapid succession, a set of legal and regulatory policies to restructure the medium-sized *chaebŏl*. There were tax breaks for restructuring firms. To permit takeovers of nonstrategic companies by foreign investors, fdi was genuinely liberalized and the ceiling raised on foreign stock ownership. The securities exchange was overhauled to facilitate mergers and acquisitions by increasing the portion of shares that could be acquired without board approval. The government also bolstered the anti-trust and fair trade acts and prohibited any new intersubsidiary debt guarantees, as well as pledging to eliminate all existing guarantees of that type by 2000.

To provide infrastructural support, the FSC promoted the Corporate Restructuring Accord, signed to run until the end of 1999, and formed a committee to assess the viability of corporate candidates for restructuring, arbitrating differences among creditors, and, if necessary, modifying "workout" plans proposed by participating creditors. Although six are banks in charge of restructuring the sixty-four corporate groups, all commercial banks now have internal workout groups. A workout may involve debt/equity conversions, term extensions, deferred payment of principal or interest, reduction of interest rates, waiver of indebtedness, provision of new credits, cancellation of existing guarantee obligations, sale of non-core businesses, and new equity issues (Lieberman and Mako 1998, 13).

As for the five largest *chaebŏl*, the government is clearly thinking long term, with an eye to producing internationally competitive enterprises, even if that involves stiff-arming the big five into business swaps, mergers, and acquisitions among themselves. Thus, in spite of pledges from the *chaebŏl* to improve their financial structure voluntarily, the state has been singularly insistent on the "Big Deal" designed to streamline business lines and reduce overcapacity. Using the threat of cutting off credit, the government has brokered a series of high-profile business swaps. Daewoo, for instance, has agreed to give up its electronics firm to Samsung, in exchange for Samsung's automobile firm. This means that Samsung will dominate Korea's consumer electronics market with 60 percent of the market share. Internationally, Samsung will control production of approximately 30 percent of microwave ovens, approximately 18 percent of videocassette recorders, and more than 10 percent of television sets (*Wall Street Journal* 17 December 1998). Daewoo, on the other hand, may become the only Korean automobile maker other than Hyundai, and the industry is likely to be consolidated from a five-player field to two. The government has also brokered a merger between the memory-chip companies of the Hyundai group and the LG Group, which will create the world's second-largest maker of DRAM chips. (The world's largest DRAM chip maker is Samsung.)

Corporate restructuring on this scale wreaks havoc on labor. The current regime has sought in a variety of ways to spread the pain of the IMF bailout fairly, throughout the society, but the layoffs related to restructuring have continued. By the end of 1998, the big five firms had slashed some 10 percent of their labor force, and they threatened to do more. Labor, in turn, has protested against corporate restructuring, but the sheer magnitude of the financial crisis has dealt it a poor hand. Even so, for the first time in Korean history, the current regime has given labor a strong voice at the bargaining table with business and government—certainly a major achievement of reform, and one that has generally kept labor from (truly) major strikes and disruptions, in the face of unemployment that tripled in one year (from 2 percent in mid-1997 to more than 7 percent in late 1998).

Lessons of the Korean Case

What does the foregoing discussion of Korea's corporate restructure suggest about reform in other East Asian countries? There may not be many lessons for the rather different political economies of Southeast Asia—although Indonesia could certainly take note of the way in which democratization has aided economic reform in Korea, Malaysia could observe the benefits of trying to accommodate legitimate Western demands for reform (rather than posturing about Western imperialism and "Asian values"), and Thailand could learn from Seoul's efforts at financial transparency and working with organized labor. Still, the main lessons relate to Korea's big neighbors—China and Japan.

The PRC is saddled with the kind of massive bad-debt problem in the banking sector that plagued Korea. From Korea's example, it might take two—albeit contradictory—lessons: either that its debt problem cannot be as bad as Western observers make it out to be (Korea had higher levels of bad debt in relation to GNP, yet grew at spectacular rates for three decades, against the predictions of leading Western economists), or that delaying reform makes the potential for disaster much greater, given the magnitude of the Asian financial crisis. Chinese policy responses suggest the second lesson has had an effect. In early 1999, Premier Zhu Rongji cited the need for decisive and quick resolution, within the next three years, of the problems in the SOEs and the banking sector. The rub will come in accomplishing this in such a way that the efficiency gains of accelerated reform and job creation mitigate the social disasters spawned by reform-related unemployment (Lardy 1998c).

There is also a rough, if curious, parallel between the Korean *chaebŏl* and the Chinese SOEs. Because the social safety net in both countries is small or nonexistent, the *chaebŏl* and the SOEs provide crucial welfare for their workers. It is well known that the SOEs provide an "iron rice bowl" of supports to their multitude of workers, including low-cost housing, health care, and retirement stipends. Less appreciated are the "company town" features of the big Korean firms. *Chaebŏl* firms provide for their employees' needs in every way. The typical Hyundai worker drives a Hyundai car, lives in a Hyundai apartment, gets his mortgage from Hyundai credit, gets health care from a Hyundai hospital, sends his kids to school on Hyundai loans or scholarships, and eats his meals at Hyundai cafeterias. If his son graduates out of the blue-collar work force and into the ranks of well-educated technocratic professionals (which is every Korean parent's goal), he may well work for Hyundai research and development. The extreme form is seen in the construction teams that Hyundai has long sent to the Middle East: every worker departs in Hyundai T-shirts and caps carrying Hyundai bags, lives and eats in Hyundai dormitories, and uses Hyundai tools and equipment to build Hyundai cities in the desert. In the same way that Kim Il Sung built a Confucian-influenced hereditary family-state in North Korea and called it communism, the Korean *chaebŏl* have built large, family-run, hereditary corporate estates in Korea and called this capitalism (Cumings 1996).

Such practices, of course, show why it has been and is so difficult to truly reform Korean corporations: it's like asking a giant cruise ship to change course abruptly while throwing 10 or 20 percent of its work force overboard. Clearly, the situation in China is analogous—the SOEs provide for more than 100 million people. How then to reform? It cannot be done overnight, or perhaps even in three years, but it can be done: both South Korea and Taiwan inherited large SOEs from Japanese colonialism but managed to dismantle or privatize many of them over the years. The tradeoff between accumulation and distribution (or employment) is always difficult, but Kim Dae Jung has shown that the worst abuses can be mitigated by severing nefarious ties between the state and the big enterprises.

A less dispiriting example can also be drawn from the Korean case. As we have seen, the reform of financial and banking structures may be aided by the very state that promoted these structures in the first place—a strong, interventionist state capable not only of restructuring the state-corporate nexus, but of maintaining a steady hand in dampening the shocks of social dislocation. Kim Dae Jung arranged for the state to play the role of broker between labor and business, with labor trading economic gains for rights of political representation. China has sought to solve the SOE problem by quickening the pace of job creation in the private sector, through Keynesian demand management. Thus far, it has been successful, but Korean-style "peak bargaining" between the state, business, and (as yet nonexistent) national unions might be necessary when private-sector job creation inevitably lags. But does China have a strong, effective state that could learn from the Korean state's role in the reform process?

The traditional conundrum of China has been the "modernization" of its central state, which—whether in the imperial, the nationalist, or the communist era—was both too centralized and too decentralized, simultaneously hyper-statized and politically parcelized. The resolution of this problem evaded Mao and Deng Xiaoping, even if Deng got the state to begin shucking off its hypertrophied central responsibilities after 1978 while deepening its provincial penetration. In this sense, some observers have interpreted the reforms in the Deng era and after as increasing the "reach of the state" (Shue 1988; see also Gates 1996).

Just what constitutes an effective state with "a long reach" is a difficult question; clearly the Communist Party–run Chinese state is both penetrative and remarkably (and often self-defeatingly) intrusive. Citizens have no inalienable rights in the face of state prerogatives. But that was also true (if in a lesser way) of the military dictatorships in Korea. This problem cannot be settled in the manner suggested by the World Bank's 1997 *World Development Report* on reforming the state, which developed an admirable if very long laundry list of how to make the state efficient while offering little advice about how the list might be implemented. Successful reform in Korea also built on the long tradition of civil service statecraft; because China was the original source of this tradition and has no lack of bureaucrats, this background still might be the source of bureaucratic renewal.

What about lessons of Korean reform for Japan? On several counts, Korea is more apt to learn from Japan: Korea is finally adopting measures that have been prevalent in Japan since the 1950s, such as "peak bargaining" with labor unions, structural reform of the *zaibatsu* (pronounced *chaebŏl* in Korean), and the provision of a wide social safety net. That Japan needs reform—especially in its banking system, which seemed so dominant in the 1980s—is not in doubt. In the face of years of recession, Japan's leaders have been unable to summon the will to do anything more than muddle along, vegetating in the teeth of a rather remarkable economic and political malaise that only seems to grow worse as time passes. Korea's relatively successful reform occurred because the depth of the financial crisis became critical during a defining presidential election; Kim Dae Jung had Korea's strong state dropped in his lap, so to speak, and, as we have seen, he has used the full panoply of executive powers to push through serious reform. If Japan's political system is often described as "a web with no spider" (Lockwood 1993), Korea's is precisely the opposite—and since Kim's inauguration, the spider has been moving rapidly through the web. This fundamental difference helps explain the dynamism of Korea's reform effort compared to Japan's political dithering.

Reform in Japan is, and no doubt will remain, a vastly slower process. If in Korea the regime of political economy collapsed of its own weight in the crisis of 1997–99, in Japan the "regime shift" has continued in subtle ways since the early 1980s, involving a transformation in socioeconomic alliances, political and economic institutions, and public policy profile, making Japanese politics in the 1990s very different from the stable regime of the 1960s and 1970s (Pempel 1998). The relationships among corporations, banks, and the state are far more legitimate and far less brittle in Japan than in Korea. (In part this is because Korea wanted to do what Japan did, but in half the time it took Japan to do it.) But to ask today for Japan to find a strong, accountable executive like President Kim and set about the business of reform is like asking Americans to adopt a parliamentary system of no-confidence voting in the middle of Bill Clinton's 1998–99 intern scandal. Japanese reform will come, but it is impossible to predict *when*; and, most likely, it will move along the twisting and evolving paths of the past twenty years rather than the "developmental state" model (Johnson 1982) that it pioneered seventy years ago.

Alternatives for Korean Reform: More Like Us, the Chinese Model, or the *Keiretsu* Model?

Considering Convergence in Corporate Governance: More Like Us?

In the midst of financial crisis and IMF reform programs, reform of corporate governance has been associated with international demands for transparency and accountability. Beyond that, however, reform of corporate governance has a neologistic ring to it in the context of societies that may be bereft of legal norms and traditions that undergirded the rise of the rational modern corporation. The traditional discourse of corporate governance was predicated on the long-standing U.S. practice of separating corporate ownership from control. In the context of "modern" enterprise, good governance is really about holding corporate management accountable to the interests of shareholders, or reducing *agency costs* (meaning the costs to shareholders of managerial behavior not consistent with their interests). Methods for achieving accountability are often formal, legalistic, and, according to some, idiosyncratic to Anglo-American traditions. In this sense, corporate governance can be thought of as a entity taxonomically separate from, say, contractual governance, which is said to characterize the "Nippo-Rhenish" model of business organization. In the latter, good governance is a matter of reducing transaction costs by building and investing in stable and long-term commercial relationships among transacting companies (Gourevitch 1996).

The debate on corporate governance in the context of global competition has been particularly fickle and prone to revaluations. In the 1980s and well into the 1990s, for instance, it was fashionable to argue that the Anglo-American style of corporate governance (and various corporate restructuring movements in particular) had the nefarious consequence of reducing investment and forcing the American managers to think short term. In contrast, Japanese corporate managers were believed to enjoy certain freedoms in retaining excess capital (rather than returning it to shareholders) and in determining long-term investment strategies (without oversight of shareholders). Once upon a time, this was viewed as the core of Japan's competitive edge.

Today, the reversal of this historical verdict is complete. Michael Jensen (1997) has argued that in periods of industrial transformation, in the late nineteenth century as at the end of the twentieth, rapid technological and organizational change leads to incentives to reduce production costs and increase average productivity of labor. Rapid change results in widespread excess capacity and reduced rates of growth in labor income, causing corporate downsizing and exit. The best example would be the merger and acquisition wave of the 1980s that ended up sharply reducing capacity (by consolidating some 1,800 U.S. firms into roughly 150); that, combined with leveraged takeovers and buyouts, represented "healthy adjustments" to overcapacity that had been building in many sectors of the U.S. economy. Corporate raiders turned out to be the ephors of modern capitalism after all. Likewise, the decline in the Japanese economy came to be seen as stemming from a structural overcapacity, fueled by lax investment criteria employed by Japanese companies and the failure to pay out excess capital in the form of higher dividends or share repurchases.

Such periodic revaluation reflects profound (or at least shifting) uncertainty about what constitutes a good system of corporate governance. We all can agree that good corporate governance is important, as are motherhood, the flag, peace, and good will to humanity; but what constitutes truly "good" governance, and how does one obtain it? The contemporary discourse on corporate governance, influenced as it is by Western practice and experience, holds out little hope of achieving a consensual understanding of what good governance actually means, which makes institutional emulation on the part of "late" developers that much more difficult. This is another way of saying that reform of corporate governance has to be plausible in the context of what *is* (not simply what *ought to be*) and must resonate with larger social goals that enjoy broad support.

Korean firms will become "more like us," to use James Fallows' phrase, only up to a point. As the reform of the corporate sector proceeds, corporations will accept more transparency, external audits, foreign participation, and more accountable management. There should be, and perhaps there will be, an effective institution guaranteeing minority shareholder rights and transparency in accounting. The power and function of the board of directors might be bolstered, and the role of institutional investors is likely to grow as well, through financial deepening. Yet, for half a century the United States has sought to make Korea "more like us"; and in 1999, the problem of reforming an economic model always more deeply influenced by Japan's industrial success remains.

More Like the Chinese?

There is an unappreciated possibility that the Korean firm might learn from the Chinese firm. This idea is worth entertaining for at least three reasons. The first is that in spite of Fukuyama's (1995) argument about social trust and forms of corporate governance, the Chinese family firms in Taiwan and in East Asia are perhaps the most flexible and adaptable entrepreneurial units in the world today. The behavior of these firms is, of course, at times a reflection of a harsh world bereft of universal trust. But the reverse is also true, that the Chinese family firm is at ease with a world of trust as Fukuyama would define it: witness the enormous success of diasporic Chinese business in highly articulated civil societies such as exist in Vancouver and Toronto. Perhaps global capitalism, with its free movement of goods and services, has made the most singularly premodern of corporate governance forms, the Chinese family firm, into a highly adaptable, multicultural, postmodern firm, able to navigate in any economic waters. The second reason is that the family-controlled *chaebŏl* is akin to Chinese enterprise—"the truth of the matter is that Korean businesses, despite their large scale, do look and behave more like Chinese businesses and like Japanese corporations" (Fukuyama 1995). If this is the case, could there be greater convergence? The third reason is Taiwan. Taiwan and Korea might have had similar structures of corporate governance and state-business relationships by virtue of a shared colonial history and the Cold War environment, but they did not. Given the profound conservatism of Taiwan's corporate sector and its stability—Taiwan has always been spared the kind of massive financial crises that visited Korea in the early 1970s and 1979–80—perhaps there is something that can be learned there, as well.

Both Korea and Taiwan formed the core of the Japanese imperium, but half a century after independence, they have radically different forms of enterprises. In Taiwan, firms are mainly small and medium sized, and even for the large enterprises the average debt to equity ratio remains one-fourth of Korea's. The reason for this was idiosyncratic to the Taiwanese predicament. Whereas in Korea, the postcolonial state sought to build a capitalist class that could in turn provide it with political support, the state in Taiwan needed big business less, because the KMT already possessed a centralized political authority, an oversized military and administrative apparatus, and a huge array of SOEs. The mainland elites sought instead to cultivate decentralized industrial structure, with the small and medium-sized firms being the broad backbone of political support, as Yun-han Chu argues in chapter 9 of this volume.

The Taiwan model has numerous merits and should be examined seriously in Korea, but such learning can only take place *after* a significant political change. Korea needs a mass-based political party that builds on a vibrant civil society, one less reliant on the kindness of big business and more reliant on grassroots membership. Why? Because the Korean failure to promote medium-sized and small firms stems less from the absence of policy (on the contrary, there are numerous policies to that effect in place) than from the lack of a political impetus to do so.

Is the Chinese firm in Southeast Asia a model of good governance? In Southeast Asia, in a context of a historical pluralism deriving from ethnically based political mobilization, the goal of the national leadership is to shape development to enhance the dominant ethnic party's political base and meet the cultural aspirations of "backward" groups (as in Malaysia). The state retains a great deal of discretionary control over the private sector and business firms, enabling it to facilitate expansion of state enterprises and enforce "affirmative action" in favor of the economically "backward" Malay majority. Hence, the Malaysian state has attempted to curtail the role of the Chinese through restrictive licenses, protective tariffs, ownership limitations, preferential credit allocations, and outright bans on Chinese activity in particular sectors. The flip side of this coin has been massive government help for non-Chinese enterprises, including placing entire sectors under state control and thus giving indigenous businessmen favored conditions for access to licenses, contracts, subsidized credits, and joint ventures with foreign companies (Lim 1983; Mackie 1993; Judason 1989).

The Chinese response has been to place adaptability at the highest premium in doing business. This has meant cultivating political patrons and sponsors, providing bribes and payoffs to local and government officials to circumvent restrictions and secure protection, and creating so-called Ali-Baba ventures with indigenous "sleeping partners" in whose names the enterprises are registered. The alliance with indigenous patrons does not seem to alter the essential character of the Chinese firm, however; indeed, the participation of indigenous partners seems to reinforce family-oriented tendencies. It is a family-oriented closed corporation, based on an individual tycoon and his family, a corporate form that is often thought to limit Chinese capacity for capital mobilization and organizational expansion. In Malaysia, for instance, there is significant participation of Malay partners in Chinese companies, including representatives from the aristocracy, the military, and the bureaucracy (but not prominent businessmen), but the Chinese entrepreneurs retain centralized control of the businesses through ownership of large blocks of shares (Lim 1983; Koon 1992).

What is the result of this "ethnic logic of accumulation" (as opposed to the "national logic of accumulation" that one might find in Northeast Asia)? It privileges the state enterprise, the surplus from which can be used for redistribution along ethnic lines, and also the foreign multinational corporation, which provides the Malaysian state with a source of entrepreneurship other than the Chinese (as well as providing employment in labor-intensive export industries). To the extent that a business alliance exists, it does not unite the state and domestic enterprises and pit them against multinationals (as might be the case in more nationalist states), but binds together the state and multinationals, often against the Chinese domestic enterprise (Judason 1989). This has been called an "ethnic bypass," meaning that Malays collaborate with foreign partners to avoid dependence on the Chinese (for example, in their national car project). There are exceptions, of course; some politically influential Chinese have managed to do well in import-substitution industries, such as cement, flour, sugar, and automobile assembly. But it would be an understatement to say that the state has not favored the Chinese entrepreneurs (who own most of the Malaysian manufacturing enterprises); Chinese entrepreneurs are often harassed for violating laws on intellectual property rights, land use, labor, and environment.

The upshot is that the Chinese manufacturing entrepreneurs prefer to remain small and family owned, engaged in a kind of "guerilla capitalism" that limits growth, economies of scale in production, technological innovation, marketing, and international competitiveness, and that has nefarious consequences for regulating wages, industrial safety, occupational health, and environmental protection. Another consequence of the harassing presence of the state in Malaysia, exemplified by the "New Economic Policy," has been to make the Chinese gravitate toward finance and real estate, investments that offer rapid, attractive returns and quick exit. The consequences of all of this are structural inefficiencies in the economy and growth rates that are dependent on commodity prices and on political priorities that lay emphasis on employment and stable wages for purposes of the political incorporation of Malays (Jomo 1997).

Back to the Future? The Keiretsu System

There is perhaps no thought more horrifying to Korean patriots than that of Korea becoming more like Japan. But the possibility that the *chaebŏl* might, *mutatis mutandis*, move in the direction of the *keiretsu* has to be entertained if we believe that history matters and institutions are reflections and repositories of norms and values of the larger society. The *keiretsu* is an advancement on the evolutionary scale of the economic combines in Japan, a rational/legal form of the earlier, more feudal *zaibatsu*. The *chaebŏl* was a postcolonial mutation of the *zaibatsu*, and it would, therefore, be wrong not to examine the logic of historical change in Japan with an eye to what is possible in Korea.

The template for the *chaebŏl* was the wartime Japanese *zaibatsu*. Korea's military leaders who served in the Pacific War (like Park Chung Hee) were familiar with the model, and the extensive wartime coordination between the Japanese state and big business, with highly centralized finance as the lynchpin, appealed to them. State control over finance not only made the implementation of industrial policy possible, but had the added benefit of bolstering the power base of the state by creating an entrepreneurial class as beneficiaries of the political leadership.

The term *zaibatsu* refers to family-dominated combines that developed after World War I, which used holding organizations to maintain control over their industries and expanded rapidly in the heavy industrialization drives and wartime conditions of the 1930s and 1940s. The goal of the *zaibatsu* was not high-market occupancy of one, two, or a few related markets, but an oligopolistic position running the gamut of the modern sector of the economy. The largest firm, Mitsui, carried on far-flung operations in coals and metals mining, shipbuilding, ordnance, aircraft, heavy and light electrical equipment, and various other fields of manufacturing, not to mention commercial banking, insurance, and trading. A series of oligopolistic positions, often accounting for 10 to 20 percent of market output, was the fundament of this *zaibatsu*—which, at the end of the war, employed an estimated 1.8 million people in Japan itself and 2 to 3 million in the whole of the Far East (Hadley 1970, 23).

What should draw our attention in the current context of *chaebŏl* reform is that even the seven-year American occupation of defeated Japan, with the war hero of the Pacific campaigns, General Douglas MacArthur, at the helm carrying the full panoply of extraordinary powers vested in him and his SCAP staff, could not decisively break the power of the *zaibatsu*, who restructured when they had to, hunkered down and waited when they could, and thus transmogrified into the postoccupation *keiretsu*: a definite improvement, but by no means the thorough breakup and reform that MacArthur had planned. There were many reasons for this outcome, which need not detain us here. But one great difficulty of that reform effort was pinpointing the line at which the state left off and private business began. The victorious Americans, used to defeating lines drawn in the sands of Pacific islands, could not find the line to draw in Japan proper.

American staff in SCAP, many of whom were New Dealers, perceived the *zaibatsu* essentially as products of tricks played with holding companies: once the secrets, like Rumpelstiltskin's name, were revealed, the whole system would come apart at the seams. Thus, the holding companies were abolished, but the system of political economy in Japan—the triumvirate of politicians (now replacing the military), bureaucrats, and business (now called the *keiretsu*)—remained intact, favoring the producers at the expense of consumers. (This experience is a strong caution to anyone who thinks the reform of the corporate sector is a matter of economic technicalities.) So, although the *chaebŏl* emerged in the last thirty years, the model goes back seventy years. This is another way of saying that we need to be sensitive to "path dependency," to a pattern of Northeast Asian development that has marked all of the twentieth century.

But what is the postwar Japanese system, which is under so much criticism today? Masahiko Aoki (1989, 265) has said that it is a system in which management acts as a mediator in the policy-making process, striking a balance between the interests of shareholders and the interests of employees. The enterprise union functions as a substructure of the firm and represents employees in the decision-making process. Before this system could come into being in Japan, three historical conditions had to be met for the firm. The first was the dismantling of family control of the firms, through occupation policies in 1946 and 1947. This involved a managerial revolution from above through the dispersal of share ownership, as part of the dissolution of *zaibatsu* holding companies, and the replacement of previous managers by young or new managers, ones not as loyal to the *zaibatsu* family. The second was a move toward Cooperative Enterprise Unions resulting from the defeat of various labor actions in the late 1950s. The third was an effective insulation from hostile takeovers through the development of mutual shareholding between companies and financial institutions, notably city banks. This was facilitated by the stock market crash of 1964–65, the government purchase and freezing of stocks to stabilize the market, and, later, a concerted action by the interlocking companies to repurchase stocks, in part to stave off foreign takeovers (Aoki 1989, 269–73).

Now observe Korea today. First, instead of the Occupation forcing anti-trust, there is the IMF and the Kim Dae Jung administration insisting on a greater injection of equity into the corporate system, further attenuating the overlap between family ownership and control. Second, given the ubiquitous presence of enterprise union organization in Korea, the Japanese example might also be used to argue for taking Korean labor reforms in this direction, which would be a good counterpart to the historically unprecedented "peak bargaining" that Kim Dae Jung directed in January 1998 between top representatives of business, labor, and government. If this were to be institutionalized, the ROK would then resemble Japan's postwar pattern of political corporatism, as a political scientist would understand it. Finally and ironically, the reform of the corporate sector may be eradicating one major difference between the Korean *chaebŏl* and the Japanese *keiretsu* (or *zaibatsu*)—the limit on the *chaebŏl* ownership of financial institutions, and vice versa.

Conclusion

In the end, Korea will probably have multiple forms of corporate governance. No one style of corporate governance fits all, even in the globalized world of unforgiving investors and school-marmish IMF officials. Some firms will look more like us, especially if there is a great participation of foreign capital; the *chaebŏl* firms are likely to look more like the *keiretsu*, whereas the small and medium-sized firms will look more like the Chinese firms in Taiwan and Southeast Asia. No matter how severe the pressure for organizational convergence, it is unlikely that we will see the emergence, at the "end of history," as it were, of one superior form of corporate government to which all can adhere. It is worth remembering that it was not visionaries standing at the doorstep of twenty-first century, but culture-bound writers of the mid-nineteenth century who "looked forward to a single, more or less standardized world where all governments would acknowledge the truths of political economy and liberalism would be carried throughout the globe by impersonal missionaries more powerful than those of Christianity or Islam had ever been; a world reshaped in the image of the bourgeoisie, perhaps even one from which, eventually national differences would disappear" (Wade 1996, 61).

CHAPTER SEVEN

Political Institutions and the Economic Crisis in Thailand and Indonesia

Andrew MacIntyre

Overwhelmingly, discussion of Asia's economic crisis has been dominated by a focus on economic and especially international economic factors. Whether the malady is deemed to be inherent flaws in capitalism, limitations in the international market mechanism, the perils of global financial liberalization, or the policy prescriptions of the IMF and the U.S. Treasury, there is a remarkable convergence on international factors as the driving force behind this crisis. (See, for example, Radelet and Sachs 1998a; Johnson 1998; Wade and Veneroso 1998; Bhagwati 1998; Krugman 1998b; Feldstein 1998.) To the extent that attention has been paid to the role of domestic and political factors, it has been in terms of vague notions of crony capitalism, weak leadership, or autocratic government. I argue that although an emphasis on the economic and the international is certainly not misplaced, it is seriously incomplete. Ultimately, Asia's economic crisis was about a sudden and profound loss of confidence on the part of local and foreign investors. Underlying this essay is a belief that the collapse of confidence was a function of investor calculations not only about the likely behavior of other investors, but also about how particular countries' governments would respond to the unfolding crisis.

When diverse countries are hit by economic crisis at the same time, it would be foolish to suggest that there were not some powerful common factors at work. We know, for instance, that engagement with the global financial system was a critical factor. Vietnam and China both have deep and systemic problems in their banking sectors, but they were much less hurt by the crisis because their financial systems were only partially opened up to international capital flows. Deep financial liberalization was a precondition for this crisis. In the context of the highly liquid global financial markets of the 1990s, financial liberalization permitted the massive inflow of mostly short-term foreign capital that fueled the growth of foreign debt and then created such havoc when it departed even faster than it came. We

143

can quickly add to this the potential perils of sustained de facto fixed exchange rates at a time of a yen-dollar realignment and declining local competitiveness—both because this promoted overvaluation of exchange rates, which contributed to the initial sell-off of currencies, and because it discouraged borrowers from insuring against currency fluctuations, leaving them very exposed when a major depreciation hit.[1]

In Thailand and Indonesia, we can see these and other problems, such as widespread bad debt among local financial institutions, combining to create serious vulnerabilities. Once a major depreciation was triggered, a serious economic crisis was unavoidable; a vicious cycle of capital flight, falling exchange rates, and loan defaults took hold. But that does not mean that these two countries were inevitably doomed to suffer a massive economic contraction—in Indonesia's case, apparently the most dramatic economic reversal anywhere since World War II. Governments can respond to economic crises in more effective or less effective ways. Once we recognize this, then the role of local politics in contributing to the crisis is inescapable. The popular wisdom in both Thailand and Indonesia is that the incumbent governments were responsible for making matters much worse. I argue that the popular wisdom is not wrong—governments in both Thailand and Indonesia did greatly compound the economic damage by exacerbating the underlying problem of investor confidence—and that the key to government mishandling in these two cases lay in the political structure, the institutional configuration, of each country. But the institutional features that caused both governments to make matters worse were very different; Thailand's political problems were not Indonesia's political problems.

In this essay, I begin by briefly outlining the theoretical literature on which I draw and setting up a simple juxtaposition between problems of policy "decisiveness" on one hand, and problems of policy "predictability" on the other. Strong manifestations of either condition can produce undesirable policy outcomes for investors, and while the conditions themselves are not strictly antonymous, the institutional conditions that underpin them are polar opposites. I then turn to specific cases—Thailand and Indonesia—but I do not retrace the ground already covered by others in more synoptic accounts of the crisis in Thailand, Indonesia, and Southeast Asia more generally.[2] My aim is *not* to present a comprehensive account of the crisis in these two countries, but, more narrowly, to explore the impact of political structure, foregoing breadth and completeness of explanation in favor of depth, to highlight the importance of local institutions. For Thailand, where indecisiveness was the problem, I focus on one key policy variable, financial sector restructuring, and trace it through the leadup to the crisis and the crisis itself to highlight the way in which repeated policy paralysis played a partially catalytic role in the outbreak of the crisis and then served to delay stabilization and recovery. By contrast, in Indonesia the core political problem was the increasingly unpredictable policy of the government. Accordingly, rather than focus on a single policy issue, I cast the net wider in my discussion of Indonesia to demonstrate that this problem afflicted policy initiatives across the spectrum.

Political Institutions and Economic Governance

Within the broad institutionalist literature pertaining to political economy, two separate but strong theoretical currents stand out. Reduced to their essences, one focuses on decisiveness of policy action and the other on the predictability of the policy environment. Both have important consequences for economic policy making and economic performance. The former is concerned with the extent to which political institutions promote qualities, such as efficiency in policy making and implementation or the ability to make and carry out difficult but necessary policy decisions in a timely fashion. The literature concerned with state "autonomy," "capacity," and "strength" falls into this category (see, for example, Katzenstein 1978; Johnson 1982; Haggard 1990; Wade 1990; Doner 1992; MacIntyre 1994; Hutchcroft 1998a). This macroinstitutionalist literature relates directly to the experiences of the high-growth economies of Asia in the 1970s and 1980s. A logically parallel body of literature, also examining the role of political decisiveness, has been concerned with the efficiency of political institutions in advanced industrial democracies, but rather than being pitched at a macro level (the state), this literature has a tighter focus on the consequences of variables, such as the division of governmental powers, the type of electoral system, and bureaucratic delegation for policy making (see Weaver and Rockman 1993; Moe and Caldwell 1994; Kiewiet and McCubbins 1991; Shugart and Carey 1992; Tsebelis 1995; Haggard and McCubbins forthcoming).

This diverse literature is united by its attention to the way in which institutional design can facilitate or hinder decisiveness in the policy process, on the one hand, and its attention to the way in which decisiveness can facilitate economic policy management, on the other. For instance, a polity in which there is a separation of powers between the executive, legislative, and judicial branches; in which the legislature is separated into two houses; in which the electoral system encourages either weak party identification on the part of legislators or perhaps multipartyism; in which bureaucrats are accountable to both the executive and legislative branches; and in which subnational governments have significant economic powers is likely to respond much less rapidly and decisively to an economic policy problem than one in which veto points are fewer and authority is more concentrated.

In contrast to this broad literature pertaining to decisiveness, the literature dealing with what I refer to here as *policy predictability* (or the credibility of policy commitments), has had almost the opposite preoccupation. Instead of perceiving executive autonomy and institutionally rooted decisiveness in policy making as a boon, this second approach views it as a problem. A number of influential studies have argued that it is firm institutional *constraints* on leaders that were critical in solidifying property rights and thus permitting the expansion of investment and growth in Europe (North 1981; Weingast 1995; Root 1989), in Asia (Root 1996; Montinola, Qian, and Weingast 1995), and cross-nationally in the telecommunications sector (Cowhey 1993; Levy and Spiller 1996).

In this context, policy predictability essentially refers to the confidence among investors that the government will adhere to its commitments. Precisely the same institutional conditions that permit a leader to make difficult but economically necessary decisions can, just as readily, permit a leader to make arbitrary, erratic, and even predatory decisions that undermine investor confidence and thus economic growth. If leaders are subject to little or no institutional constraint, their policy promises can have little credibility, and investors therefore cannot be confident that the policy environment will not change quickly in ways that erode or eliminate their profits. If the policy environment is subject to frequent, unforeseen change, investment becomes very hazardous. In this view, what is needed above all else for robust economic growth to emerge and be sustained is for private investors to feel confident that the policy commitments leaders make are credible, and this is most likely to happen if leaders must first obtain the cooperation or approval of other institutions, such as a legislature, a second chamber, an independent regulatory agency, or subnational units of government. The more veto points—the more individual institutions that must agree to a course of policy action for it to proceed—the more likely that course of policy action is to stick, because the process of reversing agreement on it will also be that much more difficult.

The theoretical arguments pertaining to both decisiveness and predictability are supported by powerful logics and substantial empirical evidence. And yet, clearly, there is a tension between the two—even if it is a tension that is seldom discussed. Indeed, in many respects the two literatures talk past each other unsatisfactorily. Whereas the concepts of decisiveness and predictability are not mutually exclusive, their enabling institutional foundations are. The more widely veto authority is dispersed, the more predictable the policy environment becomes, but the less able government is to respond to pressing problems, and vice versa. Decisiveness and predictability are provided in varying degrees depending, in large measure, on the underlying institutional framework. A severe shortage of either can be very destructive to investor confidence. I argue that Thailand's and Indonesia's ways of handling the economic crisis illustrate the perils of extreme cases of either condition. Thailand's political system tended to produce great policy stability, to the point of paralysis, because change was extremely difficult to bring about in an institutional framework antithetical to decisiveness. By contrast, Indonesia's political system had little in the way of institutional constraints on executive action and was extremely decisive, but it always carried the risk of policy uncertainty for precisely that reason. For different reasons, then, the damage caused by economic crisis was amplified in both Thailand and Indonesia beyond what might otherwise have occurred once capital was withdrawn and the exchange falls were triggered. In the case of Thailand, the institutional framework contributed directly to the outbreak of the crisis.

Thailand

As Thailand sank further and further into economic difficulty throughout 1997, the recently elected government, led by Chavalit Yongchaiyudh, was subject to mounting vilification for immobilism, indecisiveness, and corruption. Justified as these criticisms were, they were nothing new. Chavalit's government was not *unusually* incompetent, divided, or corrupt. With some slight differences from one to the next, this broad characterization applies to all fully elected governments in Thailand. The governments led by Banharn Silapa-archa, Chuan Leekpai, and Chatichai Choonhavan suffered from similar problems. All these governments were afflicted by serious and ongoing corruption scandals, rested on very shaky multiparty coalition arrangements, and implemented very little in the way of major economic reform.

The strong rate of economic growth enjoyed by Thailand from the late 1980s through the mid-1990s owes very little to policy initiatives by any of these governments. Rather, it was the two brief post-coup caretaker administrations led by the highly technocratic Anand Panyarachun that were the policy innovators in the 1990s. Anand, unelected and not a career politician, and the team working with him were subject to few of the normal constraints of Thai governments. Before this, one has to go back to the semidemocratic period in the early and mid-1980s under the unelected field marshal Prem Tinsulanond to find much major economic policy reform. And even then, it was confined largely to core areas of macroeconomic policy that were shielded by Prem from the fluid, rent-seeking imperatives of the political parties that controlled most sectorial and microeconomic policy issues (Doner and Laothamatas 1994).

This is *not* an argument that economic governance in Thailand has declined with democratization; rather, it is an argument that the *particular* institutional configuration Thailand had in place (until the constitutional overhaul in late 1997) was bound to produce serious problems of policy management and political leadership. Chavalit's government was no more venal or inept than its predecessors; indeed, part of the difficulty it faced was the accumulated legacy of reforms not made by previous administrations.

The indecisiveness of political leadership in Thailand was a function of the fragmentation of the party system and the tendency toward weak coalition governments. With parliamentary majorities composed of approximately six parties, each with its own internal weaknesses, cabinet instability was a chronic problem. Party leaders were always vulnerable to defections by factions and individuals within their own parties who could find better prospects for advancement in another party. And the prime minister, as leader of the governing coalition, was always vulnerable to policy blackmail by coalition partners threatening to defect in pursuit of better deals in another alliance configuration. This was the key political dynamic of coalition government in Thailand. Indeed, all democratically elected governments, except the Chatichai government, which fell to a military coup, met their ends in this fashion. With weak coalitions and parties, strong action on difficult public goods–oriented policy issues—whether exchange rate management or Bangkok's notorious traffic congestion—was always severely undersupplied.

The institutional root of these problems was Thailand's combination of a parliamentary structure (in which government rests on party cohesion) and a multimember electoral system (which undermined party cohesion). As Allen Hicken

(1998) has argued in important new research, Thailand's multimember electoral system strongly encouraged candidates to campaign on the basis of individualized strategies (rather than on the basis of party label), as they were compelled to differentiate themselves from competitors of the same party. Not only did this create weakly disciplined parties, but the emphasis on candidate-based rather than party-based electoral strategies also ensured that politicians would strive to deliver selective benefits to voters in their electorate to differentiate themselves from rivals from the same party (Cox and McCubbins 2000). This system encouraged vote buying and placed a premium on a politician's ability to generate a flow of cash to cover costs while in office. In short, the logic of the country's electoral system made it all but impossible for politicians to agree to economic reforms if such reforms threatened rent-taking arrangements they had put in place for themselves or their key supporters.

But let us turn from this general discussion of how Thailand's political institutions constrain policy making to focus on the crisis. To this end, I trace the government's handling of one policy variable—restructuring of Thailand's ailing financial sector—through the lead-up period and the course of the crisis. I focus on this issue because it was clearly central to the crisis[3] and, more important, because it provides a very useful window through which to view the way that the country's political institutions constrained policy making, thus helping to create the policy problems in the first place, and then compounded the loss of market confidence as the crisis unfolded.

Thailand's financial sector began to expand rapidly with the beginning of the process of financial liberalization in the late 1980s. An important part of this process was the creation of the Bangkok International Banking Facility in 1993, which was intended to launch Bangkok as an international financial center but in practice functioned to facilitate greatly the inflow of capital from foreign lenders to Thai financial institutions and real-sector companies. With hindsight, it is easy to see that one of Thailand's biggest weaknesses (as in a number of countries in the region) was the liberalization of financial markets with inadequate oversight or prudential regulation. By the second half of 1997, Thailand was beset with an estimated Bt1 trillion in bad debts held by banks and finance companies, and the government had spent an estimated Bt430 billion in propping up failing financial institutions (roughly US$28.6 billion and US$12.3 billion, respectively) (*Bangkok Post* 14 August 1997, 12 October 1997).

Early warning signs of the problems and malpractices in financial institutions came as early as 1994, when the Bank of Thailand (the central bank) began to examine the affairs of a struggling mid-sized bank, the BBC. Rolling over several years, the BBC scandal is widely regarded as one of the early and important dents in business confidence in Thailand and in the reputation of the central bank.[4] More important for our purposes, however, is what this saga reveals about the political constraints of financial-sector management in Thailand.

After becoming concerned about the situation at BBC, the Bank of Thailand failed in its clumsy efforts to gain supervisory representation on BBC's board. As the extent of mismanagement at BBC and its estimated US$3 billion in nonperforming loans became public in mid-1996 after disclosure by the opposition, there was a run on the bank. Having indulged BBC for an extraordinary period, the central bank finally stepped in forcefully in May 1994, taking formal control of BBC as it crashed and its management fled. Ultimately, a total of US$7 billion was spent to keep BBC afloat. The central bank governor was forced to resign in disgrace over the episode, but the damage to the central bank's reputation had been done. In addition to any possible impropriety on the part of the central bank governor, suspicion was directed to several politicians within Prime Minister Banharn's Chart Thai party, who, it emerged, had been the beneficiaries of large loans from BBC (*Nation* 13 March 1997, 18 April 1997; Pasuk and Baker 1998a).

In September, Banharn's government collapsed when key coalition partners deserted him. After what was widely regarded as the country's dirtiest election (with an estimated US$1 billion handed out to buy votes), and having benefited from large-scale defections from Banharn's Chart Thai party, Chavalit's New Aspiration Party narrowly emerged as the largest party in the parliament and proceeded to construct a six-party coalition comprising many of the parties from the previous government. Notwithstanding the massive vote buying on behalf of his New Aspiration Party (*FEER* 28 November 1996, 16–22), Chavalit entered government with perhaps the most promising credentials for policy action of any elected Thai government. Chavalit himself had strong military links, support from big business, and a reputation as a skillful politician. Banharn's government (of which Chavalit had been part) was widely regarded as inept and hopelessly corrupt and was blamed for presiding over the country's sagging economic fortunes. Chavalit, by contrast, declared his cabinet would be built around a so-called economic dream team. But although three respected technocrats were appointed to key ministries (most notably, Amnuay Viruwan as finance minister), the logic of Thailand's political structure very quickly reasserted itself.

The BBC saga came to life again when it emerged that criminal charges against several BBC executives had lapsed because Bank of Thailand officials had failed to act before the statute of limitations came into play in early 1997. Chavalit ordered the suspension of a deputy governor at the central bank and several other senior officials over the affair, but this did little to conceal the fact that politicians who were now members of his party maintained strong links to BBC. Problems in the Thai financial sector—and the government's inability to deal with them effectively—ran much broader and deeper than just BBC. Indeed, the area of greatest concern was not the banks themselves, but the finance companies. The country's fifteen banks dominated the financial sector, but, with entry by new banks tightly limited, finance companies came to play an increasingly prominent role in the 1990s. By the end of 1996, Thailand's ninety-one finance companies (twenty-five were pure finance companies, and sixty-six performed both finance and securities functions) accounted for nearly 25 percent of total credit (EIU 1998, 31, 50). By the beginning of 1997, their difficulties were also coming rapidly to a head as long-smoldering problems of nonperforming loans were suddenly whipped into a blaze.

Several interrelated factors came together here: the end of a prolonged property boom in late 1996 (real estate was the core collateral for much of the borrowing), mounting nervousness about the currency in the face of repeated speculative attacks, and higher interest rates designed to help support the currency and dampen inflationary pressures.

On 5 February 1997, the first Thai company (Somprasong) defaulted on a foreign loan repayment. Then, late in the month, it was suddenly announced that the largest of the finance companies, Finance One, was seeking a merger with a bank to stave off collapse. In the face of widespread fears of an impending financial implosion and the beginnings of hurried depositor withdrawals, all attention rapidly focused on the government's response to the situation. In a joint move on 3 March, finance minister Amnuay and central bank governor Rerngchai Marakanond suspended trading of financial-sector shares on the stock exchange and went on national television to announce a series of emergency measures designed to reassure nervous markets. The two key elements of the policy intervention were a requirement that all banks and finance companies make much stronger provision for bad debt and an announcement that ten of the weakest financial companies would have to raise their capital base within sixty days.

These measures did little to reassure markets, and when trading resumed the following day (4 March), financial shares fell heavily amidst reports of a rush to withdraw funds. Underlying continuing market nervousness were doubts about the government's ability to follow through with its restructuring plans. Such fears proved well founded. No sooner had Amnuay and Rerngchai targeted the ten ailing finance companies than a familiar political dynamic reemerged—the plan encountered heavy resistance from within the government. Several senior members of Chart Pattana, the second-largest party in the coalition, had controlling interests in some of the ten targeted institutions. Not only did they succeed in vetoing the plan and ensuring that no action was taken against the ten companies, but the fact that they were permitted to remain open meant that—as with BBC—the central bank had to pump in large sums of new capital to keep them afloat in the face of runs by panicked investors.

This was a critical juncture in the development of the crisis in Thailand. There was a clear and pressing need for effective government action with widespread concern among Thai and foreign investors about the scale of the bad-debt problem in the financial sector. At the same time, the currency was coming under mounting pressure, with money market players sensing exchange rate vulnerability. Amnuay and Rerngchai did not dare pursue the strict path favored by financial hawks: forcing shareholders to accept big losses by allowing ailing institutions to fail, or permitting foreign investors to take a controlling stake in these institutions. However, even the intermediate path they opted for—lifting capital adequacy provisions and singling out the weakest institutions for immediate attention—proved politically unattainable. These initiatives failed not because they were blocked by popular outcry or parliamentary opposition, but because they were, in effect, vetoed by other members of the ruling coalition. Rather than risking the collapse of his new government by alienating Chart Pattana, Chavalit preferred to gamble on compromise and delaying measures.

The finance minister's inability to follow through on even the moderate plans he had outlined had a very corrosive effect on investor confidence. In addition, there were high objective costs to deferring action: one side effect of injecting large-scale emergency funding into the ten failing finance companies was blowing out the money supply (by 10 percent in the month of June alone). This served only to sharpen the fundamental contradiction in the government's overall macroeconomic position. At the same time that it was pumping money into insolvent finance companies to keep them afloat, the central bank was also spending down reserves to prop up the exchange rate. As was increasingly recognized by markets, this was not a sustainable strategy. In the middle of May, the baht suffered its heaviest assault, but by this time it was no longer just big Thai companies and foreign investors that were betting against the baht—middle class Thais were also increasingly moving to U.S. dollars (Ammar 1997, 2).

Frustrated by his inability to persuade the coalition's leaders in cabinet to move on more extensive financial sector reforms (as well as on other fronts, such as cutting more pork from the budget), Amnuay resigned from the government on nineteen June. The leader of the government's technocratic dream team had lasted just seven months in office. With a few exceptions, his attempts at major reform had been blocked by other parties within the government, so otherwise promising initiatives never went anywhere. As one minister lamented, "To solve economic problems we cannot simply announce economic measures, we have to follow up on their progress." (*FEER* 29 May 1997, 15). But of course this was the problem; with a diverse coalition and all parties having incurred massive debts to win office, there was little prospect of the cabinet's agreeing to take tough measures that might hurt the economic interests of ministers or those of their financial benefactors. Even if a majority was in favor of taking action, a minority who were prepared to play hardball could veto the action by threatening to walk out of the coalition.

After struggling to find a prominent figure who would accept the post of finance minister, Chavalit offered it to Thanong Bidaya, the head of the Thai Military Bank. Thanong faired little better than Amnuay. Seeking to seize the initiative, on 27 June he announced the suspension of sixteen finance companies (including seven of the original ten), giving them thirty days to implement merger plans. With the central bank no longer able to sustain the exchange rate, five days later, on 2 July, it was announced that the baht was being cut loose. The baht immediately fell sharply, depreciating by 17 percent.

In his efforts to push financial restructuring, Thanong stumbled on the same obstacle as Amnuay: although he had won approval for the announcement, Chart Pattana leaders were again able to block the implementation of the initiative. Not only did Chart Pattana succeed in preventing the closure or forced merger of the sixteen finance companies, it also managed to persuade the central bank to continue injecting large sums of capital. In late July, in the context of negotiations with the IMF to obtain a rescue package, it was revealed that loans to the sixteen finance companies now totaled a staggering Bt430 billion. (This figure exceeded the actual capital funds of the finance companies themselves and corresponded to approximately 10 percent of GDP.) The government naturally sought to downplay its own direct involvement in this scandal and instead forced the resignation of central bank governor Rerngchai, as well as another senior and respected official (*Bangkok Post* 14 August 1997).

A week later, on 5 August, in an effort to regain the initiative and satisfy IMF demands for policy commitment, the new finance minister, Thanong, announced that an additional forty-two finance companies would be suspended because of the scale of their loan problems and imminent insolvency. A total of fifty-eight, or two-thirds of the country's finance companies, had now been suspended. Like the earlier sixteen, this batch was given a short period in which to meet tough new capital adequacy rules, merge with a stronger institution, or go out of business.[5] Continuing the effort to clean up the financial sector under the terms of the agreement with the IMF, Virabhongsa Ramangkura, a respected technocrat newly appointed as deputy prime minister in a hurried cabinet reshuffle in mid-August, replaced the official in charge of the committee established to vet rescue plans of the suspended finance companies. In his place, he installed Amaret Sila-on, the respected head of the Thai Stock Exchange, in an effort to counter reports of corruption and malpractice in the committee's operations (*Bangkok Post* 26 August 1997).

But as one section of the government was moving to force an overhaul of the financial sector, another was moving in precisely the opposite direction. The pattern was familiar, and the prime minister was powerless to resolve the tension. As one senior Thai business commentator put it, "What investors are worried about is political interference in the implementation of the measures, something that we have seen over the past two to three years, where previous attempts to address the problems have failed because of political interference" (*Bangkok Post* 15 October 1997). With the deadline for deciding the fate of the suspended finance companies looming, the politics intensified in early October. The Association of Finance Companies vigorously courted Chart Pattana leader Chatichai, as well as prime minister Chavalit, seeking a relaxation of the criteria for their rehabilitation. The IMF responded by publicly expressing concern that the independence of Amaret's screening committee not be undermined. Nevertheless, a week later Amaret resigned, after only a short tenure, declaring that he was being undercut by forces within the government (*Bangkok Post* 12 October 1997).

Further concessions were soon made to Chart Pattana and the finance companies when, at the same time that he announced the creation of two new independent agencies to handle the evaluation and processing of the finance companies, Thanong revealed that the deadline for their restructuring would now be extended (without a new date being set) and that loans earlier extended to the ailing finance companies by the central bank could be treated as equity—thus opening the probability that the public resources injected into these companies would never be recovered (*Bangkok Post* 14 October 1997). And in another successful rear-guard move, Chart Pattana succeeded in holding up the approval by the cabinet of the plans for the two new agencies announced by Thanong until text was inserted in the decrees specifically reversing their independence from the government (EIU 1998, 13).

By this stage however, the political situation was in a state of collapse. On 19 October, finance minister Thanong resigned over the reversal of a petrol tax a mere three days after it had been announced as part of the government's very long-awaited policy response to the IMF bailout. And in the wake of maneuvering in preparation for the formation of an expected new government led by Chart Pattana and impending defections in Chavalit's own party, the crippled prime minister announced his resignation on 3 November 1997. Thailand was in deep disarray.

My focus here has been on a single, albeit key, issue: restructuring of the financial sector. Many other issues would have yielded a similar picture (e.g., the process of designing and approving the new constitution or fiscal management). The fundamental proposition here is straightforward. Thailand's combination of a parliamentary structure with multiple weak parties (linked to the electoral system) meant that policy making was bound to be particularly indecisive. This was not a function of the character of particular personalities or the combination of interests represented in Chavalit's government; the same pattern applied in previous governments. Under this political structure, party and faction leaders were compelled to work assiduously to generate resources to hold their members together, and prime ministers had to struggle to keep their coalitions together. This meant that there were numerous veto players within the government, and it is scarcely surprising that major policy initiatives of any sort were extraordinarily difficult to undertake.

The paralysis of Thai politics had clear institutional roots. It takes little imagination to recognize how ill equipped this system was either to head off the mounting economic problems in the country in the lead-up to the fall of the currency or to manage and contain the situation once capital started rushing out. In addition to straightforward policy paralysis, the constant turnover of key personnel in this highly fluid system did little to engender investor confidence. Chavalit's government endured for twelve months and experienced three cabinet reshuffles, three finance ministers, and two central bank governors.

To summarize, then, we can see Thailand's political structure exerting a powerful negative influence over the economic policy environment—an influence that allowed serious economic problems to accumulate, thus helping to set the stage for the currency crisis and the rapid outflow of capital. We can see the same effect heightening the economic destruction suffered by Thailand once the crisis broke because of the inability of government to respond to the situation in a timely or effective manner. It is difficult to believe—especially in the context of widespread uncertainty and even panic—that this systemic governmental incapacity was not a major source of discouragement to local and foreign investors. A focus only on international economic factors misses all of this.

Drawing back from the dynamics of the crisis itself, if we take a broader view of what was happening in Thailand in 1997, it is clear that it was not only investors who despaired of Thailand's political system. Widespread public disillusionment with the system and its alarming impotence in the face of the crisis propelled the introduction of dramatic constitutional change in the latter part of 1997. This is not the place to discuss those changes, but it is worth noting that along with deep and widespread economic hardship, Thailand's economic crisis has also given birth to a new political system.

Indonesia

The political economy of Indonesia's stunning economic reversal in 1997–98 differed from that in Thailand in important ways. To be sure, there were some key shared vulnerabilities: open financial systems with weak prudential oversight; an effectively fixed exchange rate[6]; and large and rapid inflows of foreign capital, most notably short-term debt. As in Thailand, the coexistence of these conditions meant that as the currency came under pressure—in Indonesia's case, because of contagion—the economy was dangerously vulnerable. Thus, we saw the same vicious cycle at work: as short-term capital initially moved out in self-fulfilling anticipation of an exchange rate depreciation, the currency dropped and quickly created serious problems for borrowers holding unhedged foreign loans. The scramble to buy dollars by these borrowers pushed the exchange rate down further, making debt repayment even more difficult and raising the specter of nonrepayment of loans. As this caused more capital to leave and the currency to fall lower still, defaulting on foreign debt became a reality.

But there were also important differences. Many observers have pointed out that the key features of Indonesia's macroeconomy were in much better shape than Thailand's. As Hal Hill (1998, 8) put it: "almost every technical economic indicator looked safe." Inflation was moderate; although substantial, the current account deficit to GDP ratio was less than one-half that of Thailand; there was no major bubble economy effect as in Thailand (and elsewhere); and there had been no telltale sharp outflow of capital or sustained decline in the stock market before the crisis. Much less remarked upon, however, is the fact that problems in the financial sector did not play the leading role they did in Thailand (or Korea). To be sure, Indonesia's financial sector suffered from very serious weaknesses, and these did indeed compound the country's economic problems as the crisis took hold. But this was a less critical factor than in Thailand (and certainly Korea), because most of the corporate debt in Indonesia was *not* held by Indonesian banks, but by foreign banks. With a longer history of open financial markets, Indonesian companies had borrowed directly from foreign banks (both offshore and onshore). Consequently, although the solvency of the Indonesian banking system certainly became an issue, this was not where the crisis started. In Indonesia, the crisis backed into the financial sector from the real sector, rather than the other way around.

More important for the purposes of this paper than these economic contrasts are the differences in the political circumstances of the two countries. Although I argue that politics played a critical role in undermining investor confidence and intensifying the economic damage in both countries, in Indonesia this happened in a different way, for different reasons, with different timing, and ultimately with even more devastating consequences. If the basic political problem in Thailand was that the institutional framework produced hopelessly divided and thus indecisive government (of all coalitional complexions), in Indonesia, the problem was that the institutional framework imposed no constraints on executive action—thus opening the way for erratic policy behavior.[7] Not only was Indonesia's political system not democratic, it also provided for an extraordinary centralization of decision-making authority in the presidency. Quite simply, no other institution or collection of political actors had the ability to veto the implementation of the president's policy preferences or to initiate alternative policies (MacIntyre 1999).

Although it certainly produced a highly decisive policy process, such a central-ized political structure gave rise to potential problems of policy unpredictability. I argue that the unfettered power of the presidency and the resulting uncertainty about his policy commitments was highly destructive of investor confidence in the context of a regionwide economic crisis. With no institutional checks on his power and no effective mechanism for replacing him as leader—short of political upheaval—the only option open to investors, as the value of their assets continued to plummet, was exit. As local and foreign investors pulled their capital out and the economy went into a tailspin, it was only a matter of time before the resulting eco-nomic dislocation and pain produced a political backlash strong enough to force President Suharto's fall. But with such a firmly entrenched authoritarian regime, this did not happen quickly, and thus the process of economic hemorrhaging went on for much longer than in Thailand.

Before I elaborate on this argument, it is necessary to pause and address a seem-ing contradiction: if Indonesia's massively centralized political system under Suharto was inimical to investor confidence, how is it that there were thirty years of strong investment and sustained economic growth? Given that the country's political framework was much the same in 1987 as in 1977, how can it have sud-denly become a critical problem in late 1997? I argue elsewhere (MacIntyre forth-coming) that for much of the past three decades there have been factors in place that mitigated the credibility problem inherent in the political system. Briefly, the key points here are that Indonesia offered very strong rates of return, that it had a demonstrated record of reasonably sound macroeconomic management, and, importantly, that from very early on the government effectively imposed a policy constraint on its own behavior in the form of an open capital account.[8] Together, these factors served to ease the problem of policy predictability and nurture investor confidence. In seeking to illustrate my argument about the impact of polit-ical institutions on Indonesia's handling of the economic crisis, rather than tracing a particular policy issue through the crisis as I did for Thailand, I broaden the focus to capture the scope of the policy unpredictability that opened up in Indonesia in the latter part of 1997.

When exchange rate uncertainty spread to Indonesia's shores in late July 1997, investors fully expected the country to weather the storm. Not only were the eco-nomic fundamentals apparently stronger in Indonesia, but unlike Thailand,

Indonesia had a political framework in which the leadership was more than capable of taking decisive policy action in the face of economic shocks. Although Indonesia was, of course, notorious for rent-seeking practices and cronyism, if pressed by economic crisis, the government had an established track record of moving to implement tough policy measures to restore investor confidence—including measures that involved setbacks to the interests of allied business groups. This had been initially demonstrated in the late 1960s, and then, as the regime took shape, in the mid-1970s in the wake of the huge debt problem created by the state oil company; in the early 1980s as oil prices began to fall; and then again in the mid-1980s as the country was squeezed by a severe balance-of-payments crisis. And, indeed, this is how the government seemed to behave at the outset of the 1997 crisis.

Whereas Thailand spent down billions in reserves in a vain defense of the currency and then moved very slowly to introduce policy reforms, Indonesia responded decisively. Nine days after the unpegging of the baht, as currency uncertainty began to spread around Southeast Asia, Jakarta moved preemptively to widen the currency band within which the rupiah traded from 8 to 12 percent. As pressures mounted in late July and early August 1997 and the central bank found itself unable to contain the rupiah within this band, it cut the currency free rather than enter a costly and vain defense. And then, as the exchange rate continued to slide and uncertainty spread from currency markets to capital markets, the government moved to launch a series of reform measures designed to shore up market confidence by demonstrating its preparedness to deliver the policy goods.

Suharto was giving off all the right signals. His independence day speech in mid-August was notable for its sober assessment of the problems, and he set up a special crisis-management team composed of all the key technocratic ministers and placed it under the charge of widely respected former economic coordinating minister Widjojo Nitisastro. Beginning in early September, a steady stream of major reforms was unveiled. Restrictions on foreign ownership of shares in companies listed on the Jakarta Stock Exchange were lifted; cuts in public spending and new taxes on luxury goods to preserve a stable fiscal position were outlined; a range of costly high-profile infrastructure projects valued at Rp38.9 trillion (US$13.3 billion) were singled out to be postponed and another batch, valued at Rp62.7 trillion (US$21.4 billion), to be reviewed; tariff cuts on an extensive range of products were introduced with a view to helping foreign exchange earnings; and the central bank signaled preparations to move against a list of struggling banks. Particularly notable was the rescheduling of the big-ticket investment projects—because many of these were representative of the excesses of the developmental boom (e.g., the world's tallest building, the world's longest bridge), and because many of them were directly linked to the president's children or to other business people closely associated with the palace. Even though some pet crony projects were not on the list (for instance, the symbolically potent, though economically trivial, national car project), there was a sense that the president had sent a clear and strong signal that he was willing to make whatever cuts were necessary to restore investor confidence and stabilize the currency, even if it meant paring back the interests of expansionist ministers in government and crony interests in the private sector.

At the same time that Prime Minister Mahathir of Indonesia was attacking Jews and foreign speculators more generally, and Chavalit was beset by resignations and policy gridlock, Suharto seemed to present a model of sober and effective leadership in the face of crisis. Suharto was widely applauded in the regional and international media for his actions. Apparently in response to these efforts, the slide in the rupiah was checked, and it held its value through September. It was impossible for Chavalit to act in this way: if he had attempted reforms of this scope, his government would have collapsed overnight. Suharto was perceived to be acting just as he had in the past when confronted by a serious economic challenge.

By early October, the rupiah was again falling. With a fresh round of regional nervousness having been triggered by Dr. Mahathir's attack on George Soros, and as the inevitable ramifications of the falling rupiah began to work further through the economy, it became apparent that—its best efforts notwithstanding—Indonesia could not deal with the crisis on its own. On 8 October, Indonesia announced it was seeking the assistance of the IMF. The decision to approach the IMF was also seen as a positive development. Just three weeks later, an agreement was signed for a US$23 billion bailout package (shortly rising to US$38 billion), and immediately the government began releasing detailed sets of reforms, beginning the implementation of the IMF agreement—in marked contrast to Thailand, which took months. The same day, 31 October, brought the announcement that controversial import monopolies on wheat, soybeans, and garlic would be abolished. On 1 November, it was announced that sixteen small banks (many controlled by relatives or cronies) were closed. On 3 November, it was announced that there would be further major tariff cuts in industries affecting crony firms, that Indonesia would abide by whatever ruling the WTO reached on its national car project, that the strategic industries of technology minister Habibie would be reviewed with a view to cost saving, and that the wholesale and distribution sector would be opened up to foreign investors.

Again, these measures were impressive both for the speed with which they came forth and for the apparent readiness of the president to allow the privileges of allied business to be cut back. However, even as the government was apparently forging vigorously ahead on these various fronts, the picture was becoming clouded. It was from about this time that Suharto started giving off decidedly mixed signals as to his real policy intentions. The effect was very corrosive. On 1 November, amidst the flurry of IMF-related initiatives, Suharto quietly signed a decree giving a green light to eight of the large investment projects postponed in September and seven of the projects subject to review. This was disturbing for a number of reasons: all of the rescued projects belonged to relatives or close cronies; some of them would have made little commercial sense under any circumstances, let alone in the midst of an economic crisis (for instance, four new power plants at a time when the power grid was coming up against serious oversupply); and, most important, the weakness of the country's political framework was highlighted—if Suharto chose to change his mind, there was nothing anyone could do about it.

On 5 November, in an extraordinary public spectacle, the president's second son, Bambang Trihatmodjo, announced that he would sue both the central bank governor and the finance minister for their decision to close his bank. On 6 November, he was joined in this action by the president's half-brother, Probosutedjo. Investors and the public at large were left to wonder what game Suharto was playing. Finance Minister Ma'rie Muhammad would not have dared to close these banks without the president's approval. Had the president changed his mind? A few days later, Ma'rie informed a parliamentary committee that the original decision would stand, thereby indicating that the president had confirmed he would not reverse the bank closures. Shortly thereafter, the lawsuits were dropped. But by 20 November, Bambang was gloating before the press that he had just taken over another small bank and would transfer all the assets of his closed bank into the new one, making a public mockery of the decision to close the bank in the first place. On 21 November, a prominent and politically connected businessman, Aburizal Bakrie, announced that Suharto had agreed that a US$5 billion loan from Singapore could be used to help struggling Indonesian firms to pay their debts. Not only did this distress the Singaporeans (who had given more to the Indonesian rescue effort than any country other than Japan and had participated in coordinated central bank efforts to support the rupiah), it also raised further questions about Suharto's commitment to the terms of the IMF agreement, under which bailouts for banks and firms had been specifically prohibited. These countervailing signals did much to undo the confidence-building effects of all the promised reforms. Not coincidentally, near this time the celebrated crisis-management team headed by Widjojo seemed to lose momentum as their ability to influence the president was called into doubt. Throughout November, then, the rupiah fell, sped on by the outbreak of serious problems in Korea.

Indonesia was entering dangerous and uncharted waters. If the president was unwilling to adhere to his policy commitments, the economy was heading for the rocks, for no other political players could delay, alter, or countermand his decisions. In December, a new element of uncertainty was introduced when Suharto's health—indeed his survival—was thrown into doubt after he was forced to take a prolonged rest from presidential duties, officially because of fatigue, unofficially because he had suffered a stroke. The rupiah fell very sharply in response to this development, and although it strengthened briefly when it was clear that he was not about to die, it continued to fall rapidly through December as investors grappled with the uncertainty of how political succession might play out. Indonesia was now in very deep trouble. By the end of 1997, the rupiah had depreciated by 54 percent (of its precrisis value)—already equaling the lowest point in Thailand. But with Suharto's leadership and commitment to giving markets the reassurances they craved now in deep question, the rupiah still had much further to travel on its way down.

In January 1998, Indonesia parted company with Thailand (and Korea) as its problems worsened dramatically. For Suharto, the situation had become terminal.

The final straw was the unveiling of the state budget on 6 January. After the heavy fall of the rupiah through December 1997, much was riding on the budget. Although given an unfair reception in some quarters, the reality was that the budget severely disappointed commentators and markets, both in Indonesia and internationally. Among other weaknesses, the budget's core assumptions about the exchange and growth were seen as quite unrealistic and seemed to suggest that the government was simply not coming to grips with the seriousness of the situation. Local and foreign currency traders pushed the rupiah sharply down to a new all-time low of 7,000 to the U.S. dollar, and then, when it was reported that continued IMF support was in doubt in the wake of the budget, the rupiah went into free fall, dropping below the previously unimagined psychological barrier of 10,000 to the dollar. Wealthy Indonesians dumped rupiah for dollars, and poorer Indonesians dumped rupiah for food staples, triggering runs on supermarkets.

As panic broke loose, other heads of government, frightened by the possible geostrategic implications of the collapse of the regime in Indonesia, hurriedly telephoned Suharto, urging conspicuous compliance with the IMF. At the same time, senior IMF and U.S. Treasury officials rushed to Jakarta and worked with key economic ministers to draw up a stunning list of structural reforms that would radically hack at remaining restricted market arrangements enjoyed by crony businesses. This was a last-ditch effort to prop up the regime's standing with investors by seeking to demonstrate a renewed commitment to making cuts where it hurt most. Although Suharto did not hesitate to sign the new agreement on 15 January, it was all too late. By this stage, his credibility with investors inside and outside Indonesia was irreparably damaged. The promise to implement a reform package of unprecedented scope failed to impress; investors continued to dump the rupiah, and its value continued to fall through January.

Some commentators at this time began to argue that the IMF's approach was either misguided, in being overly contractionary in its fiscal posture (requiring a deficit not greater than 1 percent of GDP); incomplete, in having given inadequate attention to the issue of corporate debt; or simply politically unrealistic, in requiring the government to cut back crony privileges. Still others faulted the IMF for leaking its unhappiness with the 6 January budget to the press, arguing that this undermined what might otherwise have been a viable budget. In my view, there is substance to all of these arguments, though none is compelling. While the news of the IMF's reaction to the budget no doubt affected the markets, it is unrealistic to expect that the IMF would not express a view about the budget, under the circumstances. And while it may be that Suharto never had any intention of cutting back core crony privileges, given that this was one of the key issues on which markets were focusing in terms of the government's commitment to promoting microeconomic efficiency and export competitiveness, any program that did not include major reforms of this sort would have been instantly dismissed. More difficult to set aside, in my judgment, are the claims that the IMF's requirements were too fiscally austere and that the absence of measures to tackle the corporate debt issue constituted a gaping hole in the overall economic strategy. Nonetheless, in each case powerful complications attended any attempt to behave differently: what would have been the reaction of the U.S. Congress if the IMF was seen to be involved in bailing out "crony capitalists" in Indonesia? And though the Sachs critique of fiscal overkill has found significant support in the ensuing months, it is far from clear that markets in early January would have reacted favorably to expansionary budget settings. Indeed, part of the problem with the January 6 budget was that it was interpreted (mistakenly) by some market analysts as expansionary.

The simple reality is that there were no good economic options left for the Indonesian government by January 1998. And more fundamentally, regardless of the economic strategy the government had said it would pursue, Suharto's policy commitments were no longer of any value to the market. It no longer mattered what he said. The institutionally rooted problem of policy unpredictability that had always been embedded in the political framework of his regime had now been completely exposed. The factors that had in the past helped to ease the inevitable concerns of investors about policy reversals and predictability—strong rates of return, a solid macroeconomic track record, and the discipline of an open capital account—were all now swept away in these catastrophic circumstances. Investors were left with the stark reality that there could be no confidence in a regime in which there were no constraints on presidential power; the president could—and did—reverse earlier commitments almost as fast as he made them.

From this point on, the Indonesian economy quickly ground down. As January progressed, the rupiah continued to fall, reaching as low as 17,000 to the dollar at one point. With the currency having depreciated by as much as 86 percent since the outbreak of the crisis, the formal economy could no longer function. With firms needing three, four, or even five times as many rupiah as before the crisis to service their dollar-denominated loans, repayments simply stopped, even for the healthiest of firms. The domestic banking system was by now at the brink of systemic insolvency. All local lending had stopped. Trade fell rapidly as imported goods became prohibitively expensive, but many exports suffered as well, because international banks declined to open letters of credit with Indonesian firms. Inflation had begun to accelerate rapidly, and as firms began to cut back operations or simply close down, unemployment accelerated too.

As was by now widely recognized, the nature of Indonesia's problems had changed: the crisis had shifted and was as much political as economic. Suharto had become a fundamental obstacle to revival. The economy could not recover until the exchange rate recovered; the exchange rate could not recover until local and foreign investors brought capital back into the country; and this would not happen until investors again had some confidence in the direction of government policy and leadership. Suharto did nothing to help the situation. His decision in late January to nominate technology czar B. J. Habibie as his vice-presidential running mate panicked the markets, as did his decision to fire the governor of the central bank for his resistance to Suharto's flirtation with the idea of a currency board. As one businessman put it in early 1998, "The problem is he doesn't seem to listen to anyone any more. A feeling of helplessness prevails. You can't do anything any more. Some mid-level businessmen with a few million dollars have left the country because they think social unrest is unavoidable" (*FEER* 22 January 1998, 16). And as an Indonesian political commentator delicately put it, "There's been a real change in his political behavior. These are not normal times. We have to try and understand him and why he is thinking in such a different way" (*FEER* 26 February 1998, 14).

With Suharto's credibility terminally damaged, there was little prospect for a recovery while he remained in power. But since President Suharto effectively controlled the presidential selection process and enjoyed firm control of the military, there was not yet any prospect of replacing him. What followed was a waiting process, while rapidly rising economic hardship and dislocation generated mounting protests, violence, and elite disaffection. Finally, in late May, abandoned by almost all his supporters, Suharto stepped down amid a sea of violence and destruction.

The impact of politics on Indonesia's economic crisis is striking. There was nothing in the country's economic profile or its linkages to the global economy that would have led one to expect such massive devaluation. (Indeed, some would argue that, were it not for the contagion effect spreading currency pressures from Thailand, there was no economic reason to expect a major shakeout in Indonesia.) It is not possible to understand why Indonesia's economic reversal was *so* extensive without reference to the political situation. Rather than focusing on crony links or on the fact that Suharto was an aging, ailing, and out-of-touch autocrat, I argue that the key to understanding the utter rout of investor confidence was the political structure. The same institutional structure that had permitted the government to respond so decisively to earlier economic crises—and indeed to the initial stages of this one—proved a devastating liability once local and foreign investors concluded that Suharto could no longer be counted on to deliver the policy environment demanded by the market. Extreme decisiveness comes at the price of a highly changeable policy environment. And with the open capital account constraint now overrun by the currency crisis, there were no institutional checks at all on executive action. Suharto was in such a powerful position that it would be extremely difficult to dislodge him, and this compounded the problem. Thus, as Thailand and Korea began to stabilize in the first half of 1998, Indonesia went from bad to worse.

Conclusion

The economic crises in Thailand and Indonesia are part of a wider regional and global economic phenomenon. There are crucial shared characteristics in the severe economic problems they and other countries have experienced. However, this is not *just* a story of the perils of being exposed to fluctuating global capital flows. To complete the picture—to understand the variation across cases—we need to see how local politics played into the collapse of investor confidence. In the cases I have explored, it is local political structure that stands out as the intervening variable. I have argued that in Thailand and Indonesia we can see political structure prolonging the crisis and thus intensifying the economic destruction. Additionally, in the case of Thailand, we can see local political structure contributing directly to the initial outbreak of investor loss of confidence, a loss that then swept the region.

The nature of the institutional problems in Thailand and in Indonesia was quite different, and they played through in different ways, although they ultimately produced similar outcomes—a massive loss of investor confidence. Whereas Thailand suffered policy paralysis as a result of weak multiparty parliamentary government, Indonesia suffered from almost the opposite set of institutional circumstances—massive centralization of power that left government vulnerable to deep problems of credibility due to unreliable policy commitments. Thailand's system of government suffered from too many veto points, and Indonesia's suffered from too few.

My basic purpose in this paper has been to argue the importance of political institutions as an essential supplement to international economic factors in explaining the crisis in these two countries. Of course the crisis was a product of *much* more than political structure; my claim is simply that political structure cannot be left out of the story for Thailand and Indonesia. Further, it should be emphasized, I am not proposing that there is some optimal institutional configuration that would enable any given country to escape a major economic crisis of this sort unscathed. Although an optimal institutional configuration is, in principle, a logical possibility, I have no basis for such a claim here (nor, indeed, is there consensus on this even in the theoretical literature). The core claim advanced here is more cautious: severe cases of either indecisiveness or unpredictability are invitations to a serious loss of investor confidence. More broadly, whether the institutional framework one favors makes it hard or easy to change policy depends on whether one favors the existing policy environment. The economic crisis of 1997–98 required governments to be able to move swiftly in implementing difficult policy changes and then to be able to sustain them in the face of opposition. Thailand was unable to initiate the changes; Indonesia was unable to sustain them.

The two cases examined here represent institutional extremes—Thailand's very divided structure and Indonesia's very centralized structure—producing economic policy outcomes that were highly destructive to investor confidence. As the region moves on from the economic crisis, there are many new questions relating to the economic consequences of politics to be explored. While we can see that political structures at either extreme can produce policy behavior that undermines investor confidence, that still leaves a large moderate gray middle in the spectrum of institutional possibilities. And it is this gray middle that both countries now seem to be entering in the wake of the economic crisis as their political systems undergo radical institutional surgery.

Neither Dynamo nor Domino: Reforms and Crises in the Philippine Political Economy

Paul Hutchcroft

What has happened in Asia in the past half-century is amazing and unprecedented. . . .
In a short time, many of these economies have gone from being dominos to dynamos.

—President Bill Clinton, Remarks to the Seattle APEC Host Committee,
19 November 1993

The economic crisis that originated in Thailand in mid-1997 has since spread far beyond Southeast and East Asia to menace a range of major economies worldwide, most notably Russia and Brazil. Curiously, however, the country long derided as "the sick man of Asia" is now set apart for relatively less pessimistic prospects than those found elsewhere in the region: as many of its neighbors suffer sharply negative economic downturn, the Philippines distinguished itself with a barely positive GNP growth rate of 0.1% in 1998.[1]

As its economy seems to have merely rolled to a halt without a disastrous crash, the Philippines has once again contradicted regional trends. In the late 1980s and early 1990s, while other Southeast Asian economies were enjoying their now-legendary "tiger" growth, the Philippines was dismissed as a "perennial aspirant" to the ranks of the newly industrializing economies, "not able to combine enough positive factors from among macroeconomic stability, strong technocratic bureaucracy, export competitiveness, political stability, and policy consistency" (Leipziger and Thomas 1993; 5, 10). Even as the extensive economic reforms of President Fidel V. Ramos (1992–98) helped to push growth rates into the range of 5 to 7 percent between 1994 and 1997, the country's overall economic performance remained modest and short-lived in relation to its increasingly prosperous neighbors.

In the wake of the crisis, the Philippine economy remains far from healthy—but nonetheless seems to enjoy some remove from the cataclysms that surround it. While newly elected president Joseph E. "Erap" Estrada may grumble about the condition of the economy he inherited from Ramos, a sense of regional perspective suggests that things could be far worse. In the year before Estrada's 30 June 1998 inauguration, the peso had fallen almost 40 percent, and the stock market had lost more than 60 percent of its value. Nonetheless, in contrast to harder-hit economies nearby, large corporate meltdowns are rare, and the rise in unemployment has been modest. After more than fifteen years of recurring woes, it is indeed notable that the Philippines was held up as an example of sound management in the early months of regional travails.[2] Just as the Philippines never quite achieved the status of "dynamo" in earlier years, neither has it fallen as a "domino" in the current crisis.

The puzzle of the Philippines, and the initial focus of this chapter, is the comparative buoyancy of the economy in the face of regional crisis. In exploring this puzzle, I critique two common explanations for the country's relative insulation from crisis and support an alternative explanation that provides far less basis for complacency. I proceed to examine the political prospects for the Philippines to renew and expand the reform momentum of the mid-1990s. Amid external turbulence and domestic political change, I argue, further reform faces formidable obstacles—but is in fact essential if the Philippines is to move beyond its long-standing boom-and-bust patterns and begin to deliver greater degrees of prosperity to the nation as a whole.

Explaining the Philippines' Relative Insulation from Crisis

After years of asserting that the Philippines had joined the league of such star performers as Thailand, Malaysia, and Indonesia, Philippine policy makers are now quick to distinguish the country's recent performance from that of its neighbors and to predict that the Philippines will continue to be relatively less affected by the current crisis. The chief challenge is to convince foreign investors of the Philippines' distinctiveness, and thus reduce the "contagion" from sicklier economies next door. It is commonly asserted that the Philippines has been spared the brunt of the crisis thanks to two major factors: first, the positive impact of the Ramos administration's program of economic reforms; and second, an inherent private-sector conservatism nurtured by the crises of the 1980s and early 1990s. I critically examine each of these explanations and proceed to argue a less consoling explanation for the country's relative insulation from crisis: while neighboring high-growth economies find themselves toppled from the peaks of success, the Philippines' primary short-term advantage lies in its failure to have achieved such towering heights in years past.

The Legacy of the Ramos Reforms

The economic reforms of the Ramos administration represented the first major strategic vision of Philippine political elites since the early years of Ferdinand

Marcos's martial law regime (Rocamora 1994, 173). Although certain important initiatives of economic reform are traceable to the latter years of Corazon Aquino's presidential term (1986–92), it was with the Ramos administration that new perceptions of the Philippines' place in the world combined with new leadership to produce major goals for the wholesale transformation of the political economy. In undertaking the reforms, Ramos and his advisers were motivated by a number of factors. First, the major economic crises of the previous decade demonstrated the need for fundamental change. Second, the Philippines was influenced by global trends toward economic liberalization and by the need to make decisions about committing the country to new international fora and free trade associations (notably APEC, AFTA, and GATT). Third, more intangible but perhaps most important, the departure of the U.S. military bases in 1992 left the country feeling both more exposed and more aware of its surroundings. From the start, Ramos expressed a clear sense of the country's weakness in competing effectively in the international and regional economies. At his inauguration, the president decried an economic system that "rewards people who do not produce at the expense of those who do . . . [and] enables persons with political influence to extract wealth without effort from the economy"; the political dominance of oligarchic groups, he explained a year later, is "the reason why the Philippines has lagged so far behind the East Asian Tigers" (Hutchcroft 1998a, 23, 3).[3]

Under the banner of "Philippines 2000"—a rallying cry to join the ranks of the NICs by the end of the century—Ramos combined measures of economic liberalization, privatization, and infrastructural development with concerted attacks on what his reformers commonly referred to as "cartels and monopolies." Trade liberalization, long a priority of local technocrats, the IMF, and the World Bank, was given ongoing encouragement by the country's participation in APEC, GATT, and AFTA. Foreign exchange and foreign investment were also liberalized, and major state firms were extensively privatized. The Central Bank of the Philippines, after perishing under the weight of $12 billion accumulated debt, was resurrected as the debt-free *Bangko Sentral ng Pilipinas* in 1993. By 1994, two rival stock exchanges were at last forced to unite in the midst of extraordinary growth in the long-dormant Philippine bourse. Greater political stability emerged in the wake of major agreements with military rebels and Muslim successionists and the decline of the Communist Party. Ramos is also credited with ending the crippling power shortages that deprived Manila and other areas of electricity for as long as 8 to 12 hours a day in 1992 and 1993—the very existence of which displayed the woeful neglect of the country's infrastructure in the previous decade.

Perhaps the most dramatic initiative of the new administration, led by presidential security adviser Jose Almonte, was a very public challenge to cartels, monopolies, and the oligarchic privilege that had nurtured them. The first target was the moribund and inefficient telecommunications industry, which was transformed by new competition and came to serve as the model for thorough reform of other sectors, most clearly airlines and shipping. Although other reform efforts—such as the challenge to the banking cartel—were ultimately not very effective, that they were even attempted signaled a new orientation of the political leadership. Thanks to measures liberalizing foreign exchange and foreign investment, many of the new competitive pressures came from a major influx of international investment that had previously tended to bypass the Philippines.

By the mid-1990s, the Ramos reformers were lauded internationally for the fruits of their reform efforts—even as some of the reformers themselves freely admitted their amazement at how far their initiatives had proceeded. Growth resumed at a very respectable pace, far above the rock-bottom growth rates experienced late in the administration of Ramos's predecessor, Corazon Aquino. Unlike in earlier years, economic expansion was driven not by external debt and aid but by foreign and domestic investment. Furthermore, the growth extended far beyond Manila to include major new regional centers, including Cebu and General Santos City in the south as well as Subic Bay and other areas near Manila. There were many fresh faces on the business scene, most notably an innovative group of exporters, and a heightened prominence of Chinese-Filipino conglomerates. After years of frequently stalled reform initiatives, many observers became confident that market-oriented, outward-looking policies had at last emerged "as the unchallenged paradigm of Philippine development" (*FEER* 10 August 1995, 31).

In the wake of regional crisis, the Ramos program is credited further with the distinct achievement of enabling the Philippine political economy to weather the crisis better than its neighbors. "We've gotten away from trying to devise a national car, or steel plant, or an aircraft industry," argued former Ramos reformer and business professor Victor S. Limlingan. "What's saving us is the liberalization program. Growth has spread out" (*New York Times* 11 December 1997). Similarly, economist Manuel Montes argues that the liberal economic reforms "dampened the potential for hothouse, Asian-style growth processes" (Montes 1998a, 266).

However, whether these past efforts will continue to succeed in "saving" the country from regional trends is highly questionable. Most obviously, the greater openness of the Philippine economy makes it all the more susceptible to infirmities across the seas. More fundamentally, it is important not to forget all of the reforms that were left undone. This is not to minimize the major accomplishments of the Ramos reformers, who exercised effective and persistent leadership at a propitious crossroads and began to effect fundamental change. "By any standard," economist Emmanuel S. de Dios observed, "the Philippines has traveled a remarkable distance over the past five years" (1998, 73). The fact remains, however, that the reformers lacked the political strength to achieve their oft-stated goal of "leveling the playing field" in the economy as a whole: alongside the successes, there were also initiatives that were effectively stifled by those who were supposed to be reformed.

In assessing the current situation, it is important to recall how the political sustainability of reform was problematic from the start; even in the midst of impressive achievement, many were skeptical of future reform prospects. Most notable are the caveats of Jose Almonte, the leading figure in the Ramos reform effort, who did not hesitate to contradict the more exuberant optimism of his colleagues in the

Ramos cabinet. Speaking to the Philippine Economic Society in early 1996, Almonte proclaimed that the hardest reforms—those involving sustained administrative capacity—were yet to come. "If our country is to organize the rational economy that will move us into the mainstream of regional development," he warned, "the State must first free itself from the influence of [the] oligarchy. . . . the paradox of market reforms is that they require capable states." Despite the clear impetus for change, he further cautioned, the "rich and powerful families" could still "prove stronger" than the forces of reform (Almonte 1996).[4]

It is useful to expand on this analysis and develop a fuller taxonomy of the three major elements of a comprehensive reform effort in the Philippines. First are the various measures of *economic* liberalization described earlier, accompanied by widespread privatization and aggressive challenges to "cartels and monopolies." Even if more successful in some sectors than others, Ramos and such key advisers as Almonte nonetheless articulated a strategic vision as to how they might defeat obstructive oligarchic forces and promote market reforms as a means of democratizing Philippine society. The second category of reform goes beyond standard liberal prescriptions and involves the creation of stronger *institutional* foundations for development. The Ramos reformers did not ignore this element of reform, but, as Almonte acknowledged, such reforms as improving the quality of the bureaucracy and revamping the tax and judicial systems would prove much harder than the earlier "easy" tasks of liberalization. A concerted strengthening of institutional foundations, I argue later, is essential to the country's long-term prospects for sustained developmental success. The third broad category of reform is *political*, and it relates to efforts to reform democratic structures to encourage greater participation of and responsiveness to social forces that have long been marginalized. The Ramos administration was proud to demonstrate the compatibility of development and democracy but (as I analyze later) consistently relied on old-style politics to promote new-style economics (Rocamora 1995b, 1–3).[5]

If reform momentum was tenuous and reform content uneven during the economic successes of the Ramos administration in the mid-1990s, all the more should we anticipate problems in sustaining and expanding the reforms today. One major source of uncertainty, of course, arises from regional crisis; another, equally important element of uncertainty revolves around the leadership of President Estrada, whose close ties to former Marcos-era cronies lead many to fear that earlier efforts to curb oligarchic privilege are being undermined and may even be reversed outright. In the second part of this chapter, I return to an examination of these and other issues to assess the prospects for ongoing reform under the current administration and beyond.

The Legacy of Past Domestic Crises

The second key factor commonly cited as an explanation for the Philippines' relative insulation from crisis relates to private-sector behavior. It is asserted, in short, that after three major domestic economic crises in two decades (in the early 1980s, the mid-1980s, and the early 1990s), Philippine financiers and businesspersons have become far more conservative and prudent in their decisions. Unlike in Thailand, risk-averse strategies by both lenders and borrowers have guarded against the growth of a "bubble" economy.[6]

The most important arena in which to assess private-sector conservatism is the financial sector; this has been the site of much past instability in the Philippines, and it is in this sector as well that crisis-plagued Indonesia and Thailand seek to resolve some of their most intractable problems. The Philippine financial sector is heavily dominated by commercial banks, and commercial banks themselves are commonly the crown jewels of the diversified family conglomerates that continue to dominate the economy as a whole. Historically, familial control of a bank provided easy access to loans for related family enterprises—and rampant plundering of loan portfolios (i.e., imprudent behavior) contributed to making the Philippine financial sector the most unstable in the region (with repeated banking crises from the 1960s through the 1980s).

Does private-sector conservatism now help to insulate the Philippines from regional woes in the late 1990s? Brief examination of the current situation of the Philippine banking sector does reveal a certain validity in this argument. After years of crisis, Philippine commercial banks of the mid-1990s could boast many positive developments in their ranks. A 40 to 47 percent across-the-board increase in minimum capitalization requirements in late 1994 (after a 50 percent increase only two years earlier) posed few problems for the vast majority of banking institutions (*Business World* 29 December 1994). There has also been a marked increase in professionalization, particularly among the top banks; if one compares the 1990s to the 1980s, there are seemingly far more officers who treat their banks as profit centers in their own right (rather than as merely a source of cheap loans for related family enterprises). Additional signs of hope are found in common reports of Filipino nationals, who have been long regarded as "the most sophisticated and internationalised corps of bankers and financiers" in all of Southeast Asia, returning from overseas assignments to use their skills at home (*FEER* 24 September 1992, 70). Technological advances have accompanied this process of professionalization and contribute further to the commanding advantages of the top banks. Finally, with the rehabilitation of two banks in the doldrums since the early 1980s, BSP Governor Gabriel Singson could proudly declare in late 1995 that there is "no more weakling in the banking system" (*PDI* 25 September 1995).

Patterns of real estate lending reveal important contrasts between the Philippines and Thailand. "Partly because of high interest rates in the Philippines," explained *FEER* in late 1997, "condominium developers have been financing their projects by preselling as many as 40% of their units before they start construction" (25 September 1997, 102). With the stock market also serving as a major source of financing, debt-to-equity ratios of property firms in the Philippines were reportedly one-fourth those of Thailand. In March 1998, the ratio of real estate and property loans to total bank loans stood at roughly 14 percent— "way below the 20 percent ceiling imposed by the BSP," noted chief BSP economist Diwa Guinigundo, "and definitely better than the 20 to 30 percent ratios elsewhere in the region" (*PDI* 13 July 1998).

Closer examination, however, reveals that much of the banking sector's recent strength (particularly that of its largest members) comes from generous government handouts throughout the years of crisis and after. High-interest, low-risk Central Bank bills provided enormous profits in the mid-1980s; "[l]ocal banks snapped up the profitable bills, and their customers went without credit" (*AWSJ* 13 June 1986). In the late 1980s and early 1990s, high-interest, low-risk treasury bills became the major pot of gold, as commercial banks came to be major lenders to the government; by 1990, the value of outstanding government securities actually exceeded the value of all bank deposits. A few chosen banks were given lucrative monopoly privileges over the sale of these securities. An additional source of riches was also available in the late 1980s to an even smaller number of banks lucky enough to be chosen as the depositories of government funds. Using these low-cost or no-cost funds, the banks could turn around and invest in government securities yielding 20 percent interest and more. In other words, funds borrowed *from* the government were re-lent *to* the government at much higher rates (Hutchcroft 1998a, 172–74, 193–95)!

Drawing on these rich lodes of privilege, the five largest private domestic commercial banks increased their share of total systemwide assets from 22.1 percent in 1980 to 26.4 percent in 1985 and 38.0 percent in 1990. Their position was assisted not only by government handouts, but also by the failure of the Central Bank to stand in the way of collusive practices among the banks—despite World Bank concerns over how the more efficient banks enjoyed high profits by setting prices in accordance with the cost structure of the less efficient banks.[7] Because of the handsome advantages that they enjoyed, the banks prospered as the economy faltered. Between 1990 and 1993, the commercial banks averaged 17.9 percent annual growth in total assets and nearly 20 percent return on equity—while GDP grew at an average annual rate of only 1 percent. It is no wonder that banks adopted a conservative lending position, since the availability of government largesse made it possible to earn high levels of profits at low levels of risk.

In the end, the Filipino people had little to show for all the public money that had coursed into the country's banks. Valid arguments can be advanced for public rescue of private institutions, as long as certain benefits from that rescue are eventually realized by those who shoulder the burdens. Unfortunately, however, the banking system still did little to promote forms of financial intermediation beneficial to the vast majority of the Filipino people; government pampering strengthened the banks' balance sheets, in other words, but did not encourage the banking system to become more responsive to the developmental needs of the nation as a whole. The deficits of the Treasury weighed ever more heavily on taxpayers and consumers of essential public services, who have been further burdened since 1993 by the $12 billion debt left behind by a fatally profligate Central Bank. Meanwhile, small savers were lucky to get positive rates of interest on their deposits, and small borrowers were rarely served by the banking sector at all. Rates of financial intermediation lagged far behind the rest of the region, both in absolute levels and in rates of growth.[8]

In 1993 and 1994, Ramos administration reformers trained their sights on the banking sector—the country's most heavily fortified bastion of privilege and profits. In the end, however, the bankers had more impact on the shape of reform than did the Ramos administration; as the BAP president candidly concluded, the final law "met [our] standard in terms of balancing the national interest with the country's need for globalization without making too many unnecessary concessions" (Buenaventura 1994, 180). The reforms permitted the entry of ten new foreign banks, but a very limited loosening of branching restrictions ensured that any new competitive pressures would be confined to the very top end of the market (in those sectors "where there's already been keen competition," explained a former BAP president with perhaps unintended candor [*FEER* 9 November 1995, 65]). In addition, the reforms opened the door to new domestic banks, bringing an impressive expansion in the total number of commercial banks from thirty-two at year-end 1993 to forty-seven in early 1996. But whereas their very presence signals an important change in policy and introduces an element of new competition, it is unlikely that any of the new players—domestic or foreign—will be a significant threat to the oligopolistic structure of the banking sector. The top five banks now control some 50 percent of total assets, and their advantages in terms of capital, personnel, and technology will make it difficult for new domestic banks—all small players—to offer any significant threat in the short term. It is entirely possible, as pioneer investment banker Sixto K. Roxas earlier predicted, that the entry of foreign banks "just increases the membership of the cartel" (*Business World* 1 December 1993).[9]

In sum, while Ramos and his advisers can be credited with considerable success in confronting "cartels and monopolies" in other parts of the economy, their efforts to reform the banking sector barely made a dent. After their reform measures had been diluted by the bankers, the most hopeful speculation was that the presence of new foreign banks, by heightening competition at the upper end of the market, would at last force domestic banks to provide sound financial services to SMEs. At the end of the 1990s, however, it is clear that these hopes for eventual change have not been fulfilled; particularly in the midst of crisis, banks are doing nothing to expand out of their traditionally narrow, urban clientele. As one market analyst observed in early 1998, only the top fifty companies can readily borrow from major banks.[10]

Despite the many advantages that the banks continue to enjoy, even the strongest banks were facing new challenges at decade's end, as certain past sources of easy profit were diminished (see Hutchcroft 1998a, 225–26). At the same time, a spate of "problem banks" recalls concerns over financial stability that plagued the system in the 1980s: a large sugar-milling firm defaulted on substantial loans to three leading banks in March 1997 (*FEER* 1 May 1997); the formerly church-owned Monte de Piedad nearly collapsed in April 1997 amid reports of "anomalous loans" (and was rescued by Singapore's Keppel Group) (*Manila Times* 8 May 1997); and one of the banks newly licensed in the mid-1990s, Orient Bank, was forced to close in February 1998 after seemingly being milked to death by its majority owner, property developer Jose Go. Several other banks had also lent large sums to Go's property conglomerate and faced the risk of not getting their money back. As the president of one creditor bank explained, Go's debacle "could dent the 'we're-not-like-Thai-banks' image that Philippine banks have been trying to put up. And then people will start wondering if there could be other, even bigger, Gos out there" (*FEER* 26 March 1998, 72).[11]

At least one analyst is sure that there are, indeed, "a lot more Orient Banks out there. . . . Unfortunately, these banks won't be as lucky as Monte de Piedad was last year when it had Keppel Bank of Singapore coming to the rescue." It is particularly important to note trends in three areas. First, the ratio of nonperforming loans to total loans in the banking sector increased from 2.8 percent at year-end 1996 to 4.0 percent in June 1997, 5.4 percent at year-end 1997, 9.7 percent in July 1998, and 12.9 percent in February 1999. Although BSP economist Guinigundo correctly argues that these ratios "[compare] favorably with double-digit ratios in most Asian countries," the trends are not encouraging.[12] Second, the proportion of real estate and property lending to total loans changed little between June 1997 and June 1998, hovering in the range of 12 to 14 percent. Although one can again observe that the Philippine situation compares favorably with that of its hardest-hit neighbors, some suspect that BSP data underestimate banks' true exposure in real estate lending. Third, further uncertainties arise from greater access of Philippine bankers to foreign loans. The Philippines was a relative latecomer in its efforts to attract foreign funds, but by the mid-1990s (as analyzed later) it was beginning to claim some of the investment that had earlier bypassed the country for more attractive locales. As in Thailand, a stable currency and a large differential between international and domestic interest rates encouraged a ballooning of banks' foreign liabilities; between 1995 and 1996, there was an 89 percent increase (from $13.5 billion to $25.2 billion) (*FEER* 25 September 1997, 105).

As the condition of many banks weakens, there is little evidence that the BSP has acquired the supervisory capacity to rise to the challenges ahead. Although the BSP has been able to pay higher salaries than its pre-1993 predecessor, the Central Bank of the Philippines, compensation remains far inferior to that available in the private sector. Needless to say, this hampers efforts to attract the most qualified personnel. Just as with old Central Bank personnel, BSP officials remain personally vulnerable to being sued for acts undertaken in an official capacity. As in the past, timidity is the likely result. In the event that BSP regulators do dare attempt to curb fraudulent activities by bankers, an extremely strict bank secrecy law makes it very difficult to examine deposit transactions. Although it is heartening to note that many banks now enjoy increased professionalization, capitalization, and technological capacity, self-regulation alone does not offer sufficient protection against the considerable potential of future instability. Old problems, such as insider abuse, are unresolved, even as moves toward liberalization and globalization present new challenges to supervisory capacity. Philippine banks have long scoffed at the abilities of government regulators, who have presided over what is historically the most unstable financial system in the entire region. The greater competence of the banking profession in the 1990s only tips the balance further in favor of those who seek to circumvent prudential supervision.[14]

In short, one should draw little solace from assertions that the earlier domestic crises of the 1980s and 1990s have promoted more conservative and prudent behavior as the Philippine private sector faces the current regional crisis. The conservatism of Philippine bankers can be explained in large part by generous government handouts and the failure of the monetary authorities to challenge collusive practices; as long as government programs facilitated high profit at low risk, risk-taking strategies were largely superfluous. Despite their best efforts, Ramos reformers were defeated in their attempt to inject substantial new competitive pressures into the banking system and thereby encourage banks to promote (rather than hamper) national developmental goals. All of these advantages and victories notwithstanding, the Philippine banking sector is now showing disturbing signs of strain. By the middle of the 1990s, the banks as a whole were finding important opportunities for easy profit diminished, and since 1997 some institutions have experienced serious difficulties. Meanwhile, longstanding concerns about the regulatory capacity of the BSP endure.

The Advantages of Lower Elevation

As demonstrated, critical examination of the two common explanations for the Philippines' relative insulation from the current economic crisis provides little cause for comfort. First, the Ramos economic reforms were limited in scope and success, and their political sustainability is problematic even in the best of times (which the late 1990s clearly have not been). Second, as just summarized, the resolution of past crises does not prevent the country from sailing toward dire straits once again. A third, alternative explanation seems most consistent with current trends and underlying realities. Put in simplest terms, the country's laggard economic status in the region brought one important advantage in the midst of regional crisis: because the Philippines never achieved high peaks, it did not have as far to fall.

Thailand and the Philippines opened up their capital accounts at roughly the same time (both in the early 1990s), but the Philippines was far less successful in attracting foreign capital flows. First, as a comparison of the Philippine and Thai data reveals (Tables 8.1 and 8.2; Figures 8.1 and 8.2), it was not until 1996 that one finds a major surge in net private capital flows to the Philippines in the category *bank and trade-related lending*, and this peak was substantially less than the average level of loans flowing into Thailand annually since 1991 (i.e., flows totalled $7 billion in the Philippines at their *peak* in 1996, whereas Thailand had been pulling in an average of $10.5 billion *per year* from 1991 to 1996). Second, the Philippines attracted far lower levels of the so-called hot money of portfolio investment through the several years leading up to crisis. Third, contrasts in levels of fdi between the two countries are not nearly as dramatic, although here, too, Thailand did quite clearly outpace the Philippines in all years except 1994 and 1995. With less overall access to foreign

Table 8.1   Net Private Capital Flows in the Philippines, 1991–97 (US$ million)

	1991	1992	1993	1994	1995	1996	1997
Foreign direct investment	545	689	870	1282	1335	1340	1193
Portfolio investment	136	53	–54	256	222	–168	–4516
Bank and trade-related lending	45	318	598	1666	1854	7037	3749
Total	726	1060	1414	3204	3411	8209	426

Source: Adapted from Hill and Athukorala 1998 (36).

funds, Philippine property and stock market values did not inflate to the same magnitude as those of Thailand. Once the crisis hit in 1997, lower elevation had clear advantages: the Philippines maintained a modestly positive net private capital *inflow* of $426 million, whereas Thailand suffered a massive *outflow* of nearly $17 billion.[15]

The milder impact of the crisis may set the Philippines apart from its neighbors, but it does not thereby follow that the Philippine economy is resilient, robust, and poised for rapid growth. The inability of the country to attract such large quantities of foreign funds as Thailand did in the years before 1997 may have insulated the Philippines to a certain extent from crisis, but this relative advantage in the short term by no means connotes an impressive record of economic development over the long term. While the Thailand economy was booming from the mid-1980s to the early 1990s, it must be recalled, the Philippine economy was lurching from crisis to crisis. Even more dramatic evidence of laggard economic performance emerges from comparisons of Filipino per capita income levels over time. Had the resumption of growth during the mid-1990s endured through the latter part of the decade, de Dios (1998, 49–51) explains, Filipinos would have finally achieved the same average incomes that they had received in the early 1980s—before the long string of crises commenced. Unfortunately, the onset of crisis has delayed even this relatively modest goal; for the average Filipino, regaining the real income levels of 1981 has become an aspiration that must wait for the new millennium.

In summary, arguments about both the legacy of the Ramos reforms and the conservatism of the private sector are problematic; careful examination of these

Table 8.2   Net Private Capital Flows in Thailand, 1991–97 (US$ million)

	1991	1992	1993	1994	1995	1996	1997
Foreign direct investment	1473	1560	1377	1011	1177	1633	1989
Portfolio investment	—	557	4007	1299	3194	1089	612
Bank and trade-related lending	9037	7579	5134	10106	16981	14153	–19278
Total	10510	9696	10518	12416	21352	16875	–16677

Source: Adapted from Hill and Athukorala 1998 (36).

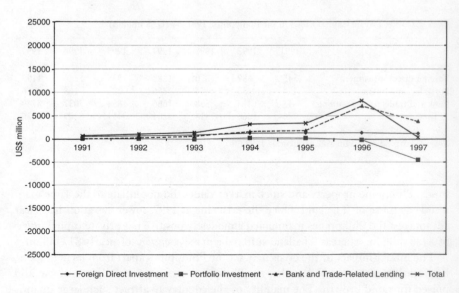

Figure 8.1 Net private capital flows in the Philippines, 1991–97

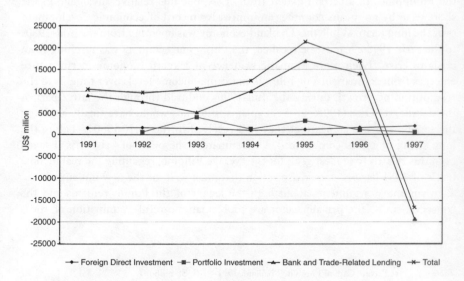

Figure 8.2 Net private capital flows in Thailand, 1991–97

factors provides no basis for complacency about the future prospects of the Philippine economy. First, while the Ramos administration did go further in the reform process than most ever imagined possible and did succeed in promoting far more productive modes of operation in the economy as a whole, it is dubious to suggest that the reforms will somehow inoculate the country from regional and global economic ailments. Second, careful examination of financial institutions (which have been at the center of crisis management in neighboring countries) makes clear that one should not be lulled into thinking that earlier domestic crises have somehow promoted more conservative and prudent behavior in the Philippine private sector. Despite the myriad advantages enjoyed by commercial banks since the major financial crisis of the mid-1980s, even some elements of this pampered sector are now showing certain signs of distress.

The Philippines may be envied for its less dramatic fall, but the ground on which it now rests remains far from secure. In other words, there are many reasons to question whether the country now possesses the institutional foundations on which sustainable growth can flourish. Further reform is necessary to shore up these foundations and begin to improve economic conditions for the nation as a whole—not only for those who easily survive when boom turns to bust, but also for those who have long been forced to struggle for a livelihood in the most challenging of circumstances. As the next section demonstrates, many diverse factors will determine whether the Philippines can sustain and expand the reform momentum in future years.

Prospects for Reform in the Era of Erap and Beyond

The preceding analysis highlights the successful elements in the Ramos economic reforms, but suggests that there are many remaining areas of incomplete reform and ongoing fragility. Although examination of these areas is beyond the scope of this chapter, it is important to note briefly some of the major problems that persist in the Philippine macroeconomy and have since before the onset of crisis: the fiscal basis of the central government remains shaky, because tax reform measures have been unsuccessful in resolving shortfalls in revenue-generating capacity[16]; spending on infrastructure and education are at levels far below what is necessary to promote the country's longer-term economic success; the domestic savings rate continues to be low (a mere 15 percent of GDP in 1995); agricultural performance has long been unimpressive (even before El Niño); performance has lagged in many sectors of manufacturing (seemingly because of the combined effect of rapid import liberalization and a long-overvalued peso); and uncompetitive structures endure in those sectors that were not reformed.[17] Most important, as I argue later, the Philippines continues to be plagued by generally weak institutional foundations for developmental success.

Unfortunately, as reform strategist Jose Almonte warned in 1996, there are daunting obstacles to building the foundations of sustainable growth. Amid external turbulence and domestic political change, one central question remains essentially the same, whether analysis is undertaken in 1994 or 1999: what are the political prospects for further reform? Whereas in 1994 the major concern was whether the reform momentum could be maintained and extended, at decade's end the major concern is whether the reform momentum will be undermined and reversed.

My analysis of the political sustainability of the reform effort concentrates on four basic levels:

1. The quality of political leadership the Philippines will experience in coming years
2. External pressures supporting or impeding the reform momentum
3. The degree to which the domestic business sector supports ongoing reforms
4. Prospects for the emergence of a broader social coalition in favor of reform

I discuss each factor in turn and examine what remains the most important end goal of the reform process, heavily dependent on all four of the factors noted above: the construction of firmer institutional foundations for future developmental success.

Political Leadership

The success of the Ramos reforms rested on the deft and savvy leadership of the president and his key advisers, most notably national security adviser Jose Almonte (who was, like Ramos, a former military officer). Liberal ideas had been floating around in Philippine policy circles for decades, yet were commonly batted down decisively by those with the most to lose from their promulgation and implementation. Ramos and Almonte adopted many liberal ideas, combined them with occasional advocacy of a "strong state" (to combat oligarchic dominance and absorb developmental lessons from Northeast Asian NICs), and pushed through the resulting program ("Philippines 2000") with very clever and well-planned maneuvers in the rough-and-tumble arena of real politics. To give two examples, the battle against the telephone monopoly involved active collaboration with consumer activists, and the cooperation of Congress in the passage of economic reforms was encouraged by intensified use of old-fashioned pork-barrel techniques (which, by 1996, consumed nearly $1 billion of the annual budget).[18]

By contrast, the new administration of Joseph Estrada has so far displayed much less sense of direction. It is significant that no major candidate in the May 1998 presidential campaign, including Estrada, challenged the Ramos economic reforms or threatened to overturn them. Estrada did make vague redistributive promises and express concern for how the poor were largely left out of the economic gains of the mid-1990s, but he has continually pledged his allegiance to market forces. Even if his self-described "pro-business, pro-poor" goals were easier to discern, however, there remain major questions about whether the administration has the resources or capacity to carry out any program of reform (*PDI* 9 October 1998). In statements that emphasize how the government is "almost bankrupt," Estrada seems to be backing away from earlier discussion of large investments in rural infrastructure (*AWSJ* 11 August 1998). His legislative agenda is strikingly sparse, and cabinet meetings are rarely convened. Since Estrada took office in mid-1998, moreover, frequent conflicts within a highly fractionated Palace often leave the impression "that he's not in control" (*AWSJ* 24 September 1998; *FEER* 13 August 1998, 20). Most troubling are the clear resurgence of former Marcos associates and the signs that brazen use of public influence for private gain is once again sanctioned at the top (see *FEER* 16 July 1998, 28; *Economist* 25 July 1998, 38–39; *New York Times* 13 December 1998). Needless to say, this is not the type of leadership that promotes optimism about the prospects for sustaining and expanding the reform momentum. Because the next presidential elections will not come until the year 2004, it is important to examine other factors that influence the political prospects for reform.

External Pressures

There are at least three distinct ways in which external pressures may be a factor in determining future reform prospects. First, the post-bases world view likely will continue to encourage a major reorientation of the economy toward more productive modes of operation, especially as tensions endure with China over disputed islands in the South China Sea. If the Philippines is to succeed in its goal of building a military worthy of regional respect, a strong economic foundation is essential. Second, as noted earlier, the Philippines has chosen to become involved in a series of associations that demand long-term commitment to economic openness—notably APEC, GATT, and AFTA. These international commitments, along with ongoing reliance on IMF assistance, will continue to condition the country's options in future years and discourage measures that reverse past liberalization. Third, given that the health of the economy has become very dependent on inflows of foreign investment, the Philippines will be forced to continue to appease the concerns of foreign investors. A reliance on portfolio investment has had real costs (most obviously in its sudden departure, but also—when it was still relatively plentiful—in its bolstering of the peso to levels that discouraged exports); nonetheless, economic policy makers show every desire to lure it back to pre-1997 levels and display no inclination to thumb their noses at liberal orthodoxies. In the wake of Malaysia's imposition of capital controls, it is notable that Philippine officials have emphasized their intention to keep capital accounts open.[19]

The Role of Domestic Business

What pressures might emerge from the pillars of large business to sustain the reform momentum? To begin, it is important to note that the oligarchy was *not* demanding to be reformed when Ramos came to power in 1992 (even if, after the laggard growth of previous years, many felt that things were gravely wrong and somehow needed to be fixed). When Almonte explained to the Institute of Asian Management on 29 April 1993 that it was necessary to "hurt the finger" of business to "save their necks," no one seems to have actually requested this form of rough manicure. Prominent business leaders were in fact highly critical of early reform initiatives, perceiving them as "a military man's anti-business sentiment" (*FEER* 6 May 1993, 45). A few years later, however, some of the same figures that had earlier denounced the Ramos administration began to sing loud praises of the liberalization measures and renewed growth with which the measures were closely associated. By 1996, one former critic, business leader Jaime Zobel de Ayala, authored a laudatory account of the reforms as "a breathtaking ride our country has not known since . . . independence in 1946. . . . The Philippines is faring better today because we have literally changed the road map to the future" (*Business World* 1 October 1996). As 1998 elections approached, business leaders fretted openly about what would happen at the end of Ramos's term.[20]

A mere shift in attitudes in the business community, however, is not sufficient to sustain pressures for further reform; far more important is an organized, pro-reform business constituency, pushing for change even when change is not forthcoming from the political leadership. Unfortunately, seemingly little evidence exists that such a group is emerging. There have at times been effective ad hoc coalitions (such as the anti-crony Makati Business Club in the late Marcos years), and the Philippine Exporters Confederation has, in the 1990s, been occasionally assertive in supporting reform and challenging more established business interests.[21] But there is not yet a large and well-organized constituency able to sustain and deepen the reform program into the future.[22] The historical weakness of Philippine business associations seems to endure, even if it is always possible—particularly in the face of adversity—that new forms of collective action may someday emerge.

The Emergence of a Broader Social Coalition for Reform

Moving beyond the pillars of the business community, what are the possibilities of a broader social coalition for reform, encompassing not only the professional middle class and small and medium-scale entrepreneurs, but also popular forces (e.g., peasants, labor, urban poor, fisherfolk)? Unfortunately, as we shall see, one cannot yet discern signs of the creation of a broad social coalition able to sustain reform pressures into future years.

The middle class has no doubt been a major beneficiary of the Ramos economic reforms, as is clearly evidenced—not only in Manila but also in provincial centers throughout the archipelago—by recent surges in ownership of private cars and other major consumer durables, the mushrooming of housing developments, and the construction of seemingly countless massive new shopping malls. Its ranks have expanded not only through renewed domestic economic growth in the 1990s, but also through the capacity of remittances from overseas workers to finance consumer purchases and nurture fledgling small business ventures at home.[23]

Assessing the political potency of this growing middle class, however, is highly problematic. On the one hand, Pinches suggests that "the middle class has become increasingly independent and critical of the old landed oligarchy and the means by which it has maintained political and economic power"; the "proliferation of non-governmental organisations over the past decade," he further notes, "is a clear measure of the crucial middle-class presence in contemporary Philippine political life" (1996, 123). In rural areas throughout the country, access to outside sources of income have served to undercut local patron-client networks (Rood 1998, 124). The Philippine middle class has a rich tradition of support for reform of corrupt and fraudulent electoral procedures (Thompson 1995, 26–32), and this tradition could be tapped for reform purposes more broadly defined.

On the other hand, it is important to recall that ties overseas can greatly under-cut the political potency of the Philippine middle class. As in the business class, analyzed earlier, it is difficult to discern a well-organized constituency for reform. In times of domestic downturn, it is often easier to leave for greener pastures than to try to cultivate parched soil at home (as long lines outside the U.S., Canadian, and Australian embassies clearly attest). Even for those who stay, support from rel-atives overseas could serve as an additional factor in curbing the potency of reformist zeal. Finally, one should not underestimate the capacity of Philippine patron-client structures to orient political action toward particularistic—rather than collective—benefits. Oligarchs at the top of these structures have been very adept at winning the personal loyalties of middle-class clients and extremely accommodating to newcomers in their ranks. Therefore, the political strength of the middle class may not grow as its numbers do; for many, it may prove far more advantageous to seek to enter and work within existing power structures than to challenge them from the outside.[24] At this stage in its development, the Philippine middle class seems more likely to be a potential supporter than a leading force in promoting reform efforts.

In contrast to the middle class, the reforms and renewed economic growth of the mid-1990s have not produced such readily apparent benefits for groups at the lower strata of Philippine society. In the Philippine context, spreading the benefits across social groups is made all the more urgent and difficult by the historical absence of any thorough program of land redistribution; unlike South Korea and Taiwan at similar stages of their industrialization process, the Philippines displays a particularly immense gulf in levels of wealth and income between the elite and the millions of workers, urban poor, and peasants below them. Despite Ramos's strong rhetorical commitment to reducing poverty, those at the bottom of society had little reason to cheer his program even in its heyday. There has been some improvement in certain indices of human development, and the administration did develop a "social reform agenda" to address the needs of the poor. But the effort was hampered by what Solita Monsod calls "a potentially deadly combination of not enough focus and insufficient funds" (1998, 98), and it did not yield many con-crete benefits for the "basic sectors" (farmers, fisherfolk, urban poor, indigenous communities, and disabled) that it was supposed to serve (Martinez 1996, 39–40).

If market reforms "are to become irreversible," warned Jose Almonte just before the onset of regional crisis, "ordinary people must see them as producing clear benefits for themselves and their families" (1997, 2). For most Filipinos, the cur-rent economic doldrums make it especially difficult to perceive such benefits. The unemployment rate has not increased substantially but has the real potential to do so if (as the U.S. Embassy suggested) the country's recent "export boom is running out of steam" (*PDI* 6 October 1998) and if (as many expect) economic troubles elsewhere bring a large repatriation of overseas workers (Montes 1998a).[25] As average per capita incomes are once again in decline, one should not be surprised by growing disenchantment—and, quite possibly, a tendency to associate liberal reforms and globalization with popular immiseration.[26] Indeed, Joseph Estrada's "pro-poor" rhetoric in the May 1998 elections won widespread support from those who have long felt excluded from the benefits of reform (as the *Asian Wall Street Journal* noted disapprovingly in a 12 May 1998 editorial, the "politics of resentment" played a role in his decisive victory).

Economic reform is likely to draw far more support from those who benefit most immediately, but no group has more incentive to support sweeping *political* reform than those lower-strata groups that have long been marginalized by Philippines-style democracy. Absent from the Ramos reform agenda was any sustained concern for improving the quality and substance of Philippine democracy.[27] Democratic institutions have indeed consolidated themselves more firmly in the Philippines, but many sectors of Philippine society remain marginal to the overall democratic process—and decidedly undemocratic forces hold sway in many localities. Democrats the world over could applaud the Ramos administration's explicit demonstration that democracy and economic growth can go hand in hand, but one must recognize that Philippines-style democracy is handicapped not only by the continuing dominance of strong oligarchic forces, but also by the weak institutionalization of both its party system and its bureaucracy. In the absence of any real reform of political structures, there is little hope that Philippine democracy will give much voice to those at the bottom rungs of society—or that economic reform programs will be crafted in ways that address their needs. Parties and the electoral process remain dominated by personalities rather than programs; legislative institutions continue to be the domain of many of the same old political clans and traditional politicians (disparagingly referred to as *trapos*, or dishrags); and the legislative process is still driven by the politics of pork and patronage. Ramos displayed considerable skill in using old-fashioned horse-trading and Philippines-style pork-barrel techniques to push liberalization measures through the Philippine Congress, but, as Joel Rocamora observed in 1995, the administration's "continuing vulnerability to the requirements of *trapo* politics has made it difficult to clinch a thoroughgoing reform image" (1995b). In many ways, the Ramos administration's concerted drive for economic reform unwittingly served to highlight the need for political reform.

Political and economic reforms can go hand in hand. In fact, one can argue that sustaining the process of economic reform actually requires reform of a political process still dominated by *trapos*. Although top-down reforms can help to initiate major political economic transformation, a more comprehensive and sustained degree of transformation requires the emergence of concerted pressures from below. The business community constitutes one important source of pressure, as discussed earlier, but broader societal pressures can serve to deepen the reforms and enhance their positive social impact.[28] The real challenge—the orderly attainment of which can only come through stronger political parties—is to insulate structures from particularistic demands (especially from the dominant oligarchy) and open them up to respond more effectively to collective pressures from societal groups whose interests have long been marginalized.

On the surface, one might view the diverse business, middle-class, and lower-class backers of Joseph Estrada as the epitome of the broad social coalition that failed to emerge under Ramos.[29] Many poor Filipinos, as well as many prominent members of the Left, jumped into a populist organization known as *Joseph E. Estrada for President* out of a conviction that Estrada the president would show as much concern for the disadvantaged in real life as Estrada the actor had earlier shown for the disadvantaged on the screen. Thus far, however, former Marcos cronies seem to be doing far better by Estrada than the *masa* (masses) whose interests he claims to represent. Unless there is a rapid change of direction, it seems that those in JEEP are destined for a very rough ride indeed.

The Necessity of Building Stronger Institutional Foundations for Development

After the many achievements of the Ramos administration in the mid-1990s (including breaking the telephone monopoly, liberalizing foreign exchange and foreign investment, furthering trade liberalization, uniting the rival stock exchanges, and turning the power back on), many observers—both foreign and local—were confident that the country had finally resolved its economic woes. Much of this confidence was nurtured by neoliberal sorcerers promising that the "magic of the marketplace" would pop out of the liberalization hat.

Unfortunately, it is now especially clear that this optimism was misguided. Despite the many positive outcomes that did emerge from the reform effort, much remained undone, and many aspects of liberalization rested on less-than-secure foundations. As Almonte warned in 1996, "market reforms . . . require capable states." Now that "hard" reforms requiring greater administrative capacity were being attempted, he continued, "the weaknesses of the Philippine State are starting to show. . . . Unless the Philippine State becomes stronger and more efficient, it will not be able to deal with our long-standing problems" (Almonte 1996).

The Philippine government has often had difficulty providing even the most basic foundation for a free market economy—whether it be supplying electricity, safeguarding the process of timber extraction, arbitrating among investors squabbling over the proper site for a petrochemical plant, or providing even-handed regulation of the financial system. The critical issue is not merely how to shrink the role of government and promote private sector initiative; more fundamentally, it is essential to improve the overall performance of government, insulate it from the plunder of oligarchic groups, and promote new *types* of private-sector initiative.

Over the long term, a more prosperous Philippine capitalism requires a government apparatus able to provide these foundations. Major institutional hurdles exist in the judicial and law enforcement systems, where extensive corruption and ineffectiveness have provoked widespread public cynicism; as Joseph Estrada himself observed when he was vice president, these systems are plagued by "hoodlums in robes" and "hoodlums in uniform."[30] It is difficult to instill investor confidence when a high degree of arbitrariness often reigns in the political and legal spheres and kidnappings plague the personal security of an important element of the business community. The country's weak fiscal position, moreover, keeps civil servants' salaries at often miserable levels and obstructs the long-term goal of strengthening the civil service and curbing the prevalence of corruption.

Sustained economic growth depends on improving the quality of the bureaucracy—described by Ramos as the "weak link" in national developmental efforts. Thus far, the most successful economic reform efforts have been those that merely remove restrictions on competition; far more complicated are initiatives requiring sustained administrative capacity. Just as liberalization of the banking sector by no means resolves ongoing deficiencies in regulatory capacity, neither do broader programs of economic reform obviate the need to address other political and institutional problems. It is one thing, for example, to liberalize agricultural imports or remove restrictions on agricultural exports, but quite another to provide the roads, irrigation facilities, extension services, and other infrastructure necessary if farmers are to improve their productivity and meet the challenges of international competition. Similarly, it is far easier to open up the economy to foreign investment and imports than to develop sustained programs of export promotion that can assist local entrepreneurs anxious to tap new opportunities in world markets.[31] In any project of institution-building, a logical place to begin would be the enhancement of administrative capacity in key institutions such as the new BSP, the Securities and Exchange Commission, and the Bureau of Internal Revenue.

On many fronts, Philippine state institutions are showing themselves to be incapable of providing the necessary institutional foundations required even by the laissez-faire model of development that the IMF, the World Bank, and the former colonial power have long been trying to peddle. Whether one is examining the Philippine political economy in the pre-crisis, crisis, or post-crisis years, the fact remains that long-term developmental success depends on careful and sustained nurturing of these foundations.

Cooking Development

In conclusion, it is worth noting that President Ramos often compared the process of development to the cooking of the bibingka, the traditional Philippine rice cake. Just as bibingka is cooked both from the top and the bottom, he observed, so must development proceed from both top-down and bottom-up initiatives. Between 1992 and 1998, President Ramos and his reformers supplied considerable heat in effecting policy change from above and encouraged new warmth from below. We can hope that the post-1998 leadership—Estrada and beyond—will sustain the heat of top-down policy momentum, supported from below not only by organized pro-reform elements of the business community, but also by a broader social coalition for growth. Most of all, we can hope that the basic institutional structures that support this cooking process will be strengthened for the future gain of all.

Unfortunately, it is also possible that considerable time may elapse before the cooking process resumes in earnest. The preceding analysis suggests that the Philippines should derive little comfort from the fact that it has been relatively insulated from regional crisis; the country's primary advantage over its neighbors lies not in the enduring legacy of past reforms or in conservative private-sector attitudes, but rather in its failure to have achieved high peaks of growth in years past. Whereas the Philippines may be fortunate to have sustained a less dramatic decline than other countries in the region, the ground on which it now stands remains insecure in many ways. Over the long term, the most important task continues to be the strengthening of institutional foundations for development. Current political prospects for further reform do not seem hopeful: while many external pressures endure, the political leadership seems to lack direction and coherence, the business community does not seem well organized to press for change, and a broader social coalition for economic and political reform shows little sign of emerging. But even if the obstacles seem daunting, further reform is essential if development is to proceed and the economy is to deliver greater degrees of prosperity to the nation as a whole.

Acknowledgments

Thanks to T. J. Pempel, Alasdair Bowie, B. J. Cohen, Ian Coxhead, Don Emmerson, Edna Labra Hutchcroft, Manuel Montes, and the participants in the University of Washington's October 30–November 1, 1998 conference for offering useful comments and advice. Valuable research assistance was provided by Gwendolyn Bevis. All errors, of course, are mine alone.

Surviving the East Asian Financial Storm: The Political Foundation of Taiwan's Economic Resilience

Yun-han Chu

In 1998, the majority of economies in East and Southeast Asia registered negligible or negative growth, with Taiwan being one of the conspicuous exceptions. Most observers credited Taiwan's huge foreign reserves, low foreign debts, high savings rate, and low bad loans ratio with the country's ability to withstand the regional financial turmoil. Some economists have moved beyond these superficial analyses and looked into the island's unique business structure, its experiences in industrial upgrading, the evolution of the regulatory regime over the banking sector and capital market, and the sequencing of financial liberalization. A full understanding of this exceptional case, however, requires more than just an economic analysis. What is also required is an analysis of the political underpinnings of these economic structures, macroeconomic policies, development strategies, and regulatory regimes. In this paper, I argue that elements of the island's economic resilience have been fostered by the state's development strategy and regulatory regimes over the long term. The state's economic strategies have been not only driven by the perceived need to facilitate the structural adjustment of its economy and to harmonize the economic relations with its major trading partners, but also shaped by a set of existing institutional arrangements and established policy orientations. These institutional arrangements and policy orientations, in the final analysis, have been embedded in Taiwan's particular security environment, political structure, and internal power configuration.

An Island of Calm in the Asian Financial Storm

It is a widely shared view that Taiwan has emerged from the East Asian financial crisis relatively unscathed. The damage to the island economy so far has been mild by regional standards. The growth momentum was slackened but not disrupted; the economy registered a 6.8 percent growth rate in 1997, and the island managed to attain a respectable 4.8 percent growth in 1998. This makes Taiwan the only mid-sized East Asian NIC to escape economic contraction. However, it would be erroneous to think that Taiwan has not been affected by the crisis. The regional economic turmoil has precipitated a sharp drop of the NT dollar and a nose dive of the stock market index. The currency (against U.S. dollars) devalued by 19.7 percent between mid-June 1997 and early October 1998. During this period, the stock market lost 23.4 percent of its total value in terms of local currency and 38.5 percent in terms of the U.S. dollar. The unemployment rate rose to 3.1 percent toward the end of the 1998, the highest level since 1985. Exports in the first ten months of 1998 shrank by 9 percent, and net exports are now estimated to be only US$5.5 billion for the entire year (*China Times* 8 November 1998)—the worst export performance since the second oil crisis. Thus, only in comparison with Taiwan's neighbors may we consider the current round of economic downturn a mild setback.

Most mainstream economists explained Taiwan's economic resilience in terms of getting the economic fundamentals right (Chiu 1998; Schive 1998; Mai and Chang 1998). Their insights can be summarized as follows: First, during the late 1980s and throughout the 1990s, Taiwan has coped with the challenge of industrial upgrading with great effectiveness. Despite a sharp currency appreciation during 1986–87, significant rises in labor costs and land prices throughout the 1980s, and growing environmental concerns, Taiwan has been able to keep up its international competitiveness through human resource development, technological upgrading, and overseas outsourcing (Chu 1995). Most notably, the high-technology industries[1] have replaced the traditional labor-intensive industries to become the backbone of Taiwan's export sector.[2] High-technology industries accounted for 39 percent of total manufacturing output and 49 percent of total exports in 1997. Since 1995, Taiwan has surpassed Germany to become the world's third largest exporter of informatics products (e.g., semiconductors, computers, telecommunications equipment), after the United States and Japan; Taiwan tops the list for design and production of such products as monitors, motherboards, keyboards, and scanners (Wang et al. 1998). The high degree of vertical integration that characterized conventional manufacturing industries in the past has continued to develop in the high-technology industries (Schive 1998, 3). In traditional export sectors, the growth of higher-value-added export activities was made possible by creating a bottom layer of international subcontracting in the region and pushing local producers to move upward in the hierarchy of international subcontracting networks (Gereffi 1995b). Unlike the ASEAN economies, which continued to compete both among themselves and with the PRC's low-waged exporters in labor-intensive manufacturing, Taiwan carved out different market niches for itself and widened its technological lead over the second-tier NICs. Also, unlike its major competitors, notably South Korea, in Taiwan the wage increase was kept largely in line with productivity gain. Between 1982 and 1997, Taiwan's labor cost registered a 237 percent increase in terms of the U.S. dollar. During the same period, South Korea witnessed a 556 percent jump (Mai and Chang 1988, 6). Thus, Taiwan has been able to run a significant trade surplus year after year since the last oil shock of 1979–80 and to accumulate a huge official foreign reserve (around US$90 billion by mid-1997), second only to Japan and the PRC. This is in stark contrast to the afflicted East Asian economies, which have all suffered from a worsened current account imbalance throughout 1990s. For example, in 1996, on the eve of the financial crisis, South Korea's current account deficit swelled to the largest level ever, US$23.7 billion.

Second, Taiwan's economic vitality is built on a decentralized industrial structure and a highly competitive domestic market. Despite the trend toward a higher degree of business centralization since the late 1980s (Chu 1994), 98 percent of all registered companies were still small and medium sized in 1997.[3] In 1997, the SMEs contributed to 34 percent of Taiwan's GDP in value-added terms. They still account for 52 percent of total production output and 78 percent of jobs. In Taiwan, the efficiency and flexibility of the SMEs have enabled them to compete with their larger counterparts at home and abroad. SMEs in Taiwan have formed comprehensive horizontal and vertical networks through cooperation and division of labor among themselves and large enterprises, creating an efficient and flexible industrial clustering (Schive 1998, 16). Most SMEs in Taiwan are constrained by limited access to bank loans or to the informal financial sector; they are charged higher interest rates, they seldom resort to overseas financing, and they tend to make efficient use of their limited and more costly capital. In a comparative light, the economy's overall efficiency in capital utilization is notable. Between 1990 and 1996, Taiwan achieved a 6.3 percent annual growth rate with a modest level of fixed capital formation, equivalent to 22.6 percent of its GDP.[4] South Korea, which is characterized by the economic dominance of the *chaeböl*, achieved a slightly higher annual growth rate (7.7 percent) with a substantially higher level of capital input, equivalent to 36.7 percent of GDP.

Third, Taiwan was partially insulated from the external financial shock, because the island's economic growth has been financed almost exclusively by domestic savings. A combination of a high saving rate and higher efficiency in capital utilization has allowed Taiwan to generate excess savings and become a major source of foreign investment in East Asia. Taiwan's average excess savings exceeded 5.4 percent of the GDP between 1990 and 1996, whereas most other East Asian NICs have depended on foreign financing to make up the shortfall in investment capital. In 1997, Taiwan's government-guaranteed foreign debts were next to nothing—0.03 percent of its GDP—and its debt-servicing payment was only 0.04 percent of its total exports. In the period between 1993 and 1996, the external liabilities of Taiwan's private sector as a percentage of GDP averaged 10.6 percent, which was much lower than other crisis-inflicted Asian economies. In addition, the gross value of the foreign assets owned by Taiwan's private sector has consistently exceeded its external liabilities. Between 1990 and 1996, fdi accounted for less than 3.5 percent of the fixed capital investment. By mid-1997, foreign portfolio investment accounted for less than 4 percent of the total market value of the securities listed in the Taiwan Stock Exchange. This means that Taiwan's economy depends very lit-

tle on foreign capital as source of financing. The stock market is much less susceptible to the cross-border movement of short-term capital than the markets of most
other East Asian economies. In contrast, South Korea had to finance its shortfall in
investment capital, which amounted to 4.1 percent of GDP in 1996, entirely
through foreign borrowing. As of the end of 1996, South Korea's total external debt
reached US$116.1 billion, approximately 23 percent of the GDP and approximately
three-fifths of it short-term debt (loans with a maturity of less than one year).

Fourth, most of Taiwan's big enterprises maintain a sound corporate financing
structure that allows them to withstand the credit crunch during economic downturns. The debt-to-equity ratios for Taiwan's enterprises averaged 160 percent on
the eve of the financial crisis (Chiu 1998). By mid-1997, the average debt ratio for
large enterprises was only 109 percent,[5] much lower than the 400 percent among the
South Korean *chaebŏl*. Actually, Taiwan's SMEs typically incur a much higher debt
ratio (around 200 percent) than their larger counterparts (Yen 1998). This is because
the large enterprises can raise most of their targeted capital through direct financing
in the capital market. Overall, Taiwanese corporations depend much less than their
South Korean counterparts on bank loans; between 1990 and 1996, bank loans
accounted for only approximately 22 percent of corporate financing (Chung 1998,
44). This is because Taiwan's financial sector is uniquely characterized by the coexistence of a conservative banking sector and a dynamic capital market. On one hand,
Taiwan's banking sector has been a drag on the process of economic restructuring.
The state-owned banks, which still dominate the banking sector, have been minimally internationalized and are very conservative in their lending policies. On the
other hand, financial deregulation in the early 1990s has led to a boom in the capital
market. Around mid-1997, Taiwan's stock market ranked sixth in the world in average trading volume and fifteenth in terms of overall capitalization.[6] Since its takeoff
in 1994, Taiwan's over-the-counter market has rapidly expanded into one of the
most highly capitalized over-the-counter markets in the world. In addition, Taiwan
is the only place in Asia that has successfully followed the United States' lead in pursuing venture capital (*FEER* 10 September 1998, 62–63). As a result, high-growth
firms raised capital mainly through rights issues and initial public offerings, through
which approximately US$26.6 billion was raised between 1994 and 1997. Also, ven-
ture capital fills a void created by the unwillingness of the island's conservative banks
to invest in risky start-ups. By mid-1998, 108 venture-capital funds were licensed.
The total pool of the venture-capital funds is approximately NT$60 billion. The
bulk of the funds have been funneled into high-technology companies.

Fifth, Taiwan had brought an overheated stock market and real estate sector partially under control before the regional financial crisis broke out. The government
had taken some strong measures to curb the flow of capital from the banking and
insurance sectors into the real estate market since early 1989. The bubble economy
was effectively cooled down by 1993. Since mid-1996, both the stock and real estate
markets have been in the process of slow recovery. Therefore, the impact of the
regional financial crisis on both markets was not too significant—it simply prolonged the process of recession. Nevertheless, the health of the banking sector was

still damaged somewhat. In particular, the protracted recession in the real estate sector was largely responsible for the rise in the ratio of nonperforming loans from 2.67 percent of total outstanding loans in 1992 to 4.13 percent by the end of 1997, which is still much lower than in most afflicted Asian economies.

Lastly, Taiwan has diversified its export markets since the late 1980s. Mainland China has risen to be Taiwan's second largest export market and single largest source of trade surplus over the last ten years. ASEAN, South Korea, and Japan accounted for 27.3 percent of Taiwan's total exports in 1996 and 19.6 percent in 1997. During the financial crisis, Taiwan's three leading trading partners, the United States, China (plus Hong Kong), and the European Union, were still in a phase of economic expansion and generated strong demand for Taiwan's exports. The three leading markets accounted for 61.4 percent of Taiwan's total exports in 1996 and 63.4 percent in 1997. Otherwise, Taiwan would have experienced even worse export performance.

Political Foundation of Taiwan's Economic Resilience

In Taiwan, state policies, more than anything else, have fostered the development of a decentralized industrial structure, a flexible labor market, the module of domestically financed growth, the dualistic nature of its financial sector, and a unique pattern of corporate financing. Elements of economic resilience have been nurtured both by the state's development strategy and policy guidelines for macroeconomic management over the long run and by its policy responses to the twin challenges of globalization and democratization over the short to medium run. The state's longstanding policy guideline for macroeconomic management is characterized by its overriding concern over monetary and financial stability and fiscal balance. Also, its established pattern of industrial targeting is in part designed to address the deficiency of the SMEs in financing and research and development (Chu 1995). In response to the challenge of globalization, the state has chosen a sequence of financial liberalization that gives priority to deregulating the domestic capital market over internationalization (i.e., foreign participation). Despite the trend toward an integrated global financial market, the state has been keen in safeguarding its ability to set monetary targets by preventing the internationalization of local currency and controlling the volatility of cross-border movement of short-term capital. Amid the trend of politicization of economic policy making that came with the island's democratization, the state has managed to protect the autonomy of the monetary authority and contain the erosive effect of "money politics" on the health of the banking sector through institutional adjustments.

The state's economic strategies have not only been driven by the perceived need to harmonize economic relations with Taiwan's major trading partners and facilitate the structural adjustment of the economy, but they also have been shaped by a set of existing institutional arrangements and established policy orientations. These institutional arrangements structure the power relations among different economic agencies within the overall state apparatus and constrain the scope of political participation in economic decision making by business, labor, and other interest groups. These policy orientations, which reflect the collective memories and learning that the incumbent elite has acquired over a long period of time, set the parameters for policy discourse and deliberation within the state apparatus. At a more fundamental level, the incumbent elite inherited, established, maintained, and adjusted these institutional arrangements and policy orientations to cope with changing security environments and to meet the challenge of institutionalizing a one-party dominant regime amid rapid socioeconomic transformation. These institutional arrangements and policy orientations are not immutable, but they tend to have strong staying power as long as the KMT continues to enjoy undisrupted one-party political dominance.

Autonomy of the Monetary Authority

A long-standing institutional characteristic of Taiwan's economic decision making is the privileged status of the CBC within the overall state apparatus. The CBC is formally a part of the cabinet,[7] but in practice it is always under the direct control of the president. The governor of the CBC is almost always hand-picked by the president, rather than the premier.[8] The bank occupies a unique position in the state apparatus, because it is at the same time a part of the economic bureaucracy and a part of the national security apparatus, which falls under the exclusive purview of the president. As a result, the CBC has long occupied the commanding heights of the state economic bureaucracy; its governor is always considered the most senior economic minister.[9] The CBC has been staffed by elite technocrats, who enjoy a prestige unmatched by any other economic ministries. The CBC's governor is protected by a renewable term of five years; most governors stay on for a long period of time, much longer than the cabinet.[10] Virtually all governors serve two terms or more.[11]

The CBC is more than just a monetary authority. It is also entrusted with an extensive regulatory authority over the banking sector and capital market. Some of its supervisory and investigative authority overlaps with the Ministry of Finance (Yin 1998), and many finance ministers were themselves former deputy governors of the CBC. The Ministry of Finance traditionally has played second fiddle to the CBC as far as banking regulation is concerned. The bank can overrule the Finance Ministry, which deals with the constituencies in the financial sector more directly, over the sequence and timetable of financial deregulation and internationalization. The CBC also serves as a check on the expansionist tendencies of the planning technocrats and sets the limits on the use of credit policy in industrial targeting. The steering power of the CBC over the banking sector was further buttressed by an array of state-owned banks that virtually monopolized the first-tier banking (i.e., commercial banks). Before the opening up of the banking sector in 1992, the state-owned banks accounted for more than two-thirds of total outstanding loans and discounts. Private participation was limited to the second-tier money banks, consisting of regional savings and loans, city credit cooperative associations, and credit departments of farmers' and fishermen's associations at the grassroots level.

During the authoritarian years, the governor of CBC usually had more say than the premier, let alone the Finance Ministry or the governor of Taiwan province, in the appointment of senior bank officials (S. Chen 1998, 64). As a result, the CBC can pull a number of disciplinary strings over the lending policy of state-owned banks through the rediscount window, financial inspections, and appointment power.

This arrangement was originally designed to prevent a replay of the disastrous hyperinflation and currency crisis of 1947–48, which had contributed to the defeat of the KMT leadership by the Communist regime in 1949 (Cheng 1993). The CBC was entrusted with the authority to protect the island's economic stability in the name of national security and for the sake of the political security of the KMT regime.[12] The CBC became the institutional embodiment of the incumbent elite's overriding concern for monetary and financial stability. During the 1970s, the two oil shocks and the crisis of diplomatic recognition, which functionally replaced the fading memory of the civil war, reinforced the political rationale for a privileged and autonomous CBC.

Under the steering authority of the CBC and the Finance Ministry, for almost four decades the Nationalist government has invariably maintained a positive real interest rate, minimum public-sector foreign debt, small fiscal deficit, a fixed exchange rate pegged to the U.S. dollar, restrictions on the convertibility of the NT dollar, a rigorous regulatory regime over financial institutions, and a conservative ethos that permeates the entire banking sector. State-owned banks almost always demand collateral for their loans. Most state-owned banks have maintained their capital-to-assets ratio above 12 percent (Yin 1998, 127), which is much higher than the International Bank of Settlement's 8 percent requirement. Also, Taiwan's reserve requirement has been among the highest in the world, hovering around a weighted average reserves-to-deposits ratio of 9.26 percent. As a check on the expansionist tendencies of the planning technocrats at the Ministry of Economic Affairs, the CBC and the Finance Ministry have customarily insisted that targeted lending to the private sector be backed up by government-financed specialized funds, so that the ceiling of policy loans can be kept under tight control. It would therefore be hard for the Ministry of Economic Affairs to force the banks to make loans to private industrial development projects unless the projects are worthy financially.[13]

However, even during the authoritarian years, the banking sector was not entirely immune from unduly political influences. First, the seventy-plus credit cooperative associations and three hundred credit departments of farmers' and fishermen's associations were subject to more relaxed banking inspection schemes not only because of their limited banking functions and small operations, but also because these grassroots financial institutions have long served as the cash cows for the KMT-affiliated local factions. The seven leading state-owned commercial banks, which were formally under the Provincial Government, were under constant pressure to offer soft loans to individual members of the Provincial Assembly. However, the rent-seeking activities by corruption-prone local factions did not go without being checked. First, the KMT has intentionally created rivalry among competing factions in a given locality. Thus, a system of "competitive clientelism" was installed throughout the island. The rival factions served as countervailing forces against each other in the distribution of political rents. Furthermore, to contain the encroachment of political cronyism, the CBC and the Ministry of Finance have imposed on local financial institutions a strictly limited scope of deposit/loan operations and geographical span, and a requirement to redeposit their surplus reserves in designated state-owned banks (Huang 1998). The CBC and the Finance Ministry always stand ready to close down insolvent local financial institutions through forced merger and acquisition. With the encouragement of the ruling party, as a measure of expedience, the state-owned commercial banks were allowed to offer an implicit quota of soft loans to individual provincial assemblymen on an equal basis. With these controlling measures, the CBC and the Finance Ministry have been able to keep the nonperforming loan ratio of the overall banking system at a sustainable level.[14]

The deregulation of the financial sector in the late 1980s and early 1990s was prompted by economic exigency. A series of ominous economic signs—the mushrooming of underground financial institutions, bubbles in the real estate and stock markets, and rapid deterioration of private-sector investment—compelled the government to take decisive measures to overhaul the anachronous financial sector (Chu and Lee 1998). Since 1989, the government has introduced a series of measures to deregulate the banking sector. Fixed interest rate schemes were abolished. New licenses for commercial banks were issued to qualified private investors. Regional savings and loans were upgraded to medium-sized business banks. Restrictions on the operations of foreign banks were relaxed. However, the privatization plan for state-owned commercial banks, the centerpiece of the banking reform, was held off until mid-1998,[15] and the new privatization timetable announced in 1997 has been subject to further delays. The privatization plan is slow to come because, on the one hand, it has been strongly resisted by the Provincial Assembly to protect the prerogatives of individual members, and, on the other hand, it never received strong backing by the CBC. By mid-1998, the seven leading commercial banks under the Provincial Government still accounted for close to one-half of the total outstanding loans of the banking sector. As an alternative, the Finance Ministry moved at full speed to deregulate the capital market and provide the private sector with an expanding source of direct financing. In 1988, the Finance Ministry lifted the long-time ban on setting up new brokerage houses. In 1995, to promote money market transactions, new, privately-owned bill financing companies were licensed to compete with the three existing semi-official institutions.

The CBC has consciously built up Taiwan's shock-absorbing capacity to withstand potential diplomatic shocks, military tension, or economic sanctions that the PRC might instigate to bring the island to its knees. The government has purposely built up not only a huge foreign reserve, but also an exceptionally large oil and food reserve. A big cushion is justified, because Taiwan would have to survive on the basis of self-help if its relationship with the PRC should worsen. Taiwan has not been a member of the IMF or the World Bank since 1978 and could not count on an international rescue package during a currency crisis or on bilateral emergency loans from its security partner. With dwindling diplomatic recognition, official foreign reserves have almost become a benchmark measure of Taiwan's self-confidence.

This mentality explains why the CBC was very hesitant to remove foreign exchange controls despite a clear trend of soaring trade surplus from the early 1980s on. The bank put off foreign currency deregulation until mid-1987, when the U.S. Trade Representative Office started putting the undervalued NT dollar in the political spotlight, when the current account surplus reached a staggering 19 percent of GNP, and when the accumulation of the trade surplus and domestic savings started to wreak havoc on the real estate and stock markets. In July 1987, the CBC finally decided to remove most restrictions on private holding of foreign currencies and to nurture the growth of a foreign exchange spot market and, later, a futures market. However, since then the CBC has established a panoply of monitoring schemes and has continued to intervene heavily to prevent excessive short-term fluctuation. Restrictions on the futures market were loosened only gradually. Until the end of 1996, the CBC still required banks to keep their foreign exchange derivatives positions below 33 percent of their total foreign exchange positions. More important, the CBC was resolved to prevent an internationalization of its local currency. The CBC still prohibited domestic banks from offering local currency accounts to their customers abroad and restricted the outbound movement of the NT dollar. In essence, the CBC has been keen in curbing the growth of an offshore foreign exchange market of the NT dollar. In so doing, the CBC can retain its position as the sole market maker of NT dollars. Furthermore, the foreign borrowings for Taiwan's banks were traditionally low, because the CBC restricted banks' holding of foreign assets and owing of foreign liabilities. Despite the flood of cheap yen in the international money market in the early 1990s, domestic banks did not engage in heavy short-term foreign borrowing or participate actively in the global financial markets.

Bowing to pressure from the United States, Taiwan's stock market was opened to foreign institutional investors in early 1991. Under the influence of the CBC, the Finance Ministry imposed a strict investment cap on foreign investors. Initially, each foreign institutional investor could invest up to US$50 million, and the cap for total foreign investment was set at $2.5 billion, which represented only approximately 2 percent of total market capitalization. Each institution was allowed to buy up to 5 percent of a single company, and total foreign ownership of each company was limited to 10 percent. As part of the down payment during the WTO negotiation with the United States, the Finance Ministry was compelled to raise the investment cap step by step. By early 1997, the capital ceiling for individual foreign institutional investors was raised to US$600 million. The cap on ownership by an individual foreign institutional investor in any listed company was raised to 15 percent, and no more than 30 percent for all foreign investors.[16]

The island's economic resilience was put to a rigorous test when the PRC employed saber-rattling strategies in the summer of 1995 and in March of 1996. During the first missile crisis of July 1995, the stock market lost approximately one-third of its total value, and the local currency dived by 9 percent. The CBC intervened heavily to support the NT dollar; the Finance Ministry was instructed to set up a stock market stabilization fund, and all government-run investment funds were required to chip in and to buy in. Managing the missile crisis, as it turned out, functioned as an unintended rehearsal of the East Asian financial shock that came a year later.

Changing State-Business Relations

At the zenith of the one-party authoritarian rule, the KMT relied on a proven formula for maintaining the entrenched political dominance of the mainlander elite (the émigré group that fled to the island after its members were defeated by the Chinese Communists on the mainland in 1949) at the national level and controlling a limited popular electoral process implemented at the local level. The institutionalization of the paramount leader in the party power structure laid the foundation for the autonomy and coherence of the party-state. At the grassroots level, the KMT used the existing patron-client networks to establish complex local political machinery within the party structure throughout the island. The KMT appropriated the economic premiums generated by local government procurement, zoning policies, and regional oligopolistic sectors, such as public utilities, transportation, and local credit unions to cultivate the political allegiance of the local native elite.

The development of Korean-style conglomerates was virtually impossible in the first three decades of the post-War era. The mainlander elite discouraged concentration of wealth for both political and ideological reasons. First, the KMT had implemented a comprehensive land reform (i.e., a redistribution of wealth) between 1948 and 1951 to prevent Communist insurgence in the rural area. Second, a decentralized industrial structure served the political interests of the ruling elite well. Overconcentration of industrial power and wealth not only might pose a potential political threat to the mainlander elite, but could undermine the KMT's claim that it embodies the interest of all classes. On the other hand, the myriad of SMEs that grew around the state-sponsored, export-oriented industrialization strategy has enabled the KMT to broaden its social base; the emerging industrial structure addressed both growth and equity issues with a high degree of effectiveness. More importantly, the monopoly or near-monopoly of the SOEs had preempted the private participation in the financial sector, the public utility sector, and most of the capital-intensive industries from the very beginning.

Formidable institutional cleavages were erected between the party's national leadership and the private business community. The mainlander state elite and native business elite shared very little in the way of lineage bonds, marital ties, or common social backgrounds. The formal channel between government officials and private-sector business leaders was through the state-sponsored industrial associations that were created throughout the economy. Business was not able to assert itself as an autonomous and organized political actor in the policy-making process, and neither were its interests well represented in the party power structure. The KMT-directed political structure encouraged businessmen to seek particularistic ties rather than attempt group-based coalition politics. Business was politically weak because big businesses depended on the state for essential economic resources. The private sector lacked organizational and ideological endowment for autonomous collective actions. More important, the state was relatively strong in relation to private business, because it was endowed with a centralized political authority, an oversized military and administrative apparatus, and a huge array of SOEs. The party-state could shape the patterns of segmentation and association within the business community through its control of the organizational bases of interest intermediaries and its power of institutional creation. Finally, the political support of the business community was not a weighty factor in sustaining the political security of the regime, which has based its legitimacy on international recognition, its irreplaceable function in protecting the island from the aggression of mainland China, and its effectiveness in bringing about economic prosperity. None of these required a full-fledged political recognition of the business sector. The relative autonomy of the economic technocrats derived from the fact that they answered only to the party's top leadership and were responsible mainly for the overall performance of the economy and the success of the targeted sectors.

The political ascent of the business elite was not fully actualized until the end of the 1980s. With the 1988 death of the last strong man, Chiang Ching-kuo, the cohesion of the party's central leadership deteriorated, and the pace of democratization quickened. Personnel turnovers, a split within the party leadership, and the new democratic institutions provided the business community with a strategic opening that was sometimes beyond its conception.

First, an expanded electoral avenue and an ascending parliament provided the business elite with new opportunities to pursue influence buying at strategic junctures in the policy-making process. Structured corruption that had long been fermenting in local electoral politics was rapidly transferred to the national electoral arena. This structured corruption involved candidate-centered election financing and campaigns; institutionalized vote-buying mechanisms; and relentless pursuit of pork barrels, economic prerogatives, and bribes for replenishing the campaign chest (Bosco 1994). The diversified business groups suddenly became the most sought-after patrons of elective politicians and local factions. Starting from the 1995 Legislative Yuan election, even some of the opposition candidates have been trapped into addictive soliciting of money.

Second, the old institutional insulation between the party-state central leadership and the business sector began to melt down. As the trend of indigenization of the party-state power structure accelerated, the infiltration of social forces through interpersonal connections revived.

More important, the power struggle over political succession, which was entwined with division over the scope of political reform, compelled competing power blocs within the party's central leadership to bring in new allies from the outside. The only visible and ideologically compatible social forces in the civil society were the family-controlled diversified business groups. In a race to build a broad-based constituency in the business community, party leaders and government officials began to turn a ready ear to business leaders. The business community as a whole began to be accorded a more prominent position in the party power structure, and the selective incorporation of the past was replaced by a more inclusive approach (Chu 1994).

In the new political climate, economic officials began to embrace a pro-business outlook. They took long-awaited reform proposals out of the pigeonhole and expedited their passage through the bureaucratic process. Between 1988 and 1991, the state economic bureaucracy made more deregulation decisions than it had in the preceding three decades. The government removed the entry restrictions in a series of sectors, such as the commercial banking, investment banking, construction, mass transportation, airlines, and midstream petrochemical sectors, which had been dominated by SOEs. A number of state-harbored oligopolies, such as security brokerage, newspapers, and insurance, were also opened to new entrants.

The emerging political clout of the business elite has weakened the autonomy of the state economic bureaucracy. The Legislative Yuan has become an arena for horse-trading among economic officials, party officials, and lawmakers, who act as surrogates for special business interests. Many economic and financial legislative proposals became the targets of intensive lobbying. An immediate consequence of the politicization of economic decision making is that the Cabinet can no longer force its will upon the Legislative Yuan.

However, the influence of the special business interests over economic policy making has clear limits. The business community as a political force has many weaknesses. The big-business elite still craves particularistic ties and proprietary return from political investment, but it shuns building the permanent organizational base and impersonal links necessary for broad-based collective actions. As a result, the business community is a far from cohesive entity in both organizational and ideological terms.

Moreover, the KMT, being an oversized, richly endowed, and autocratically governed political machine, provides the institutional foundation for the undisrupted political dominance of its national leadership over local factions and big business. Unlike the Liberal Democratic Party in Japan or the ruling parties in South Korea, the KMT, which owns a huge array of business interests itself, relies little on political donations by the business community. Through the exercise of purse power, business interests can capture individual lawmakers or even an entire local faction, but not the ruling party. The political democratization, so far, has not transfigured the KMT's power structure at the core.

Most vital economic measures, measures that have economy-wide ramifications, are still within the purview of the cabinet. As a last resort, economic officials can take their cases to the premier or the president and ask those figures to throw their weight behind key economic proposals that are deemed crucial to achieving priority development objectives. After all, under the existing institutional arrangements, the KMT's leadership still has a final say over nomination decisions, and no individual legislator is politically indispensable or electorally invincible. The economic planning technocrats are encouraged by the overall success of the past development strategy, which relied more on SMEs than on big business as an agent of industrial upgrading and technological innovation. The industrial upgrading strategy of the 1980s and 1990s did not discriminate against SMEs. On the contrary, the state economic bureaucracy has been keen in addressing the deficiency of SMEs: through public-funded support of research and development and of technological transfer, the provision of venture capital, and a lending guideline stipulating that all medium-sized business banks must extend at least 60 percent of their outstanding loans to SMEs. The bulk of these loans is backed by the Small and Medium Business Credit Guarantee Fund, which helps enterprises with great developmental potential to readily obtain funds from financial institutions without collateral.

Economic technocrats in the CBC and the Finance Ministry still have a decisive say in devising the priority and timetable of deregulation and liberalization and in the design of the new regulatory scheme and mechanism. The opening-up of the banking sector, the most far-reaching financial deregulation over the last ten years, is a good example. The original design of the Finance Ministry was largely kept intact as it came out of the legislative tunnel at the end of 1989. The revised Banking Law was designed to ensure stability, promote diversified ownership, and prevent the emergence of Japanese-styled keiretsu. In its finalized version, the minimum capital requirement is set at NT$10 billion (US$400 million); the share of a single corporate investor is limited to 5 percent, and that of a diversified business group to no more than 15 percent (S. Chen 1998, 82–84). The only major concession made to lawmakers is a 50 percent reduction of the minimum capital requirement from the proposed NT$20 billion, which is extraordinarily high by international standards and probably was used by the Finance Ministry simply for bargaining leverage.

Another case in point lies in the high-handed measures implemented by the CBC to bring an overheated real estate market under control between 1989 and 1993. To curb the excessive capital flow into the real estate market, on 28 February 1989 the CBC imposed a new ceiling capping the amount of secured loans that a bank could extend on real estate. The restriction was in force for almost six years. In 1992, on the recommendation of the Finance Ministry and the CBC, the Insurance Law was revised to lower the ceiling ratio of real estate investments to total capital from 33 to 19 percent for insurance companies. To prevent the weaker local financial institutions from crumbling over a protracted downturn in the real estate sector, the Finance Ministry pushed through a compulsory deposit insurance scheme in 1992 to cover almost 90 percent of local financial institutions, despite strong resistance from local politicians.

Three trends helped the KMT's central leadership regain its coherence and steering capacity as it entered the second half of the 1990s. First, the intraparty power struggle over political succession and political reform turned out to be an aberration rather than the norm. By early 1993, Lee Teng-hui had successfully marginalized the so-called non-mainstream faction and recentralized power in the hands of the party chairman. Second, after the democratization process had run its full course, the opposition parties steadily lost their electoral momentum. They could no longer galvanize voters with a fresh democratic reform agenda.[17] Third, the presidency was strengthened, rather than weakened, by the democratization process. Both the popular base and the constitutional power of the president, the pinnacle of state power, were further buttressed by the introduction of popular elections in 1996. The latest constitutional change was favored by both the KMT and the major opposition, the DPP. Out of concern for national security, both parties believed that a popular election for the highest executive office would not only boost Taiwan's international visibility, but would also strengthen the government's position in both cross-Strait negotiation and domestic political bargaining.

The autonomy of the economic bureaucracy, in the final analysis, is built on the autonomy of the party's top leadership. So far, the political ascent of the business elite is still quite circumscribed when it comes to leverage over the top party leadership. The KMT remains essentially a hierarchically structured constellation of entrenched state and party elite based permanently in the state and party apparatus. As long as there is no alternative power pact in sight, the incumbent party can effectively use its unabated staying power and incontestable hegemonic presence in society to make long-term policy commitments and to construct an unequal partnership with the business elite, in which the party-state elite set the limits on influence buying and policy contestation. And as long as the "garrison state" mentality prevails among the KMT's top leadership, the CBC and the Finance Ministry will continue to enjoy privileged status within the overall state economic bureaucracy. There is little ground for doubting that the "garrison state" mentality will wane over time. After all, safeguarding the country's military and economic security has been the raison d'être of the KMT's long-term political dominance.

At the same time, it has been intrinsically difficult for the principal opposition, the DPP, to capture any major social groups with a distinctive set of socioeconomic programs. Beneath Taiwan's long-running economic prosperity and full employment is a very fluid class structure. A highly decentralized private sector exists, which generates a large number of owner-operators and a sizable temporary working class. A large portion of the male population experiences vertical social mobility (i.e., class mobility) during their lives or within their families. The economic structures inhibit the growth of independent union movements in an even more decisive way. Most companies and work-units are relatively small. This means most laborers do not enjoy much collective bargaining power over their employers to begin with. Also, the majority of the industrial laborers are first-generation working class. Their social identities are still heavily shaped by their primary social bonds rather than by class status. By the time the second-generation working class arrived on the scene in the early 1990s, Taiwan's economy was already moving into a service-based and brain-intensive economy. Thus, in Taiwan, there was never a politically active working class that might have provided the opposition a solid social foundation. As a result, the DPP has become a mirror image of the KMT in terms of its all-class appeal.

Coping with the Financial Crisis

The Asian currency crisis has preoccupied economic policy makers in Taiwan since September 1997. When the tidal wave of competitive currency devaluation hit Taiwan in September 1997, the CBC spent more than US$7 billion resisting the market's efforts to drive the local currency below NT$28.6 to US$1. However, it became clear around mid-October that the CBC's intervention would only increase speculative pressure and invite more hedge funds to the gambling table, because the market expectation for devaluation was so overwhelming. In a high-level meeting among the president, premier, and CBC governor, the government decided on October 17 to change its strategy by allowing the NT dollar to float. Over the following weeks, the Taiwan currency lost ground and fell to NT$31.4 to US$1. Toward the end of November, the descent of the South Korean wón further dragged the NT dollar down, to NT$33 to $US1.

The CBC did not give up its fight to halt the slide of Taiwan's currency. It was simply waiting for the best moment to intervene again (i.e., when the Japanese yen started to stabilize). At the same time, the CBC took steps to consolidate its attacking position. On 25 May 1998, without advance warning, the CBC closed down the no-deposit future trading for domestic institutional investors. The CBC also reintroduced an old monitoring measure, requiring all foreign exchange traders to report any transaction exceeding US$0.5 million by individuals and US$1 million by corporations to the CBC immediately and to submit the required documentation of every such transaction for inspection. Lastly, the CBC occasionally took disciplinary measures to punish unruly currency traders, such as imposing a punitive overnight lending rate on targeted foreign banks, zeroing in on the most infamous currency arbitragers to make sure that they would lose big, and phoning select high-wired traders directly to give moral persuasion. By late August, the Taiwan currency finally settled at approximately NT$33 to US$1. It rebounded to approximately NT$32.2 to US$1 by the end of 1998.

At the same time, the government took swift measures to extend liquidity to afflicted Taiwanese firms in Southeast Asia. On 12 March 1998, the CBC earmarked US$1.36 billion (through depositing a fraction of the official reserve in overseas branches of domestic banks) for the relief financing of Taiwanese investors in Southeast Asia. The next day, the cabinet approved a package that provided a special fund of NT$10 billion through the China Export-Import Bank for issuing export insurance to domestic firms exporting to Southeast Asian countries. The rescue operation was followed by a new initiative, led by the KMT-owned China Development Trust, to hunt for good bargains. With government endorsement, a new investment trust (the Southeast Asia Investment Holding Company) was created with initial capital of NT$20 billion for investing in the stock market and financing the acquisition of troubled financial institutions in Southeast Asia.

The government responded to signs of domestic economic slowdown by adopting an expansionary fiscal policy. In the summer of 1998, it put together an NT$652.6 billion expansionary package of government spending for the fiscal year ending June 1999. Of this amount, NT$541.8 billion was designated to expedite already planned projects, and the remaining NT$110.8 billion was earmarked for newly initiated projects. This fiscal stimulus package was estimated to boost growth by approximately 0.6 percent. The Finance Ministry also pumped more money into the SME Credit Guarantee Fund to create an additional NT$78.8 billion liquidity for the SMEs.

While the government was busy writing the expansionary fiscal package into the actual budget, the private sector in Taiwan began to show serious signs of trouble in the fourth quarter of 1998. The situation reached a semi-crisis level in late October and November 1998, when a number of big business groups' checks bounced and prices of their stocks plummeted, amid the eruption of large-scale defaults in stock transactions. In addition, at least two bill financing companies and one commercial bank were taken over by government-designated financial institutions. The bank experienced bank runs of approximately NT\$55 billion in three days; the NT\$32.1 billion run on 25 November 1998 set the record for the biggest single-day withdrawal in Taiwan's post-War financial history (*United Daily News* 27 November 1998). These threatening developments prompted the government to (1) announce a "special rescue program to aid enterprises in need of funds" and (2) arrange for public and private institutions to purchase stocks to bolster the stock market.[18] The CBC also intervened by loosening the money supply (raising the interest rate paid on the reserve B account by 0.3 percent, from 2.4 to 2.7 percent). Furthermore, the governor of the CBS reportedly indicated that, for those banks restricting credit to the business sector, help from the CBS would not likely be forthcoming in the future (*China Times* 20 November 1998). With these stimulus programs in place, the Taiwan Stock Exchange rose 645 points between 13 and 19 November, or 9.69 percent in five trading days. However, it is too early to assess at this point whether the current round of financial troubles will soon be pacified or will deteriorate further in the future.

The financial fiascoes of the last half of the 1990s suggest that the rapid expansion of the capital market in the early 1990s has created an apparent trade-off between market efficiency and financial risk. An important example is the liberalization of the bill financing companies, which has been the driving force leading to financial turmoil. In 1995, the Ministry of Finance, which is more susceptible to political pressures than the CBC, agreed to open the lucrative commercial paper and unsecured corporate bond markets before setting up an adequate supervisory framework. The threshold for paid-in capital was set at NT\$2 billion, compared to NT\$10 billion for commercial banks, and the bill-financing companies are allowed to endorse commercial papers amounting to as much as 12.5 times their equity. Thirteen new bill-financing companies were approved in all. However, the regulatory regime was very rudimentary (e.g., no provision was made for handling troubled bill financing companies). Moreover, the regulation of cross-holding of ownership among (related) companies in general was inadequate. The combination of the two regulatory weaknesses proved to be calamitous. After the forced merger of two bill financing companies, the Ministry of Finance finally took remedial measures—freezing the license for bill financing companies indefinitely and setting up a credit rating agency, Taiwan Ratings Corporation, to make risk at the bill financing companies more transparent.

Generally speaking, the financial shock of the Asian crisis in Taiwan once again accentuated the role of the CBC in safeguarding the island's economic stability. The CBC did not shy away from intensive intervention but acted swiftly and decisively, with the assistance of the healthy financial institutions. No doubt the fact that the government still maintains de facto control of the major commercial banks (despite technical privatization) is also an important factor. Deposits at public banks, including the Postal Savings, and "private" banks in which the government remains the largest shareholder, account for approximately 70 percent of total deposits as of November 1998.

The storm also reinforced the long-standing fiscal and financial conservatism of the CBC and the Finance Ministry. It prompted economic officials to reexamine both the rationale and the timetable for further capital market liberalization. Government leaders are now actively looking for "off-mainstream" views, not from Mahathir Mohamad, but from Jagdish Bhagwati, Paul Krugman, and Jeffrey Sachs, to support their suspicions about the merit of free cross-border capital mobility and the wisdom of the "Washington consensus."[19] There are clear signs that Taiwan will back off from its pledge that, by the year 2000, it will liberalize all restrictions on portfolio investment.

Conclusion

It would be erroneous to think that Taiwan has not been affected by the Asian crisis. It would also be premature to believe that Taiwan's economy can independently maintain high growth rates regardless of the conditions in the rest of Asia. Nevertheless, by mid-1999, Taiwan remains one of the strongholds against the contagion of the Asian financial crisis. Its unique capacity to absorb external financial shocks is built on a successful implementation of industrial upgrading strategies throughout the 1990s, a flexible labor market, a vibrant capital market, the efficiency and adaptability of Taiwan's SMEs, a sound corporate financing structure enjoyed by a great majority of big businesses, low dependence on foreign portfolios and investment, and very limited exposure to short-term foreign borrowing.

Elements of economic resilience have been nurtured by the state's development strategy and policy guidelines for macroeconomic management over the long run and by its policy responses to the twin challenges of globalization and democratization over the short to medium run. The state's long-standing policy guideline for macroeconomic management is characterized by its overriding concern for monetary and financial stability and fiscal balance. The state has enjoyed direct control over the bulk of the banking sector, maintained a rigorous regulatory regime over the non-state banking sector, and refrained from an extensive use of credit policies in promoting targeted industries. The state's strategy for industrial targeting is in part designed to address the deficiency of the SMEs versus the big businesses and multinationals in the areas of financing and of research and development. In response to the challenge of globalization, the state has chosen a sequence of financial liberalization that gives priority to deregulating the domestic capital market over internationalization. During the process of democratization, the state has managed to protect the autonomy of the monetary authority and contain the erosive effect of "money politics" on the health of the banking sector. The island's decentralized business structure has preempted the growth of independent union movements despite the removal of outright political suppression.

The state's policy responses to globalization and democratization emanated from existing institutional arrangements and established policy orientations. The state's economic bureaucracy was characterized by its relative insulation from influence buying, by the supremacy of monetary authority over planning technocrats, and by a professed "garrison state" mentality among top economic officials. The KMT leadership established and maintained these institutional arrangements and policy orientations in light of the need to cope with the security challenge posed by the rival regime across the Taiwan Strait and to protect the long-term political security of the ruling party. The KMT top leadership, because it is buttressed by a more extensive social support for its development strategy, an elaborate party apparatus, and ingenious electoral design, has been able to construct an unequal partnership with big business and local factions and to set limits on influence buying and policy contestation amid the process of democratization. In turn, the long-term political dominance of the KMT and the centralization of power at the apex of the ruling party enhance the relative autonomy of the state economic bureaucracy versus rent-seeking social actors.

In contrast, South Korea's high-debt model, which was characterized by a national industrial strategy of channeling state-mediated capital into large firms trying to conquer foreign markets, ran into serious troubles under globalization and democratization. The often-cited structural features of the South Korean model (the supremacy of the planning agency over the monetary authority, the slight autonomy enjoyed by domestic banking institutions with respect to lending criteria and responses to nonperforming loans, the high debt to equity ratio in the *chaebŏl*, and the extensive mutual payment guarantees among companies of the *chaebŏl* [Woo 1991; Cho and Kim 1995]) might have continued to fuel the industrialization of Korean economy without risking a financial crisis with the help of five supporting conditions: First, the state could act as an effective risk partner of the private sector, standing ready to write off bad loans through either inflationary refinancing of the nonperforming loans to bail out firms or through expansion of the state's equity share in the banks. Second, the planning agency could maintain the capacity to monitor and regulate the business strategies of the *chaebŏl* to minimize the moral hazard. Third, the state could maintain the cleavage between the domestic financial sector and foreign financial market. Fourth, the regime could withstand the political backlash against the trend toward high concentration of economic power. Fifth, the South Korean government could knock on the door of U.S. and Japanese governments, its ultimate security guarantors, for concessional loans in times of balance-of-payments crisis. The *chaebŏl* were able to expand rapidly and aggressively because they faced a basically risk-free environment. Their profit remained high because they were protected economically from foreign competition in the home market and politically from strong unions.

However, in the 1990s, the implicit co-insurance scheme among the state, banks, and industry began to unravel. Under foreign and domestic pressures for liberalization and deregulation, the government gradually lost its capacity to monitor and supervise the business operations of Korean firms and banks, especially with respect to short-term foreign borrowing and risky financial investment in the foreign markets. In addition, democratization aggravated the legitimacy crisis of the high-debt model. All democratically elected governments were compelled to introduce economic reforms. Every new government vowed to promote reformist labor policies and to take the measures necessary to moderate the market power of the *chaebŏl* and enhance their competitiveness, but, in almost every area of reform, the government oscillated between reform and the status quo. New governments began with ambitious reform projects, but finished by backsliding at the end of their administrations (Mo and Moon 1998, 15–17). The inconsistency in government policy toward labor and the *chaebŏl* eventually undermined the confidence of the international financial community, which had always assumed that the Korean government would stand behind the *chaebŏl* and the banks in a time of trouble. Specifically, the government's indecisiveness in handling the Hanbo bankruptcy in January 1997 and the Kia crisis between July and October 1997 sent a shock wave not only through Korea but also through the international financial community, which began to call in loans and deny roll overs. After failing to secure a bilateral rescue package from the U.S. government, the South Korean government had no choice but to apply for IMF standby loans. Thus, in the South Korean case, there is a clear link between democratization and the economic crisis; the fluctuations of reform efforts have clearly followed electoral cycles. Under a democratic regime, and with an underdeveloped party system, the state could no longer act effectively as the risk partner of the *chaebŏl*. In a nutshell, democratization and globalization have eroded the institutional foundation for the South Korean high debt model.

In comparative terms, Taiwan's economic resiliency is, in the final analysis, founded on the resiliency of its "one-party dominant regime" (Pempel 1990). The KMT's ability to achieve its historical projects—security, development, and international legitimacy—remains unhampered under democracy. The incumbent elite continued to deliver a streak of electoral successes while the principles of popular accountability and open political contestation were being legitimized and institutionalized. The KMT has built its winning coalition around a development strategy that brings about growth with equity and around a set of macroeconomic priorities that underscore monetary autonomy, financial stability, and fiscal conservatism. Undisrupted hegemonic presence in society, in turn, has enabled the ruling party to shape the terms of policy discourse over the issue of financial liberalization. A government confronted with the famous "trilemma" of macro policy—free capital movement, a stable exchange rate, and an effective monetary policy—can have only two of the three (Wade 1999, 7). The incumbent elite has always been able to resolve the conflict in favor of a stable exchange rate and an effective monetary policy. These proved politically critical in Taiwan's survival of the Asian economic crisis.

CHAPTER TEN

China: Domestic Restructuring
and a New Role in Asia

Barry Naughton

Given China's new openness to the world market, the Asian financial crisis has inevitably had an important impact on the domestic economy and politics. Yet, despite important economic effects, the Asian crisis is not the main force changing the Chinese political economy. Instead, China is in the midst of an important *domestic* economic and political transition that is recasting its political economy. The Asian crisis is important for China because it changes the terms on which this domestic transition will take place.

The latest changes make up the latest phase of the country's long march from socialism. Yet the current phase has important characteristics that distinguish it from the country's other key stages of transition since 1978. Since the death of Deng Xiaoping in February 1997, the leadership team of Party Secretary Jiang Zemin and Premier Zhu Rongji has cobbled together a distinctive and generally coherent strategy whose purpose is to accelerate domestic transformation, consolidate power, and give their regime longevity. A more aggressive role for domestic policy was developing just as the Asian crisis broke out. Indeed, the financial crisis in Thailand emerged literally within days of the reversion of Hong Kong to Chinese sovereignty, which—because it was seen as successful—was a key milepost in the consolidation of the post-Deng regime. On balance, the Asian crisis has made the risky domestic transformation even more difficult.

This chapter begins with economics and moves into political economy; it concludes with some speculations about the future of Chinese politics. (The first sections describe the effects of the Asian crisis on China and the interaction between the Asian crisis, Chinese macroeconomic policy, and economic reform strategy.) Later sections discuss political economic aspects of the domestic transformation and the interaction between Chinese domestic politics and the Asian crisis. A key point is that the recent evolution of Chinese politics is in many respects counterintuitive: despite the passing of the old guard, Chinese politics may be moving toward a more decisive form of authoritarianism with few purely political checks on decision making.

Impact of the Asian Crisis

There are many reasons to expect that China would be vulnerable to the economic turmoil that began in Thailand. China became a relatively open economy in the 1990s. Exports as a share of GDP increased rapidly, from 12 percent in 1988 to 22 percent in 1994, and then stabilized. Openness to foreign investment is even more striking. Since 1993, China has been the second largest recipient of fdi in the world, after the United States; even when scaled to China's large economy, inflows have been large, surpassing 5 percent of GDP annually. Of the total inflow of fdi, slightly more than one-half came from Hong Kong alone and approximately two-thirds from the predominantly Chinese industrializing economies together: Hong Kong, Macau, Taiwan, and Singapore. Nearly 80 percent of total inflows have come from East Asia. Clearly, China's economic fate is increasingly intertwined with that of its East Asian neighbors.

The pattern of investments in China is similar to the patterns of investment in the Southeast Asian countries most seriously affected by the crisis. Beginning in the early 1990s, China and the ASEAN-4 (Indonesia, Malaysia, Philippines and Thailand) all benefited from the restructuring of East Asian export networks, made possible by the inflow of investment from the predominantly Chinese indus-trializing economies and Japan; all five economies quickly moved into new export sectors and experienced rapid growth. China is thus in the same structural position in the world economy as the economies of the ASEAN-4. China produces simi-lar—though not identical—labor-intensive export goods, and China and the ASEAN-4 are competitive for new export markets and for new inward fdi flows. During 1992–93, China began to exploit the additional advantage of its huge domestic market, granting significant market access to foreign-invested firms, and it was rewarded with a flood of incoming investment. For a period, China seemed to be overshadowing ASEAN as an attractor for investment, but further liberaliza-tion in ASEAN and some disillusionment with China worked to reestablish bal-ance after the mid-1990s (Tan 1997).

Krause (1998) argues that, "for several years and through different mechanisms, China and Japan had been putting tremendous pressure on the entire Asian region. This trend may account for the virulence of the Asian flu." Krause locates the Chinese pressure in export competition. But, although in a few relatively small commodity classifications there is a direct trade-off between Chinese and Southeast Asian exports, in numerous examples of commodities there is a clear division of labor between the regions. For example, China produces virtually all the toys and telephone handsets imported by the United States, whereas ASEAN countries produce virtually all the hard disc drives. Although a generalized export competition of course exists, it is important to stress that, until 1996, whatever

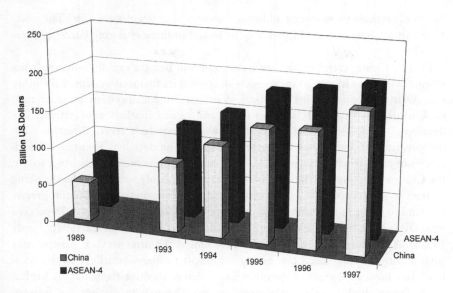

Figure 10.1   Comparative exports: China and ASEAN-4

competition existed was experienced within the context of very rapid growth of both regions. As Figure 10.1 shows, the ASEAN-4 export more than China does, and the exports of each have been growing with nearly equal rapidity (IMF 1998). Between 1989 and 1995, Chinese exports grew 19 percent annually, and those of the ASEAN-4 grew 17 percent. Export growth slowed dramatically in 1996, but Chinese exports actually slowed more abruptly (to less than 2 percent, versus nearly 5 percent for the ASEAN-4), due to problems with the Chinese export tax rebate program. It was not until the second quarter of 1997—with crisis in ASEAN already looming—that Chinese exports began to rebound significantly, ending the year with a sharp recovery to 21 percent growth, significantly outper-forming the 5.4 percent growth registered by the ASEAN-4. Thus, although com-petition exists, the really striking fact is the commonality of experience: extremely rapid export growth through 1995 and increased difficulties since 1996. China and ASEAN have, arguably, both faced similar challenges of saturated markets and excess capacity in some export sectors.

Like the ASEAN nations before crisis, China has effectively pegged its currency to the U.S. dollar, and it has experienced real currency appreciation as domestic inflation exceeded U.S. and world inflation levels. China devalued the reminbi by approximately 40 percent at the beginning of 1994, when it unified its exchange rate and set a new dollar rate that has changed little since (the HK dollar was already linked to the US. dollar). By 1997, though, China's real exchange rate against the dollar had returned to its 1993 level and, indeed, was slightly higher. In addition, as the Japanese yen depreciated against the dollar, China and other dollar-linked currencies experienced additional appreciation against the yen. The post-1996 export slowdown could plausibly be linked to these changing currency rates as well.

Finally, China resembles the crisis economies in being a rapidly industrializing economy that has in important respects outgrown its financial system. Like other East Asian economies, China has a bank-dominated financial system, in which total bank lending is large in relation to GDP, and capital markets are relatively less developed. Banks—in China's case, state-owned—regularly accept direction from the government. Government interference in lending decisions is entangled with cronyism and favoritism at both local and central government levels. As a result, the Chinese banking system is no better off, and probably worse off, than banking systems in the rest of East Asia. Estimates of nonperforming loans are not precise but tend to hover in the range of 20 percent of total loans, equivalent to 18 percent of GDP, a huge number (*New York Times* 16 July 1996; Naughton 1997c; Lardy 1998b). A fundamental cause of these problems is the utter lack of transparency surrounding lending decisions and government-business relations at the local level. In China, as in many of the other East Asian economies, the banks are big but weak. When these fragile giants stumble, they threaten to disrupt the forward march of economic development.

Despite the fundamental structural similarities, there are nonetheless even more profound differences between China and the Southeast Asian developing economies. First, the Chinese system is more closed, politically and economically. Despite China's emergence as an export power, important limits to its economic openness exist; these limits reflect the ways in which China adapted its economic policy to the opportunities provided by the East Asian restructuring described earlier. China liberalized policy toward fdi to a much greater extent than it did other aspects of its external economic relations. As a result, the flood of investment into China in the 1990s has been overwhelmingly in the form of fdi. From 1993 to 1997, China tapped a total of $250 billion in foreign investment capital, of which 78 percent, or $194 billion, was fdi and only 22 percent, just over $55 billion, was in the form of loans. That means that China was spared the destabilizing impact of "hot money" flows into and out of domestic markets. By contrast, the ASEAN crisis nations got into really serious trouble only after the inflow of fdi was augmented by other, more liquid forms of finance. The Chinese renminbi is convertible only on the current account (meaning that documentation of a legitimate trade or other approved transaction is required to change money). The capital account is still closed. This does not mean that businesses and individuals cannot find ways to move money in and out of China, but it does mean that it is difficult to place large, leveraged bets for or against the currency. As a result, the currency is much less vulnerable to speculative pressures.

China's opening to foreign trade has been similarly circumscribed (Naughton 1996). The most liberal part of the trade regime is "processing trade," under which imported inputs intended for export production enter the country duty free and without significant administrative obstacles. Liberal policies toward export processing facilitated the movement into China of Asian export production and complemented the liberal policies toward fdi. As a result, processing trade was the main force driving China's export expansion; it accounted for 55 percent of China's exports in 1997. By contrast, imports directly to the Chinese market continue to be hobbled by various kinds of non-tariff barriers, including, most importantly, the restriction of import trading rights to small numbers of foreign trade companies, nearly all of which are state owned. The government thus retains more tools to influence trade flows than would be the case in a fully open economy. In essence, these systemic features, which provide some insulation to China, reflect the particular nature of its integration with its East Asian neighbors: by serving as the "factory in the back room" for merchants in neighboring economies, China gives up some share of the profits, but it is also buffered from some of the financial instability.

Second, the Chinese government has followed relatively conservative policies that have limited its vulnerability to crisis. China had accumulated $140 billion in foreign exchange reserves at the end of 1997, which was the third largest reserve in the world and equal to a full year's imports. More important is that most of that reserve was built up after 1994, due to large, persistent surpluses in the balance of payments. In 1997, China had a trade surplus of $46 billion and, even after accounting for deficits in services of almost $6 billion and a net outflow of profits of foreign-invested firms of $16 billion, ran an overall current account surplus of almost $30 billion. At the same time, given the massive inflow of $45 billion of fdi, the capital account also showed a large surplus—$23 billion by year-end 1997. As a result, even after deducting $17 billion of "errors and omissions," reflecting primarily smuggling and capital flight, China accumulated foreign exchange reserves of $35 billion in 1997 alone (SSB 1998, 92–93). Thus, despite the trend toward currency appreciation, China has avoided the deterioration of its current account position that we would normally expect, while continuing to enjoy capital inflows. It is not simply that China's stock of reserves is abundant, but also that current flows are highly favorable. Although China also has a significant foreign debt— $131 billion at year-end 1997—only 14 percent is short-term, and of the remainder, a large part is loans from governments and international organizations, often at concessionary rates (*China Daily* 6 April 1998).

China thus differs from the most seriously affected crisis countries both because its economic system provides more insulation and because its current economic condition (a large surplus) provides it with more room to maneuver. Yet, both these differences reflect policy choices. They spring from the preference of China's current leadership to maintain a modicum of control, particularly over aspects of the economy that relate to the world economy. The systemic features remain because China's leaders have consistently moved slowly, resisting advice that they open their economy more rapidly to the outside. The current accumulation of foreign reserves is equally the outcome of a cautious policy. Standard economic advice was that China's reserves were more than ample, and that it would be sound—and contribute to growth—to use some of those reserves to finance larger imports of investment goods. China resisted that advice out of a desire to maintain a more conservative and secure position.

These basic features help to clarify both the nature of Chinese vulnerability to the Asian crisis and the trade-offs facing Chinese policy makers. Susceptibility to financial *contagion* is limited, because the financial markets that spread contagion have limited influence on China. But, on the other hand, China is potentially vulnerable to transmission of crisis through economic *competition*. China produces goods similar to those produced by the crisis economies and must compete with those countries for foreign investment. Foreign investment has been an important driving force behind China's export growth in the 1990s, and the most important source countries for investment are themselves liable to suffer from a protracted crisis and invest less in China. As the Asian crisis spread, all of China's neighbors devalued their currencies, with the exception of Hong Kong (now a Special Administrative Region of China). China's currency was already overvalued—arguably so against the dollar, and certainly against the yen—and appeared increasingly out of line as all other Asian currencies dropped lower against the dollar. Beginning in 1998, China faced the danger of a very substantial slowdown, and perhaps even a shrinkage, of export growth. Inevitably, this meant that the growth impetus from rapidly growing exports in previous years would be lost.

These pressures help to explain Chinese policy choices during 1997 and 1998. Because China was not susceptible to large capital flows and thus financial contagion, it could not be *forced* to devalue. However, because its long-term competitive position was seriously undermined, it had important reasons to devalue. Thus, the question of a possible Chinese devaluation emerged as one of the most watched and speculated-about issues of 1998. A devaluation was feared because it might lead to a further spiral of competitive devaluation among affected countries, but also because it would indicate a willingness on China's part to take advantage of crisis to improve its own position at the expense of its East Asian neighbors. In fact, China was able to resist devaluation through 1998, in a decision that proved to be surprisingly easy. While the devaluation of all the other Asian currencies in theory made China less competitive, in practice the economic disruption of the crisis was so severe—particularly the disruption in trade financing—that competitor economies really did not provide an attractive alternative to China throughout most of 1998.

Indeed, during the first seven months of 1998, Chinese exports grew only 7 percent—a significant slowdown—but the distribution of growth was somewhat reassuring. Exports to Asia dropped, but exports to developed-country markets grew almost 20 percent (CSICSC 1998). This was only a temporary reprieve, though, and from October 1998, Chinese exports began to decline. Ironically, China's position will become most difficult when crisis countries begin to recover: when export financing resumes and normal economic relations are restored, crisis countries will pose formidable competition as they desperately try to expand exports to retire huge debt loads. In this sense, some of the most serious economic repercussions of the Asian crisis on China will only begin to unfold in 1999.

Silver Linings

During the first eighteen months of the Asian crisis, China was unusual not only because it suffered relatively few harmful effects, but also because it was one of the very few countries that actually benefited, however slightly, from the crisis. The crisis was both a warning to China and an opportunity: a warning, because China's financial system has all the characteristics and all the flaws of the financial systems in the rest of East Asia, which had proven so vulnerable; an opportunity, because the sharp setbacks experienced by the other economies in the region and the relatively limited impact of the crisis on China provided the country with an unprecedented opportunity to exert leadership in Asia.

In the face of crisis, China has been able to demonstrate responsibility and leadership through its policy choices. Most important has been the Chinese willingness and ability to maintain the value of the Chinese currency against the U.S. dollar, whereas the currencies of every other Asian nation have been devalued. This choice has won wide praise and contributed to a perception of China as a responsible power. Of course the policy is not selfless, because it is based on a calculation that devaluation, by contributing to a deepening of the crisis, would end up providing little or no benefit for China. But it is nonetheless responsible, because China bears all the economic costs of keeping its currency high, whereas the costs of devaluation would be shared with its neighbors. Further responsible actions have been evident in the Chinese willingness to provide financial aid to crisis countries, culminating in a $4.5 billion commitment to the IMF in November 1998 (*Wall Street Journal* 2 September 1998; CND 1998a).

Both the United States and Japan, in their own very different ways, contribute to a perception of China's enhanced international stature. Clinton's June 1998 visit to China, his apparent lack of prior consultation with Japan over some key political issues, and his failure to stop in Japan on the way contributed to a perception in some parts of Asia that the United States was "tilting" toward China and away from Japan. As for Japan, although it has attempted to play a responsible role in the Asian crisis—offering to sponsor regional credit facilities—good intentions have been swamped by Japan's remarkable and persistent failure to get its own economic house in order. Japan has thus marginalized itself. China lacks the power and weight to launch itself into the group of leading powers on its own, but China is moving into a responsibility vacuum in Asia, created by the abdication of Japan and the absence of any other credible middle-ranked powers. Ezra Vogel (1998, 8) has recently declared a "new 'Era of Three Kingdoms,' . . . the first time in history that China, Japan, and the United States have all been strong Asian powers at the same time."

The short-term effect of these aspects of the crisis has been to strengthen the Chinese leadership. The heightened respect China seems to be commanding plays into the neonationalist appeals that are the basis of recent Communist Party claims of legitimacy. The role of the Chinese currency has become entangled with national pride and self-perception. A particularly curious occurrence has been the latest addition to the East Asian "No" literature; a recent book entitled *The Renminbi Can Say No* (Tong 1998) is a novel expression of national pride.[1] The current premier, Zhu Rongji, has a reputation within China as an effective economic policy maker. The Asian crisis strengthens his hand by showing the dangers of economic policy mistakes and increasing the esteem in which his talents are held. At the same time, the Asian crisis is a warning to the Chinese leadership about economics and the transitory nature of power. Chinese policy makers have been following fast-breaking events closely (see Xiong 1998). It has confirmed their belief in the basic correctness of their own approach to economic transformation. But it has also given increased urgency to the tasks and challenges that confront the Chinese leadership today: dealing with the financial system, dealing with discontent caused by unemployment and corruption, and navigating through the economic demands of foreign countries. Increased urgency, however, does not automatically reveal the appropriate direction or speed of the response. Does the increased danger of financial crisis, for example, mean there is less time to fix things (and thus indicate a faster pace) or greater danger from mishandling reforms (and thus a slower pace)? The crisis has confirmed Chinese leaders in their belief that they need to be tough, maintain control, and proceed cautiously, but also that they have to keep moving ahead, because those who fail to develop will not survive.

The Economics of Domestic Transformation: The Zhu Rongji Policy Regime

The impact of the Asian crisis on China must be seen in the context of changes in China's domestic political economy. The first year of the crisis was also the first year in which the post–Deng Xiaoping Chinese leadership was established and making policy on its own. The current heads of the Communist Party (Jiang Zemin) and of the government (Zhu Rongji) were named to their positions by Deng Xiaoping and served for several years while Deng was still around to watch over them. But it is only since the February 1997 death of Deng—and the deaths of a handful of other revolutionary elders—that they have shaped a fully independent policy package. In the post-Deng era, Jiang and Zhu have taken policies they had already established and pushed them further, in more fundamental and more radical directions. From their past actions, we have substantial information about their preferences and policy choices. In the economic realm, the most important policies are closely associated with the premier, Zhu Rongji.

Zhu began to put his personal stamp on economic policy making during 1993. A wave of Deng Xiaoping–supported reform was in process, packaged in a typical (for China) combination of decentralization, marketization, and slackening of rules and oversight. Although important breakthroughs were made in the transition to a market economy, the burst of reforms in 1992 and 1993 was accompanied by enormous financial laxity, rampant speculation and corruption, wide-scale diversion of public resources, and significant inflationary pressures. In this sense, it was a clear continuation of past patterns of macroeconomic policy cycles, in which major periods of reform and decentralization were also major periods of macroeconomic disorder and inflationary growth. In 1993, China undeniably was experiencing a "bubble economy," and its vulnerability to financial contagion would have been at a maximum at that time.

Zhu immediately set out to burst the financial bubble that had formed and quickly ended some of the most speculative financial activities. Moreover, he set in motion a consistent set of policy initiatives that have persisted. Zhu's policy regime consisted of two main pillars: macroeconomic restraint and regulatory reforms. Macroeconomic restraint was initiated in 1993, and it was held steadily for the next four years. After a lag, the rate of inflation fell: from a peak annual rate of 24 percent in 1994, growth of the consumer price index slowed annually, and it began to fall in early 1998. Most remarkably, inflation was controlled with only moderate costs in terms of economic growth. Real GDP growth for 1997 was 8.8 percent, according to Chinese official figures, below the unsustainable 14 percent growth in 1992, but still quite rapid. During 1997, Chinese economists and policy makers spoke with understandable pride of their success in achieving a "soft landing."

The fundamental factor leading to the control of inflation was a shift in the relative bargaining position of enterprises and banks. Zhu Rongji—serving for part of this time as the head of the central bank—was able to create a banking system that had a certain amount of independence from the state enterprise system. At the least, the banks gained bargaining power that enabled them to resist some of the many demands placed upon them. Zhu was able to give the banking system the power to say "no," at least some of the time. How was he able to do this?

Clearly, the foundation of macroeconomic restraint was a conservative monetary policy. The real growth rate of credit was restrained, and much irregular credit generated off the books by the banking system during 1992–93 was recalled. Standard administrative tools were used to increase monitoring and keep credit growth down. As in the past, tools such as credit quotas were crude but effective in breaking inflationary momentum, slowing the economy, and beginning to restore macroeconomic discipline. Moreover, as inflation came down, real interest rates rose. Although nominal interest rates were reduced repeatedly, they did not decline as rapidly as the inflation rate, so real interest rates for bank loans increased from −10 percent in 1994 to between 7 and 8 percent in 1997. As enterprises found themselves paying substantial interest rates, they began to rethink their dependence on easy access to bank credit. The endless supply of cheap credit having disappeared, and bankers having become increasingly assertive about the need to pay on time, many firms found themselves unwilling to increase already high levels of bank debt.

Along with these changes in basic economic conditions, important changes were made in the way the banking system functioned. First, the 1995 banking laws recentralized the banking system, making local bank branches more dependent on their Beijing headquarters and correspondingly less attentive to local government officials. Second, Zhu Rongji personally laid down the law to the (Beijing) bank heads: he is reputed to have said that any bank head who didn't turn a profit would be fired, period. Third, it was made clear that the banks had decision-making authority—at least veto power—over the use of their own money. At the same time, new restrictions were put in place that substantially limited some of the flexibility bank officials had enjoyed during the 1992–93 episode, which brought widespread diversion of funds and questionable speculative activity. Bank officials were subject to greater monitoring but clearly gained more authority within their authorized scope of business. It should be emphasized that these changes did not amount to central bank independence. Rather, they implied central bank subordination to a policy line clearly established by the top leadership. The central leadership lent its own authority temporarily to the banking system and then put in place a modest package of regulations and incentives that tended to keep at least some of that authority with the banking system.

At the same time, the financial pressures resulting from a large trade surplus and capital inflow were used to place the banking system itself under greater externally imposed discipline. With intense pressure from the top to carry out a domestic policy of macroeconomic austerity, the banking system had to contain overall credit growth within strict limits. Internal balance required slow credit growth. At the same time, the central bank had obligations to achieve external balance, meeting government policy objectives in foreign exchange markets. Specifically, the central bank was instructed to prevent (nominal) currency appreciation after large trade surpluses emerged in 1994. This meant that the central bank had to buy up the foreign exchange revenues China's exporters were generating, building up foreign exchange reserves and releasing renminbi into the domestic marketplace. Because most of the growth of the money supply was coming from the buildup of foreign currency reserves, the central bank had almost no leeway to create money through central bank lending. The share of total central bank base money creation that was attributable to the increase in foreign exchange reserves was 61 percent in 1996 and a whopping 79 percent in 1997 (G. Chen 1998). The central bank was sterilizing capital inflows, so it was unable to make significant new loans to commercial banks; as a result, it could credibly refuse to bail out local commercial banks if they overspent their reserves.

In short, the budget constraint for banks was being gradually hardened; as bankers found themselves with harder budget constraints and more decision-making authority, they in turn imposed tougher requirements on their customers, and especially on SOEs and their local government patrons. Bargaining power had swung away from the enterprises and to the bankers.

Along with macroeconomic austerity, Zhu Rongji presided over a new, more regulatory approach to economic reform. The new reforms were regulatory in the sense that they introduced new rules (and new prices) that, at least in principle, applied equally to all economic actors. There was more focus on creating and regulating competition as a force for economic change, and less on direct government action in restructuring organizations and providing new incentives.[2] Although this represented a real change of emphasis, it also reflected a natural movement from one stage of reform to another. Reform during the 1980s had introduced markets and incentives. By the 1990s, the economy having "grown out of the plan," the most important tasks were to improve the legal and regulatory environment, create a "level playing field," and reduce some of the most obvious distortions in the economy (Naughton 1995). As regulatory reforms proceeded, they led to a greatly enhanced emphasis on restructuring state enterprises. State enterprise restructuring has meant converting vaguely defined public ownership into more explicit, legally defined ownership categories, sometimes involving privatization. Restructuring is related to regulatory reforms in that both envisage the creation of a legal framework that allows market forces to work. As I argue later, restructuring is driven primarily by market forces and is itself an adaptation to increased market competition. Such reforms were in harmony with the tough macroeconomic policies that were adopted. Regulatory reforms and the new macroeconomic policies both stressed the need to adhere to tough and objective rules; moreover, macroeconomic austerity made market conditions more difficult and thus tended to strengthen market discipline.

Regulatory reforms have been promulgated in nearly every area of the economy. The most important were the foreign trade reforms and the fiscal and tax reform of 1994, and a number of important financial regulations covering banks (1995) and equity markets (1996–97). The foreign trade reforms—particularly the devaluation and unification of the exchange rate on 1 January 1994—quickly brought about impressive results. China's exports surged, and the country began to run the sustained trade surplus discussed earlier. The fiscal reform was an especially important turning point. Over the course of more than fifteen years of reform, China's fiscal position had eroded significantly. Reform strategy through 1993 stressed decentralization and distribution of benefits and tolerated slackening of oversight and some corruption. Not surprisingly, government tax revenues slid, dropping from 35.8 percent of GDP in 1978 to only 11.2 percent at their low point in 1995 (Figure 10.2). No doubt marketization and dismantling of government monopolies were responsible for most of the fiscal decline. Still, the chosen reform strategy also contributed to it, and by the early 1990s, it was widely perceived that China had a serious fiscal crisis

Fiscal reforms in 1994 were designed to arrest this slide by introducing new taxes, such as the value-added tax, with relatively low, uniform rates that applied to all economic actors. Reforms were not immediately effective, but by 1997 the corner had apparently been turned. The low point in budgetary revenues as a share of GDP was in 1995. The revenue share of GDP increased two years in a row and reached 12 percent of GDP in 1997 (see Figure 10.2). In a related manner, the central government share of revenues and expenditures, which continued to erode in the immediate aftermath of fiscal reform, stabilized (Figure 10.3). These trends indicate an increasing degree of compliance with the legal provisions of the fiscal system. Although the changes are neither enormous nor unambiguous, they are significant, because they represent changes in the direction of powerful, longstanding tendencies. It is a difficult task to shift 1 percent of GDP into the gov-

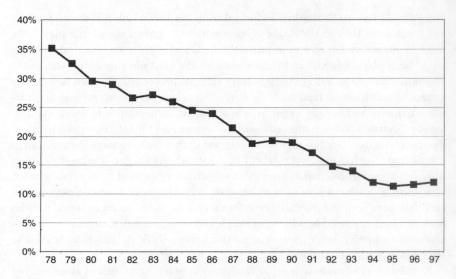

Figure 10.2 Fiscal revenues as a share of GDP: China, 1978–97

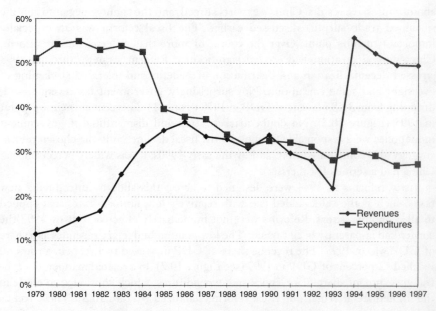

Figure 10.3 Central share of revenues and expenditures (excluding borrowing): China, 1979–97

ernment revenue column. In both banking and fiscal areas, the Zhu Rongji policies are associated with a stronger, more authoritative set of institutions.

During 1997, the economic conditions described earlier were allowed to drive a restructuring, and shrinkage, of the state enterprise sector. After the Fifteenth Communist Party Congress in September, local government officials were given an almost free hand to proceed with state-sector reforms that included bankruptcy, sales and auctions, mergers, and "corporatization." The result was a new wave of enterprise reform, diverse and multiformed, generally labeled *enterprise restructuring*. This wave of reform is still unfolding, and it is too early to draw up a comprehensive summary of the reform's bottom line. It is beyond question, however, that the current wave is an important change that is in the process of fundamentally recasting the economic landscape. Throughout almost twenty years of economic reform between 1978 and 1995, although the state sector shrunk in relative importance, it continued to grow in absolute terms, both in output and in employment. Only since 1995 has policy shifted to permit state-sector employment to decline absolutely.

Given the decentralized nature of the Chinese economy, the progress of SOE restructuring depended predominantly on the incentives facing local governments, which "owned" the majority of SOEs. The policies that followed in the late 1990s shifted that incentive environment in crucial ways: reducing access to easy credit, decreasing profitability, and increasing competition. Given the shift in bargaining power to the financial system, enterprises were unable to turn to government patrons to secure bank-funded bailouts. In Kornai's terms (1980), the enterprise "soft budget constraint," under which SOEs could always incur short-term losses, ceased to be a guaranteed option for firms.

SOEs have ceased to be cash cows on which local government officials can always draw for financial and material resources and for employment. Due to changes both in real competitive ability and in the taxation and accounting system, SOE industrial profits, which once were huge, are now quite modest. Industrial SOE profits were 15 percent of GDP in 1978, but fell below 2 percent of GDP in 1996–97. Because loss-making enterprises lost approximately 1 percent of GDP through most of the period, net profits of industrial SOEs sank to only 0.6 percent of GDP in 1997. The financial relationship between SOEs and local governments had already begun to change with the initiation of the new tax system: instead of drawing an ill-defined "surplus" from local SOEs, local governments now rely primarily on taxes, which are, in principle, levied on SOEs at the same rate as on any other ownership. Moreover, as SOEs found themselves under enormous pressure from the marketplace, due to intensified competition, and from the financial system, due to the enhanced bargaining position of bankers, local governments began to rethink the value of possessing their own SOEs. Increasingly, local governments began to conclude that they derived few advantages from local state ownership that could not equally be derived from a generally prosperous local economy, even if that economy were based on private ownership. If, moreover, the emerging private entrepreneurs were linked to government officials through ties of kinship, patronage, or friendship, that would further tilt the calculus in favor of privatization.

Local governments rushed to use "corporatization" to rationalize local industrial systems and reduce burdens. At its least significant, such restructuring involved the merger of various enterprises and the creation of various forms of joint ventures. Some of these were "shotgun marriages" in which financially healthy enterprises were compelled to take over less solvent firms, sometimes to gain access to land or other assets the insolvent firms possessed, sometimes simply because they were ordered to do so by superior organs. The steel industry is notorious for a number of economically irrational and clearly coerced takeovers of this sort.

Far more significant, however, has been a wave of sales, privatizations, and bankruptcies of local enterprises. The Fifteenth Party Congress essentially removed any remaining ideological barriers to local restructuring. As long as restructuring can plausibly be presented as in the public interest, local governments are free to carry out almost any program, including one that involves significant de facto privatization. Although the word *privatization* is still avoided, the reality is that an enormous wave of privatization is in fact occurring in China. The number of employees of manufacturing SOEs has declined from a peak of 35.3 million in 1992 to 30.1 million at the end of 1997, and the process is accelerating (SSB 1998, 138).

Because of the variety of local experiences, it is not yet possible to get a comprehensive sense of the scope of enterprise restructuring. It is not clear how much of the 5 million-worker reduction in state manufacturing employment corresponds to privatization, how much to bankruptcy, and how much to formation of joint stock companies that may be effectively state-controlled in all but name. It is clear that the number of joint stock companies is increasing rapidly, and, although most have a government agency as the controlling shareholder, some do not. The number of companies listed on the Shanghai and Shenzhen stock exchanges—a small but important subset of all joint stock companies—increased from 530 to 745 during 1997, and total capitalization of all listed companies jumped from 14 to 23 percent of GDP during the same period (Zhong and Zhuang 1998). There is little doubt that an important process is under way that will dramatically reshape China's economic landscape.

Through 1997, an extremely coherent economic policy configuration prevailed. Macroeconomic austerity, combined with regulatory reforms, was being used to drive a substantial downsizing of the state sector. The most important impact of the Asian crisis on China was that it made this policy package unsustainable in its original form. During 1997, the Chinese economy was already slowing, due to the delayed effects of the macroeconomic austerity program. Growth in 1997 had come to a significant extent from an expansion of net exports, and the Asian crisis made it inconceivable that growth of that magnitude would continue through 1998. Further slowing of the economy would be difficult to accept, because it would increase unemployment, already increasing rapidly in the wake of enterprise restructuring. As a result, beginning in December 1997 and throughout 1998, a series of policies was rolled out with the intention of maintaining GDP growth at 8 percent for the year. Those policies included increasing the growth rate of state fixed investment, lowering interest rates, stepping up mortgage financing to convert housing privatization into a growth opportunity, liberalizing conditions for fdi, and increasing the value-added tax rebate for exporters. A common theme of most of these measures is that they relax, to varying degrees, the intense macro-economic austerity and financial discipline that were biting into enterprise opera-tions, particularly in the state sector.

It makes perfect sense to use domestic stimulus to replace external demand lost as a result of the Asian crisis. This is straightforward Keynesian aggregate demand management. Many of the Asian crisis countries have been deprived of this option because of their open capital accounts. They are unable to set an autonomous domestic policy of lowering interest rates and stimulating credit and investment, because capital would simply continue flowing out. China, however, having already foregone full access to world capital, now has the extra flexibility of being able to wage an independent domestic macro policy. But the new policies have substantial costs and risks. Relaxing macroeconomic discipline and propping up the economy through rapid growth of bank credit would upset recent achieve-ments by reversing the tremendously important shift of bargaining power away from enterprises and toward the banking system. There is much more at stake than the ordinary economic arguments about macroeconomic management. This is specifically evident in the fear of increasing unemployment, which led to an obvious reduction in the urgency with which the central government has been promoting enterprise restructuring. To see what is at stake, we must look at broader political economy issues.

Redefining the Urban Social Compact

State-sector restructuring reflects a historic turn in the political economy of China. For four decades—and throughout most of the reform era—urban workers were a privileged social and political class in China. Within urban areas, incomes and social benefits were evenly distributed. Membership in the privileged group of urbanites in and of itself produced higher incomes and benefits, with workers in SOEs having slightly more generous benefits than workers in other types of organ-izations. Returns to education were nil, and remaining differentiation among urbanites was due largely to political status (Griffin and Zhao 1994). Moreover, workers were almost never fired. Even through the first fifteen years of the reform process, this basic arrangement did not change. Reforms introduced some flexibil-ity into the system, but layoffs, and quits and fires from the state sector, remained extremely small through 1992. China has now dismantled the system of central planning and adopted a market economy. Thus, the privileged position of urban workers has been the single remaining feature of the socialist regime that most sharply distinguishes China from her East Asian neighbors.

Since 1993, the guarantees given China's urban workers have largely evaporated. The clearest indication of this change is the rapid growth of unemployment. Unemployment in China's cities is composed of two classes of worker: registered

Table 10.1   Urban Unemployment and Layoffs (Year-End, in Million Workers)

	Registered Unemployed	Laid-Off Workers
1993	4.2	3.0
1994	4.8	3.6
1995	5.2	5.6
1996	5.5	8.9
1997	5.7	11.5

Sources: Yang Yiyong 1998; SSB 1998.

unemployed and laid-off workers. Registered unemployed workers have no links to existing enterprises and have filled out forms at local labor offices indicating they are looking for work. Their numbers have increased moderately, from 4.2 million in 1993 to 5.7 million at the end of 1997 (Table 10.1). Far more striking is the rapid increase in the number of laid-off workers (*xiagang renyuan*), which jumped from 3 million in 1993 to 11.5 million at the end of 1997. Laid-off workers retain ties to their former workplaces but have no current jobs with those firms. Their ties to the workplace are kept to ensure some access to various benefits, to possible early retirement pensions, and to enterprise-supplied housing. Some laid-off workers in fact have found new employment, particularly in the informal sector, and retain ties of convenience to their former enterprise because it is in their interest to do so. Moreover, there may be some double-counting of individuals in the registered unemployed and laid-off categories. Total unemployment, therefore, cannot be calculated simply as the sum of these two numbers. I estimate that urban unemployment has increased from less than 4 percent in 1993 to between 7 and 8 percent at the end of 1997.

State enterprises are under enormous economic pressure, and they are simply unable to shield their own workers from it. Chinese workers are now fully at risk from layoffs and unemployment. Even those workers who retain ties with their former work units frequently find that payments are sporadic and well below the minimum benefit level established by most municipalities. Many workers fall through holes in the social safety net.

Not all urbanites will suffer from the current changes: there will continue to be an urban elite, more privileged in relation to the rest of society than ever before. But that elite is defined by wealth and skills, not simply by residence in an urban area. Urban workers without special skills or education, wealth, or connections to the wealthy and powerful increasingly find themselves in competition with China's vast reservoir of rural workers. That competition stems from the increased mobility of China's workers, which has brought rural residents into urban job markets in unprecedented numbers, but also from the deepening progress of state enterprise reform, which pushes workers into the same job markets that are attracting rural workers (Beijing University 1998).

These changes are far more important to the Chinese leaders than is the Asian crisis as such. Chinese leaders believe that a restructuring and shrinkage of the state sector is necessary if the Chinese economy is to develop and grow into a world-class economy. Economic competition between China and other East Asian economies—and also between different regions within China—dictates leaner enterprises that have the flexibility to trim surplus workers. At the same time, Chinese leaders have always displayed enormous sensitivity to the political activity of the urban working class. They understand that an urban working class in active opposition to Communist Party rule will spell the end of their system. Fear of working-class opposition was a major reason that no leader dared dismantle this system during the reforms of the 1980s.

This is the context within which the impact of the Asian crisis needs to be understood. The previous section described the shift in macroeconomic policy during 1998 designed to prevent the economy from slowing too abruptly. Similarly driven by the gravity of the Asian crisis, concern with rapidly increasing unemployment led central government leaders to shift emphasis during 1998 away from the urgency of enterprise restructuring and toward the importance of creating re-employment opportunities for laid-off workers. The emphasis moved from efficiency to welfare considerations. With the shift in central government rhetoric and the reduced pressure of macroeconomic austerity, the impetus to enterprise restructuring clearly diminished during the course of 1998.

These events show that Chinese leaders will be managing the Asian crisis with an eye toward the main game: the transition in the role of urban workers. China's leaders would prefer to unwind the privileged position of urban workers gradually and "safely." The Asian crisis presents the frightening possibility that the compact would disintegrate rapidly, causing massive social dissatisfaction and unrest. As a result of these concerns, the central government has done some back-pedaling on enterprise restructuring.

But, whereas China's dramatic transformation of the role of urban citizens faces formidable challenges, it is also driven by a powerful economic and social logic. Most important, the restructuring process is driven primarily at the local level. Each restructuring initiative brings powerful local interests into play and creates new opportunities for personal gain. Moreover, the dominant interest is that of local government. Rapid SOE restructuring occurs in those localities where local government leaders have concluded that restructuring is in their interests; restructuring limps along slowly when local government leaders decide it is against their interests. Moreover, as Solinger (1998) shows, local governments interpret central government re-employment policies stressed during 1998 according to their own interests as well. Some local governments give re-employment a predominantly free market spin, stressing more rapid absorption by the private sector, while others give it a predominantly welfarist spin, emphasizing ongoing obligations by state firms to laid-off workers.

The fundamental logic driving enterprise restructuring is powerful enough that it is unlikely to be substantially altered by short-term fluctuations in central government policy. The emergence of an increasingly fluid and competitive society, on the one hand, combined with the government's hunger for revenues and a disciplined macroeconomic policy, on the other, implies that the pressures reshaping the state enterprise sector will continue to be intense. Regions that restructure promptly and thoroughly will enjoy a competitive advantage over regions that delay and carry larger subsidy burdens into the future. Over time, the incentives pushing local governments to restructure their public enterprise sectors are likely to intensify, rather than moderate, regardless of central government proclamations.

Conclusion: The Changing Political Process

We can further clarify the political changes in China by placing them in the context of the dichotomy between policy credibility and policy decisiveness used by MacIntyre in chapter 7. In this framework, policy credibility is provided by an institutional setup with sufficient checks and balances built into the system to provide a real assurance that established policies and political rights or property rights will be fully respected. By contrast, policy decisiveness is most easily achieved on the basis of an opposite institutional setup—one without significant checks and balances, allowing an authoritative policy maker to promptly and fully respond to changing conditions. It is important to recognize that China is moving toward a much more decisive type of policy making. This shift appears to be deeply rooted, reflecting economic, political, and institutional factors.

Economically, one of the main lessons Chinese policy makers have drawn from the Asian crisis is the need to maintain economic positions that permit a high degree of policy decisiveness. For example, the Chinese leaders see that the financial setup in Taiwan, described by Chu in chapter 9, gives policy makers a high degree of autonomy in setting financial and macroeconomic policy, and this has arguably contributed to their ability to weather the Asian crisis more effectively than other economies. Conversely, Chinese leaders see that the decline in policy decisiveness associated with political transitions in the region has contributed to the severity of the crisis. Zhu Rongji himself clearly believes that greater government decisiveness is needed to clean up financial irregularities and prevent the emergence of speculative bubbles.

Perhaps surprisingly, an image of decisiveness and toughness also contributes to Zhu Rongji's political standing. Zhu Rongji is an unusual politician by Chinese standards. He is much less closely associated with Communist Party insiders than are other top Chinese leaders (such as Li Peng). Indeed, Zhu was designated a "rightist" in 1957, and was only "rehabilitated" at the end of the 1970s (Gao and He 1995). He spent his entire career as an economist, until he was suddenly appointed mayor of Shanghai in 1987. In the Chinese context, he is a technocrat. He has no foreign degrees but possesses considerable economic and administrative expertise. An image of tough impartiality and competence makes him quite popular. Although no opinion poll published in the PRC would be credible, it is interesting that a poll in Hong Kong—which retains freedom of speech and of the press—reports approval ratings of 77 percent for Zhu Rongji and 73 percent for Jiang Zemin, but only 46 percent for the Beijing-appointed chief executive of Hong Kong, Tung Chee-hwa (CND 1998b). Of course, Zhu Rongji carefully tends his image, and he has shown a knack for displaying—for example, at press conferences—an image that is simultaneously authoritative and informal.

During 1998, even as Zhu Rongji and Jiang Zemin were in some respects retreating from their agenda with respect to SOE restructuring, they took care to maintain the impression of authoritative, decisive action. Most striking was the launching of simultaneous campaigns against smuggling and military involvement in business. These campaigns have significant economic benefits, reducing imports that threaten to surge because of the overvalued currency, facilitating increased monitoring and nontariff barriers to legal imports, and increasing government revenues; but they also alienate potentially powerful interest groups. Similarly, Zhu has vowed to push ahead with government downsizing, designed to reduce the number of government employees by one-half within three years (Mo 1998, 28–29). To China's urban workers, government downsizing sends a strong message that government employees are not exempt from the pain of unemployment. Thus, rather than retreating, Zhu has chosen to capitalize on his political assets, and the resulting "strong man" approach to economic policy is evident across the board: toward the renminbi (no devaluation); toward state enterprises and government (slimmed down to face market forces); and toward smuggling and military involvement in business (crackdown).

More surprising is the fact that the institutional underpinnings of the Chinese system are shifting in a way that favors greater policy decisiveness. One would normally assume that a nondemocratic authoritarian system, run by a hierarchically organized Communist Party and dominated by charismatic individuals like Mao Zedong and Deng Xiaoping, would always display a high degree of decisiveness. However, the lack of decisiveness in Chinese policy making during the 1980s is well attested. During this period, Communist Party elders, most crucially Deng Xiaoping but also, importantly, Chen Yun and several other, more conservative elders, had significant veto power and an important influence over policy. Next-generation leaders, such as the premier Zhao Ziyang and the party secretary Hu Yaobang, faced important constraints on their decision-making authority. Various central leaders, in competition over specific policy choices, sought to mobilize winning political coalitions by "playing to the provinces," in Shirk's evocative term. The result was an indecisive policy process that nonetheless in many respects "muddled through" to some important successful outcomes (Shirk 1993). There were many checks and veto points in decision making, but they were dependent on personalities rather than formal institutions. This political process allowed local political elites and privileged urban workers to maintain their privileges, because the political coalition building required made it virtually inconceivable that such important groups would be seriously excluded.

Jiang Zemin and Zhu Rongji have already begun to change some of the economic phenomena consistent with this institutional setup, including declining government revenues and a declining central government share of revenues. Not surprisingly, they would also like to change the institutional underpinnings to consolidate their personal political positions. In this they have the advantage that the formal institutions at hand are highly authoritarian, reflecting the organizational principles of the Communist Party and its dominance of the government. Now that the elders are gone, there are many fewer informal veto gates that must be crossed, and formal positions correspond better with real authority.

Substantial dangers are associated with this process. First, increased decisiveness brings with it, almost inevitably, decreased credibility. The policies are more highly associated with a single individual, and although individual policy outcomes may be desirable, they retain a degree of fragility. Precisely because policies have not passed through multiple veto gates, they do not have the broad-based support they would have acquired had more decision makers signed off on them. In this respect, it is striking that Zhu Rongji and Jiang Zemin have invested far more in building up *personal* credibility than in building up the credibility of the policy process as a whole. Outside core economic strategy, Chinese government policies fluctuate significantly, but Zhu and Jiang display an ability to make their personal views stick.

Second, the current leadership is forsaking some of its traditional pillars of support. The desire to develop more policy-making autonomy inevitably means that some social groups that (at least passively) supported the regime in the past will now have less motivation to do so. It is not clear whether the regime can forfeit the support of urban workers or the military and still survive. The pressures are great, and the potential for open political opposition from the urban working class is significant. In this context, the events that took place in Mianyang, a medium-sized city in the Sichuan province, cannot have escaped the notice of Chinese politicians. Mianyang, a city in interior China with intense economic problems, was selected in 1996 as a keypoint test city for industrial restructuring. In the subsequent two years, sixty-two SOEs were declared bankrupt, with more than twenty-one thousand workers (7 percent of the municipal total) laid off (Mo 1998, 18). But there were major demonstrations in Mianyang, caused not only by the layoffs, but also by failures to pay wages and pensions at these and other firms. Demonstrations apparently met with a brutal police response that, according to one report, led to scores of deaths and hundreds of injuries (CND 1997). Despite the remoteness of Mianyang, reports of these demonstrations made their way through China's dissident network to the West, where they were given significant play in human rights publications and newspapers. Although the link with government economic policies was not noted in the Western press, it certainly would not have escaped Chinese leaders, particularly those with doubts about the policies. If the Zhu policies provoke excessive resentment and unrest, and if they are perceived to be unsuccessful, it would be easy enough for other leaders—including Jiang Zemin—to distance themselves from Zhu and let him fall.

It is hard for China's leaders to believe that they can get through this transition without authoritarian political controls. The Asian crisis brings greater costs and greater vulnerability to China than would otherwise be the case. This intensifies the Chinese leadership's fear of economic disruption and political challenge, because they perceive this as perhaps the most delicate and contested step in the entire economic transition. Now, of all times, they would like to maintain control. The Asian crisis strengthens their desire for control, while also throwing up another set of unpredictable and potentially threatening economic developments. Thus, although the underlying economic processes driving change in China are deeply rooted and likely to persist for the foreseeable future, the political institutions are being reshaped in new and sometimes surprising ways. Whether these institutions are adequate to cope with the broad social changes occurring in China must remain an open question.

Conclusion

T. J. Pempel

Crisis fosters reexamination. Conventions and routines are most frequently challenged during upheavals. Only when prevailing practices demonstra-
bly fail does the search for alternatives begin in earnest; it is in hard times that
existing rules of the game are most typically altered (Gourevitch 1986). The Asian
crisis is proving to be precisely such a period. In its wake, long-standing verities
have come under challenge at all three levels of politics. The Asian economic crisis of 1997–98 may prove to be the same kind of politically redefining event regionally as the Great Depression of the 1920s and 1930s or the breakdown of the
Bretton Woods system and the oil shocks of the early 1970s were worldwide.

At the national level, well-entrenched political patterns in numerous Asian
countries have undergone radical reconfigurations. Some have been changed more
radically than others, but few have been spared scrutiny. At the regional level,
existing institutions and power balances have been changed, and at the international level, after the Asian meltdown, there has been considerable conflict about
the uses of economic power by the United States and the IMF. National governments are engaged in an ongoing struggle over the political wisdom of allowing
free movement of capital worldwide versus politically regulating capital and monetary markets. Beneath this debate lurks the long-standing confrontation between
alternative models by which to structure national political economies.

This conclusion explores the main political issues that have arisen. Because
events are ongoing, highly interconnected, and complex, the focus will be, not on
assessing the latest micro-developments, but instead on isolating the broad dynamics and political contests that have arisen as a result. Paralleling the introduction to
this volume, this conclusion concentrates on developments at three different levels: national, regional, and international.

224

National Political Reassessments

The diverse political economies that prevailed across East Asia ensured that the general crisis highlighted in part I of this book would affect individual countries in particular ways. This point was made apparent throughout the chapters in part II. The initial shocks generated considerable debate, particularly within the most severely affected countries, about where to locate the burden of blame and how best to enact changes.

High growth allows, although it by no means guarantees, that politics can be a positive-sum game. During the wave of Asian growth, politics and economics were locked in just such a positive upward spiral. As growth rushed forward at 6 to 10 percent per year in many countries, issues of income inequality, ethnic tension, environmental degradation, and cronyism were subordinated. Throughout most of Asia between the late 1980s and the mid-1990s, domestic politics was decidedly low volume. Political discontents were difficult to mobilize in an era of broadly expanding wealth: better to hold one's political tongue and benefit from a rising bank balance.

Slow to no growth, by way of contrast, transformed domestic politics within many Asian countries into zero-sum confrontations. As economic conditions worsened, internal cleavages previously smoothed over by the lubricant of rapid growth rose quickly to the political surface.

Such conflicts appeared in many guises: civil versus military, intraethnic, technocrat versus politician, personalistic, sector versus sector, banks versus corporations, and the like. But, regardless of their specific manifestations, most of these contestations arose over two big issues: first of all, who was to blame for the crisis; and second, how extensively, and by what mechanisms, should the country plug into international finance and trans-border capital flows.

Within Japan, since at least the bursting of its asset bubble in 1990–91, these have been the prevailing and unresolved issues (Pempel 1998). Tensions between the country's internationally competitive sectors and its noncompetitive sectors have been exacerbated by the political necessity to pursue policies that favor one over the other. This tension contrasts with the earlier era of high growth, when policies generated benefits for both sides. Japanese politics through the 1990s has largely reflected the struggle to find some politically acceptable resolution for this fundamental economic division.

In Indonesia, the massive collapse of the rupiah, extensive inflation, and high interest rates caused the economy to contract by approximately 15 percent in 1998. Widespread unemployment and a sharp downturn in living conditions resulted. When longtime strongman Suharto proved unable to soften these economic blows, ethnic scapegoating broke out, and he was eventually toppled by violent street protests and a loss of military support.

In Thailand, the government of Prime Minister Chavalit Yongehaiyudh was also held politically responsible for high levels of corruption, failure to ensure financial oversight, and an overabundance of "politics" in economic management. Public demonstrations, led by members of the middle class, forced Chavalit's resignation and brought about a takeover by Chuan Leekpai of the Democratic Party. In an effort to forestall future cronyism, technocrats were charged with implementing financial reforms, and a new constitution was put in place in October 1997. As Donald Emmerson points out (1998, 51), one of the interesting anti-crony mechanisms contained in the new constitution is a clause that prevents any individual from simultaneously being a member of parliament and of the cabinet. This provision seeks to eliminate the previous cycle of corruption in which an aspiring parliamentarian needed to raise huge sums for election. Once elected, he then sought a cabinet post from which to extort bribes so as to pay off his political creditors and to raise more money for the next election.

The old regime was politically reconfigured in South Korea as well. Newly installed president Kim Dae-jung aggressively used the crisis to attack the country's long-powerful *chaebŏl* and to force through financial restructuring. As was true elsewhere, IMF assistance had come with a host of stipulations requiring structural changes in the Korean financial system and in corporate governance. But unlike both Indonesia and Thailand, where official resistance to the wholehearted acceptance of such conditions was strong, in Korea, President Kim welcomed IMF conditionality as congruent with his own reform agenda. He consequently strong-armed institutions weakened by the liquidity crisis to open themselves up to foreign takeovers or mergers, thereby advancing his own anti-establishmentarian program of economic democratization.

The penetration of foreign firms into the core of Korean finance and manufacturing has drastically undercut the previous dominance of key sectors of the economy by Korean-owned firms. As David Hale (1998b, 25) points out, at the onset of the crisis, Korea, despite its much higher GNP and per capita income, was far less open to fdi than many other developing economies. Korea was host to only $12.5 billion in fdi, compared to $67 billion in Singapore, $42 billion in Malaysia, $72 billion in Mexico, and $20 billion in Thailand. But from May 1998 onward, fdi increased monthly, with $1.9 billion committed in December 1998 alone (*FEER* 28 January 1999, 43). Layoffs have also been legalized, leading Korean unemployment to skyrocket. Although labor protested, the magnitude of the economic crisis left workers in an extremely weak bargaining position. President Kim has only partially assuaged and empowered labor by enhancing its legal voice in the corporate restructuring process. Yet this represented another important recalibration of political power within the country.

Domestic political tensions were also sharpened within Malaysia leading up to and following Prime Minister Mahathir's sacking and the subsequent arrest and trial of former finance minister and designated heir Anwar Ibrahim. The dispute between the two centered on resuscitation measures for Malaysia's flagging economy. Long an outspoken critic of international finance, speculators, and currency traders, Mahathir resented the hard choices forced on his country by what he criticized as unelected and faceless financiers. Anwar, in contrast, sought to follow strict austerity programs congruent with IMF conditions elsewhere. In early

September 1998, Mahathir fired Anwar, imposed capital controls, ended the convertibility of the ringgit, and used public funds to stimulate the national economy. Woven into this economic and personalistic clash were a host of additional problems involving cronyism; frictions within the ruling party, UMNO; and the power of Muslim religious associations. But ultimately the central issue in Malaysia, as elsewhere, hinged on how to deal with capital mobility, financial regulation, and corporate restructuring.

Even countries that escaped the worst effects of the crisis began reassessing established political practices, often in response to the vulnerabilities demonstrated by their neighbors. China in particular struggled with the political trade-offs between social stability and economic efficiency, as Barry Naughton's chapter in this book stresses. In one major shift, for example, on 10 January 1999, the Chinese government announced to stunned foreign bankers who had lent enormous sums to the failed Guangdong International Trust and Investment Corporation that Chinese bankruptcy law would give no priority to foreign creditors (*FEER* 21 January 1999, 53). From one perspective, the national government's announcement was a totally unexpected blow to the previously protected foreign investment community. From another, it was a sharp articulation of the national government's commitment to internal financial reform and a rejection of the long-standing expectation that *quanxi* (connections) between Guangdong International Trust and provincial administrators would guarantee the safety of Western investment capital.

In the Philippines, too, a new axis of political cleavage reemerged, although one that was not completely obvious. The administrations of Aquino and Ramos had brought about some reduction in the cronyism of Marcos' rule and a rise in private entrepreneurs. The result was the creation of a new middle class heavily tied to ethnic Chinese families, many of the most successful of which were in turn linked to businesses in Taiwan and Hong Kong. These groups came to control perhaps 30 percent of the top five hundred Philippine corporations (Robison and Goodman 1996, 120). Under President Estrada, however, there was a backlash against this new middle class and against the wave of financial liberalization that was presumed to have benefited them while leading to the problems of 1997–98. With Estrada's election having been built around support from the poor and the left-of-center, and with unemployment at 13 percent in 1998, the focus of his administration logically shifted to providing safety nets for the poor and poverty alleviation.

Heightened political cleavages in themselves did little to ensure victory for reformers, however. Not surprisingly, entrenched power has proven more difficult to dislodge than to challenge. With the notable exception of South Korea, where the power of the presidency has been mobilized forcefully and self-interestedly behind reform, structural changes challenging entrenched elites and power configurations have been slow to materialize in most of Asia. Quite the contrary: even as the financial crisis highlighted the need for various reforms, the accompanying problems of increased unemployment, slower growth in the economy, crime, hunger, and smaller government budgets have made comprehensive changes much more painful to implement.

Thus, despite the fact that Indonesia's economy was the most severely affected by the crisis, shattering old power relations was far from the top of the agenda for the interim government of President Habibie. Of the thirty-six ministers in the Habibie cabinet in early 1999, at least twenty had served under Suharto. Moreover, as one observer put it, "Removing Suharto is a simple matter—relieving his children of their businesses will not be very easy" (Keenan 1998, 246). Two years after the crisis first hit, the Suharto family retained control over a sprawling array of businesses, including toll roads, satellite communications, broadcasting, car making, power projects, domestic airlines, taxi services, water-supply utilities, and trading ventures. Many of these involve joint ventures with prominent Indonesian-Chinese groups, the military, and the ruling Golcar Party. Business reforms have consequently been sluggish, and domestic flight capital and new investment monies have been slow to return.

Much the same story of intensified domestic conflicts confronting calcified resistance could be told for Thailand, Malaysia, Hong Kong, and Japan. Two points remain true throughout most of Asia: first, the economic crisis has brought new issues to the political surface and led to more conflictual domestic politics, but second, and at the same time, preexisting power arrangements have usually remained stolidly resilient. For most countries in the region, mending their fractured economies will require more than a technocratic decision to opt for one package of macroeconomic measures over another. Instead, the central domestic issue will be how to perform the delicate balancing act between what is advantageous economically and what is possible politically. Nor will these decisions be made in a regional or international vacuum; instead, domestic policy makers will continually confront outside pressures—some constant and some changing.

Regional Power Realignments

Two central political issues have emerged at the regional level. First, the longstanding issue of Asian regional institutionalization has resurfaced, largely in the form of weakened national commitments to already limp institutions. Second, there has been a reconfiguration of regional power, primarily with China gaining regional influence at the expense of Japan, and secondarily with Singapore gaining strength as a regional financial hub at the expense of Hong Kong.

As I noted in chapter 3, few formal political, security, or economic organizations connected the countries of Asia before the crisis (see Grieco 1997). ASEAN and APEC, the two major regional associations, have been institutionally thin with limited secretariats and even less authority to shape national behavior or regional events. In the aftermath of the crisis, these inherent weaknesses became even more blatant.

Formed to manage relationships among countries that would otherwise be at odds, ASEAN long adhered to the principle of mutual noninterference in one another's domestic affairs. Cooperation and consensus prevailed over hierarchically based leadership. The economic crisis exposed many previously hidden fault lines among the member countries as well as the inherent difficulties of responding quickly to crisis through procedures demanding consensus. For at least the first year afterward, ASEAN leaders proved incapable of agreeing on any united response to the problems besetting so many of its members' economies.

The July 1998 meeting of ASEAN offered some prospect of change. Thai Foreign Minister Surin Pitsuwan, joined by his Philippine counterpart, Domingo Siazon, proposed that members be allowed to discuss one another's domestic troubles when these had cross-border impacts. Critical to Surin's proposal was the replacement of the principle of noninterference with "flexible engagement" and "constructive intervention." But the other ASEAN members were vehemently opposed, arguing that any reassessment of the principle of noninterference could occur only after the crisis had passed. Indonesian Foreign Minister Ali Alatas argued, for example that the dividing line between talking about transborder problems and interfering in domestic affairs was thin, and crossing it during a crisis could lead to organizational disaster (*FEER* 6 August 1998).

APEC was no better in providing solutions to the economic crisis. Like ASEAN, it had not been designed to deal with trans-Pacific crisis management. Instead, it sought to provide a forum for voluntary moves toward trade liberalization. Not surprisingly, at the December 1997 APEC meeting in Vancouver, participants did little to address the economic crisis, despite efforts by Philippine President Ramos to raise them. U.S. and Canadian representatives avoided the subject completely; Japan's delegation made it clear that it would not be "so conceited" as to think it could be the region's locomotive. Only Chilean and Mexican leaders, quite familiar with financial crises in their own right, were interested in offering advice to their Asian counterparts—but, beyond advice, they could offer little more.

The final declaration of the meeting said little about the economic turmoil, announcing emptily but optimistically that "the fundamentals for long-term growth and prospects for the region are exceptionally strong." With the United States and Canada pushing the hardest, attendees universally re-committed themselves to the allegedly common goal of deregulation of the banking and insurance industries and nine other economic sectors (*FEER* 4 December 1997). But no sooner had participants announced their agreement for trade liberalization than Japan's spokesman admitted that abolishing tariffs on fish and forest products was essentially out of the question.

In the following year's meeting at Kuala Lumpur, Malaysia, APEC was dealt a serious blow in President Clinton's last-minute decision not to participate. Again, the organization did little to address the regionwide economic problems.

In short, the crisis exposed the deep-seated limitations of Asia's regional organizations. Neither ASEAN nor APEC was structured to address seriously the collective economic problems that beset so many of their members. Instead, most countries were forced to rely on nation-specific solutions.

A second shift in regional politics can be noted. During the 1980s, Asia, along with the world more broadly, was pregnant with speculation about Japan's rising economic influence throughout Asia. Fueled by a stronger yen and an expanding world market for Japanese products, Japanese-owned manufacturers undertook a wave of investment that expanded their production facilities throughout Asia. Japanese banks increased their regional lending operations simultaneously. Japan became the world's number-one foreign aid donor, with roughly 70 percent of that money targeted for Asia. At the time, pundits and serious analysts alike agreed that Japanese economic strength was catapulting the country into unquestioned regional preeminence.

What a difference a decade makes. Approaching the turn of the century, Japan's economy was mired in nearly ten years of economic stagnation with little prospect for any short-term turnaround. Japanese politicians, business leaders, and financiers, consumed by the seeming intractability of their country's domestic problems, were slow to direct attention beyond the four main islands of Japan. Governmental aid has fallen since 1995. Japanese fdi in ASEAN and in China have also dropped sharply since the crisis (Ministry of Foreign Affairs 1998). Japanese imports from ASEAN have been in decline since the fourth quarter of 1996, and imports from the NIEs have been in decline since the second quarter of that year. So have imports from China (Ministry of Foreign Affairs 1998). Meanwhile, Japanese banks—in dire straits at home—have pulled back substantially from their overseas operations (*FEER* 5 November 1998). In the single fiscal year 1997–98, overseas assets fell $387 billion, to a level (¥92.9 trillion) that was less than half the peak of ¥198 trillion reached in March 1990 (*Japan Digest* 13 January 1999, 3). As a result, private Japanese loans to Asia have also shrunk as banks have been reluctant to roll over outstanding loans or to make new ones (*Wall Street Journal* 29 January 1999).

Japan has hardly lost all influence in the region, nor has the government given up attempting to shape events there. In September 1997, during the early stages of the Asian crisis, Japan proposed a $100 billion "Asian Monetary Fund" to provide liquidity to the troubled economies. Although only vaguely sketched, the fund would have had Japan provide one-half of the money, and the remainder of Asia would have supplied the other half. The idea was almost immediately rejected. Other Asian countries (most notably China) were neither anxious to see Japan increase its regional influence nor to part with their own riches to help their impoverished neighbors. Even more importantly, U.S. Treasury Secretary Rubin and his deputy Larry Summers were lividly opposed to the plan, seeing it as a potential institutional competitor with the IMF, as well as undercutting American interests and influence in Asia (*New York Times* 17 February 1999, A8). Only as the crisis deepened did American views soften. In November 1998, a modified plan was accepted that involved Japan's putting up a more modest $10 billion toward assistance with no actual institutionalization of an Asian Monetary Fund.

The decline in Japanese influence has also been underscored by the inability of Japanese government officials to generate serious regional or world interest in making the yen a truly worldwide reserve currency, parallel to the U.S. dollar and the Euro. Finance Minister Miyazawa made a number of unsuccessful efforts in late 1998 and early 1999 to convince European leaders of the yen's importance; he was similarly rebuffed in his efforts to have Asian leaders tie their currencies to an international basket of currencies, of which the yen would be a large component.

The declining influence of Japan and the corresponding rise in China's leverage was perhaps most tangibly demonstrated when President Clinton opted to skip a stopover visit to Japan in June 1998, after a nine-day stay in China. During the China stay, in exchange for continued trade, Clinton was quick to offer an array of verbal assurances that the United States accepted various foreign policy conditions demanded by China. By mid-1999, the United States also appeared committed to supporting China's longstanding bid for WTO membership.

China's regional influence has been on the rise with its reabsorption of Hong Kong, the anticipated return of Macao, and what Selden (1997, 339) has labeled "the growing if fragile Taiwan-China links." That influence took on an enhanced economic character with China's announcements that the country would not devalue the renminbi despite the wave of currency depreciations sweeping across Asia. That guarantee elicited almost universal praise from both Asians and Westerners. With it, Chinese leaders managed to convey the impression that their country and its currency had become the lynchpins of Asia; by holding firm on their currency, they would prevent the contagion from getting further out of hand. The announcement and the consequent praise are particularly ironic, given China's relatively small economic contributions to the rest of the region, but even more so because China's devaluation in 1994 was seen by many as the trigger that had set off the subsequent round of regionwide currency instabilities in 1997.

Nonetheless, Chinese influence was at least nominally recognized in August 1998, when Malaysia's new special functions minister, Kiam Zainuddin, announced that "Malaysia's new currency controls are based on China's model" (Wade 1998, 8) It seems clear that until Japan's domestic economy is thriving, that country will continue to be seen as increasingly marginal to broader developments within the region and throughout the world, whereas Chinese influence will continue to rise.

The regional chaos and the lack of cohesion within ASEAN also allowed China to enhance its regional territorial expansion by resuming construction in October 1998 on Mischief Reef, a tiny outpost in the disputed Spratley Islands. The reef is located one thousand kilometers from China's nearest coast (and only three hundred kilometers from the Philippines, which claims it). From 1992 onward, statements of concern by ASEAN had checked Chinese actions in the Spratleys. But with the economic crisis consuming the attention of ASEAN members, and with none of them anxious to engage in a regional arms race, the issue was only vaguely referenced in the communiqué from the ASEAN leaders' December 1998 meeting.

The balance between Japan and China will almost certainly continue to be defined heavily by their respective economic strengths. Although there is little evidence in mid-1999 to show that it will do so soon, Japan is certain to recover at some point, and when it does, its phenomenal economic resources could again be turned to enhancing its regional influence. China, in contrast, is temporarily on the economic upswing; however, its long-term prognosis remains vulnerable to a shaky banking system, bloated state-run enterprises, rising unemployment, and the chances of social unrest. Yet the crisis itself and actions in its aftermath dramatically tilted the regional balance from Japan to China.

Finally, the balance of influence between Hong Kong and Singapore has also shifted. Long in competition to become the most important financial and service hub for the region, the two city-states have found their competition exacerbated since the crisis. Although Hong Kong has long held the lead, particularly in finance, Singapore has gained ground. Singapore's managed float allowed the country to fare better than Hong Kong did with its peg. Hong Kong's reversion to Chinese control has left many international financiers nervous about possible political interference with commercial transactions. Roughly one-half of the equities on the Hong Kong exchange are now owned by Chinese "red chip" state enterprises, and Hong Kong's stock market, currency, and regional service exports proved more vulnerable to both recession and speculative attacks than Singapore's (Lim 1999).

Meanwhile, the Monetary Authority of Singapore has advanced the liberalization of that city-state's financial sector and is allowing foreign funds to manage portions of the extensive and compulsory savings in the massive CPF. It has pledged to remove restrictions on foreign ownership of local brokerages, and in October 1998 it announced a one hundred–project pipeline of investments that were expected to emerge over the next two to three years. Perhaps most significant in its competition with Hong Kong, the Singapore stock exchange began offering a host of derivatives on the Hong Kong market, despite the absence of such instruments in Hong Kong and over Hong Kong's strong objections.

International Political Ramifications of the Asian Crisis

The political reverberations of East Asia's crisis have extended well beyond the immediate region. The early stages of the Asian crisis saw a satisfied triumphalism in the IMF, among major banking houses, within schools of classical economists, and across the U.S. policy community generally. Asia's economic problems, in addition to the IMF's restructuring packages, were quickly accepted as self-evident proof by those already predisposed to such beliefs that (1) global markets would ultimately discipline any who sought to defy them; (2) IMF conditions attached to its financial ministrations would encourage recipients to move toward greater financial responsibility; and (3) if Asia had ever posed any serious threat to U.S. economic hegemony, that threat had passed. Subsequent analysis and changing events in Asia, however, have delayed the universal embrace of such conclusions.

Certainly, with much of Asia on its economic back, it is hard to sustain credibility for the once-popular post–Cold War scenario that anticipated a world divided into three main blocs, each built around one of the three largest national economies: NAFTA, including much of Latin America orbiting the United States; the European Union, unified around a German core; and Asia, forging a third bloc centered on an economically powerful Japan. With Japan having registered virtually zero growth for almost all of the 1990s, and with South Korea and much of Southeast Asia facing empty office buildings, massive bankruptcies, idle construction cranes, and severe damage to their "real economies," it is tempting to begin writing Asian epitaphs. Certainly the Asian leg had become by far the weakest in any tripolar world.

As of early 1999, however, South Korea's economy began to turn around. Stock markets in Thailand and Indonesia were among the developing world's most rapid risers—albeit from the abysmal lows that followed their collapse—and with far less effect on the domestic economy per se. In February 1999, Malaysia relaxed its currency controls and began actively courting foreign capital. The Malaysian currency was stable, the stock market more than doubled, and foreign exchange reserves rose sharply.

Economic growth projections for 1999 were positive for South Korea, three of the ASEAN five, Taiwan, and China. Admittedly, such projections range from barely positive (Singapore at 1.5 percent) to normal euphoria (8.2 percent for China), whereas negative growth was still predicted for the important economies of Japan, Indonesia, and Thailand (*FEER* 4 February 1999, 56–57). At the same time, the relatively rapid turnaround of so many Asian economies underscores their substantial infrastructural resources in ports, roads, industrial capacity, and education, as well as the multiple layers of personal talent and diligence within their political and business communities.

Asian growth rates have unquestionably been fueled at times by classic asset bubbles that simultaneously concealed serious institutional weaknesses. Nonetheless, most of Asia's economies have foundations strong enough to sustain aggressive rebuilding. To restate the obvious, despite their current problems, these countries and many of the companies within them are far better poised for renewed growth than they were in the 1950s or 1960s, or than many of the developing economies in other areas of the world are at century's end.

At the same time, Asian economies as a whole, or Northeast Asian "developmental states" more particularly, no longer present anything like the threat that they once did, namely, the promise of an alternative and more appealing model of capitalism (Albert 1993; Berger and Dore 1996; Crouch and Streeck 1997; Esping-Andersen 1990; Hollingsworth, Schmitter, and Streeck 1994; Katzenstein, 1985; Pauley and Reich 1997; Woo-Cumings 1999; inter alia). For the moment, at least, many elements of the peculiarly Asian vessel of capitalism lie foundered on the shoals of poor performance or else drenched by the tidal wave of Western triumphalism.

Yet much of Asia remains highly skeptical of the purportedly unvarnished merits of market forces unchecked by social and political considerations. With very few exceptions, prior Asian developmental patterns rejected, among other things, the Anglo-American emphasis on market over government, individual over community, short-term profit over long-term market share, equity over bank financing, short-term spot contracts over networks of relational contracting, and transparency over informational control. These biases were shared by many of the countries in continental Europe, and they have hardly disappeared as a simple outgrowth of the recent crisis. This ongoing tension between competing approaches to economic growth was exacerbated in the aftermath of U.S. and IMF actions vis à vis the Asian crisis and the subsequent responses and criticisms these actions induced within much of Asia.

Prime Minister Mahathir's proclamations about the threats to national economic and political sovereignty posed by currency manipulation, Western acquisition of endangered corporations, and IMF restructuring may strike many as the atavistic embrace of Confucian xenophobia. But such fears and Malaysia's actions in closing capital markets resonated positively throughout much of Asia, reverberating as they did with long-standing issues of national and regional pride (and the frustration of having limited leverage in any confrontation with the world's current power holders).

By the early months of 1999, this confrontation between views on the eastern and western shores of the Pacific had widened into a much broader worldwide debate about general problems of global finance, capital mobility, and more specific issues concerning the role and behavior of the IMF. The Asian crisis and the subsequent financial crises in Russia and Brazil generated intense conflicts about just how global finance should be designed. From the January 1999 Davos Forum of top bankers in Switzerland to 10 Downing Street to the U.S. Federal Reserve, as well as in the pages of numerous journals specializing in finance, economics, and international politics, a widespread debate had begun over possible revision of the arrangements governing global finance (see, for example, *Economist* 30 January 1999).

The primary catalyst for such rethinking was the recognition of the havoc played on Asia by the "hot money" phenomenon discussed in earlier chapters of this book. Countries with the lowest levels of such fast flows—Taiwan, China, the Philippines—were the least hurt during the crisis. Malaysia also appeared to have benefited from its decision to end convertibility of the ringgit. Elsewhere, Chilean monetary and economic stability was also attributed to that country's restrictions on easy capital flows. It has always been clear that the highest short-term return to instantly mobile capital could often conflict with long-term national political and social goals. But in the aftermath of the Asian economic crisis, the choices between these competing goals were reexposed and increasingly debated. Most of official Asia has continued to resist the Anglo-American advocacy of freely mobile capital.

Short-term capital mobility was only one aspect of the problem, however. At least as important was the growing perception—in Asia, but also within the World Bank (*New York Times* 11 February 1999) and the U.S. Treasury (*New York Times* 17 February 1999) and among economists such as Jeffrey Sachs (*Economist* 12 September 1998, 23–25), Jagwash Bhagwati (1998b, 14), and Martin Feldstein (1998)—that the IMF and the U.S. government had failed on numerous fronts in their dealings with the Asian crisis.

Criticisms of the IMF have ranged from U.S. Congressional fears that it is an agent of world governance to economists' concerns that as the lender of last resort, it poses an inevitable problem of "moral hazard." Most of these debates can not be seriously addressed here. But three broad criticisms deserve particular attention because of their explicit implications for international relations: first, that the IMF failed adequately to foresee and forestall the crisis; second, that it misdiagnosed the problems; and third, that its economic medicine aided lenders (usually Western) at the expense of borrowers (usually Asian), while simultaneously shifting the burden of adjustment primarily to the shoulders of those least responsible for the problems.

That the IMF failed to anticipate the Asian crisis seems clear from its public pronouncements about Asian strength immediately before the crisis hit. As late as November 1996, barely eight months before it began demanding pervasive structural changes in the Asian economies, the fund sponsored a conference in Jakarta in which the central conclusion was headlined as "ASEAN's Sound Fundamentals Bode Well for Sustained Growth." This upbeat projection went on to suggest that "ASEAN's economic success remains alive and well . . . the region is poised to extend its success into the twenty-first century . . . " (*IMF Survey* 25 November 1996, 377–78). If Asia's economic fundamentals seemed so right to the IMF in November 1996, it is hard to see why they were so wrong six months later.

That the IMF did not foresee the scope and timing of the Asian crisis is itself less surprising than was the organization's quickness in determining that its long-standing economic biases remained the correct ones from which to suggest a cure. Yet, the Asian financial problems stemmed not from *government* profligacy and a *solvency* crisis, as was the case in so many earlier IMF bailouts, but rather from overborrowing by the *private* sector and a consequent *liquidity* crisis. Moreover, Asia's various crises hit countries that were enjoying strong fiscal positions, low inflation, and high growth rates; where there were large current account deficits, these were represented by capital formation, *not consumption* (Bosworth 1998, 8).

As David Hale has shown (1998b, 24), the IMF failed to understand the importance to Thailand of exchange rate stability. The Thai private sector had accumulated large dollar liabilities (through foreign currency loans), and they were thus vulnerable to an upsurge of bankruptcies if exchange rates adjusted dramatically. When Thailand *did* devalue, the result contagiously rippled throughout the region. Corporations rushed to hedge their dollar liabilities, generating the subsequent wave of uncontrollable selling. The exchange rates of Thailand, Indonesia, Malaysia, and other countries fell far more than could be justified by inflation rates, budget deficits, or even trade accounts.

Furthermore, in Thailand and Indonesia, the IMF did not rely on private banks for the resolution of the liquidity crisis but instead took the lead in providing credit itself (Eichengreen and Fishlow 1998, 55–59; Feldstein 1998, 23–24). In addition, in all cases of assistance it was the local government, not the private sector, that was charged with making the changes the IMF claimed would prevent future problems.

It is the explicitly political biases built into many of the IMF's actions and the actions of the IMF's main backer, the United States, that generated the sharpest reactions from those with little power to resist. Financial crises in Mexico, Russia, and Eastern Europe predisposed both the U.S. government and the IMF toward saving the lenders and forcing austerity measures and "structural reforms" on the borrowers (Feldstein 1998). Similar measures were pursued in Asia. Actions by both the IMF and the United States served to bail out the lenders while putting the burden of adjustment on the shoulders of the governments and citizens in crisis. Not least important, structural changes threatened to require the sell-off of major national assets to foreign purchasers at fire-sale prices.

U.S. political interests were also clear in its different reactions to the problems of Thailand and Indonesia, on the one hand, and South Korea, on the other. In the case of Thailand, the United States signed on to a standard IMF plan of spending cuts, high interest rates, and reform of Thai banking practices. Over IMF criticisms, however, the United States refused to contribute financially to the assistance package. The U.S. reaction was similar in Indonesia.

In contrast, when South Korea ran into trouble in November 1997, officials in Washington spent the bulk of the Thanksgiving weekend securing a $57 billion IMF package for the country and urging U.S. banks to reschedule outstanding loans (*New York Times* 17 February 1999). Critics were quick to note that the United States had thirty-five thousand troops in South Korea but none in Thailand or Indonesia, and that American banks had more than double the exposure in South Korea that they had in either Indonesia or Thailand.

U.S. banks, including Citibank, J.P. Morgan, Chase Manhattan, and Bankers Trust, were rewarded for their help in restructuring with interest rates only two to three percentage points over LIBOR. In addition, they received government guarantees that passed the risk of default from the banks' shareholders to Korean taxpayers (*New York Times* 17 February 1999). Meanwhile, tighter monetary policies and reduced budget deficits from tax hikes and cuts in government spending shifted much of the adjustment burden away from borrowers to the general citizenry. Extremely high borrowing rates simultaneously left many Korean companies at great risk of bankruptcy.

Political linkages were most unmistakable in the conditions established for IMF assistance. When the IMF entered Thailand in August 1997, its support package included measures to freeze finance corporations, an act which Jeffrey Sachs (1998) labeled the IMF's screaming "fire" in a theater. Uninsured depositors panicked, as they subsequently did in Indonesia, when the IMF imposed the closure of domestic banks holding uninsured deposits (Wade 1998, 6).

Conditions were even more severe in Korea. There, the IMF demanded a host of structural changes designed to allow foreign ownership of corporations, an opening of domestic financial markets to foreign banks and insurance companies, the import of foreign cars, an end to government encouragement of loans to favored industries, and the like, most of which had little direct relationship to the liquidity problems faced by private Korean borrowers. All of these steps involved a wide departure from the IMF's officially stated role and previous actions, and even from the advice of many economists. As Martin Feldstein put it, "Lenders who listened to the IMF could not be blamed for concluding that Korea would be unable to service its debts unless its economy had a total overhaul" (1998, 31).

Korea undeniably faced a serious problem of short-term private-sector indebtedness. Yet, overall the economy was structurally sound, and it was the eleventh largest in the world. Total Korean debt was only 30 percent of GDP, a level among the lowest for developing countries and one that would be envied by many developed countries as well. Clearly, the IMF could have solved most of South Korea's short-term temporary illiquidity problem through a far simpler bridge loan and coordination of action among creditor banks aimed at restructuring the country's short-term debts.

Whether the more comprehensive measures were economically justified or not, they were surely congruent with the broader U.S. goal of dismantling many of the instruments previously critical to South Korea's long-term economic success. Indeed, as Deputy Treasury Secretary Larry Summers put it at a conference of the Bretton Woods Committee, "The IMF has done more to promote America's trade and investment agenda in East Asia than thirty years of bilateral trade negotiations."[1]

That U.S. and IMF actions had dire long-term social consequences was clearly argued in a two hundred-page report issued in December 1998 by the World Bank. The report concluded that the effort to push up Asian interest rates was a crucial blunder that worsened the crisis. The report contended further that, in their combined efforts to reassure investors and to stabilize currencies, the IMF and the American government opted for a strategy of higher interest rates that in turn spread the economic pain far beyond the banks, investment funds, and real estate companies that had been the key sources of the problems. The recipient countries were plunged into deep recessions that sent thousands of small businesses into bankruptcies, setting off substantial unemployment and removing the gas from the national engines of long-term growth. Indeed, IMF officials themselves conceded that they had mistakenly believed what was happening in Asia to be simply a repeat of past currency crises, such as the Mexico crisis in 1995 (*New York Times* 3 December 1998, 1).

Looking Ahead

In an ironic way, the Asian economic crisis has restored the United States to economic superpower status in the Asian region, at least in terms of being the country that sets the prevailing economic and financial norms. At the same time, those norms were resisted by many in Asia. As was noted previously, in the discussion of domestic political actions, numerous political economies have been slow to reconfigure their most powerful institutions or to sweep aside long-standing personal connections derived from pre-crisis power bases. Japan has been among the strongest resisters to U.S. pressures for economic restructuring, but government leaders in Malaysia, Thailand, and Indonesia have also been vocally reluctant to accept an international monetary and capital regime that threatens national political autonomy.

The capacity for collective regional resistance, however, has proven quite limited. Diverse national self-interests throughout Asia have taken center stage, whereas regionwide institutions have failed to become focal points for any unified political agenda that would challenge U.S. political primacy or the open capital markets favored by the U.S. government and its private-sector investment and banking managers.

Any Asian resistance to the presumed U.S. and IMF agenda favoring national structural reforms to ensure open capital markets is likely, curiously, to find its strongest allies in Europe. There, too, a greater focus on national social and political stability has gained institutional primacy with convergence on the euro, the acceptance of common minimal social programs, and the return to office of many social democratic governments. Although few countries in Asia share the domestic political orientations of European social democrats, they do share a reluctance to allow any single economic model to become dominant throughout the world. Moreover, the euro is likely to become a far more popular reserve currency in places like China, Taiwan, Singapore, and even Japan as a possible counterweight to a dollar-driven world.

The chronologic proximity of the Asian crisis makes secure predictions about the future highly risky. But three broad directions seem clear. First, domestic politics across Asia have become and are likely to remain far more conflictual than they were in the decade or so immediately before the crisis. Second, the regional balance of power within Asia has shifted, and those shifts are likely to continue unless economic fundamentals among the major players of the region change. And third, the Asian economic crisis has become a defining moment in international relations, one that is likely in hindsight to be credited with having catalyzed a substantial recalibration of the currency of international power. The extent to which that debate is resolved in favor of national governments or unregulated capital remains the most open question.

NOTES

Chapter 1

1. I am indebted to Mr. Hale for sending me this paper.
2. Pierre Bourdieu (1998, 126) wrote that the fetishism of productive forces is found not in old Marxist texts but "in the prophets of neoliberalism and the high priests of the Deutschmark and monetary stability . . . it is becoming a sort of universal belief, a new ecumenical gospel."
3. Chinese banks dominate the financial system, accounting for 90 percent of all financial transactions; their incentives for underpricing loans are many, and huge state-owned firms, like South Korea's conglomerates, get preferential lending at low rates. Excess credit availability has led to surplus capacity in Chinese industry (see Lardy 1998a, 78–88).
4. An important nationwide poll of American attitudes on foreign affairs found in 1995 that while the mass of Americans (62 percent) continued to worry about economic competition from Japan, far fewer among the American elite (21 percent) still did. Five years earlier, the figures were 60 percent for the public, 63 percent for the "leaders" (Reilly 1995, 25).
5. Japanese credit agencies continued to give Korea their highest ratings through mid-1997; according to the Bank of International Settlements, bank lending to East Asia rose to a record peak of $14.1 billion in the third quarter of 1997 (Hale 1998a, 5–7).
6. See, for example, *Chicago Tribune* 14 December 1997 (originally printed in the *Boston Globe*) and Mallaby 1998 (14); also Richard W. Stevenson and Jeff Gerth (*New York Times* 8 December 1997), who wrote that "The United States is the fund's largest shareholder, at 18 percent, and effectively wields a veto over major programs and policies." Stevenson and Gerth also said that the IMF "is pushing far more deeply than even before into the day-to-day operations" on a foreign economy—"the Korean one."
7. Even the $6 billion in usable reserves left on 2 December was in jeopardy because of $6.2 billion in committed forward contracts to sell dollars at a set price at a future date (*Wall Street Journal* 10 December 1997).
8. Alan Murray quotes a German analyst on Summers-as-MacArthur in *Wall Street Journal* 8 December 1997.
9. Quoted in *New York Times* 28 January 1998. See also the study by the Institute of International Finance, reported in *New York Times* 30 January 1998.

239

10. Quoted in *Wall Street Journal* 8 December 1997.

11. Yardeni's "zombie" remark was broadcast widely on CNN television news; see the full quotation in *Washington Post* 11 December 1997.

12. GNP figures assume purchase-power parity or PPP; 1995 and 1996 figures are multiplied by 1996 and 1997 growth rates. Figures for 1998 are from LG Economic Research Institute, reported in *Korea Herald* 21 February 1998.

13. The *Choson ilbo* acquired the full, classified text of the bailout package and posted it on its Web site on 4 December 1997. Rubin's personal role in holding up the agreement was reported by Stevenson and Gerth (*New York Times* 8 December 1997).

14. Kanter is quoted in Kapur 1998 (115). Kapur also wrote that, according to fund sources, "conditions such as the one asking Korea to speed up the opening of its automobile and financial sectors reflected pressures from major shareholders (Japan, and the United States)."

15. Clay Chandler discusses Rubin's critical role (which included intensive consultations with leaders of the IMF and G-7) in *Washington Post* 13 December 1997; Bergston is quoted by Chandler in *Washington Post* 11 December 1997.

16. Sanger's reporting on the Asian crisis has been by far the best in the American press.

17. The *Wall Street Journal*'s editors (17 December 1997) wrote that the IMF "seems to be finding ways to socialize the world economy."

18. David Sanger (*New York Times* 25 December 1997) gives the best account of Rubin's Christmas Eve meeting. Information on Korea's bad loans comes from Hale (1998a, 13).

19. Timothy O'Brien (*New York Times* 30 January 1998) wrote that the two Wall Street firms came to Seoul in late November, led by Jeffrey Shafer (Salomon Smith Barney) and Robert Hormats (Goldman, Sachs), "precisely to help the country design and implement a new financing plan for 1998," when it was not yet clear that international banks would be willing to renegotiate the bad loans. O'Brien said delicately that some have questioned whether "the two investment banks have conflicts of interest in simultaneously advising the South Korean government in its negotiations with banks and being the first in line to lead any bond offerings," and that "While Rubin's ties to Goldman, Sachs undoubtedly allow the firm to engage in occasional name-dropping, none of its competitors have suggested the firm's representation of South Korea is inappropriate because of Rubin's tenure there." The U.S. Treasury's top international troubleshooter, David Lipton, is a former IMF official.

20. In other words, from the Cato Institute to Harvard theorist Michael Sandel, to *Tikkun Magazine*'s Foundation for Ethics and Meaning, and to the host of intellectuals roped into various new forums hoping to reinvigorate civility and civil society. The Cato Institute advertised its publications in a 1996 brochure entitled "How You Can Help Advance Civil Society," with a bust of Thomas Jefferson on the cover. See also Michael Sandel's *Democracy's Discontent: American in Search of a Public Philosophy* (Harvard University Press, 1996).

21. Although dissidents in both countries argue that thousands were massacred, it appears that about seven hundred protesters were killed in China. In Korea the exact number has never been established; the Chun government claimed about two hundred died, but recent National Assembly investigations have suggested a figure no lower than one thousand.

22. All information from Asia Watch 1987 (21–22, 31–33, 88–89, 84–95, 123–24).

23. Quoted in *New York Times* 20 November 1997.

24. The rate increased dramatically between November and July to 6.5 percent, with nearly 1.5 million unemployed (according to many Korean newspaper accounts); in mid-1999, it was just over 8 percent.

25. See also the government white paper "The New Administration's Directions for State Management February 1998" (Korean Overseas Culture 1998), which called for

financial transparency, good accounting, improvement of capital adequacy, and no "unrestricted diversification" by the *chaebŏl*—but made no mention of breaking them up.

26. Minister of Finance and Economy Lee Kyu-sung said Kim's reforms were not aimed at diminishing the power and size of the *chaebŏl*, but rather at using various incentives and tax reductions to encourage restructuring (*Korea Herald* 10 April 1998). Later, President Kim told reporters he had no intention of breaking up the *chaebŏl*, but merely wanted them to "run their firms in the black" (*Korea Herald* 2 June 1998).

27. For the backgrounds of new appointees, see *Korea Herald* 11 March 1998 and Hoon 1998 (14).

28. External debt–to–GNP ratios exceed Latin America's in the 1980s: Indonesia, 114 percent; Thailand, 97 percent; the Philippines, 91 percent; South Korea, 62 percent.

29. On the race in electronics exports, see *Korea Herald* 16 July 1998; see also Johnson 1998a.

30. Quoted in *New York Times* 17 January 1998.

31. Taiwan's formal treaty relations with Washington ended in 1979, and no U.S. troops are based there; but Congress' Taiwan Relations Act indicated strong continuing concern for Taiwan's independence from the mainland, and in 1996 President Clinton sent two aircraft carrier task forces to shadow Taiwan while Beijing rained missiles down in tests near the island.

Chapter 2

1. A nearly comprehensive list of these articles is found on Nouriel Roubini's website devoted to "What Caused Asia's Economic and Currency Crisis and Its Global Contagion?" The address is http://www.stern.nyu.edu/~nroubini/asia/AsiaHomepage.html.

2. Prices for products and services are assumed to be set through an equilibrating process between all buyers and all sellers, in which selling price would include (1) inputs, with prices set by foreground institutions (e.g., markets in credit and in commodities), (2) labor, with wages set competitively, and (3) value added in manufacturing.

3. These are my terms for what other observers have also seen. I take no credit for discovering these changes. I have attached new labels because I wish to emphasize the large-scale organizational qualities of the changes (Hamilton and Feenstra 1998).

4. The following argument is developed more fully in Gereffi and Hamilton 1996.

5. Gary Gereffi has pioneered the global commodity chain approach. For good descriptions of it, see Gereffi 1994 (also see Gereffi and Korzeniewicz 1994; Bonacich et al. 1994; Gereffi and Hamilton 1996).

6. This discussion of reflexive manufacturing systems is based on my own research, first in Taiwan (Hamilton 1997) and later in the United States. Some discussion of this research is found in Gereffi and Hamilton 1996.

7. The best of this literature (e.g., Lim and Pang 1991; Lim 1995; Stallings 1995; Chen and Drysdale 1995; Naughton 1997a) traces shifting patterns of export development to changing factors of political economy (e.g., government policy) and technology, including fdi. Although subtle in many ways, this highly descriptive literature is, generally speaking, not sensitive to substantial organizational differences that exist between economies having very similar political economies and the same access to the advanced technology. For an analysis that emphasizes crucial differences in economic organization among countries, see Whitley 1992; Lazonick et al. 1997; Hollingsworth and Boyer 1997; and Orrù, Biggart, and Hamilton 1997.

8. I should note that an artifact of this mode of analysis is to place the explanations of development on a continuum between the strong state, at one end, and the free market, at

the other end. For a preliminary exploration of this bias and its perniciousness, see Hamilton 1994.

9. Economist Robert Feenstra and I (Hamilton and Feenstra 1998; Feenstra and Hamilton forthcoming) have developed a simulated model of industrial structure that produces multiple equilibria and clearly shows both the importance of embedded structure for economic outcomes and the sensitivity of these structures to price structures. We have corroborated these models with empirical data from Taiwan and South Korea.

10. For a first-rate comparative analysis of the level of debt leverage in South Korean manufacturing firms against levels found in a selected sample of other countries, see Zeile 1993.

11. The move toward merchandising in the United States was directly enhanced by the Japanese and Korean successes. More than a few former manufacturers began to subcontract, on an OEM basis, with Korean and Japanese firms. Ford and Chrysler had models of their cars build in Korea. Once an industrial strength of the United States, television production moved almost entirely to Asian production sites, even though the brand names of the former producers, such as RCA and Magnavox, persisted for a while.

12. The accelerating success of East Asian countries in global export trade and the expanding trade deficit in the United States prompted the Plaza Accord meeting, at which U.S. negotiators successfully argued that Asia's currencies had been kept artificially low and ought be allowed to float to find their "true" level.

13. The effects of these currency adjustments increased even further in 1991 when China devalued its currency, thereby making China Asia's low-cost producer for many labor-intensive manufactured goods. China's reevaluation had the effect of undermining Southeast Asia's competitive advantage, since currencies there were rising or were stable in value against U.S. currency.

14. For some indications of the difficulties that began to surface, see Roubini, Corsetti, and Pesenti 1998.

Chapter 3

1. Quoted in Frieden 1987 (114–15).

Chapter 4

1. Now, the World Bank struggles to convince leaders of the advanced industrial countries that it is still useful. In a 1996 speech, the bank's president, James Wolfensohn, argued that the real significance of the World Bank was not in the levels of resources it provides, but in the leading role it plays as chief reformer on behalf of private capital controllers: "Indeed, the post–Cold War world has increased, not reduced the Bank's relevance—not only because of the Bank's ability to reach out to new centers of influence such as civil society, but because the Bank, focusing on systemic change, is perfectly positioned to create the kind of enabling environment so necessary to attract private capital" (1996).

2. On these important changes in capital flows, see Armijo 1999b. For a focus on portfolio capital, see Haley 1999. For an assessment of the impact of these flows on Indonesia, see Winters 1999.

3. BIS 1998b, 10.

4. The ratio of short-term debt to exports of goods, services, and transfers grew from 40 to 60 percent for Thailand and Indonesia and from 29 to 43 percent for South Korea between December 1993 and December 1996. (The same ratio for Mexico peaked at 42 percent in December 1994, when the Tequila crisis hit, but fell back to 25 percent once a

rescue had been implemented.) The ratio of short-term debt to foreign reserves was slightly below 1 for Indonesia and Thailand and at 1.4 for South Korea in December 1993. The ratios rose to 1.2 for Thailand, 1.5 for Indonesia, and 1.8 for South Korea by June of 1995. In June of 1997, on the eve of the crisis, the ratios had increased still further to 1.4 for Thailand, 1.6 for Indonesia, and a staggering 2.6 for South Korea, the highest rate in the region (BIS 1998a, 6).

5. There can be no doubt that exclusionary and crony politics helped set the stage for economic collapse in places like Indonesia. But Suharto had been building and expanding his crony empire for three decades when the crisis hit. The implosion of Indonesia needed a catalyst that was not necessarily endogenous to "booty capitalism" as practiced in Southeast Asia. See Hutchcroft 1998a.

6. James Riady, a leading Indonesian banker with the Lippo Group, estimated that 80 percent of Indonesia's private sector debt was directly committed to overseas parties, without the involvement of Indonesia's local banks (*Antara* 18 February 1998).

7. In September 1997, short-term debt in the Philippines was roughly $9 billion, which was only 93 percent of gross international reserves. Ratios under 1 are considered good. China's short-term debt was less than 33 percent of gross foreign exchange reserves (AFX News 24 February 1998).

8. The largest Korean company is sixteen times bigger than the largest Taiwanese firm.

9. Quoted in Chowhury and Paul 1997.

10. It is crucial that any analysis of the crisis and the responses to it (including one that strongly emphasizes external factors, as I do here) be linked analytically to the struggles over power within the governments of the region. For instance, one consequence of the close arrangement in Southeast Asia between the state and its clients in business and politics is that there is a built-in tendency for economic reformers in government who are marginalized from power in normal times to seize moments of crisis as windows of opportunity to ram through as many fundamental changes in the domestic political economy as possible. Some of these policies may help address the immediate crisis, but just as often they extend it. Far from being a rational, methodical, planned, phased, or integrated set of policies to stabilize the economy and set it on a more prosperous course, the actions of frustrated reformers are sometimes driven by a desire simply to get as many sweeping changes in place as possible before the window closes and power swings back to those who enjoy it during the intervals between crises. For a fuller development of these relationships, see Winters 1996.

11. One consequence of this bedrock belief in the regional dollar pegs was that most companies in the region who had borrowed billions of dollars abroad did not hedge their debt—meaning they did not buy futures and options to protect them against exchange rate fluctuations.

12. Even Paul Krugman's (1994) mild observation that as GDPs in Asia grew, annual growth rates on a much larger base would have to slow down, was dismissed as overly pessimistic.

13. There are indications that many EMFMs in fact did not act prudently and responsibly. "Before [the crisis], people could just close their eyes and blindly buy Asia as a whole," said Nitin Parekh, regional strategist at Credit Suisse First Boston (HK) Ltd. "Now you can't do that; you have to pick carefully what you buy and why you're buying it." Is this not what the high-paid EMFMs were supposed to be doing all along? It would have been a lot cheaper to pay someone to throw darts at a stock market dartboard, if all one wanted to do was close one's eyes and blindly buy Asia (Tam 1997, 18). According to one of the world's leading specialists on financial markets, "When the market rises, there may be a rush of 'noise traders' wanting to get in on the action. Noise traders care little about underlying values [of companies' stock] and are simply betting that the rising trend will continue. Their buying can drive prices up, providing them with the capital gains they hoped for. This, in turn, spurs more buying, and so on" (Kohn 1994, 727).

14. Richard Hazlewood was "reassigned" from his position as the EMFM in Hong Kong for Fidelity Investments to the lowly position of "analyst" back in Boston. Hazlewood, who was thirty-seven years old, had managed the emerging market fund since July 1993. His fund was deeply invested in Malaysia when the crisis began to unfold. Hazlewood was so overinvested in Malaysia that he became trapped, "unable to sell his investments . . . because of chaotic market conditions, which would be made worse if a big investor like Fidelity dumped even more stock." Hazlewood found himself "not selling what you want to sell, when markets go down, they go illiquid." By any objective standard, Fidelity, one of the world's largest and most reputable mutual funds, should not have been so deeply invested in Malaysia. At the beginning of 1997, the ratio of the country's stock market capitalization to its GDP was 325 percent, the highest ratio of any country in the world. Attractive markets have ratios of less than 50 percent. According to people who knew Hazlewood, he had been courted personally by Malaysian politicians and businessmen, and he "relished the attention." Not only did this attention flatter Hazlewood's ego, but it gave him a false sense of security in the Malaysian market that caused investors in his fund to endure huge losses (*AWSJ* 22 October 1997, 8).

15. The situation I just described applies to banks as well, although with one important difference. If depositors think a bank is in serious trouble, they will rush to take out their money because banks honor withdrawals on a "first come, first served" basis, until their resources are depleted. Even someone who happens to know that the bank is not in serious trouble will rush to withdraw deposits, recognizing that all the other depositors, who lack privileged information, will withdraw, and that the bank has only a small reserve to cover routine withdrawals (moreover, if other bankers also believe the bank is in trouble, it will not be able to borrow on the interbank market to cover the rush of withdrawals). The big difference between a bank and a capital market is that when a bank collapses because of a run, people lose their deposits and the story is over (unless, of course, a "contagion effect" transforms a run on a single bank into systemic bank panic). But capital market crashes are not so final. Because of the nature of share trading, they tend to be temporary and self-correcting, meaning that after shares hit rock bottom, they will rise again as investors start buying eagerly at bargain prices. After the 1987 U.S. market crash, investors regained their losses relatively quickly. The rebound took longer after the 1929 crash, but investors still did very well over the medium and long term. For more on crashes and panics, see Kohn 1994.

16. Soon after Bambang dropped his suit, one of his father's close business associates allowed Bambang to buy out his banking license and name and, after a change of costumes and signs, reopen for business.

17. The IMF was asleep and silent during other crashes as well, including the European Rate Mechanism (1992 and 1993) and the Czech Republic (1997) crashes (*Wall Street Journal* 25 August 1997).

18. But then, why should they? As long as the IMF and bilateral rescuers can be relied on to bail out companies and their incompetent and even criminal managers, why bother to look at the financial ratings? The point is that creditors will be paid, and, if that is all they care about, then looking at the financial ratings only spoils an otherwise pleasant day (*International Herald Tribune* 22 November 1997, 1).

19. It also appears that this political impasse in Indonesia undermined progress on rescheduling the private debt of Indonesian companies. According to one report,

> U.S. commercial banks, which were pressured by the Treasury Department and the Federal Reserve to roll over their loans to South Korean banks, are not getting similar pressure with regard to loans to Indonesian corporations for a number of reasons. In South Korea, which has just elected a prominent advocate of democracy to be its new president, United States and International Monetary Fund officials could argue to bankers that the fundamentals in the country, which happens to be a key United States military ally, were positive—if only it could

*get through a short-term credit crunch. Indonesia, in contrast, is plagued by the political instability of President Suharto's 32-year regime—and his certain victory when he stands for a seventh five-year term next month. (*Wall Street Journal *2 February 1998, 6)*

Chapter 5

1. Short selling in the currency markets involves borrowing local currency at the prevailing domestic interest rate and exchanging it immediately for foreign currency (in this case, U.S. dollars) in anticipation that the exchange rate will depreciate before the domestic loan is due, which would enable the speculator to buy back the local currency he owes at a lower rate (for fewer units of the foreign currency), pocketing the difference (between dollars bought at the higher local currency rate and sold at the lower rate).

2. For example, Argentina's currency board is credited with preventing the bouts of hyperinflation that plagued the country in the past, but price stability has been achieved at the expense of employment, with unemployment remaining at a high 16 percent many years after the currency board was established. In this case, the political costs of renewed hyperinflation are considered to be lower than the political costs of continued high unemployment, so the board system remains intact.

3. For example, a monthly Merrill Lynch–Gallup survey of global fund managers in September 1997 found that one-half of the Asia-based managers polled believed that the government's intervention to prop up the market had made them more worried about the future of the HK dollar. Whereas in the August survey, not one Asian fund manager believed the peg would float in 1998, in September, approximately 11 percent of the respondents believed it would float in 1998, and 47 percent said it would float in 1999 (*South China Morning Post* 8 September 1998).

4. *FEER* weekly Asian Executives Poll of 17 September 1998 (page 34) found that 91.5 percent of top company executives polled in Hong Kong agreed that the territory's economy was too dependent on property, the highest proportion of respondents in any of the ten countries polled.

5. Ronnie Chan, chairman of one of Hong Kong's large real estate companies, the Hang Lung Group, quoted in Brauchli and Guyot 1998.

6. These include the unwinding of the short positions in Hong Kong of global hedge funds adversely affected by the Russian debt default and three successive reductions in U.S. interest rates (*Economist* 31 October 1998, 79). Because the HK dollar is pegged to the U.S. dollar, a fall in U.S. interest rates will also occasion a fall in Hong Kong interest rates.

7. Devaluation would increase the competitiveness of China's exports relative to those of its now-cheaper, crisis-hit Asian neighbors and alleviate some of the rising unemployment likely to result from the (now delayed) reform of overstaffed SOEs. But it would also increase the prices of imports, especially capital equipment and technology, and the cost of servicing China's sizable foreign debt. The fact that China still runs a current account surplus and reportedly has over $140 billion in foreign reserves (although this figure, like that of China's supposed 1998 growth rate of 7 or 8 percent, is challenged by many observers) removes the immediate need to devalue. China also has regional political status invested in its repeated promise to its neighbors not to devalue "this year" (i.e., 1998).

8. There is extensive literature on Singapore's industrial policy. For a contribution by this author, see Lim 1995.

9. The same relative buoyancy has been enjoyed by Taiwan for the same reasons: both economies allowed their managed-float currencies to depreciate by about 15 percent; export mainly high-technology products to growing world markets; and maintain low domestic debt, large current account surpluses, and large foreign exchange reserves. Hong Kong, in contrast, maintains a—now overvalued—fixed exchange rate, exports mainly services to

depressed or slowing regional markets, runs a current account deficit, and maintains much smaller per capita foreign exchange reserves. The Hong Kong government is now considering a switch to a high-technology industrial policy, but skeptics abound.

10. Foreign nationals account for more than 20 percent of Singapore's labor force and more than 50 percent of manual or low-skilled jobs in manufacturing, where they complement local workers who are too scarce or expensive for these jobs.

11. Depreciation was not, however, uncontroversial, because it would increase the cost of imported goods in a highly import-dependent economy and also, some felt, could potentially undermine Singapore's role as a regional financial center, which might require a strong, stable currency.

12. Steven Choo, executive director of the private rental agency Jones Lang Wootton, quoted in Chua 1998 (14).

13. All statements by Steven Choo, quoted in Chua Mui Hoong 1998 (14).

14. In interviews I conducted in Singapore in July 1998, many private-sector professionals—lawyers, bankers, and businessmen—questioned why GLC senior managers in their forties continued to keep their jobs and draw annual salaries in the range of US$500,000 to US$1 million despite being responsible for bad investment decisions incurring massive losses for shareholders in their publicly listed companies. Ever aware of and sensitive to public opinion, the government subsequently announced salary cuts and freezes for civil servants that included GLC officers. Cabinet ministers—the most highly paid in the world—would take a 10 percent pay cut.

15. Senior Minister Lee Kuan Yew, quoted in an interview in *FEER* 24 September 1998 (11).

16. A survey of four hundred people in September 1998 found that 42 percent were worried about a CPF cut and 26 percent about repaying housing loans (Ching 1998, 7).

17. See speech by Deputy Prime Minister Lee Hsien Loong, reported in Veloor 1998 (24).

Chapter 6

1. Here I use the term *regime* in the sense T. J. Pempel (1998, 20) uses it, as a midlevel complex of legal and organizational features consisting of particular patterns of socioeconomic alliances, political economic institutions, and public policy profile.

2. For a full discussion of the political economy of Korea's financial policy, see Woo 1991.

3. Maurice Meisner (1996) uses the term "bureaucratic capitalism" to describe China's socialist market reform. *Booty capitalism* is a variant of *adventure capitalism*, referring to a system in which rulers raid the population for treasures. Paul Hutchcroft (1998) uses the term to describe the predatory behavior of the oligarchy in the Philippines, especially in the Marcos years.

4. In other words, 1998 was not the first year in which Korea recorded a –6 percent growth, nor was the 1997–98 crisis the worst since the Korean War, as is often reported in the press. The economic crisis of 1979 was worse in terms of its social and political consequences and was followed by a military coup.

5. Remark by the Korean head of McDonald's, quoted in Clifford 1995 (325).

6. This is calculated, at the firm level, as earnings before interest and taxes in local currency over total assets minus the annual inflation rate in the country.

7. For a fuller account, see *New York Times* 25 March 1998.

8. Quoted in Hadley 1970 (455).

Chapter 7

1. Identifying these factors as key elements in the crisis does not necessarily imply that the policies behind them were hopelessly misguided. Financial liberalization can bring

important benefits in terms of capital mobilization, and stable or predictable exchange rates greatly facilitate international transactions. The lesson here is not that these earlier policy reforms were wrongheaded, but simply that financial liberalization without adequate regulatory oversight can be very dangerous, as can be a fixed exchange rate if it fails to respond to major currency realignments or encourages borrowers to disregard currency risk.

2. There are a number of comprehensive accounts of events, particularly economic events, in Thailand (Ammar 1997; Bhanupong forthcoming; Warr 1998; Pasuk and Baker 1998a; Pasuk and Baker 1998c; Yos and Pakorn 1998; Laothamatas 1998) and in Indonesia (Soesastro and Basri 1998; Pincus and Ramli 1998; McLeod 1998; Azis 1998; Tubagus 1997), and of empirically based comparative studies (Hill 1998; Krause 1998; Garnaut 1998; McLeod and Garnaut 1998; Jomo 1998; Montes 1998b).

3. Radelet and Sachs (1998a, 28) even go so far as to say that if this issue had been handled differently by Thai authorities, Thailand might have avoided a major economic crisis.

4. Another dimension of the institutional story of Thailand's handling of the economic crisis that I do not have space to pursue here is the changing status of the central bank. There is a clear and fascinating story to be told about the rise of ministerial control over the central bank (and the bureaucracy more generally) as a normal consequence of democratization.

5. The government also announced that all depositors would be protected and that a deposit insurance would be set up for the remaining healthy institutions. But, as before, this failed to prevent a three-day bank run.

6. Although not actually fixed, the rupiah had been weighted heavily to the U.S. dollar in a managed float, and, in a well-established policy, it had been permitted to depreciate at a gradual but highly predictable rate of 4 to 5 percent per year. As in Thailand (before the baht came under pressure in late 1996), investors believed there was little or no risk of major exchange rate fluctuation.

7. There is an extra dimension to this story that I do not pursue here: Suharto's motives. The institutional framework permitted him to behave erratically, but it did not cause him to do so. Identifying Suharto's political preferences is a highly speculative exercise. Among the most frequently encountered guesses are that he was simply unwilling to cut back the business privileges of his children (cf. his willingness to cut back crony privileges in previous crises); that he suffered from seriously inadequate information on the true precariousness of the economic situation because his advisers no longer dared to bring him unwelcome news; or that he suffered from seriously diminished political judgment through some combination of age and hubris.

8. The open capital account was important for two reasons. First, and most obviously, it promoted investor confidence by enabling investors to get their money out easily at any time. Second, and more subtly, the existence of an easy exit option for investors served as something of a constraint on the policy behavior of the government—if the government allowed the overall business environment to deteriorate or to become too uncertain, it would be punished swiftly by an outflow of capital. In a sense, then, by opening the capital account in 1970, the government was tying its own hands. It could of course always untie its hands by imposing capital controls, but to do so would have been very costly in terms of investor confidence.

Chapter 8

1. It is also worth noting that with an annual population increase of at least 2.32 percent (the officially acknowledged rate), even mildly positive aggregate growth translates into negative per capita growth.

2. The Philippines "has eschewed the hubris that has infected many Asian tigers," reported the *New York Times* on 11 December 1997. "The thunder of collapsing banks and the cracking of economic hubris elsewhere are even making Filipinos a bit smug." Before

the crisis as well, a World Bank representative declared that the country "is emerging as one of the star performers within the East Asia region" (*FEER* 27 February 1997, 43).

3. For more comprehensive analysis of the motivations behind the reform effort, see Hutchcroft 1998a (241–46).

4. As I argue, the characteristics of the Philippines' "patrimonial oligarchic state" have made it particularly resistant to reform initiatives: selective measures, initiated from the top by the political leadership, have commonly been inhibited by a lack of bureaucratic coherence and by the tremendous power of oligarchic interests, whereas far more sweeping measures, initiated from below, are discouraged by the tendency of economic growth not to nurture new social forces but merely to strengthen the oligarchic social forces that are *already* the major beneficiaries of patrimonial largesse (Hutchcroft 1998a, 53–55).

5. The term *political reform* can encompass a broad range of processes, from the promotion of political stability (noted earlier) to the installation and consolidation of democratic institutions (the Philippine experience of which is most ably analyzed in Thompson 1996) to reform of electoral, party, and legislative structures (with the goal of improving the quality of democracy). In this paper, I am dealing with the third aspect of the term.

6. Manuel Montes (1998a, 249), for example, writes of "the inherent conservatism of Philippine banks, especially the bigger ones, because of memories of previous crises" (see also Montes 1998b, 13–14).

7. According to a 1988 World Bank study, pre-tax profit margins in the Philippines were roughly 300 percent higher than the average of such margins in eight other countries. The banks' oligopolistic power was unchallenged by the Central Bank, and prices for important banking services were seemingly set by the actions of a cartel. See Hutchcroft 1998a (67, 204).

8. Data on bank profits and growth come from Bautista, Ybañez, and Agulto 1995 and Sycip, Gorres, and Velayo (various issues, 1980–95). On rates of financial intermediation, see Hutchcroft 1998a (9, 230).

9. This discussion draws from Hutchcroft 1998a (212–20).

10. Carlos Jalondoni of UBS Securities, quoted in Ebias 1998.

11. Also notable is the loan exposure of two leading banks in the highly troubled Philippine Airlines, one of the country's largest corporations. See *FEER* 8 October 1998 (106).

12. The pessimistic analysis is that of UBS Securities' Carlos Jalondoni, quoted in Ebias 1998 (56–58); Guinigundo is quoted in *PDI* 13 July 1998. Data on nonperforming loans come from *FEER* 25 September 1997 (104); *PDI* 13 July 1998; and *FEER* 15 October 1998 (75), and *PDI* 10 May 1999. Out of concern for increasing levels of nonperforming loans, the BSP announced in early 1998 that it would require banks to implement loan-loss provisions in 1998, 1999, and 2000 (Ebias 1998, 56–58). In late 1998, Standard & Poor's lowered the ratings of many banks and predicted that nonperforming loans would "easily exceed" 20 percent of total loans in 1999 (*AWSJ* 4 September 1998). Governor Singson refuted this prediction and said the Philippines had adopted criteria for assessing levels of nonperforming loans that are stricter than international standards (*AWSJ* 17 September 1998).

13. *AWSJ* 9 October 1998; *PDI* 13 July 1998. On the underestimation of loan exposure, see *FEER* 25 September 1997 (102). UBS Securities, in a February 1997 report, also expressed concern that Philippine banks were overexposed in property loans (*FEER* 1 May 1997, 53). UBS Securities subsequently predicted that as much as 30 percent of loans to real estate developers could become nonperforming (Ebias 1998, 57).

14. Problems of supervisory capacity in the 1990s are discussed in greater detail in Hutchcroft 1998a (210–12, 223–24, 229–30). It is notable that in late 1997 the BSP actually accused banks of unfair profiteering and required them to post notices disclosing the differential between loan and deposit rates. The banks resisted pressure to alter their rates, but one can hope that this episode represents a new willingness of the BSP to question

bank practices (*AWSJ* 5 September 1997). Nonetheless, as in earlier years, "many observers worry about the central bank's ability to supervise the banks" (*AWSJ* 24 November 1997).

15. "What we have going for us," one government official noted, "is that our hubris is much younger" (*AWSJ* 7 November 1998). A banker similarly observes that "our little asset bubble is only three years old" (*AWSJ* 7 October 1998).

16. Throughout the Ramos administration, fiscal difficulties were generally obscured by proceeds from privatization—but by the time Estrada took power, almost all of the big-ticket assets had already been sold off. The tax effort remains very low (a mere 16 percent), revenue collection fell nearly P20 billion short of its 1997 target, and the budget surplus of earlier years is forecast to become a P40 billion (US$1 billion) budget deficit in 1998. See de Dios 1998 (52–55, 69–72); Montes 1998a; and *AWSJ* 9 September 1998. Estrada's proposed tax amnesty will not be likely to improve matters (*AWSJ* 11 August 1998).

17. For an excellent overview of the Philippine economy, see de Dios 1998.

18. On the centrality of a military perspective to reform motivations and execution, see Hutchcroft 1998a (242–46). On the financial ties binding the Philippine Congress to Ramos, see Hutchcroft 1998b (38–39).

19. After all the earlier trumpeting about the Philippines finally extracting itself from IMF supervision, the country once again drew on IMF loans (and submitted to IMF conditions) in September 1998 (*AWSJ* 10 September 1998). The impact of "hot money" on export competitiveness is noted in Montes 1998b (21); on capital accounts, see *AWSJ* 17 September 1998.

20. But this did not necessarily translate into support for those in the Ramos administration who were hoping to amend the constitution to permit the president to run for another term. Many business leaders supported the late-1997 mass demonstrations that effectively squelched "charter change" (or "cha-cha") proposals. See *AWSJ* 5 September 1997.

21. Historically, Philippine business is well organized at the level of the family conglomerate but very poorly organized at any broader level of aggregation. There is little separation between the enterprise and the household, and—given the highly diversified character of most family conglomerates—it is difficult to discern larger segments of capital divided along coherent sectorial lines. In such an environment, business associations generally remain weak and poorly institutionalized (Hutchcroft 1998a, 21, 37–39, 185, 250).

22. One major business organization has revitalized itself in recent years: the BAP has built up a professional staff and played a major role in promoting the collective interests of its membership. Unfortunately, the BAP's major success has been to obstruct, rather than to promote, liberalizing reforms in the banking sector (supporting reforms in general terms, but curbing them as much as possible in their specifics); see Hutchcroft 1998a (214–20).

23. On the growth of the middle class, see Pinches 1996 (106-7, 122–23) and Rood 1998 (124).

24. This degree of social mobility highlights the appropriateness of the term *oligarchy*—not *aristocracy*—to analysis of the Philippine political economy. See Hutchcroft 1998a (21–22).

25. *PDI* 6 October 1998; Montes 1998a. The export boom has been primarily based on electronics products, which account for over two-thirds of goods exports (de Dios 1998, 67). Remittances from overseas workers totalled $7 billion in 1996 (the last pre-crisis year) and were expected to total $6.5 billion in 1998 (*FEER* 23 October 1997, 92; 15 October 1998, 75).

26. The presence of such sentiment, of course, does not imply that redistributive measures will actually be implemented. Obstacles to redistributive change noted by Kurt Weyland (1996) in his analysis of Brazil (clientelism, weak party organization, narrow interest associations of better-off sectors, and a fragmented state apparatus) seem similarly important in the Philippines.

27. As Rocamora points out, the (unsuccessful) proposals for reforming legislative institutions that did come from Almonte's National Security Council were anything but democratic in content (e.g., a parliamentary system that lacked "provision for bringing down a Prime Minister through a vote of no-confidence"!) (1995, "The political requirements of economic reform," 3). The Ramos administration did actively promote a far-reaching 1991 Local Government Code that devolved significant levels of authority and resources to provinces, cities, and municipalities. It remains to be seen, however, whether this measure will bolster or challenge undemocratic structures at the local level. For a generally optimistic analysis, see Rood 1998; for a less detailed but more cautionary appraisal, see Hutchcroft 1998b (39–41).

28. Although the Philippines has always had far more embeddedness than autonomy, there are certain parallels here to Peter Evans' argument for "a more encompassing form of embedded autonomy." By including a "broader range of societal groups," he proposes, it may be possible to "counterbalance the weight of a more powerful business community so that embeddedness is less likely to degenerate into capture." Social groups such as labor, he points out, can be expected to have "a direct interest in binding capital's search for profit to productivity-enhancing investments." See Evans 1997 (83–84).

29. Although attacks on "cartels and monopolies" and oligarchic privilege showed a potential to construct a populist coalition for change, the Ramos administration did not seize the opportunities to do so. Reformers presented their economic policy changes as an element of "people empowerment," building on the restoration of democratic institutions since 1986, but other Ramos policies—particularly those that perpetuated regressive revenue structures and sought to curb civil liberties—undercut any hope for building a more inclusive coalition (see Rocamora 1994, 179–80; 1995a, 40–43; de Dios 1998, 71).

30. *PDI* 19 September 1995. Similarly, Archbishop Jaime Cardinal Sin has denounced the "judicial Judases" found throughout the system and observed that the study and practice of law in the Philippines are "as different as heaven and hell" (*PDI* 27 April 1996). A rash of kidnappings and bank robberies (widely thought to involve "law enforcement" officials) highlighted the corruption and incompetence of judicial and police officials. See *AWSJ* 23 May 1997 for a detailed account of corruption in the Philippine Supreme Court.

31. Because the country's commitment to liberalization has not been matched by a similar commitment to export promotion, the result has been a kind of reverse mercantilism. The mercantilists of Northeast Asia, it is worth recalling, restricted imports while promoting exports; in the Philippines, on the other hand, the ports have been opened up to a stream of foreign goods without any concomitant effort to promote higher-value-added exports. The one success story in Philippine exports, electronics equipment, remains highly dependent on imported inputs.

Chapter 9

1. The high-technology industries fall into four categories: power and electrical machinery (including informatics products), chemical, biotechnology, and precision machinery.

2. See Mai and Chang 1998 (7–10) for a detailed account.

3. Officially, SMEs are defined as companies with capital less than NT$50 million.

4. This ratio is commonly known as the *capital coefficient* in economics textbooks.

5. It is worth noting, however, that the degree of leverage could be much higher than the apparent figure for many business groups in Taiwan, because of the cross-holding of stocks and the mutual endorsement of checks (Chu and Lee 1998).

6. In comparison, as of mid-1996, Taiwan's stock market in terms of market value was twice as big as South Korea's. The market value of the Taiwan market stood at US$274 billion (or 87 percent of GDP), whereas the South Korea market stood at US$139 billion (or 40 percent of GDP).

7. This has only been the case since 1979. Before that, the CBC was formally under the presidential office.

8. The only exception occurred when late president Chiang Ching-kuo served as the premier between 1971 and 1978.

9. Two former CBC governors, Yu Hong-jun and Yu Kuo-hua, later became premier. Also, two governors served formerly as minister of finance, and quite a few ministers of finance were formerly vice governors of CBC.

10. Before the political opening of the late 1980s, the average tenure of a premier was five years and eight months, while the average tenure of the governor of CBC was nine years and four months. See S. Chen 1998, 62–64.

11. The two exceptions, Liang Kuo-shu and Hsu Yuan-tung, were both forced out of office by accidental causes. Excluding these two, the average tenure of the CBC governor between 1961 and 1997 was about eight years.

12. 1949 and 1961, as a temporary measure, the Bank of Taiwan actually performed the function of the central bank. After 1961, the CBC was reinstated when the Nationalist government began to retreat from its goal of "recovering the mainland."

13. In addition, Taiwan's highly institutionalized civil servant system also enhanced conservatism in the banking sector. As public servants, most bank employees enjoy solid job security, on the one hand, and, on the other hand, are subject to criminal prosecution for corruption or negligence should the loans they approve turn bad. Strong incentives therefore exist for employees to protect themselves by being very risk-averse. If they are pressured to approve particular loans that otherwise do not meet certain requirements, they typically request written (overriding) orders from their superiors, who are then exposed to the same risk of prosecution.

14. During the 1980s, the nonperforming loan ratio of the local financial institution was kept below 2 percent most of the time. However, it once reached an alarming 7.6 percent for credit cooperative associations in 1985 due to the bankruptcy of Taipei's Tenth Credit Cooperative Association. Two finance ministers, former and incumbent, were forced to resign over the Tenth Credit incident.

15. Even after privatization, the government will remain the largest shareholder.

16. However, foreign investors have chosen to stay out of Taiwan's stock market. Foreign investment totaled only US$11.1 billion, well below the legal limit (equivalent to US$91.4 billion or 30 percent of the market's total capitalization). There are several reasons for this: (1) All portfolio investment capital was required to stay in Taiwan for at least three months before remission. The three-month requirement amounted to a hidden tax on "hot money." (2) Many foreign fund managers worried about the uncertainty inherent in cross-Strait relations and the associated exchange rate risk, which had reached a boiling point during the 1995–96 missile crises. (3) Many foreign investors were disappointed by the government's insistence on restricting cross-Strait economic exchange. (4) Foreign fund managers found their analytical skills of limited use in a market dominated by numerous hyperactive small investors. (5) Other high-growth Asian markets simply seemed more attractive to Taiwan.

17. The major opposition party, the DPP, managed to capture no more than one-third of the total seats in four consecutive Parliamentary elections since its founding. In the election of December 1998, the DPP actually suffered a small setback in terms of both seat ratio and popular vote.

18. The government will accept applications for special loans from temporarily financially stranded enterprises "that are otherwise healthy" (*United Evening News* 10 November 1998). It asked all financial institutions to extend the maturity of loans by six months and declared that bad loans directly resulting from such extensions will not be "counted" as such when the Ministry of Finance reviews their performances—a move that has drawn some criticism from the press (e.g., *China Times* 8 November 1998).

19. The "Washington consensus," so dubbed by the Institute for International Economics in 1990, refers to the new prevailing ideology on the primacy of market-based

policy reform as being promoted by the IMF and Reagan administration since the late 1980s. See John Williamson (1990) and Barbara Stallings (1995, 349–89).

Chapter 10

1. The genre was created by Ishihara Shintaro's *A Japan that Can Say No*, in 1991. In 1995, the book *China Can Say No* appeared, and the commercial success of this neonationalist treatise provoked an outpouring of related books, including *China Can Still Say No*, *Why Does China Say No?* and *China Cannot Become Mr. No*. For an interesting perspective on this literature illuminating the relationship between individual respect and national dignity, see Fitzgerald 1998.

2. This approach to reform is sometimes called *parametric reform* in Chinese, because it stresses getting right the external parameters (including prices) that shape enterprise activity. It is contrasted to *enterprise reform*, which stresses improving incentives and restructuring organizations to make them more sensitive to economic opportunities. For further discussion, see Naughton 1995 (chap. 5).

Conclusion

1. Quoted in Hale 1998b (25).

REFERENCES

AFX News. 1998. Philippine Central Bank governor says "no solid basis" for S&P ratings cut. *AFX News*, 24 February.

Alagappa, Muthiah. 1993. Regionalism and the quest for security: ASEAN and the Cambodian conflict. *Journal of International Affairs* 46, no. 2 (winter): 439–67.

Albert, Michel. 1993. *Capitalism vs. capitalism*. London: Whurr.

Almonte, Jose. 1993. Speech to the Asian Institute of Management, 29 April.

———. 1996. Building state capacity for reform. Speech to the Philippine Economic Society, Metro Manila, Philippines, 9 February.

———. 1997. Philippine politics and society: Moving toward the nation we wish to be. Speech to the Asia Society international conference on the Philippines, 7 May, Los Angeles.

Ammar Siamwalla. 1997. Why are we in this mess? J. Douglas Gibson Lecture, School of Policy Studies, Queen's University, Ontario, Canada, 15 October.

Amsden, Alice H. 1989. *Asia's next giant: South Korea and late industrialization*. Oxford: Oxford University Press.

Antara. 1998. Indonesia monetary crisis caused by excessive short-term debts, businessman says. February 18. Jakarta: Antara Indonesia National News Agency.

Aoki, Masahiko. 1988. *Information, incentive, and bargaining in the Japanese economy*. Cambridge: Cambridge University Press.

———. 1989. The Japanese firm in transition. In *The political economy of Japan*. Vol. 1, *The domestic transformation*, edited by Kozo Yamamura and Yasukichi Yasuba. Stanford: Stanford University Press, 263–88.

———. 1992. Decentralization-centralization in Japanese organization: A duality principle. In *The political economy of Japan*. Vol. 3, *Cultural and social dynamics*, edited by Shumpei Kumon and Henry Rosovsky. Stanford: Stanford University Press, 142–69.

Aoki, Masahiko, and Ronald Dore, eds. 1994. *The Japanese firm: The sources of competitive strength*. London: Oxford University Press.

Arase, David. 1995. *Buying power: The political economy of Japan's foreign aid*. Boulder, Colo.: Lynne Rienner.

Armijo, Leslie Elliott. 1999a. *Financial globalization and democracy in emerging markets*. New York: St. Martin's Press.

——. 1999b. Mixed blessing: Expectations about foreign capital flows and democracy in emerging markets. In *Financial globalization and democracy in emerging markets*. Ed. Leslie Elliott Armijo. London: St. Martin's Press.

Asher, David. 1996. Economic myths explained: What became of the "Japanese Miracle." *Orbis* (spring): 1–21.

Asher, David, and Andrew Smithers. 1998. Japan's key challenges for the twenty-first century: Debt, deflation, default, demography, and deregulation. Washington, D.C.: SAIS Policy Forum Series.

Asian Development Bank. 1996. *Key indicators of developing Asian and Pacific countries*. Manila, Philippines: Asian Development Bank.

——. 1998. *The currency crisis in Southeast Asia and the Republic of Korea*. Manila, Philippines: Asian Development Bank.

Asia Watch. 1987. *A stern, steady crackdown: Legal processes and human rights in South Korea*. Washington, D.C.: Asia Watch, May.

AWSJ (Asian Wall Street Journal). 13 June 1986–87 November 1998.

Azis, Iwan J. 1998. Indonesia and the Asian crisis: Assertions and propositions. Paper presented at the Pacific Council on International Policy: Fourth Annual Members Retreat, Santa Monica, Calif., 16–18 October.

Bacani, Cesar. 1998. Expensive city. *Asiaweek*, 7 August, 50–53.

Banfield, E. 1958. *The moral basis of a backward society*. Glencoe, Ill.: Free Press.

Bangkok Post. 14 August–15 October 1997.

Barron's (weekly). 11 January 1999.

Bautista, Carlos C., Roy C. Ybañez, and Gerardo Agulto, Jr. 1995. The behavior and performance of the Philippine commercial banking industry, 1980–1994. In *The Philippine financial services industry: Prospects and challenges in the next decade*. Ed. Rafael A. Rodriguez. Quezon City, Philippines: University of the Philippines Press.

Beijing University Chinese Economics Research Center, Urban Labor Market Research Group. 1998. Shanghai: Stratification and integration of urban and rural workers. *Gaige* 4:99–110.

Berger, Suzanne, and Ronald Dore, eds. 1996. *National diversity and global capitalism*. Ithaca: Cornell University Press.

Bernard, Mitchell. 1999. East Asia's tumbling dominoes: financial crisis and the truth about the regional miracle. Paper prepared for *The Socialist Register* (draft manuscript).

Bernard, Mitchell, and John Ravenhill. 1995. Beyond product cycles and flying geese: Regionalization, hierarchy, and the industrialization of East Asia. *World Politics* 47, no. 2 (January): 171–209.

Bhagwati, Jagdish. 1998. The capital myth. *Foreign Affairs* 77, no. 3:7–12.

Bhanupong Nidhiprabha. 1998. Economic crises and the debt-inflation episode in Thailand. *ASEAN Economic Bulletin* 15, no. 3: 309–18.

BIS (Bank for International Settlements). 1998a. International banking and financial market developments. *BIS Quarterly Review* (May).

——. 1998b. International banking and financial market developments. *BIS Quarterly Review* (November).

Bluestone, Barry, and Bennett Harrison. 1982. *The deindustrialization of America*. New York: Basic Books.

Bonacich, Edna, Lucie Cheng, Norma Chinchilla, Nora Hamilton, and Paul Ong. 1994. *Global production: The apparel industry in the Pacific Rim*. Philadelphia: Temple University Press.

Bosco, Joseph. 1994. Taiwan factions: guanxi, patronage, and state in local politics. In *The other Taiwan: 1945 to the present*. Ed. Murray Rubinstein. Armonk, NY: M.F. Sharpe, 1994.

Bosworth, Barry. 1998. The Asian financial crisis: What happened and what can we learn from it? *Brookings Review* (summer): 6–9.

Bourdieu, Pierre. 1998. A reasoned utopia and economic fatalism. *New Left Review* 227 (January/February).

Bremner, Brian, et al. 1997. Rescuing Asia. *Business Week*, 17 November, 116.

Brinton, Mary C., and Takehiko Kariya. 1998. Institutional embeddedness in Japanese labor market. In *The new institutionalism in sociology*. Ed. Mary C. Brinton and Victor Nee. New York: Russell Sage Foundation, 181–207.

Buenaventura, Rafael B. 1994. At the forefront of change. Manila: *Fookien Times*, 180.

Business World. Manila, Phillipines, 1 December 1993–1 October 1996.

Castells, Manuel. 1996. *The rise of the network society*. Oxford, England: Blackwell.

Cerra, Valerie, and Sweta Chaman Saxena. 1998. Contagion, monsoons, and domestic turmoil in Indonesia: A case study in the Asian currency crisis. Paper presented at the conference on The Asian Crisis: The Economic Front, Seattle, Washington, University of Washington, 29–30 December.

Chan, Wee Chuan. 1998. Simex HK futures' debut. *Straits Times*, 28 November, weekly edition, 17.

Chandler, Alfred D., Jr. 1977. *The visible hand: The managerial revolution in American business*. Cambridge: Harvard University Press.

———. 1990. *Scale and scope: The dynamics of industrial capitalism*. Cambridge: Harvard University Press.

Chandler, Alfred D., and Herman Daems, eds. 1980. *Managerial hierarchies: Comparative perspective on the rise of the modern industrial enterprise*. Cambridge: Harvard University Press.

Chang, Ha-joon. 1999. The hazard of moral hazard: Untangling the Asian crisis. Paper presented at the American Economic Association Annual Meeting, New York, 3–6 January, 1999.

Chen, Chieh-hsuan. 1994. *Xieli wangluo yu shenhuo jiegou: Taiwan zhongxiao qiye de shehui jiji fenxi* (Mutual aid networks and the structure of daily life: a social ecomonic analysis of Taiwan's small- and medium-sized enterprises). Taipei, Taiwan: Lianjing.

———. 1995. *Huobi wangluo yu shenhuo jiegou: Difang jinrong, zhongxiao qiye Taiwan shisu shehui zhi zhuanhua* (Monetary networks and the structure of daily life: Local finances, small and medium-sized enterprises, and the transformation of folk society in Taiwan). Taipei, Taiwan: Lianjing.

Chen, Edward K. Y., and Peter Drysdale. 1995. *Corporate links and foreign direct investment in Asia and the Pacific*. Pymble, Australia: Harper Educational.

Chen, Guangxin. 1998. Appropriate growth of the money supply; striking growth of foreign exchange reserves. *Zhongguo Jinrong* 3:19–20.

Chen, Shang-mao. 1998. Taiwan jinrong zhengce de zhengzhi jingji fenxi (The political economy of Taiwan's banking policy). M.A. thesis, National Cheng-chi University.

Cheng, Tun-jen. 1993. Guarding the commanding heights: The state as banker in Taiwan. In *The politics of finance in developing countries*. Ed. Stephan Haggard, Chung H. Lee, and Sylvia Maxfield. Ithaca: Cornell University Press.

Chicago Tribune. 14 December 1997.

China Daily. Beijing, China, 6 April 1996–98.

China Times. Beijing, China, 8–20 November 1998.

Ching, Leong. 1998. Six in ten hit by downturn. *Straits Times*, 2 September, weekly edition, 7.

Chiu, Paul C. H. 1998. ROC's experiences in responding to the Asian financial crisis. *Economic Review* (International Commercial Bank of China) 304:1–7.

Cho, Yoon Je, and Joon-Kyung Kim. 1995. Credit policies and industrialization of Korea. *World Bank discussion papers*. Washington D.C.: The World Bank, 286.

Chowhury, Neel, and Anthony Paul. 1997. Where Asia goes from here. *Fortune Magazine*, 24 November.

Chu, Yun-han. 1993. Industrial change and developmental state in two East Asian NICs: A case study of the automotive industries in South Korea and Taiwan. *Proceedings of the National Science Council Part C: Humanities and Social Sciences* 3, no. 2 (July): 203–23.

———. 1994. The realignment of business-government relations and regime transition in Taiwan. In *Business and government in industrializing Asia*. Ed. Andrew MacIntyre. Ithaca: Cornell University Press.

———. 1995. The East Asian NICs: A state-led path to the developed world. In *Global change, regional response*. Ed. Barbara Stallings. New York: Cambridge University Press.

———. 1999. Surviving the East Asian financial storm: The political foundation of Taiwan's economic resilience. In *The politics of the East Asian economic crisis*. Ed. T. J. Pempel. Ithaca: Cornell University Press.

Chu, Yun-peng, and Thomas Tunghao Lee. 1998. From bubbles to new rounds of Asian monetary cooperation—with reference to the Taiwanese. Paper delivered at a conference on contemporary Taiwan cosponsored by the Institute for National Policy Research and the French Center for Contemporary China Studies, Taipei, Taiwan, 16–17 December.

Chua Mui Hoong. 1998. Whither, property? Myths punctured, lessons learned. *Straits Times*, 19 September, weekly edition, 14.

Chung, Chun-wen. 1998. A study of direct financing and indirect financing. In *Huobi yu jinrong zhengce yantaohui lunwenji* (Proceedings of a seminar on monetary and banking policy). Ed. Po-chi Chen. National Taiwan University.

Claessens, Stijn, Simeon Djankov, and Larry Lang. 1998a. East Asian corporates: Growth, financing and risks over the last decade. Working paper, The World Bank.

———. 1998b. Who controls East Asian corporations? Working paper, The World Bank.

Clifford, Mark L. 1996. Troubled tiger: Businessmen, bureaucrats, and generals in South Korea. Armonk, N.Y.: M.E. Sharpe.

Clifford, Mark L., and Sheri Prasso. 1998. A heavy hand in Hong Kong. *Business Week*, 2 September, 46–47.

CND (China News Digest). 1997. Latest development on workers demonstrations in Mianyang, Sichuan. *China News Digest*, 20 July.

———. 1998a. China pledges $4.5 billion to aid Asian economies in crisis. *China News Digest*, 18 November.

———. 1998b. Hong Kong residents approve PRC leadership more than local chief. *China News Digest*, 23 November.

Colletti, Lucio. 1975. Introduction to *Karl Marx: Early writings*, translated by Rodney Livingstone and Gregor Benton. New York: Vintage Books.

Cox, Gary, and Matthew McCubbins. 2000. Political structure and economic policy: the institutional determinants of policy outcomes. In *Structure and policy in presidential democracies*. Ed. Stephan Haggard and Matthew McCubbins. New York: Cambridge University Press.

Courtis, Kenneth. 1992. Japan in the 1990s. *Business and the Contemporary World* IV (winter), no. 2: 62–68.

Cowhey, Peter. 1993. Domestic institutions and the credibility of international commitments: Japan and the United States. *International Organization* 47, no. 2:299–326.

Crouch, Colin, and Wolfgang Streeck. 1997. *Political economy of modern capitalism*. London: Sage Publications.

CSICSC (China Statistical Information Consultancy Service Centre). 1998. China's most recent economic statistics. Hong Kong: CSICSC, August 1998.

Cumings, Bruce. 1987. The origins and development of the Northeast Asian political economy: Industrial sectors, product cycles, and political consequences. In *The political economy of the new Asian industrialization*. Ed. Fred Deyo. Ithaca: Cornell University Press.

——. 1989. The abortive *Abertura*: Korean democratization in the light of the Latin American experience. *New Left Review* (March–April).

——. 1991. *The origins of the Korean War*. Princeton: Princeton University Press.

——. 1996. *Korea's place in the sun*. New York: W.W. Norton.

——. 1999. *Parallax visions: making sense of American–East Asian relations at the end of the century*. Durham, N.C.: Duke University Press.

de Dios, Emmanuel S. 1998. Philippine economic growth: Can it last? In *The Philippines: New directions in domestic policy and foreign relations*. Ed. David G. Timberman. New York: Asia Society, 49–84.

Dicken, Peter. 1992. *Global shift: The internationalization of economic activity*. New York: Guilford Press.

Doner, Richard F. 1990. *Driving a bargain: Automobile industrialization and Japanese firms in Southeast Asia*. Berkeley: University of California Press.

——. 1992. The limits of state strength: Toward an institutionalist view of economic development. *World Politics* 44, no. 3: 398–431.

Doner, Richard F., and Anek Laothamatas. 1994. Thailand: Economic and political gradualism. In *Voting for reform: Democracy, political liberalization, and economic adjustment*. Ed. Stephan Haggard and S. Webb. New York: Oxford University Press.

Dong-A Ilbo. Seoul, South Korea, 3 December 1997.

Dore, Ronald P. 1986. *Flexible rigidities: industrial policy and structural adjustment in the Japanese economy, 1970–80*. Stanford: Stanford University Press.

Ebias, Jun. 1998. Banking on the hard lessons. *Filipinas* (May): 56–58.

Economist (weekly). 31 October 1993–30 January 1999.

Eichengreen, Barry, and Albert Fishlow. 1998. Contending with capital flows: What is different about the 1990s? In *Capital flows and financial crises*. Ed. Miles Kahler. Ithaca: Cornell University Press, 1998, 23–68.

EIU (Economist Intelligence Unit). 1998. *Country profile: Thailand*. London: Economist Intelligence Unit.

Emmerson, Donald. 1998. Americanizing Asia? *Foreign Affairs* 77, no. 3 (May–June): 46–56.

Esping-Andersen, Gosta. 1990. *The three worlds of welfare capitalism*. Princeton: Princeton University Press.

Evans, Peter. 1997. State structures, government-business relations, and economic transformation. In *Business and the state in developing countries*. Ed. Sylvia Maxfield and Ben Ross Schneider. Ithaca: Cornell University Press, 63–87.

Faber, Marc. 1998. Who profited from the intervention in Hong Kong? *Asian Wall Street Journal Weekly*, 14 September, 20.

Fallows, James. 1994. *Looking at the sun: The rise of the new East Asian economic and political system*. New York: Pantheon Books.

Feenstra, Robert, and Gary G. Hamilton. Forthcoming. The organization of the Taiwanese and South Korean economies: A comparative analysis of networked equilibria. In *Integrating networks and markets*. Ed. James Rauch. New York: Russell Sage.

FEER (Far Eastern Economic Review) (weekly). 24 September 1992–94 February 1999.

Feldstein, Martin. 1998. Refocusing the IMF. *Foreign Affairs* 77, no. 2 (March/April): 20–33.

Financial Times. London, 8 August–31 December 1997.

Fitzgerald, John. 1998. Between individual dignity and nationalist indignation: The irrational roots of liberalism and nationalism in contemporary China. New York: Columbia University, East Asian Institute, Institute Report, July 1998.

Frieden, Jeffry A. 1987. *Banking on the world: The politics of international finance*. New York: Basil Blackwell.

——. 1993. Domestic politics and regional cooperation: The United States, Japan, and Pacific money and finance. In *Regionalism and rivalry: Japan and the United States in Pacific Asia*. Ed. Jeffrey A. Frankel and Miles Kahler. Chicago: University of Chicago Press.

Frieden, Jeffry A., and David A. Lake, eds. 1995. *International political economy: Perspectives on global power and wealth*. New York: St. Martin's Press.

Fruin, W. Mark. 1992. *The Japanese enterprise system: Competitive strategies and cooperative structures*. Oxford, England: Clarendon Press.

Fukuyama, F. 1995. *Trust: The social virtues and the creation of prosperity*. New York: Simon and Schuster.

Gao Xin and He Bin. 1995. *Zhu Rongji Zhuan*: [A biography of Zhu Rongji]. Hong Kong.

Gao, Bai. 1997. *Economic ideology and the Japanese industrial policy: Developmentalism from 1930 to 1965*. New York: Cambridge University Press.

Garnaut, Ross. 1998. The financial crisis. *Asian-Pacific Economic Literature* 12, no. 1:1–11.

Gates, H. 1996. *China's motor: A thousand years of petty capitalism*. Ithaca: Cornell University Press.

Gereffi, Gary. 1994. The international economy and economic development. In *The handbook of economic sociology*. Ed. Neil Smelser and Richard Swedberg. Princeton: Princeton University Press, 206–33.

——. 1995a. Global production systems and Third World development. In *Global change, regional response: The new international context of development*. Ed. Barbara Stallings. Cambridge: Cambridge University Press, 100–42.

——. 1995b. Industrial upgrading, state policies, and organizational innovation in East Asia. Paper delivered at the Association for Asian Studies annual meeting, Washington, D.C., 6–9 April.

Gereffi, Gary, and Gary G. Hamilton. 1996. Commodity chains and embedded networks. Paper presented at the Annual Meeting of the American Sociological Association, New York City, August.

Gereffi, Gary, and Miguel Korzeniewicz. 1994. *Commodity chains and global capitalism*. Westport, Conn.: Praeger.

Gerlach, Michael. 1992. *Alliance capitalism: The social organization of Japanese business*. Berkeley: University of California Press.

Gold, Thomas B. 1986. *State and society in the Taiwan miracle*. Armonk, N.Y.: M.E. Sharpe.

Goldstein, Morris. 1998. *The Asian financial crisis: Causes, cures, and systematic implications*. Washington, D.C.: Institute for International Economics.

Gourevitch, Peter J. 1986. *Politics in hard times: Comparative responses to international economic crises*. Ithaca: Cornell University Press.

——. 1996. The macropolitics of microinstitutional differences in the analysis of comparative capitalism. In *National diversity and global capitalism*. Ed. Suzanne Berger and Ronald Dore. Ithaca: Cornell University Press.

Greenspan, Alan. 1998a. Statement before the Committee on Banking and Financial Services, January 30, 1998. U.S. House of Representatives. *Federal Reserve Bulletin* 84, no. 3:186.

——. 1998b. The current Asia crisis and the dynamics of international finance. Testimony of Chairman Alan Greenspan before the Committee on Banking and Financial Services, January 30, 1998. U.S. House of Representatives. Available at http://www.bog.frb.fed.us/boarddocs/testimony/1998/19980130.htm.

——. 1998c. The current Asian crisis and the dynamics of international finance. Testimony of Chairman Alan Greenspan before the Committee on Foreign Relations, February 12, 1998. U.S. Senate. Available at http://www.bog.frb.fed.us/boarddocs/testimony/1998/19980212.htm.

Greider, William. 1997. *One world, ready or not: The manic logic of global capitalism*. New York: Simon and Schuster.

Grieco, Joseph M. 1997. Systemic sources of variation in regional institutionalization in Western Europe, East Asia, and the Americas. In *The political economy of regionalism*. Ed. Edward D. Mansfield and Helen Milner. New York: Columbia University Press, 164–87.

Griffin, Keith, and Zhao Renwei, eds. 1994. *The distribution of income in China*. London: Macmillan, 1994.

Griffith-Jones, Stephany, and Barbara Stallings. 1995. New global financial trends: Implications for development. In *Global change, regional response: The new international context of development*. Ed. Barbara Stallings. Cambridge: Cambridge University Press.

Habermas, Jürgen. 1992. Interview. In *Autonomy and solidarity: Interviews with Jürgen Habermas*. Rev. ed. Ed. Peter Dews. London: Verso.

Hadley, Eleanor. 1970. *Antitrust in Japan*. Princeton: Princeton University Press.

Haggard, Stephan. 1990. *Pathways from the periphery: The politics of growth in the newly industrializing countries*. Ithaca: Cornell University Press.

Haggard, Stephan, and Matthew McCubbins, eds. Forthcoming. *Structure and policy in presidential democracies*. New York: Cambridge University Press.

Hale, David D. 1998a. Developing country financial crises during the 1990s. Zurich Group, June 1998.

——. 1998b. Dodging the bullet—this time. *Brookings Review* (summer): 22–25.

Haley, Mary Ann. 1999. Emerging market makers: The power of institutional investors. In *Financial globalization and democracy in emerging markets*. Ed. Leslie Elliott Armijo. London: St. Martin's Press.

Hamilton, Gary G. 1994. Civilizations and the organization of economies. In *The handbook of economic sociology*. Ed Neil Smelser and Richard Swedberg. Princeton: Princeton University Press, 183–205.

——. 1997. Organization and market processes in Taiwan's capitalist economy. In *The economic organization of East Asian capitalism*. Ed. Marco Orrù, Nicole Woolsey Biggart, and Gary G. Hamilton. Thousand Hills, CA: Sage Publications, 237–96.

——. 1999. Hong Kong and the rise of capitalism in Asia. In *Cosmopolitan capitalists: Hong Kong and the Chinese diaspora at the end of the twentieth century*. Ed. Gary G. Hamilton. Seattle: University of Washington Press, 14–34.

Hamilton, Gary G, and Nicole Woolsey Biggart. 1988. Market, culture, and authority: A comparative analysis of management and organization in the Far East. *American Journal of Sociology*, Special Issue on Economic Sociology (July): S52–94.

Hamilton, Gary G, and Robert Feenstra. 1998. The organization of economies. In *The new institutionalism in sociology*. Ed. Mary C. Brinton and Victor Nee. New York: Russell Sage Foundation, 153–80.

Hanguk Ilbo. Seoul, Korea, 28 July 1998.

Harberger, Arnold C., et al. 1993. Economic integration and the future of the nation-state. *Contemporary Policy Issues* 11 (April): 1–22.

Harrison, Bennett. 1994. *Lean and mean: The changing landscape of corporate power in an age of flexibility*. New York: Basic Books.

Hatch, Walter, and Kozo Yamamura. 1996. *Asia in Japan's embrace*. Cambridge: Cambridge University Press.

Harvey, David. 1990. *The condition of postmodernity*. Oxford, England: Basil Blackwell.

Henderson, Gregory. 1968. *Korea: The politics of the vortex*. Cambridge: Harvard University Press.

Henning, C. Randall. 1994. *Currencies and politics in the United States, Germany, and Japan*. Washington, D.C.: Institute for International Economics.

Hicken, Allen. 1998. From patronage to policy: Political institutions and policy making in Thailand. Paper presented at the Midwest Political Science Association Annual Meeting, Chicago, 23–25 April.

Hill, H. 1998. Southeast Asia's economic crisis: Origins, lessons, and the way forward. Paper presented at the ISEAS Thirtieth Anniversary Conference: Southeast Asia in the Twenty First Century, Singapore, 30 July–1 August.

Hill, Hal, and Prema-chandra Athukorala. 1998. Foreign investment in East Asia: A survey. *Asian-Pacific Economic Literature* 12, no. 2 (November): 36.

Hollingsworth, J. Rogers, and Robert Boyer. 1997. *Contemporary capitalism: The embeddedness of institutions*. Cambridge: Cambridge University Press.

Hollingsworth, J. Rogers, Philippe C. Schmitter, and Wolfgang Streeck, eds. 1994. *Comparing capitalist economies: The embeddedness of institutions*. Oxford: Oxford University Press.

Hsing, You-tien. 1998. *Making capitalism in China: The Taiwan connection*. New York: Oxford University Press.

Huang, Po-yi. 1998. Taiwan's local financial institutions. In *Huobi yu jinrong zhengce yantaohui lunwenji* (Proceedings of a seminar on monetary and banking policy). Ed. Po-chi Chen. National Taiwan University.

Hughes, Helen. 1997. The threat of regionalism to trade liberalization in East Asia. *The Asia Pacific Journal of Economics and Business* 1, no. 1 (June): 4–17.

Hutchcroft, Paul. D. 1998a. *Booty capitalism: The politics of banking in the Philippines*. Ithaca: Cornell University Press.

——. 1998b. Sustaining economic and political reform. In *The Philippines: New directions in domestic policy and foreign relations*. Ed. David G. Timberman. New York: Asia Society, 23–47.

Ibrahim, Zubaidah. 1998. Government decides on $10.5 b. cost cuts. *Straits Times*, 28 November, weekly edition, 1.

IMF (International Monetary Fund). 1998. *Direction of trade statistics*. Washington, D.C.: International Monetary Fund.

——. *IMF survey*. Washington, D.C.: International Monetary Fund.

——. 1995. *Direction of trade statistics yearbook*. Washington, D.C.: International Monetary Fund.

——. Various (annual). *Direction of trade statistics yearbook*. Washington, D.C.: International Monetary Fund.

International Herald Tribune. Paris, 22 November 1997.

Japan Digest. Tokyo, 13 January 1999.

Japan Times. Tokyo 20 June 1994.

Jensen, Michael. 1997. The modern industrial revolution, exit, and the failure of internal control systems. In *Studies in corporate finance and governance systems: A comparison of the U.S., Japan, and Europe*. Ed. Donald H. Chew. New York: Oxford University Press.

Johnson, Chalmers. 1982a. *Industrial policy debate*. San Francisco: Institute for Contemporary Studies.

——. 1982b. *MITI and the Japanese miracle: The growth of industrial policy, 1925–75*. Stanford: Stanford University Press.

——. 1998. Economic crisis in East Asia: The clash of capitalisms. *Cambridge Journal of Economics* 22, no. 6: 653–61.

Jomo, K. S. 1997. In *Essential outsiders: Chinese and Jews in the modern transformation of Southeast Asia and Central Europe*. Ed. Daniel Chirot and Anthony Reid. Seattle: University of Washington Press.

——, ed. 1998. *Tigers in trouble: Financial governance, liberalisation, and crises in East Asia*. London: Zed Books.

Judason, J. 1989. *Ethnicity and the economy: The state, Chinese business, and multinationals in Malaysia*. Singapore: Oxford University Press.

Kahler, Miles, ed. 1998. *Capital flows and financial crises*. Ithaca: Cornell University Press.

Kang, T. W. 1989. *Is Korea the next Japan? Understanding the structure, strategy, and tactics of America's next competitor*. New York: The Free Press.

Kapur, Devesh. 1998. The IMF: A cure or a curse? *Foreign Policy*, 111 (summer): 115.

Kato, Kozo. 1999. Open regionalism and Japan's systematic vulnerability. In *Asian regionalism*. Ed. Peter J. Katzenstein. Ithaca: Cornell University Press.

——. 1978. *Between power and plenty: Foreign economic policies of advanced industrial states*. Madison: University of Wisconsin Press.

——. 1985. *Small states in world markets: Industrial policy in Europe*. Ithaca: Cornell University Press.

——, ed. 1999. *Asian regionalism*. Ithaca: Cornell East Asian Series.

Katzenstein, Peter J., and Takashi Shiraishi. 1997. *Network power: Japan and Asia*. Ithaca: Cornell University Press.

KCTU (Korean Confederation of Trade Unions). 1997. Struggle for labor law reforms. *Campaign News*, no. 24, 28 February.

Kiewiet, D. Roderick, and Matthew McCubbins. 1991. *The logic of delegation: Congressional parties and the appropriation process*. Chicago: University of Chicago Press.

Kim Dae Jung. 1985. *Mass participatory economy*. Cambridge: Harvard East Asian Center.

Kim Dae Jung, Corazon Aquino, and Oscar Arias. 1995. *Democracy in Asia: Its problems and prospects*. Seoul, South Korea: Asia-Pacific Peace Press.

Kim, Eun Mee. 1997. *Big business, strong state: Collusion and conflict in South Korean development 1960–1990*. Albany: State University of New York Press.

Kim, Nyong. 1996. *Han'guk chngch' i wa kyohoe—kukka kaldng* (Korean politics and church-state conflicts). Seoul, South Korea: Sonamu.

Kohn, Meir. 1994. *Financial institutions and markets*. New York: McGraw-Hill.

Kokuseisha. 1997/98. *Nihon kokusei zue* (Japan statistical databook). Tokyo: Kokuseisha.

Koon, H. 1992. The Chinese business elite of Malaysia. In *Southeast Asian capitalists*. Ed. Ruth McVey. Ithaca: Southeast Asia Program, Cornell University.

Korea Herald. Seoul, Korea, 22 January 1997–16 July 1998.

Korean Overseas Culture and Information Service. 1998. The new administration's directions for state management. February.

Kornai, Janos. 1980. *Economics of shortage*. Amsterdam: North-Holland Publishing Company.

Koschmann, J. Victor. 1996. *Revolution and subjectivity in postwar Japan*. Ithaca: Southeast Asia Program, Cornell East Asia Program.

Krasner, Stephen D. 1993. Westphalia and all that. In *Ideas and foreign policy: Beliefs, institutions, and political change*. Ed. Judith D. Goldstein and Robert O. Keohane. Ithaca: Cornell University Press.

Krause, Lawrence B. 1998. *The economics and politics of the Asian financial crisis of 1997–98*. New York: Council on Foreign Relations.

Krugman, Paul. 1994. The myth of Asia's miracle. *Foreign Affairs* 73, no. 6 (November/December): 62–78.

Laothamatas, Anek. 1998. The Thai financial crisis. East Asia Institute, Institute Reports, Columbia University, New York.

Lardy, Nicholas R. 1994. *China in the world economy*. Washington, D.C.: Institute for International Economics.

——. 1998a. China and the Asian contagion. *Foreign Affairs* 77, no. 4 (July/August): 78–88.

——. 1998b. *China's unfinished revolution*. Washington, D.C.: Brookings Institution.

Lazonick, William, Ronald Dore, Henk W. De Jong, and P. H. Admiral. 1997. *The corporate triangle: The structure and performance of corporate systems in a global economy*. Oxford, England: Blackwell.

Lee, Samsung. 1988. Kwangju and the American perspective. *Asian Perspective* 12, no. 2 (fall–winter).

Lee, Sheng-Yi. 1990. *Money and finance in the economic development of Taiwan*. London: Macmillan.

Leifer, Michael. 1989. *ASEAN and the security of South-East Asia*. London: Routledge.

Leipziger, Danny M., and Vinod Thomas. 1993. *Lessons of East Asia: An overview of country experience.* Washington, D.C.: World Bank.

Levy, Brian. 1988. Korean and Taiwanese firms as international competitors: The challenges ahead. *Columbia Journal of World Business* (spring): 43–51.

——. 1991. Transactions costs, the size of firms, and industrial policy: Lessons from a comparative case study of the footwear industry in Korea and Taiwan. *Journal of Development Economics* 34:151–78.

Levy, Brian, and Pablo Spiller, eds. 1996. *Regulations, institutions, and commitment: Comparative studies of telecommunications.* New York: Cambridge University Press.

Lieberman, I., and William Mako. 1998. *Korea's corporate crisis.* Washington, D.C.: World Bank.

Lim, Linda Y. C. 1983a. Singapore's success: The myth of the free market economy. *Asian Survey* 23, no. 6 (June 1983): 752–64.

——. 1983b. The ownership and control of large corporations in Malaysia: The role of Chinese businessmen. In *The Chinese in Southeast Asia.* Vol. 1, *Ethnicity and Economic Activity,* edited by Linda Lim and L. A. Peter Gosling. Singapore: Maruzen Asia.

——. 1987. The state and private capital in Singapore's economic development. *Political Economic Studies in the Surplus Approach* 3, no. 2: 201–22.

——. 1989. Social welfare in Singapore. In *Singapore: the management of success.* Ed. Keranial Singh Sandhu and Paul Wheatley. Singapore: Institute of Southeast Asian Studies, 171–97.

——. 1995. Southeast Asia: Success through international openness. In *Global change, regional response: The new international context of development.* Ed. Barbara Stallings. Cambridge: Cambridge University Press, 238–71.

——. 1998. Whose "model" failed? Implications of the Asian economic crisis. *The Washington Quarterly* 21, no. 3 (summer 1998): 25–36.

——. 1999. Asia beyond the crisis: The challenges for government policy and business practice. *Asia Society; Asian Agenda Report* (February).

Lim, Linda, and Pang Eng Fong. 1991. *Foreign direct investment and industrialization in Malaysia, Singapore, Taiwan, and Thailand.* Paris: OECD Development Centre.

Lin, Pao-an. 1991. The social sources of capital investment in Taiwan's industrialization. In *Business networks and economic development in East and Southeast Asia.* Ed. Gary G. Hamilton. Hong Kong: Centre of Asian Studies, University of Hong Kong.

Lincoln, Edward J. 1998. Exploring the Asian financial crisis. *Brookings Review* (summer): 4–5.

Lockwood, William, ed. 1965. *The state and economic enterprise in Japan: essays in the political economy of growth.* Princeton: Princeton University Press.

——. 1993. *The economic development of Japan : growth and structural change, 1868–1938.* Ann Arbor, Mich.: Center for Japanese Studies, University of Michigan.

Los Angeles Times. 8 February 1998.

Lowi, T. 1975. Toward a politics of economics: The state of permanent receivership. In *Stress and contradiction in modern capitalism.* Ed. Leon Lindberg. Lexington, Mass.: D.C. Heath.

MacIntyre, Andrew, ed. 1994. *Business and government in industrialising Asia.* Ithaca: Cornell University Press.

——. 1999. Political parties, accountability, and economic governance in Indonesia. In *Party systems, democracy, and economic governance in East Asia.* Ed. Jean Blondel, Takashi Inoguchi, and Ian Marsh. Melbourne, Australia: Cambridge University Press.

——. Forthcoming. Investment, property rights, and corruption in Indonesia. In *Corruption: The Boom and Bust of East Asia.* Ed. J. E. Campos.

Mackie, J. 1993. Changing patterns of Chinese big business in Southeast Asia. In *Southeast Asian capitalists.* Ed. Ruth McVey. Ithaca: Cornell University Press.

Mai, Chao-cheng, and Pei-cheng Chang. 1998. Asian financial storm: Taiwan's experience and prospect. Chung-hua Institute for Economic Research. Taipei, Taiwan: Mimeograph.

Mallaby, Sebastian. 1998. In Asia's mirror: From Commodore Perry to the IMF. *The National Interest*, 52 (summer): 14.

Manila Times. 8 May 1997.

Martinez, Edmund. 1996. Fidel Ramos' unfinished business. *Politik* 2 (February).

Marx, Karl. 1973. Bastiat and Carey. In *Grundrisse: Foundations for the critique of political economy*. Trans. Martin Nicolaus. New York: Vintage Books.

McLeod, Ross. 1998. Indonesia. In *East Asia in crisis: From being a miracle to needing one*. Ed. Ross McLeod and Ross Garnaut. London: Routledge.

McLeod, Ross, and Ross Garnaut, eds. 1998. *East Asia in crisis: From being a miracle to needing one?* London: Routledge.

Meisner, Maurice. 1996. *The Deng Xiaoping era: An inquiry into the fate of Chinese socialism*. New York: Hill and Wang.

Ministry of Foreign Affairs. 1998. Asia graph. Available at http://www2.nttca.com/info-mofa/policy/economy/measure98.

Mo, Jongryn, and Chung-in Moon. 1998. Democracy and the origins of the 1997 Korean economic crisis. In *Democracy and Korean economy*. Ed. Chung-in Moon and Jongryn Mo. Stanford: Hoover Institution Press.

Mo, Rong. 1998. *Jiuye: Zhongguo de shiji nanti* (Employment: China's problem of the century). Beijing: Jingji Kexue, 1998.

Moe, Terry, and Michael Caldwell. 1994. The institutional foundations of democratic government: A comparison of presidential and parliamentary systems. *Journal of Institutional and Theoretical Economics* 150, no. 1: 171–95.

Monsod, Solita. 1998. The war against poverty: A status report. In *The Philippines: New directions in domestic policy and foreign relations*. Ed. David G. Timberman. New York: Asia Society, 85–110.

Montes, Manuel F. 1998a. The Philippines as an Unwitting Participant in the Asian Economic Crisis. In *The Causes and Consequences of a Financial Crisis*. Ed. Karl Jackson. Boulder, Colo.: Westview Press.

———. 1998b. *The currency crisis in Southeast Asia*. Updated ed. Singapore: Institute of Southeast Asian Studies.

Montinola, Gabriella, Yingyi Qian, and Barry Weingast. 1995. Federalism, Chinese style: The political basis for economic success in China. *World Politics* 48, no. 1: 50–81.

The Nation (weekly). 13 March 1997–23 February 1998.

Naughton, Barry. 1995. *Growing out of the plan: Chinese economic reform, 1978–1993*. New York: Cambridge University Press.

———. 1996. China's emergence and future as a trading nation. *Brookings Papers on Economic Activity* 2: 273–344.

———, ed. 1997a. *The China circle: Economics and technology in the PRC, Taiwan, and Hong Kong*. Washington, D.C.: Brookings Institution Press.

———. 1997b. Financial reform and macroeconomic instability in China. Working paper 1997–11, Graduate School of International Relations and Pacific Studies, University of California, San Diego.

New York Times. 16 November 1996–12 February 1999.

Nietzsche, Friedrich. 1983. *Untimely Meditations*. Trans. R. J. Hollingdale. New York: Cambridge University Press, 128.

Noble, Gregory. 1996. *Regimes and industrial policy: The politics of collective action in Japan and Taiwan*. Ithaca: Cornell University Press.

Norman, E. H. 1975. *Origins of the modern Japanese state*. Ed. John Dower. New York: Pantheon Books.

North, Douglass. 1981. *Structure and change in economic history*. New York: Cambridge University Press.

Ogle, George E. 1990. *South Korea: dissent within the economic miracle*. Atlantic Highlands, N.J.: Zed Books.

Orr, Robert M., Jr. 1990. *The emergence of Japan's foreign aid power*. New York: Columbia University Press.

Orrù, Marco, Nicole Woolsey Biggart, and Gary G. Hamilton. 1997. *The economic organization of East Asian capitalism*. Thousand Hills, Calif.: Sage Publications.

Osman, Ahmad. 1998. Home owners get help on loan payments. *Straits Times*, 28 November, weekly edition, 3.

Park, Kie-duck. 1993. Fading reformism in new democracies: A comparative study of regime consolidation in Korea and the Philippines. Ph.D. diss., University of Chicago.

Park, Won-soon. 1993. *The National Security Law*. Los Angeles: Korea NGO Network for the UN World Conference on Human Rights.

Park, Yung Chul. 1998. Investment boom, financial bust. *Brookings Review* (summer): 14–17.

Pasuk, Phongpaichit, and Chris Baker. 1999. The political economy of the Thai crisis. *Journal of the Asia Pacific Economy* 4, no. 1: 193–208.

———. 1998a. *Thailand's boom and bust*. Bangkok: Silkworm Books.

———. 1998b. Thailand's economic crisis: Neo-liberal agenda and local reaction. Mimeo, Chulalongkorn University, Bangkok.

Pauly, Louis W., and Simon Reich. 1997. National structures and multinational corporate behavior: Enduring differences in the age of globalization. *International Organization* 51:1–30.

Pempel, T. J. 1995. Trans-Pacific Torii: Japan and the emerging Asian regionalism. In *Network power: Japan and Asia*. Ed. Peter J. Katzenstein and Takashi Shiraishi. Ithaca: Cornell University Press.

———. 1998a. *Regime shift: Comparative dynamics of the Japanese political economy*. Ithaca: Cornell University Press.

———, ed. 1998b. *Uncommon democracies: The one-party dominant regimes*. Ithaca: Cornell University Press.

———. 1999. The developmental regime in a changing world economy. In *The developmental state*. Ed. Meredith Woo-Cumings. Ithaca: Cornell University Press.

PEO (Pacific Economic Outlook). 1995. *Capital flows in the Pacific region: Past trends and future prospects*. Osaka: Japan Committee for Pacific Economic Outlook.

———. 1995. The interdependence of trade and investment in the Pacific. In *Corporate links and foreign direct investment in Asia and the Pacific*. Ed. Edward K. Y. Chen and Peter Drysdale. Sydney, Australia: Harper Educational.

PDI (*Philippine Daily Inquirer*). Metro Manila, Philippines, 25 September 1995–9 October 1998.

Pillay, Subramaniam. 1998. Bailout blues. *Aliran Monthly*, May, 2–5.

Pinches, Michael. 1996. The Philippines' new rich: Capitalist transformation amidst economic gloom. In *The new rich in Asia: Mobile phones, McDonalds, and middle class revolution*. Ed. R. Robison and D. Goodman. London: Routledge, 105–33.

Pincus, Jonathon, and Rizal Ramli. 1998. Indonesia: From showcase to basket case. *Cambridge Journal of Economics* 22, no. 6: 723–34.

Piore, Michael J., and Charles F. Sabel. 1984. *The second industrial divide: Possibilities for prosperity*. New York: Basic Books

Polanyi, Karl. 1944. *The great transformation*. Boston: Beacon Press.

Prestowitz, Clyde. 1988. *Trading places: How we allowed Japan to take the lead*. New York: Basic Books.

Pugh, Cedric. 1989. The political economy of public housing. In Management of success: The moulding of modern Singapore. Ed. Keranial Singh Sandhu and Paul Wheatley. Singapore: Institute of Southeast Asian Studies, 833–59.

Putnam, Robert D., with Robert Leonardi and Raffaella Y. Nanetti. 1993. Making democracy work: civic traditions in modern Italy. Princeton: Princeton University Press, 1993.

Radelet, Steven, and Jeffrey Sachs. 1998a. The East Asian financial crisis: Diagnosis, remedies, prospects. *Brookings Papers on Economic Activity* 1: 1–90.

———. 1998b. The East Asian financial crisis: Diagnosis, remedies, prospects. Harvard Institute for International Development unpublished paper, 20 April.

Redding, S. Gordon. 1990. *The spirit of Chinese capitalism*. Berlin: Walter de Gruyter.

Reich, Robert B. 1991. *The work of nations*. New York: Knopf.

Reilly, John E., ed. 1995. *American public opinion and U.S. foreign policy 1995*. Chicago: Chicago Council on Foreign Relations, 25.

Robinson, William I. 1996. *Promoting polyarchy: Globalization, US intervention, and hegemony*. New York: Cambridge University Press.

Robison, Richard, and David S. G. Goodman, eds. 1996. *The new rich in Asia*. London: Routledge.

Rocamora, Joel. 1994. *Breaking through*. Metro Manila, Philippines: Anvil Publishing, Inc.

———. 1995a. Dodging the authoritarian temptation. *Politik* (November): 40–43.

———. 1995b. The political requirements of economic reform. *Issues and Letters* 4 (October): 1–4.

Rood, Steve. 1998. Decentralization, democracy, and development. In *The Philippines: New directions in domestic policy and foreign relations*. Ed. David G. Timberman. New York: Asia Society, 111–35.

Root, Hilton L. 1989. Tying the king's hands: Credible commitments and royal fiscal policy during the old regime. *Rationality and Society* 1, no. 2: 240–58.

———. 1996. *Small countries, big lessons: Governance and the rise of Asia*. Hong Kong: Oxford University Press.

Roubini, Nouriel, Giancarlo Corsetti, and Paolo Pesenti. 1998. What caused the Asian currency and financial crisis? In *What caused Asia's economic and currency crisis and its global contagion?* [website]. Ed. Nouriel Roubini. Available at http://www.stern.nyu.edu/~nroubini/asia/AsiaHomepage.html.

Saxenian, Anna Lee. 1994. *Regional advantage: Culture and competition in Silicon Valley and Route 128*. Cambridge: Harvard University Press.

Schive, Chi. 1998. Taiwan's economic role after the financial crisis. Paper presented at the Conference in Memory of Kuo-Shu Liang, National Taiwan University, Taipei, 14 September.

Schumpeter, Joseph. 1951. *Imperialism/social classes*. New York: Meridian Books.

Selden, Mark. 1997. China, Japan, and the regional political economy of East Asia, 1945–1995. In *Network power: Japan and Asia*. Ed. Peter J. Katzenstein and Takashi Shiraishi. Ithaca: Cornell University Press, 306–40.

Sen, Sunanda. 1998. Asia: myth of a miracle. *Economic and Political Weekly*, January 17.

Sheard, Paul. 1986. Main banks and internal capital markets in Japan. *Shoken Keizai* 157: 255–85.

Shieh, G. S. 1992. *"Boss" Island: The subcontracting network and micro-entrepreneurship in Taiwan's development*. New York: Peter Lang.

Shiraishi, Takashi. 1997. Japan and Southeast Asia. In *Network power: Japan and Asia*. Ed. Peter J. Katzenstein and Takashi Shiraishi. Ithaca: Cornell University Press.

Shirk, Susan. 1993. *The political logic of economic reform in China*. Berkeley: University of California Press.

Shue, Vivienne. 1988. *The reach of the state: Sketches of the Chinese body politic*. Stanford: Stanford University Press.

Shugart, Matthew, and John Carey. 1992. *Presidents and assemblies: Constitutional design and electoral dynamics*. New York: Cambridge University Press.

Soesastro, Hadi, and M. Chatib Basri. 1998. Survey of recent developments. *Bulletin of Indonesian Economic Studies* 34, no. 1: 3–54.

Solinger, Dorothy. 1998. The impact of openness on integration and control in China: Migrants, layoffs, labor market formation, and the antinomies of market reform in Guangzhou, Shenyang, and Wuhan. Working paper, University of California, Irvine.

Soulard, Francois. 1997. *The restructuring of Hong Kong industries and the urbanization of Zhujian Delta, 1979–1989.* Hong Kong: Chinese University of Hong Kong.

South China Morning Post. Hong Kong, 27 August–8 September 1998.

SSB (State Statistical Bureau). 1998. *Zhongguo tongji nianjian* (China statistical yearbook). Beijing: Zhongguo Tongji.

Stallings, Barbara, ed. 1995. *Global change, regional response: The new international context of development.* Cambridge: Cambridge University Press.

State Department. 1998. Singapore economic overview. In *Market reports, national trade data bank.* Washington, D.C.: Department of State, 10 November.

Sung, Yun-wing. 1997. Hong Kong and the economic integration of the China circle. In *The China circle: economics and technology in the PRC, Taiwan, and Hong Kong.* Ed. Barry Naughton. Washington, D.C.: Brookings Institution.

Sycip, Gorres, and Velayo & Co Various annual issues. *A Study of Commercial Banks in the Philippines.* Metro Manila, Philippines: Sycip, Gorres, and Velayo & Co.

Tam, Pui-Wing. 1997. Fund flows to Asia shrink. *Asian Wall Street Journal Weekly,* September 1.

Tan, Kong Yam. 1997. China and ASEAN: Competitive industrialization through foreign direct investment. In *The China circle: Economics and technology in the PRC, Taiwan, and Hong Kong.* Ed. Barry Naughton. Washington, D.C.: Brookings Institution, 111–35.

Thompson, Mark R. 1995. Off the endangered list: Philippine democratization in comparative perspective. *Comparative Politics* 28, no. 2: 179–205.

Tong, Chuan. 1998. *Renminbi keyi shuo "bu"* (The renminbi can say "no"!). Beijing: Zhongguo Chengshi.

Toronto Star. 29 August 1998, 1.

Tsebelis, George. 1995. Decision making in political systems: Veto players in presidentialism, parliamentarism, multicameralism, and mulitpartyism. *British Journal of Political Science* 25, no. 3: 289–325.

Tubagus, Feridhanusetyawan. 1997. Survey of recent developments. *Bulletin of Indonesian Economic Studies* 33, no. 2: 3–39.

Turner, Matthew. 1996. Hong Kong design and the roots of Sino–American trade disputes. *The Annals of the American Academy* 547 (September): 37–53.

United Daily News. Taipei, Taiwan, 27 November 1998.

United Evening News. Taipei, Taiwan, 10 November 1998.

United Nations. 1998. *World investment report 1998.* New York: United Nations.

Uriu, Robert M. 1996. *Troubled industries: Confronting economic change in Japan.* Ithaca: Cornell University Press.

Veloor, Ravi. 1998. S'pore will stick to open markets. *Straits Times,* 19 September, weekly edition, 24.

Vogel, Ezra. 1998a. For Asian stability, a China–US–Japan triangle. *International Herald Tribune,* 18 September, 8. Quoted in the second Goh Keng Swee Lecture on Modern China, Singapore.

——. 1998b. Taking the road to a peaceful Asia, step by step. *International Herald Tribune,* 19–20 September, 6. Quoted in the second Goh Keng Swee Lecture on Modern China, Singapore.

Wade, Robert. 1990. *Governing the market: Economic theory and the role of government in East Asian industrialization.* Princeton: Princeton University Press.

——. 1996. Globalization and its limits: Reports of the death of the national economy are greatly exaggerated. In *National diversity and global capitalism.* Ed. Suzanne Berger and Ronald Dore. Ithaca: Cornell University Press.

——. 1998. The Asian crisis and the global economy: Causes, consequences and cure. *Current History* (October): 1–15.

——. 1999. Is this the end of the Asian model? Paper presented at the 32nd Annual Meeting of the Asian Development Bank, Manila, Philippines, 30 April.

Wade, Robert, and Frank Veneroso. 1998. The Asian crisis: The high debt model versus the Wall Street-Treasury-IMF complex. *New Left Review* 228 (March/April).

Wallerstein, Immanuel. 1983. *Historical Capitalism*. London: Verso.

Wall Street Journal. 25 August 1997–29 January 1999.

Wang, Chien-chuan et al. 1998. *Zhongxiao qiye zai gaokeji chanye de diwei* (The role of SMEs in high-tech industries). Taipei, Taiwan, Chung-hua Institute for Economic Research.

Wang, Hui Ling. 1997. Tung pledges changes to better the lot of HK people. *Straits Times* (Singapore), July 2, weekly edition, 1.

Warr, Peter. 1998. Thailand. In *East Asia in crisis: From being a miracle to needing one?* Ed. Ross McLeod and Ross Garnaut. Routledge: London.

Washington Post. 21 November 1997–27 August 1998.

Weaver, R. K., and B. A. Rockman. 1993. *Do institutions matter? Government capabilities in the United States and abroad*. Washington, D.C.: Brookings Institution.

Weber, Max. 1951. *The religion of China*. New York: The Free Press.

——. 1958. *The protestant ethic and the spirit of capitalism*. New York: Charles Scribner's Sons.

Wei, Chu-Llin. 1991. The development of the strategies for Taiwan's big and small enterprises. Paper presented at seminar: Relationship Among Government, Enterprises, and Society. Institute for National Policy Research, Taipei, Taiwan, 14 September.

Weingast, Barry. 1995. The economic role of political institutions: Market-preserving federalism and economic growth. *Journal of Law, Economics, and Organization* 11, no. 1: 1–31.

West, James M. 1987. South Korea's entry into the international labor organization: Perspectives on corporatist labor law during a late industrial revolution. *Stanford Journal of International Law* 23, no. 2.

Westney, D. Eleanor. 1996. The Japanese business system: Key features and prospects for change. *Journal of Asian Business* 12, no. 1: 21–50.

Weyland, Kurt. 1996. Obstacles to social reform in Brazil's new democracy. *Comparative Politics* 29, no. 1: 1–22.

Whitley, Richard. 1992. *Business systems in East Asia: Firms, markets, and societies*. New York: Sage Publications.

Williams, Raymond. 1975. *The country and the city*. New York: Oxford University Press.

Williamson, John, ed. 1990. Latin American adjustment: How much has happened? Washington, D.C.: Institute for International Economics.

Winters, Jeffrey A. 1996. *Power in motion: Capital mobility and the Indonesian state*. Ithaca: Cornell University Press.

——. 1999. Indonesia: On the mostly negative role of transnational capital in democratization. In *Financial globalization and democracy in emerging markets*. Ed. Leslie Elliott Armijo. London: St. Martin's Press.

Wolfensohn, James. 1996. Speech before the G-7 meeting. Available at http://www.worldbank.org.

Womack, James P., Daniel T. Jones, and Daniel Roos. 1990. *The machine that changed the world*. New York: Harper Perennial.

Wong, Siu-lun. 1985. The Chinese family firm: A model. *British Journal of Sociology* 36: 58–72.

——. 1988. *Emigrant entrepreneurs: Shanghai industrialists in Hong Kong*. Hong Kong: Oxford University Press.

Woo, Jung-en [Meredith Woo-Cumings]. 1991. *Race to the swift: State and finance in Korean industrialization*. New York: Columbia University Press.

Woo-Cumings, Meredith. 1995. Developmental bureaucracy in comparative perspective. In *The Japanese civil service and economic development*. Ed. Hyung-Ki Kim, Michio Muramatsu, T. J. Pempel, and Kozo Yamamura. New York: Oxford University Press.
——, ed. 1999. *The developmental state*. Ithaca: Cornell University Press.
World Bank 1997a. *Global Development Finance*. Washington, D.C.: World Bank.
World Bank. 1997b. *World development report: The state in a changing world*. New York: Oxford University Press.
Xiong Xianliang. 1998. (Lessons that China can draw from the financial crises in Mexico and Thailand). In *Zhongguo fazhan yanjiu: Guowuyuan fazhan yanjiu zhongxin yanjiu baogaoxuan* (China development studies: Selected reports of the State Council Development Research Center). Ed. Ma Hong. Beijing: Zhongguo Fazhan, 197–205.
Yang Yiyong. 1998. (China's unemployment problem: Current conditions, trends, and appropriate measures). In *1998 Nian Zhongguo jingji xingshi fenxi yu yuce: Jingji lanpi shu* (1998 China economic conditions, analysis and projections: Economic blue book). Ed. Liu Guoguang, Wang Luolin, and Li Jingwen. Beijing: Shehui Kexue Wenxian.
Yen, Ching-Chang. 1998. Taiwan's fiscal policy: Its role in the Asian financial turmoil. Ministry of Finance. Taipei, Taiwan: Mimeograph.
Yin, Nai-Ping. 1998. The system of financial regulation: a review and suggestions. In *Proceedings on a conference on monetary and fiscal policies*. Ed. Po-Chi Chen. Taipei, Taiwan: National Taiwan University.
Yos Vajragupta and Vichyanond Pakorn. 1998. *Thailand's financial evolution and the 1997 crisis*. Bangkok: Thailand Development Research Institute.
Yu, Sungmin. 1996. *Nanumyonso k'oganda* (Sharing, growing). Seoul: Mirae Media.
Zeile, William J. 1993. *Industrial targeting, business organization, and industry productivity growth in the Republic of Korea, 1972–1985*. Ph.D. diss. Department of Economics, University of California, Davis.
Zhang Chenghui, Zhang Yongsheng, and Liu Renhui. 1998. (The 1997 financial situation and prospects for 1998). In *Zhongguo jingji xingshi yu fazhan* (Economic situation and prospect of China). Ed. Ma Hong. Beijing: Zhongguo Fazhan, 109–27.
Zhong Rongsa and Zhuang Mou. 1998. (China's stock market development and prospects). In *Zhongguo shichang fazhan baogao* (China market development report). Ed. Ma Hong. Beijing: Zhongguo Fazhan, 74–88.

INDEX

Note: Page numbers followed by *t* indicate tables; page numbers followed by *f* indicate figures; page numbers followed by *n* indicate endnotes.

269

Cornell Studies in Political Economy
A SERIES EDITED BY
PETER J. KATZENSTEIN